AF735498

Debt Recovery Through the Courts

Debt Recovery Through the Courts

First Edition

By

CLAIRE SANDBROOK

CHIEF EXECUTIVE OFFICER, SHERGROUP LEGAL AND FINANCIAL SERVICES / LL.B (Hons), F.I.C.M

Solicitor of the Supreme Court

SWEET & MAXWELL

THOMSON REUTERS

First edition 2008 Debt Recovery Through the Courts

Published in 2008 by
Thomson Reuters (Legal) Limited (Registered in England & Wales,
Company No 1679046. Registered Office and address for service:
100 Avenue Road, London, NW3 3PF) trading as Sweet & Maxwell.
For further information on our products and services,
visit www.sweetandmaxwell.co.uk
Typeset by Servis Filmsetting Ltd, Stockport, Cheshire
Printed and bound in Great Britain by
Athenaeum Press Ltd, Gateshead, Tyne & Wear

No natural forests were destroyed to make this product;
only farmed timber was used and re-planted.

British Library Cataloguing in Publication Data

A CIP catalogue record for this book
is available from the British Library

ISBN 978-1-84703-256-0

Foreword

For too long, Litigation and Enforcement have often been considered the "last resort" in the credit manager's collections strategy. The apparent cost—both in terms of manpower and capital outlay—has been viewed as a barrier to entry, especially when low-value debts are involved, and culturally litigation has been seen as having to admit defeat.

For the smarter credit manager, and the smarter collector, Litigation and Enforcement can be a powerful and cost-effective tool, with a very high chance of recovering even the smallest of balances outstanding. Far from being on the periphery of the credit management process, it is rapidly becoming at the very heart of that process.

The secret, if there is one, to successful use of Litigation and Enforcement is information and information sharing. You need to have the right information at your disposal and use it intelligently—this is what makes the difference between success and failure. Litigation should only be used where appropriate; information will determine which cases should be taken to Litigation, and which should not.

For example, an account where the debtor has the means to pay and assets of value, but clearly no intention of paying, is worth taking to court. Conversely, those without the means or any assets could end up costing you dearly. In short, there is little point in throwing good money after bad. The lesson therefore is to be highly selective before making your decision, and to select those accounts with a real chance of success.

The accumulated information at hand needs to be assessed and used intelligently to determine potential pitfalls. This is where the fundamentals of credit management come to the fore: the process starts with "knowing your customer" and understanding their payment record. In terms of individuals, basic details—addresses, employment history, etc. should be checked and confirmed. More importantly perhaps, if the account has any outstanding disputes then these need to be resolved prior to any court action, or the consequences could be costly.

If your selection criteria are good, more often than not the case will go uncontested and the court will issue an order for payment. At this point, assuming your debtor has not co-operated, the method of Enforcement needs to be determined.

Most frequently the first line of Enforcement starts with the bailiff. An example of the importance of using good quality information to aid the decision process is clearly illustrated by statistics produced by the court service which show that almost half of all warrants issued are unenforceable, mainly because the debtor is not at the address. Whilst there is a cost to instigating a "trace", this has to be balanced with the fact that when the debtor is found to be at the address, around 80 per cent of warrants result in payment.

A more involved method of Enforcement is an attachment of earnings, where payments are effectively deducted at source, via the debtor's pay-packet. Of course such an action is only relevant where the individual is in regular employment, but if so it is extremely effective.

A further route is to take a charge on the debtor's property (or other assets). This is useful in that it secures the debt on the equity of the property, such that if that property is subsequently sold, or re-mortgaged (as is happening currently in a very buoyant housing market), then the money owing is immediately recovered. The thought of a charge on the property as far as the debtor is concerned can focus the mind.

Only in the most drastic and dramatic of circumstances would one force a sale of a property to recover a debt, but the option is there if it needs to be taken. (The main potential pitfall is in ensuring that the property does not already have a charge or charges against it with a prior claim on any equity realised).

Again the key is in assessing each account individually and making a judgement on the most appropriate course of action to pursue. It is important to weigh the cost of the procedure against the value of the debt to be recovered. Selective Litigation and Enforcement as a credit management tool per se can be used for debts as low as £25 (and can serve as a useful wake-up call for the habitual debtor), so its appropriateness spans a broad spectrum of debt.

Despite its benefits, Litigation remains one of the most under-used weapons in the credit manager's armoury. However, the court service has, over the last few years, streamlined many cumbersome enforcement procedures, and continues to do so, which is yet another attraction to the discerning credit manager.

At the Institute of Credit Management, our mission is to empower credit management professionals, supporting them with the latest training and resources to keep them at the top of their game. I am delighted, therefore, to be writing the foreword to Claire's book, which I believe will become essential reading to every serious-minded professional.

I wish it every success.

Philip King
Director General of the Institute of Credit Management

Dedication

To my parents
Jin and John Goldie
who have always believed
in me and my husband Steve
without whose love and support
I would not be where I am today

Preface

At the time of writing this book, Britain is on the edge of an economic recession and the issue of debt recovery is climbing in importance for politicians and policy makers alike.

Britons owe more than £1.4 trillion and with the "credit crunch" on the horizon the topic of how to recoup and recover what is owed is a recurring theme for debt recovery professionals.

In writing this book I hope myself and my team have produced a guide which can help practitioners achieve more from the court system. The book is designed to help those working in the field of debt recovery who may not be very familiar with the Civil Procedure Rules or the nuances of the regulatory environment within which debt is recovered.

Our approach is to make things easy to understand, so the book contains straightforward notes, a case study with a set of completed forms, flowcharts, and other materials which we have developed over the years.

My reason for writing this book has been to consolidate nearly 20 years of qualifying as a solicitor into a Guide which can be used by all sorts of practitioners, both legally and non-legally qualified. Debt is no respecter of qualifications!

I was delighted that Philip King, as the Director General of the Institute of Credit Management, was able to write the Foreword and I thank him for that. I have been very inspired by Philip's leadership of the ICM and I am sure over the coming years the Institute will have an increasingly loud voice in how debt is recovered in the court system. It is a voice of experience and reason and I hope it will be heard.

Over the years I have gained much inspiration in my career from leading lights in the legal and credit industry too numerous to mention, although I do offer a special mention to Master Robert Turner and indeed all the Masters both past and present in the QB corridor. It was here, as a young solicitor, that I cut my teeth on interlocutory applications with a case that was always well prepped and presented—how I wish I had the time to do that now!

Of course my main interest has been in the enforcement of judgments and I hope that by reading this book practitioners will appreciate that the enforcement will not work without real strategies for the recovery of their debts. It's a selfish thought really, but if some of my ideas can be picked up on it does mean more judgments should become enforceable.

I must also thank my faithful team within Shergroup. Sharon Housden, as a Fellow of the Institute of Legal Executives, has been my trusty assistant and I thank her for her patience and hard work in helping me draw together the strands of this work. I would also like to thank Lalit Karira and my transcription team in India who have worked so hard to transcribe my dictation, and listen to the frequent references to cases and statutes which can be hard going—thank you.

And to my colleagues and supporters both in Shergroup and outside, I thank you for your support of my ideas within Shergroup itself and for working with us in ways of adding some level of ingenuity to the debt recovery industry. It has been our pleasure to serve all of you and we look forward to working with you in the years to come.

Finally, we will be donating all royalties from this book to our latest venture, "The Sherbet Foundation", which is being set up to help families affected by enforcement action. As enforcement officers we have a unique vantage point to see families affected by the worst aspects of poverty. We wanted to do something positive to help them and by buying this book you will have helped our cause. Thank you.

Claire Sandbrook
August 2008

Contents

4 Recovering the Cost of Debt Recovery through the courts

5 Preparing a Debt Recovery Claim

9 Tactical Applications In Debt Recovery

10 The Enforcement Arena

12 Third Party Debt Orders—CPR 72

13 Charging Orders–CPR 73

14 Using Writs and Warrants–CPR Schedules 1 and 2

Appendices

Table of Cases

Table of Statutes

Table of Statutory Instruments

Table of European Legislation

Table of Practice Directions

Chapter 1

Credit Management as a Prelude to Debt Recovery

Introductory Comments

The purpose of this book is to offer debt recovery practitioners a guide to the law and procedure surrounding the subject of debt recovery through the courts with some practical hints on how to get the most from the court system. **1–01**

At the outset of debt recovery, before litigation has even been contemplated, the process should start with some form of credit management process. In a large organisation this may be headed by a Credit Manager or a Financial Director, in a smaller operation it may be a Credit Controller. In a one-man band or sole trader organisation it might simply be the book keeper. However, whatever size of business, all businesses depend on proper management of their cash flow to ensure the management of any debts are handled as efficiently as possible.

At its simplest debt recovery should be a straight forward procedure. But there are plenty of issues which crop up to ensure debt recovery is anything but routine. This book will endeavour to show how, when that happens, action can be taken to deal with non-routine matters so they are less disruptive to the smooth running of a debt recovery department.

What is the starting point?

At the outset of credit being granted a customer should be checked to ensure they are "good for the money". Often in debt recovery procedures we find a person who has been lent money or given credit is in fact worth nothing. This can be for a variety of reasons including the most fundamental of which is that the creditor has not checked who **1–02** he has traded with. This can make subsequent recovery action frustrating and difficult. Pro-active credit management at the outset of the customer relationship, which continues throughout the lifetime of that relationship, will ensure that any risk of loss is minimised because the purpose of credit management is to manage the credit risk.

What steps should be taken to ensure that customers are creditworthy?

1–03 Before offering credit or allowing a consumer to borrow money, a credit management process will be an assessment of the level of risk that the transaction involves. The output of that process should be a decision as to the level of risk a creditor is prepared to offer by way of credit. Again, in large organisations this will be a sophisticated process probably based around a computer model which will "score" the customer's credit rating. Even in smaller organisations access to online credit reports and tools to check whether a customer should be granted credit are easily accessible through a variety of suppliers.

The starting point to find out what level of credit can be granted to a customer should come from a credit application form which can be tailored to the organisation's requirements. Wherever possible the credit application form should be completed before *credit is advanced* and when the customer is happiest to oblige in giving all relevant information to enable a decision to be made as to the amount of credit to be granted.

In this book we have used a casestudy called "Tom and Margot" to explain both the credit function and the debt recovery process of a case based on two characters which those of a certain age may remember. The casestudy is in essence the set up of a simple contract for the supply of goods which goes awry and Tom's attempt to get back his money from the court system. Readers are encouraged to read that section of the book as we move through the chapters to see how the various pieces of documentation fit together as a complete set of papers.

The first such piece of paper is the credit application form which Tom will ask Margot to complete and which can be found in the Appendix.

What are the standard methods of assessing the ability of a customer to pay?

1–04 The table below provides a simple summary of the ways in which a creditor can check a debtor's ability to pay or meet invoice terms:

Method	Description
Credit Reference Agency Report	A credit reference agency check can provide detailed information about new and existing customers on an ongoing basis. The information supplied can be very comprehensive and can include financial results, payment experienced by suppliers, county court judgments and recommended credit ratings. The trick with these reports is being able to identify the salient facts and ensure the risk is clearly identified. There are a number of brand names which supply such reports which are set out in the Matrix for Sources of Information in the Appendix. In a busy credit department creditors should take time to constantly evaluate and compare information from suppliers and if budgets allow to have credit information from more than one source. The three major credit reference agencies operating in the UK are Experian (*http://www.experian.co.uk*) Equifax (*http://www.equifax.co.uk*) Callcredit (*http://www.callcredit.co.uk*) There are also a number of resellers of credit information which can add additional insight to information in the main credit report. An example of this might be Graydon or ICC.
Customer Payment Behaviour	The payment behaviour of existing and previous customers can be invaluable in providing an indication of future behaviour when it comes to paying on time. Credit professionals will have experience of their sectors and they should be able to calculate customers who have been slow payers or have raised unjustified queries about invoices. These types of customers should be subjected to a more rigorous check and stricter terms and conditions before credit is advanced.
Companies House Webcheck	The Webcheck system of Companies House is an invaluable tool to ensure that a limited company actually exists. The check is free and it can confirm that a limited company is solvent because the solvency history is stated as part of the check. It can also confirm if a limited company is up-to-date with its annual returns (again an indicator of a company's solvency and its reliability in its processes to meet its obligations). Copies of annual accounts and other documents filed by a limited company can be obtained for a fee ranging from £1 to £5 per document. Companies House can be telephoned on 0870 333 3636. The web check system is available at *http://www.companieshouse.gov.uk*. However, the system is available only from Monday to Saturday 7pm–12am midnight UK time. It is vital that the Companies House Webcheck is built into any upfront process before credit is given for trade debt and continues to be made throughout the life of a debt recovery action.

Method	Description
	It is a simple check but a fundamental one to ensure the existence of a limited company as opposed to a non-limited business such as a partnership or firm. Often customers are confused about the legal status of their trading entity. A Companies House search will quickly and cheaply confirm whether the business is limited or not.
Other Supplier References	It should be standard practice to ask customers for references from their other suppliers before agreeing to give credit to them. There is of course the question as to the reliability of these references, particularly if the customer has chosen the trade referee. As a matter of good practice it is important not to allow customers to choose their own referees as there may be an unrepresentative sample of how a customer really behaves in paying its bills. The Institute of Credit Management (ICM) advises that the name of suppliers of particular services or goods be requested such as cleaners, accountants, stationers or other suppliers which are vital to the customer's business process and therefore the customer will need to pay on time to ensure a good line of credit. Questions which should be asked of trade referees in a standard process include: • How long have you been dealing with the customer business? • What are your terms of business, i.e. 30 days or 60 days? • How promptly does the business pay in accordance with the trade referee's terms of business? The ICM warns that this approach does not provide a guarantee other than as to the business reliability of a customer, but is nevertheless a useful starting point on whether a customer will pay his or her bills on time. The ICM has a useful website resource at: *http://www.icm.org.uk*
Industry Credit Circles	Credit circles usually operate on an informal and rather discrete basis by industry and trade associations and also by credit recovery departments of larger accountancy firms, whose apparent motive for organising credit circles is business development. Often shrouded in mystery these groupings tend to be organised on a sector by sector basis where competitors exchange information about late paying customers and customers who are identified as a risk. Such discussions are of course subject to the provisions of the Data Protection Act 1998 (see Chapter 2). Credit circles can be effective in uncovering businesses which slip through normal credit agency checks and often highlight customers who turn from one supplier to another as soon as their credit line has been exhausted.
Bank References	The value of bank references in debt recovery has apparently little real value, largely because banks are reluctant to disclose

<table>
<tr><th>Method</th><th>Description</th></tr>
<tr><td></td><td>information which could be a breach of Data Protection in relation to a customer's affairs (see Chapter 2 for more information about this Act).

However, as a prudent policy it may be advisable to seek a bank reference from a customer as part of a wider account opening procedure. To obtain a bank reference a creditor must ask for the customer's permission to apply for the same and then pay a fee to the appropriate bank of around £10.

The language used in bank references is extremely subtle and will need some decoding. The matrix below shows how to read between the lines!
<table>
<tr><th>Acceptable risk—words such as:</th><th>Proceed with caution—alarm bells should be ringing!</th><th>Do not grant credit—phrases such as:</th></tr>
<tr><td>"undoubted"
"good for your figure"
"considered good"
"should prove good for £"<br>"good for normal business"
"trust worthy"
"should prove good"
"should prove trustworthy"
"respectably constituted"</td><td>"figure larger than normal"
"preferred in a series"
"should prove good"
"would not enter into"</td><td>"fully committed"
"capital fully employed"
"cannot speak"</td></tr>
</table>
It should be remembered that the differences between each category can be very slim, so this sort of information should only be used with caution and as part of a series of information which is evaluated.</td></tr>
<tr><td>Credit Insurance Risk Assessments</td><td>Credit insurance companies can also perform credit checks for their clients who take out insurance to cover potential bad debts. Information about how to go about applying for trade credit insurance can be obtained from the Institute of Credit Management (telephone: 01780 722 900) or their website at http://www.icm.org.uk. Another source of information is the UK Credit Insurance Brokers' Committee which operates under the auspices</td></tr>
</table>

Method	Description
	of the British Insurance and Investment Broker's Association (telephone: 020 7623 9043). Credit insurers look to minimise the risk of insuring bad debts and these organisations have sophisticated systems to assess risk. As a result credit insurers will expect their insured clients to have certain processes and checks in place as part of their credit management procedures to minimise their extent of risk and some may require that their own credit checking system be used before issuing credit insurance. A credit insurer may refuse to insure credit for some customers and this might be a useful warning about the particular customer's ability to pay. The credit management recommendations of the insurer and its credit checking facilities can also be of substantial benefit to a creditor both at the start of the customer relationship and through the ongoing trading relationship. Under most policies the insurer only covers a percentage of the debt, usually between 75 per cent to 95 per cent. It is also worth bearing in mind that claims of protracted default (late payment) are usually payable only after six months have elapsed from the date on which the default occurred. As a result the creditor's own cash flow can be adversely impacted by the delay in a credit insurer paying out under the policy.

Is there a model form of credit application?

1–05 Before agreeing to offer credit to a customer on this basis, it is essential for the customer to complete a credit account application form. The information which the customer enters into this form allows the supplier to decide how much credit it is safe to provide. The credit application form should also clarify the supplier's terms of trade, reducing the risk of late payment problems later on. The best form of credit application form is available as part of the Order to Obtain Information Procedure under CPR Pt 71 of the Civil Procedure Rules (see Chapter 11) being court form EX140. In effect, the questions posed on this form for either an individual debtor or the officer of a company are usually the questions that should be asked *before any credit is granted* and certainly at the outset of any litigation process. Form EX140 can be found as part of the Appendix and as part of the case study which is referred to throughout the book.

A review of this form will show the extent of questions which could be included as part of the account opening process to avoid the very same questions having to be asked after a county court judgment has been entered. At a post judgment stage a former customer may be less than co-operative to give the necessary information to enable the enforcement of the court's judgment.

In fact a very cynical approach to the granting of credit is to view every new application for credit as one where the customer could default. Credit managers and those involved in granting credit should really be asking themselves if that were to happen, how would they enforce any county court or High Court judgment! The question to ask is, "if I ended up with a judgment against this customer, how would I be able to enforce it?" If this question were asked at the outset of the customer relationship, would credit be offered or would it be subject to more rigorous terms? There is always a need to sell goods and services, but the risk of default needs to be understood at an early stage and creditors should really examine whether their own polices and procedures protect them in the event of default.

In Chapter 3 we will look at this in more detail in the section headed "Know your debtor".

Subject to the nature of the supplier's business, it is always good practice to have a professional account opening process. A welcoming letter can be sent to the customer advising them of their credit limit and confirming that regular statements will be sent as the credit facility is used. Again, the supplier's terms and conditions of business should be printed on the reverse of any standard documentation issued at this stage to ensure they are incorporated into the contract with the customer which becomes important should litigation become necessary (see "Know Your Contract" in Chapter 3).

How much credit should a customer be allowed?

In the business-to-business sector or in the business-to-consumer sector once credit checks have been made it should be possible to "score" the customer and arrive at a decision on how much credit is to be allowed. Credit card companies are doing this all the time with their customers with some very sophisticated credit policies. 1–06

A model credit application form taken from the Forum of Private Businesses Credit Control Guide is set out in the Appendix to this book. Even if credit has already been granted a debt recovery practitioner should appreciate the terms of the existing credit policy or set one up where none is found to exist in any credit organisation.

Some of the most important strands to a credit policy can be summarised as follows:

1–07

Credit Policy Requirement	Reason for Inclusion
A credit policy should set the overall amount of credit for an organisation's customers.	The credit policy should determine the total amount of credit which a supplier business will allow its customers.
Setting credit limits for types of customers according to risk.	Another key component of the credit policy is dividing customers into categories of risk. The lower the risk the more credit to be allowed and vice versa. Customers may be classified into high, medium and low risk and unacceptable risk. The amount of credit to be given to high risk customers should be controlled and 20 per cent of total debt being owed to the supplier is a common maximum limit to the amount of credit to be given to high risk debtors. Deciding upon a limit can be difficult as sometimes selling to the high risk customers offers higher profit margins. An example below shows how a business could allocate the credit limit to its high risk customer. A business has a net worth of £1,000,000 and has working capital of £400,000 in its debtor's figure. The overall amount of credit to be allowed is the lower of 10 per cent of net worth, i.e. £100,000 or 20 per cent of working capital being £80,000. The overall credit exposure should be £80,000. The maximum amount of credit to be given to a high risk debtor would therefore be 20 per cent of the £80,000, i.e. £16,000.
Setting credit limits for individual customers	There are many methods of setting individual credit limits. These can be set as a percentage of the total credit limit for a particular category of business or according to the anticipated value of sales over a period of say three months. The overriding principle to adopt is to avoid having all the risks as "eggs in one basket". The customer can be advised of his or her credit limit in the welcoming letter in the set up of the new account or in the regular statements sent to existing customers.
Policy for reviewing customer credit limits	This task should be performed frequently for new and fast growth customers. An overall periodic review of credit limits should be encouraged as part of the culture for credit management within an organisation.
Procedure for informing sales staff of customer credit limits.	A situation should never arise in which customers are allowed more credit than has officially been agreed. Sales staff in particular, who might be anxious to sell

Credit Policy Requirement	Reason for Inclusion
	more to achieve better commission rates, should be made aware of the policy on credit and managed to ensure they stick to the limit unless they can seek approval for a higher credit limit being granted for a particular case.
Staff responsibilities for operating credit policy	Staff should be assigned the responsibility of giving credit limits for individual customers on an ongoing basis.
Policy for businesses which are too high risk for credit to be given	Diplomacy is essential here as a customer could be offended when told they are "high risk". The trick is to offer the customer other terms such as "cash on delivery" or an "advance payment" basis, so that goods are not actually delivered until the cash is in the bank.

How is a credit account set up with a new customer or an existing customer?

Customers who purchase from the supplier on a regular basis often have their own credit accounts with that supplier. This arrangement is preferred by many customers who find it convenient so they do not have to make an individual payment for each purchase but instead can pay for a group of invoices at any one time and which they find more convenient. **1–08**

For the supplier, customer credit accounts also have many advantages. Firstly, they encourage customers to keep buying from them in future as customers are reluctant to change supplier and set up another credit account. Secondly, the procedure through which the customer applies for a credit account is a useful way of obtaining information about them which makes it a more secure trading relationship.

How can terms and conditions of business help in the management of creditor risk?

If a customer signs a credit application form agreeing to the terms and conditions of business he or she is more likely to pay in the accepted timescale. Should he or she fail to do so further action will be easier to take. **1–09**

A copy of the creditor's terms and conditions which are signed by the customer will also be an *invaluable* piece of evidence in the event legal action is necessary for non-payment of the debt—creditors should always keep this original paperwork or a scanned copy in a safe place.

In fact terms and conditions of business should be inserted into every piece of written documentation issued by the supplier business and particularly in the order confirmation form, form of contract and delivery note. The customer should be asked to sign that he or she accepts, that before any goods are delivered, or services are performed of any significant value, the terms are agreed.

This approach may be thought unnecessary for every sale, especially for those of little value; in this situation a minimum amount should be set.

1–10 Terms and conditions of business can also be varied for different customers depending on what is the most appropriate for the particular circumstances, although variations have to be managed to ensure that credit control staff appreciate which customers are on which terms.

It is always worth raising the subject of terms and conditions with customers at an early stage, especially when negotiating large contracts, to prevent misunderstandings later on and to ensure that terms and conditions particularly in relation to payment are mutually agreed. This is discussed more fully in Chapter 3 under "Know Your Contract". The minimum terms and conditions which should be included in relation to terms of payment are as follows:

1–11

Length of Credit Period	Usually this will be 30 days but changes from industry to industry and what is the norm in one sector may be different elsewhere. Practitioners should work within accepted norms when offering credit and require high risk customers to have a shorter period such as 7–14 days.
A clause which asks the customer to sign that he or she agrees the terms and conditions of sale	For example the standard wording might read "We have read your terms and conditions and agree to abide by them". This clause should be inserted for the customer to sign in the order confirmation/contract to purchase.
Interest for late payment	The creditor should insert a clause requiring that interest is paid on overdue debts, for example, "interest charges of X% per month will be levied on overdue accounts". For contracts agreed on or after November 1, 1998, The Late Payment of Commercial Debts (Interest) Act 1998 enables small businesses to automatically claim interest on overdue debts owed to them by large organisations and public sector organisations. For contracts agreed after November 1, 2000, this legislation was extended so that small businesses could automatically claim interest from any size of business and public sector organisation. This legislation is referred to throughout this book. The final

	phase of the Act extended the right to claim interest to all businesses and public sector contracts dated after August 7, 2002. Even if an express clause is not inserted into the contract a creditor will still be eligible to claim late payment interest. However, as part of good business practice it is advisable to state the intention to claim interest under the Act rather than ambush the customer with interest at a later date. The benefit of stating the intention to charge interest in accordance with the Act is that on contracts agreed from August 7, 2002 a creditor business can also claim a sum to recover the costs of collections as stipulated in the legislation. This cannot be done if the claim is limited to just contractual interest.
Retention of Title Clauses	Retention of Title Clauses/"Romalpa" agreements/"all money clauses" are widespread where goods are supplied to customers in certain circumstances. Under this type of clause the seller retains ownership of the goods until they are paid for in full. If the buyer does not pay the seller can take possession back of the goods subject to a series of rules about how and when such a clause can be invoked. At its simplest, the creditor must be able to identify the goods by codes, numbers, markings or labels. Goods which have been processed into something else for example bricks or nuts and bolts, cannot be returned to the seller once they have been "processed".
Customer's own terms and conditions.	Disputes can arise when a supplier has signed the customer's conditions of purchase. These are sometimes included in small print on the reverse side of a purchase order. It is essential for the supplier to check that these are acceptable before signing otherwise these may become incorporated into the contract and be less favourable than the supplier's own terms.

Which party's terms control the contractual position?

This is often referred to as the "battle of the forms". When a supplier agrees to sell to a customer he or she is entering into a contract which has legal consequences even if the contract is only verbal in nature. So to prevent misunderstandings it is always advisable to ask the customer to sign his form and order confirmation before goods are dispatched or services are performed. This means that the supplier's terms of business become paramount because effectively the contract **1–11.1** was signed with those terms and conditions becoming the ones which are binding on the customer.

As a minimum the contract or order confirmation from the supplier's point of view should include the following terms:

- a clear specification of the goods or services to be supplied;
- the terms and conditions regarding the remedy for late payment;
- the price of each item excluding VAT;
- the total price of the contract excluding VAT;
- a clause stating that VAT will be added at a prevailing rate;
- the correct name of the customer (again this is of paramount importance) as an incorrect name can cause confusion in possible future legal action and enforcement options;
- the delivery date or any key dates or schedules to be complied with;
- the date or dates of invoicing or the issue of certificates or equivalent milestone documentation;
- the customer order number;
- the period allowed for inspection of goods or certification of work done;
- the procedure for resolving disputes which may relate to mediation or arbitration services.

Extra precautions that can be taken to ensure there is no delay or ambiguity relating to payment in relation to the contract order can also include the following:

- A term seeking part payment—when dealing with a high risk customer a supplier may ask for an advance payment before forwarding goods or providing the service. The customer is required to pay the remaining amount according to the agreed terms and conditions once the goods have been delivered or the service has been supplied.
- A third party guarantee—written commitments can be sought from third parties who then agree to be legally liable to pay in the event of a customer not doing so. They are often worth considering for newly established businesses without a track record for payment (often shown up on the credit searches which are made at the outset of the customer relationship).

Before granting credit to a new limited company a personal guarantee should be sought from the Directors of the new company to guarantee the company's debts. They will be personally liable for those debts in the event that the limited company cannot meet its obligations. As limited companies are designed to limit liability this can be a very sobering decision by the new directors and will show their commitment or otherwise to meeting the Company's obligations.

What is the importance of a delivery note?

The signing by the customer of a delivery note for the goods delivered or a certification statement for services performed can be very important to avoid disputes. **1–12**

Delivery notes can serve as very useful evidence if legal action is taken against the late paying customer as contemporaneous confirmation that at the time the goods or services were delivered, everything was in order.

A copy of the creditor's terms and conditions of business should be included in the delivery note as a reminder to the customer of the terms of the contract. Again, these are usually printed on the reverse in standard documentation.

What are the benefits of efficient invoicing?

An efficient process for issuing invoices and following them up will mean that customers will be clear as to where they stand and indeed will see the supplier organisation as well organised. An efficient process means that invoices will be issued and sent immediately when they are due and at least within 24 hours of production of a chargeable event by first class post or email as agreed with the customer. **1–13**

Invoices can often be dispatched with the goods to which they relate. It is strongly recommended that invoices are sent to a named individual to ensure that person takes responsibility for payment. A well displayed invoice should include:

- the date payment is due;
- the description of each item ordered or service performed;
- the quantity of each item ordered;
- the price for each item excluding VAT;
- the VAT rate for each item;
- the VAT amount per item;

- the total amount due excluding VAT;
- the total amount of VAT;
- the total amount due including VAT;
- the invoice date—again very important as evidence in legal proceedings;
- the delivery date and method;
- the terms and conditions of sale (although at this stage the terms and conditions are already included in the contract and act only as a reminder because these should have been agreed before any business was transacted). If advising a creditor it is important to stress that at this stage it is too late to include further terms of business as the work has been done;
- the address to which payment should be made;
- the method of payment;
- the details of the name of any payee for a cheque payment;
- the customer's name;
- the invoice number;
- the customer order number (the number allocated by the supplier to the customer's account); and
- bank details for easy payment through the BACS system.

It is essential that all information on the invoice is accurate as any error can provide a customer with reasonable grounds for delaying payment through raising a query. The easier it is for the customer to check the invoice with his or her ledger, the quicker the creditor will be paid.

Where do statements fit into the debt recovery process?

1–14 It is standard practice for customers with credit accounts to be sent regular statements which show the value of each purchase and the payment amount that is due. Even for non-credit account customers, it is good practice to send a statement to the customer as soon as payment is due, as some customers will only pay when they receive a statement.

The statement should display:

- the total amount due;
- the amount for each invoice;

- the cumulative total;
- the reference number for each item;
- the order number for each item;
- a copy of the terms and conditions of sale;
- the date of the statement;
- the address to which payment should be sent;
- the method of payment and bank details again to encourage payment by BACS; and
- the customer's name and address.

How can invoices and statements be effectively managed in a debt recovery process?

The creation of invoices and statements is all part of the organisation's management of its debtors. There are a number of ways in which a business can employ data and accounting information to measure the effectiveness of its debt recovery systems. It is certainly a vital practice for any business to regularly monitor the collection of its debts. This is necessary for priorities to be identified and assessments to be made. **1–15**

Calculating the average time for a debt to be collected is one such measurement. A formula for calculating the average time for debt to be paid is as follows:

$$\frac{\text{Amount owed at end of year}}{\text{Total amount of sales during the year}} \times 365 = \text{average number of days to be paid}$$

If a firm sold £500,000 of goods the previous year and was owed debts totalling £100,000 at the end of that year, the average period of payment would be:

$$\frac{£100{,}000}{£500{,}000} \times 365 = 73 \text{ days}$$

Of course the result of this calculation can be distorted if a particularly large order has been delivered towards the end of the previous year for which payment has not been made. In that case the accuracy of the figure produced against the average collection time for a random sample of invoices from the same year. Ideally, the average collection time should be equal to the supplier's terms of payment, i.e. 30 days. In the example given above a 73 day period would show that it was taking nearly twice as long for a business to recover its debts, as its terms of business allow which could be having a very adverse affect on cash flow.

How can the cost of late payment be measured?

1–16 Once a business knows how long on average it takes to be paid, it can gauge the size of its late payment burden by calculating the cost of that late payment per month and adding in estimates for the monthly cost of:

- Telephone calls, stationery and postage use in the recovery of its debts.
- Staff time used collecting debts calculated by:

  Hours worked × hourly pay rate + overheads.
- The extra cost of borrowing or interest lost due to late payment which is calculated by multiplying the total overdue at the end of last year × the interest rate on borrowings (or if in credit by the base rate) and then dividing that amount by 12.

What is the benefit of carrying out an aged debt analysis?

1–17 Debts should be analysed in order to establish debt collection priorities and to help identify problem customers. One of the most effective tools is the aged debt analysis which analyses debts by customer, and by the age of the debt.

An aged debt analysis can be performed manually, but often accounting software will calculate the "day's sales outstanding" figure or "DSO" which is a standard measure for credit professionals. Standard reports can be manipulated in a number of ways to show customers with the oldest debts, the highest amounts outstanding and the lowest balances so that the credit policy can be applied to tackle each customer in line with the credit policy.

The aged debt analysis report can be used to track progress and to review the situation on an ongoing monthly basis. It should form part of the monthly management accounts.

What is an ideal timetable for recovering debts?

1–18 Debt recovery should always follow a clearly defined process on which all relevant staff are trained, both in the process and in the technology, i.e. the accounting system which supports the process. Records should be kept of action taken regarding each debtor and of course some computer software packages allow for details to be entered on a note pad within the programme.

Although it is only natural that policies on debt management will vary from business to business, the following timetable can serve as a model for an in-house debt recovery function.

1–19

Time Scale	Action
Day 1—Send a Statement	This should be sent as soon as possible after the end of the stated payment period. The statement details as set should be similar to the invoice, but in essence the statement must state the amount of money due and the date that payment must be made by. As in all correspondence sent to debtors, a statement should be sent to a named person or to a job title such as the Credit Controller, Finance Director or even Managing Director. It is also advisable to restate the terms and conditions on the back of the statement as they appeared in the original order.
Day 8—Send First Written Reminder	This should be sent seven days after sending the statement. The first reminder should politely draw the customer's attention to the fact that the invoice remains outstanding and enquire if there is any problem behind the delay. The reminder letter should not appear to be a standardised document. Debtors always take more notice of personalised correspondence. In any event, the letter should be concise and clear. For an example of a first reminder letter, see the case study again at pages 444
Day 12—Make Telephone Contact	Four to five days after the reminder letter is sent a telephone call should be made to the customer pointing out that the debt is still outstanding. When speaking to the customer, the following points should be borne in mind: • The telephone call should be directed to the person who has responsibility for paying the invoices, i.e. the Purchase Ledger Clerk or perhaps the Finance Director. • The creditor's representative should always be polite and calm. • All relevant information should be at the Credit Professional's fingertips including dates of documentation, dates of previous contact, the amounts of previous payments received and the date of payment and any invoice numbers, etc. • The customer should be asked if they have any queries and if so they should be carefully listened to and where possible resolved. • It should be decided beforehand what the policy is regarding payment by instalments if the customer offers to pay in this way and procedure to record any agreement to pay by instalments.

Time Scale	Action
	• At the end of the telephone call, the creditor should try to ensure that the agreement has been reached and asked for it to be confirmed in writing so as to avoid misunderstandings later on.
Day 19—Send Debt Collection Letter	Seven days after the first reminder letter, if telephone calls prove unsuccessful the first debt collection letter should be sent which will tell the customer in clear terms the action that the creditor is going to take as a result of the non-payment of its invoice. This might, for example, mean putting a "stop" on the further supply of goods or credit until the invoice is paid or issuing legal proceedings or a statutory demand (see Chapter 3 on "Know Your Remedy")

Is there a model form of debt recovery letter?

1–20 Usually every organisation has its own suite of debt recovery letters and system of sending these as part of a process. It is important to remember that the more letters that are sent the less likely it is to receive a response. The statement accompanied by one or two well-worded and well laid out letters is going to be more than ample to cover off the initial stages of debt recovery.

Should the debt recovery letters be changed?

1–21 A system which regularly changes the wording of its recovery letters is essential to demonstrate to debtors that the debt recovery system is being managed and reviewed on a periodic basis and as a result late payment is not accepted. If the debt recovery process is reviewed and updated debtors will be less likely to be complacent when receiving letters which change emphasis and wording in an ongoing trading relationship. This will be particularly true if they point out the consequences of not paying in accordance with the terms of business.

The expression "You only have one chance to make a first impression" is extremely true in relation to how the debt recovery letter should be presented. A scruffy, poorly laid out letter which lacks information will send a signal to a debtor that the recovery process is poorly managed and therefore further delay in payment will not be reduced.

To avoid this it is important that the letter has an immediate effect. It should be well-written, informative, clear and point out the consequences of non-compliance. Vital information such as the amount outstanding should be highlighted.

There is also much to be said for making it easy at this stage for the debtor to pay the outstanding amount. Enclosing details of how to pay by credit or debit card or enclosing a payment slip and a reply-paid envelope will all encourage debtors who have forgotten to pay to put a cheque in the post or give you their card details for processing.

Is there a structure to a well-presented debt recovery letter?

An example of a well-prepared debt recovery letter is set out in the case study in this book within the Appendix. Good business practice will assist the debt recovery practitioner in building a series of templates for letters which will send the right signals to the debtor that payment must now be made. Some simple rules to follow include the following: **1–22**

Identify the correct address for your debtor	An incorrectly addressed letter is only going to end up on the incorrect desk of the person that you want to ensure makes the payment. It is important to ensure that through the sales or account opening process the name of the person responsible for paying overdue accounts is noted and that in future correspondence, and indeed telephone calls, are addressed to that person. Use information from the steps taken in setting up the account to get this right.
Salutation	Assuming the name of the person to whom the letter is addressed is known, the letter should be addressed to them personally and depending on the familiarity with that person it should read either Dear Mr Bloggs/Mrs Bloggs/Miss Bloggs or Dear Jane or Fred.
Heading	The letter should state in the heading what it is about so if it is to do with an overdue payment it should state "Overdue payment in the sum of £__" so that the recipient is clear as to why you are writing to them and apart from anything else this is good business practice.
The body of the letter	The letter should clearly set out the amount which is owed and where available the invoice number should be included to ensure that it cannot be ignored for lack of detail. The letter itself should never just refer to the "Overdue amount" or "Outstanding amount" without detailing what that amount is and how it is arrived at.
Reminder on terms	This is an ideal opportunity to remind the debtor of the creditor's terms of business and, where it is possible, to point out how far beyond terms the payment is now overdue.

Seeking the demand for payment	The letter should ask for the payment to be made by a deadline which should be stipulated in the letter, for example, "May we please have your payment by Friday, 1st August 2008". The letter should not state "Please can we have your payment by "return of post" or worse still "the next few days" or even the next "seven days" because there can be arguments about how to compute that time so it is much better to stipulate a deadline.
Leeway	Because at this stage there is still an ongoing customer relationship, it is important to recognise that customers may simply have forgotten to make payment so offering some leeway in a debt recovery letter for some customers will be appreciated and might read "if your payment has been sent in the last few days please disregard this letter".
The threat	It is actually good debt recovery practice and indeed becoming a compliance issue (see Chapter 2) that a clear signal is sent to the debtor as early as possible as to the possible action which may be taken if they fail to make payment. We will deal with this when looking at the Office of Fair Trading Guidance in Chapter 2 but there is no harm in spelling out to a debtor at an early stage the consequences of non-compliance. That said if something is threatened in a debt recovery letter then the creditor needs to be in a position to carry out that threat at some future date. Idle threats will often leave creditors at a disadvantage if they fail to carry them through. If the letter states there is an intention to sue then the creditor needs to be in a position to do that at the end of any period given for payment. More leeway can however be added to the threat so that it is worded, for example, "If you fail to pay this account by close of business on Friday, August 1, 2008 we will have to consider you for legal action". For some debtors the fact you have given leeway encourages them to pay.
Sign off	Wherever possible, the debt recovery letters should be signed in ink with a signature or initials. This sends a signal to the debtor that the creditor has taken the time to sign the letter. A letter which is signed with a PP or not at all sends a signal "If you cannot be bothered to sign your letter why should I as a customer be bothered to read it?"

How can the telephone be used to assist in the recovery of debt?

The telephone is perhaps the most effective method of recovering overdue accounts before a debt is escalated to legal proceedings and even then it can be used throughout the legal process and indeed the enforcement process to keep open channels of communication so that any issues can be resolved and queries dealt with. **1–23**

Again simple rules on telephone collection include:

1–24

Training	If telephone collection training is not something that a Debt Recovery Practitioner has undertaken in the past it is well worth investing in specialist training on how to use the telephone as an effective tool and to ensure that it is included in part of the debt recovery process. Debt recovery by telephone takes confidence and underlines the need to rehearse the facts of any particular debt recovery matter so that when speaking to the debtor the facts are at one's fingertips. There is no point in speaking to a debtor unless all facts are known and the figures are understood. The Institute of Credit Management provides specialist training courses and can be contacted on 01780 722900 and their training program can be viewed on their website at *http://www.icm.org.uk*.
Greeting	In a debt recovery call it is important that the debtor is greeted appropriately such as Mr Bloggs/Mrs Bloggs/Miss Bloggs or if the debtor is well-known to the Debt Recovery Practitioner then "Jane" or "Fred". However, over-familiarity should be avoided if the debt recovery call is made to someone who is not well-known. It is a question of degree and common courtesy.
Introducing yourself	The Debt Recovery Practitioner should introduce him or herself using their title and surname, i.e. Mr Jones/Mrs Jones/Miss Jones and again use of one's first name should only be used if one is well-known to the debtor and indeed this has been used in the past.
Identifying creditor Organisation	The Debt Recovery Practitioner should identify his or her organisation and his/her position.
Identification of client	Where the Debt Recovery Practitioner is telephoning on behalf of a client in the case of a debt collection agency or a solicitor's practice, the identity of the client company should be given in the opening comments to the debtor.
Account details	The Debt Recovery Practitioner should explain the account that he or she is telephoning about giving details of the outstanding amount with a reason for the call, stating the balance outstanding and asking for payment in full today.

Logical questions	The Debt Recovery Practitioner should set out (usually by developing training) a series of logical questions that he or she will ask the debtor about the account and indeed a series of open probing and closed questions regarding the debtor's current financial situation to enable the Debt Recovery Practitioner to determine the "debtor type", i.e. an individual in the home, sole trader, partner, director of a limited company. Throughout this conversation the Debt Recovery Practitioner should be listening carefully to what the debtor is saying and should be taking notes contemporaneously within the notes facility of any software system or simply using a humble desk diary if no computer system is available.
Encouraging payment	The debtor should be encouraged to pay in full and where necessary the Debt Recovery Practitioner can empathise with the debtor's situation. The Debt Recovery Practitioner should be aware of the consequences of non-compliance and should outline these to the debtor as a result of the information that he or she has been given.
Negotiating payment	The debtor should be asked how they can arrange for payment either through a BACS/CHAPS or a debit or credit card. The Debt Recovery Practitioner should refuse the first offer and should ask how the balance will be cleared before accepting an increased offer. The debtor should be asked to repeat back what has been promised to take ownership of the promise and again the Debt Recovery Practitioner should reinforce the consequences if that promise is not fulfilled.
Closing a debt recovery call	Calls should be closed with a routine which: • confirms the amount to be paid; • confirms the date the payment will be sent; • results in the payment being sent first class or by the BACS or CHAPS system; and • confirms the date payment will be made and uses the debtor's name to close the call.

What are the classic delaying tactics for non-payment?

1–25 Handling delaying tactics are a part of life for Debt Recovery Practitioners. Simple rules to tackle a debtor who is deliberately delaying payment include taking the reason away for the debtor not to pay by:

- creating a mood of cooperation; and
- being confident and assertive on the telephone.

Classic excuses on why not to pay include the debtor never being available or stating they require a copy statement even though the creditor knows that one has been sent or sending in a cheque which has been unsigned or saying that there has been problems with cash flow or benefits. In fact the Better Payment Practice Group (BPPG) has collated these into a page on its website at *http://www.payontime.co.uk*.

Whatever the excuse, the debtor should continue to be reminded that a consequence of non-payment will result in legal proceedings being issued and subsequent to that enforcement action being taken.

Which outside agencies can help in the recovery of debt?

If all the above fails and the customer still refuses to pay there are **1–26** a number of ways in which Credit Professionals can seek external assistance for the recovery of their debt prior to legal action being commenced. One such avenue is to choose a third party to intervene and seek to collect the debt on behalf of the creditor organisation. It is the intervention of a third party which will often cause a debtor to pay. Such third parties include Debt Collection Agencies (DCAs) and solicitors specialising in debt recovery and litigation.

Debts should be referred to third parties as soon as all the internal steps to recover the debt have been exhausted. The older the debt the more difficult it will be to collect and this can be statistically proven in many cases. DCAs are helpful for businesses who have limited time in which to chase their debts and therefore the debt is outsourced to the agency that takes the debt on and applies their own debt recovery process to its collection. Disputed debts are usually best sent to solicitors specialising in debt recovery rather than to Debt Collection Agencies although of course both types of organisation offer a service. Letters sent by solicitors threatening legal action are a popular choice for Credit Professionals who want to ensure the debt is paid.

What will it cost to use a third party?

Most DCAs charge a percentage of the debt recovered as a com- **1–27** mission for their services. This can range from 5 per cent for larger debts to perhaps 10 per cent for an overall portfolio of debt which is outsourced for collection. Many agencies work on a "no collection, no fee" arrangement while others charge only a very small fee. For more information about the work of collection agencies and to seek a professional organisation please see *http://www.csa-uk.com* being the Credit Services Association within the UK and also see Chapter 4.

Solicitors are governed by their Professional Code of Conduct on what they can charge and this is dealt with more fully again in Chapter 4.

How does a creditor select a third party collection partner?

1–28 The following factors will be part of a decision-making process when selecting a third party as a collection partner:

- Performance—This is possibly the most important of all selection criteria and cannot be underestimated. Measurement of results and cash banked are clear indicators that a third party is actually doing the job which they are employed to do and that is to recover the debt. The speed of which debt is recovered is of paramount importance of course to the creditor's own cash flow and again proper management information as to how this is being achieved is vital. In selecting a partner the reporting process should be outlined at the beginning of the relationship so it can be fully understood before a decision is made.
- Regulatory Compliance—Any third party should be licensed under the Consumer Credit Act 1974 to collect debt. Licences are issued by the Office of Fair Trading (see Chapter 2 on The Regulatory Environment for Debt Recovery) and guidance is issued by the Office of Fair Trading to Consumer Credit Act licence holders.
- Professional Associations—The third party should preferably be either a member of the Credit Services Association (CSA) as mentioned above or if they are solicitors then they will automatically be members of the Law Society. Both sets of organisations will carry professional indemnity insurance as to the services that they offer. The CSA does not recommend firms but will send a list of its members to any creditor who makes an enquiry. The Law Society website does mention firms which specialise in debt recovery at *http://www.lawsociety.org.uk/choosingandusing/findasolicitor.law*
- Information on charging—If charges are based on commission, the question needs to be asked what is the percentage and does this vary according to the size of the debt? Whether a DCA or a solicitor operates on a "no collection, no fee" basis is clearly important.

- Debt Profile—The makeup of the debt or debts to be collected should be set out so that the third party applies the best collection strategy. Debts which are old in age—say more than two years—need a different approach to debts which are relatively fresh in terms of Days Sales Outstanding (DSO) of say 60 days.
- Escalation to legal proceedings—The question should be asked as to whether the third party will pursue the debt through to legal action and indeed whether the service for collection is all encompassing. The client should also check the process for how debts will be selected for legal action, the costs and fees involved (see Chapter 4) and the legal formalities to be adhered to, i.e. the signing of the Statement of Truth process (as dealt with in Chapter 5).

Can personal visits assist in collecting pre-legal debts?

Personal visits, field visits, or status reports can all be carried out as part of a pre-legal process to collect a debt, however, care must be taken to ensure the visit does not constitute harassment and that data protection rights are not violated in discussing the outstanding account with anyone other than the debtor. **1–29**

A well constructed status report to record information is always useful and again Form EX140 based on the Order to Obtain Information procedure under CPR Pt.71 provides a useful model on the questions to ask either a debtor or neighbours as to the debtor's circumstances.

What external help is available to collect disputed debts?

For disputed debts commercial mediation can be a useful tool for reaching agreement without having to resort to legal action. Due to the cost of mediation, this is only really worth considering for larger debts—the major advantage of this process is that it is likely to cause less damage to the supplier/customer relationship than the claim route alternative. **1–30**

Commercial mediation does require the consent of both parties and if both parties have been unable to agree to mediation the mediating organisation can contact the unwilling party to discuss this.

Both sides will be asked to present a written statement to the mediator which provides details about the dispute and copies of supporting documents such as invoices and correspondence.

The mediator will then discuss the case with each party separately in private and in the strictest of confidence. The mediator may need to spend two or three hours dealing with the case although more complicated cases can take up to a day or more. If an agreement is reached both sides will be asked to meet again and prepare a written settlement which, on the consent of each party, becomes legally binding.

1–31 Mediation does not guarantee an agreement will be achieved and both parties are free to go to court if they are still dissatisfied at the end of the process. Costs for mediation can vary from £60 to £100 an hour and there are various providers appearing on the internet who can be applied to for a quote.

Alternatively arbitration is used for disputes between two parties, but unlike mediation the decision of the arbitrator is legally binding. Again, this is only appropriate for larger debts and the cost of arbitration can amount to several hundred pounds running into thousands in a large dispute.

To work, arbitration is based on the agreement of both parties who agree arbitration will be used for the resolution of their dispute. It is particularly prevalent in the construction industry.

Once the arbitrator has reached a decision, an appeal against that decision can only be made if one of the parties considers the arbitrator has misunderstood, misapplied the law or worse still is guilty of misconduct. The arbitration procedure can require a considerable amount of paperwork for establishing the conditions for arbitration exist and then in hearing and preparing the case.

Can trade associations bring any weight to bear in achieving payment?

1–32 If a debtor is a member of a trade association scheme then a complaint could be made to that association which may instigate a conciliation process. This will involve contacting the debtor to arrange an agreement which is acceptable to both sides. If conciliation fails then possibly arbitration may commence. The cost of any arbitration will be borne by either the business in dispute or the trade association but clearly an agreement from the conciliation process is going to be more cost effective.

How can statutory demands be used as an alternative to court action?

1–33 A statutory demand is an alternative method to issuing a claim in the county court though, it should not be used lightly as it is a formal allegation that the customer's business is in fact insolvent. If the debt is not paid within 21 days of the statutory demand being served then the Credit Professional can file a petition for a compulsory winding up of the debtor business (if it is a limited company) or, for bankruptcy in the case of a proprietor.

Statutory demands can also be used following judgment where a county court bailiff or High Court Enforcement Officer has levied execution on goods (more about this process will appear in Chapter 14).

Statutory demands can only be used where the debtor owes at least £750 in England and Wales and that sum rises to £1,500 when they are used in Scotland although the use of the statutory demand in Scotland is outside the scope of this book.

The advantage of a statutory demand is that it is relatively inexpensive, however, it is a quite draconian tool. Forms are available from legal stationers for around £1 or can be downloaded from the Internet or the insolvency service website, see *http://www.insolvency.gov.uk*.

The statutory demand must be handed to the debtor and not **1–34**
posted and this process is dealt with more fully in Chapter 17.

If a debtor business can actually afford to pay a debt but for some reason is delaying payment then usually the service of a statutory demand will prompt payment to be made rather than running the risk of being wound up or the proprietor being made bankrupt. If the debtor, however, is really in a desperate situation the Credit Professional has to decide whether there is anything likely to be gained by filing the petition for compulsory winding up or bankrupting the debtor. The problem with taking this course of action is that all the other creditors will expect to receive a percentage of their debt in the event of insolvency and furthermore a solicitor will be needed to help in relation to the legal work.

For many creditors insolvency does not result in payment of their debt, it is the threat of insolvency which creates the payment.

So the service of a statutory demand is a very drastic form of action which should only be used when the debt is undisputed or a court judgment has been obtained and when it is accepted the relationship with the debtor has broken down irretrievably.

Although the service of a statutory demand may intimidate a **1–35**
debtor sufficiently into paying if the threatened action is not taken when the debtor still fails to pay then the debtor will not take further debt seriously.

An example of a statutory demand in the case study of this book is set out at page 510.

Chapter 2

Regulatory Environment for the Collection of Debt

Introductory Comments

Over the last 10 years the regime in which debt recovery operates has seen an increase in the amount of regulations which affect the process. There are now a number of major statutes along with the Civil Procedure Rules and regulatory guidance coming from government agencies which all create a framework in which debt recovery in England and Wales is carried out. 2–01

The drivers for creating a framework, undoubtedly due to the pressures of over-indebtedness, has been the subject of a number of major Government reports and is clearly a major social issue which must be tackled.

For Practitioners this means that failing to appreciate the extent of the regulatory environment and how debt must be collected within it are ignored at one's peril. Debt Recovery Practitioners must ensure that they are trained and train their teams to understand how to operate and ensure they comply with all the various aspects of regulation.

This Chapter aims to highlight the major areas of compliance on a subject by subject basis.

The Data Protection Act 1998

Introductory comments

The Data Protection Act (DPA) is probably one of the most important statutes which affects debt recovery practices and processes in England and Wales today. The Data Protection Act itself requires all organisations who handle "personal information" to comply with a number of important principles regarding privacy and disclosure. 2–02

The Act requires all personal data to be processed in accordance with the principles of the Act.

Definitions

2–03 "Data" is defined under s.1(1) of the DPA as "information processed or recorded in specified ways". "Personal data" is then defined as data which relates to a living individual who can then be identified either from that data or from that data and other information which is in the possession of, or is likely to come into possession of a data controller.

Information kept in any type of debt recovery system about a debtor is going to be on the face of it personal data. Moving on through the definitions in order for something to constitute "personal data" it must, however, consist of information relating to an identifiable living individual. One could argue as companies are not living individuals data kept on a company is not personal data and therefore the DPA does not apply.

Introducing departmental policies

2–04 However, rather than trying to make artificial distinctions about what is and is not personal data and who is and who is not a data controller, a better way to use the principles of the Act is to build systems and policies that ensure that anything that is recorded about any type of debtor is recorded in accordance with the principles of the Act so one cannot fall foul of its requirements to process data fairly. Trying to distinguish between different data sets and situations can be dangerous and difficult to control particularly in a busy department.

Policies need to embrace the Eight Principles of the Act which can be summarised as follows:

1. All data must be processed fairly and lawfully.
2. Data must be processed for the purposes which is stipulated or agreed.
3. The processing of the data must be adequate, relevant and not excessive.
4. The data process must be accurate and up-to-date—the policy must ensure data is managed in accordance with best practice and ideally a data management standard such as ISO 27001.
5. The data must not be kept for longer than it is necessary—the policy needs to include a destruction procedure.

6. The data must be processed in accordance with the individual's rights.

7. The data must be kept securely—there have been horror stories of laptops being left on trains and CDs with full database information being lost in government departments, clearly if data is allowed to escape the organisation this is a breach of the Act.

8. The data must not be transferred to other countries without adequate protections being in place which is a consideration if debts are being managed and recovered offshore.

Handling Data Subject Access Requests

In debt recovery, the DPA allows those who are being chased for payment of their account to find out what personal information is held about them within the debt recovery process. They can call for information held on computer or paper records and can seek full disclosure of credit reference details. If a member of the public thinks he or she is being prevented from seeing the information, they can ask for help through the Information Commissioner's Office (ICO) for the records to be made available. **2–05**

The ICO is responsible for ensuring that an individual's rights are enforced and that personal information is not misused. The ICO's website is a useful source of information on everything to do with the DPA and can be found at *http://www.ico.gov.uk*.

If a person wishes to enquire about the use of his or her personal data he or she can make a Data Subject Access Request. The ICO publishes a guide, "Subject Access–A Guide for Data Subjects". This guide can be found on the ICO website.

As these requests can come at anytime a process needs to be in place in the debt recovery team to handle one when it arrives. The guide itself gives the procedure—basically the data controller has 40 days to respond to the request which should be in line with an approved policy and procedure.

The data subject can call for all the personal data held about them **2–06** in the data controller's file. This means whatever is in the personal record of the data subject will need to be disclosed.

A good practical suggestion to Debt Recovery Practitioners is never to write anything about anyone in a file note that they would not want to see written about themselves! It is a simple rule for most people in the office to follow. Of course from time to time the fact a debtor is abusive, upset, suffering a serious illness, or on state benefits all adds to the decision making process on whether to accept a proposal. However whatever is written should be viewed as being open to scrutiny both in terms of internal processes and if a data subject request is received. In a busy department notes will be taken all day long about conversations with debtors. Managers of departments have to consider how they will manage the substance and quality of these notes to ensure compliance with the DPA.

Instructing a tracing agent

2–07 Another area of compliance for Practitioners to be aware of is how suppliers acting on their behalf use the personal data of debtors. Tracing agents are a good example of how a Debt Recovery Practitioner can slip into non-compliance under the DPA. As recently as May 2006 the Information Commissioner's Office issued a damming report highlighting instances of where the protection of privacy and in particular violations of s.55 of the Data Protection Act had occurred. This important section of the DPA which makes it an offence to obtain, disclose or "procure the disclosure of" confidential personal information "knowingly or recklessly" without the consent of the organisation holding the data were disclosed. Indeed activities of debt collection agencies and tracing agents were highlighted as one area of concern by the ICO which even went as far as publishing the names of those individuals who had been found to be guilty of breaching s.55 and indeed have been prosecuted for that offence.

Debt Recovery Practitioners should therefore consider implementing policies to audit suppliers of tracing information on a periodic basis. The ICO itself provides guidance including good practice notes on how to comply with the Act and the ICO website is well worth visiting to ensure that current DPA knowledge is kept up-to-date.

The site can also be used as a way of checking whether tracing agents or other suppliers notify their business activities in the proper form to the ICO and if it can even be used as a form of check on whether a debtor is registered and has notified under the DPA. On occasion this can even lead to a result in finding a new address for a debtor.

Processing data lawfully

2–08 It is also an offence to process personal data without notifying the Information Commissioner that this is being done and is a criminal offence under s.21 of the DPA. Debt Recovery Practitioners should take a moment to check their own organisation is registered correctly to handle personal data under the DPA and should not rely on this being done for them by someone else. Checking an organisation's notification is easy and can be done through the ICO website.

Inevitably, all debt recovery operations of any size must have clear processes for dealing with data to ensure that the principles of the DPA are complied with and to ensure they respect the principles of the Act and stay on the right side of compliance. Much of what the Act wants to achieve in the management of personal data is common-sense and indeed good practice. Practitioners should work with their IT departments and quality audit colleagues to create policies surrounding the handling and management of personal data of debtors and indeed clients so that should there be a problem they can look to the policy and benchmark what is going wrong.

The Human Rights Act 1998

The Human Rights Act 1998 confers rights on citizens whether or not they are debtors or whether judgment has been entered against them as judgment debtors. Debtors themselves can take the form of individuals, sole traders or limited companies and since the introduction of the Human Rights Act 1998 into domestic legislation, there have been a series of cases particularly in relation to art.6 of the European Convention on Human Rights (ECHR) involving the right to a fair hearing. **2–09**

In relation to debt recovery the areas of the Human Rights Act which have particular focus include:

- Article 6 being the right to a fair trial. The European Convention on Human Right states that under this Article in the determination of civil rights and obligations or of any criminal charge against the citizen each person is entitled to a fair and public hearing in a reasonable time by an independent and impartial tribunal established by law. Clearly the default judgment regime under the Civil Procedure Rules is not a public trial but of course debtors are given the opportunity to apply to set aside any order that is made and to appeal any order should this become necessary.
- Article 8 states that every citizen has the right to respect for his or her private and family life, his home and his correspondence and that where there should be no interference by public authority with the exercise of this right such interference is permissible where it is in accordance with the country's domestic law and where it is necessary in a democratic society and in the interest of national security, public safety or the economic well being of the country, for the prevention of disorder or crime or for the protection of health and morals, or for the protection of the rights and freedoms of others. Of course, this Article centres closely on the activities of debt recovery

procedures in contacting citizens to recover debts by letter, telephone, field visit or ultimately by legal procedures.

- Finally, an area which acutely affects the debt recovery process in England and Wales is Pt 2 of the First Protocol of the European Convention on Human Rights and Art.1 which involves the protection of property. In this Article, it is stated that every natural or legal person is entitled to the peaceful enjoyment of his possessions and no one should be deprived of those possessions except in the public interest and subject to the conditions provided for by law and by the general principles of international law. These provisions however do not in any way impair the right of a state to enforce its laws as it deems necessary to control the use of property in accordance with the general interest or to secure the payment of taxes or other contributions or penalties. Clearly in this context the impact of the enforcement of the court's judgment to ensure the debtor pays the amount due using either bailiffs or other enforcement options is going to be in compliance with the European Convention on Human Rights even though there is a clear interference with the property of the individual citizen.

2–10 There have been cases which have come before the European Commission and have been narrowly interpreted. In the case of *James & Others v United Kingdom* (1986) 8 EHHR 123 it was stated that the court would "respect the legislature's judgment as to what was in the public interest unless that judgment was found to be manifestly without reasonable foundation". In the case of *Gasus Dosier v The Netherlands* (1995) 20 EHHR 403 the European Commission, when looking at activities by the Dutch Tax Authorities to collect arrears, who had seized and sold third party assets in satisfaction of the tax payer's liability, found the Dutch collection mechanism was not uncommon and not in itself incompatible with the Protocol even though the case ended up with a third party's assets being sold who had no connection with the outstanding tax bill.

Similarly, in the case of *K. v Sweden* (1991) Application N.13800/8871 DR 94 the European Commission held that even though tax authorities had forced entry to a private house, the door lock had been changed and the debtor's belongings were thrown on the floor, the action of the authorities could be justified on the basis that they were carrying out their responsibilities in accordance with the law and it was necessary in a democratic society for tax to be collected. The "necessity" was required to meet the social need in that people should pay their taxes and this requirement was in proportion to the legitimate aim being pursued by the state in the action taken against the tax payer.

Limitation Act 1980

All Debt Recovery Practitioners need to be aware of the impact of limitation on any action they wish to bring to the courts. If an action is not brought within six years of the debt becoming due it will become "statute barred". This means that no legal action can be taken on the debt in any shape or form. Debt Recovery Practitioners should look at the date that the debt was incurred to see what has happened since the debt became due to assess whether debt recovery action can still proceed. **2–11**

It should be noted that if the debt, however, relates to a "specialty", being a document which is executed by a deed such as a mortgage deed, the limitation period increases to 12 years.

Under s.29(5) of the Limitation Act 1980 if a debtor acknowledges his indebtedness or makes a part payment in respect of the debt, then the creditor's right of action is "deemed to have accrued on and not before the date of the acknowledgment or payment". The policy behind this exception to limitation is that a creditor should be given more time to negotiate for the payment of an admitted debt without the fear that the claim will become statute barred.

To be effective for the purposes of s.29 an acknowledgment must be "in writing, and signed by the person making the acknowledgment" (see s.30).

In *Bradford & Bingley Plc v Rashid* [2006] 1 W.L.R. 2066, the **2–12**
House of Lords held unanimously that so long as the acknowledgment admitted the liability for the debt it did not need to contain an admission of a definite amount, or an amount ascertainable by mere arithmetic. The Law Lords also held, but only by majority, that an admission made in the course of "Without Prejudice Negotiations" could not be relied upon as the acknowledgment for the purposes of the Act. Section 29(7) does, however, provide that a limitation period can be repeatedly extended by further acknowledgments or payments, but a right of action once statute barred cannot be revived by any subsequent acknowledgment or payment.

The acknowledgment itself can be made by an agent on behalf of the debtor (see s.30).

It will be for the court to determine whether the acknowledgement is a sufficient acknowledgment bearing in mind the comments made in the case of *Bradford & Bingley Plc v Rashid.*

In relation to judgment debts under s.24(1) of the Limitation Act, no action can be brought upon any judgment after the expiration of six years from the date on which the judgment became enforceable. In *Lowsley v Forbes* [1998] 3 All E.R. 897 the question was raised as to whether or not s.24 barred the execution of a judgment after six years or whether it only barred the bringing of a fresh action on the judgment. The House of Lords held that "action" in s.24 meant "fresh action" and did not include proceedings by way of execution. It is therefore permissible to enforce judgments more than six years old, but the Civil Procedure Rules require the judgment creditor to obtain the court's permission in order to take this step. This is dealt with in Chapter 14 of this book. The rationale of this case was also explored in the more recent case of *Ridgeway Motors (Isleworth) Ltd v ALTS Ltd* [2005] EWCA Civ 92 in which the six year limitation period under Limitation Act s.24 was found not to apply to bankruptcy or winding up proceedings based on judgment debts (see Chapter 17 of this book).

Consumer Credit Act 1974

2–13 The Consumer Credit Act 1974 (as amended by the Consumer Credit Act 2006) regulates consumer credit and consumer hire agreements. The legislation is designed to protect individuals, sole traders, partners and unincorporated associations in agreements with traders. It does not cover agreements between traders and limited companies.

John Hutton the newly Secretary of State for Business and Enterprise was quoted as saying that as a result of the new legislation, "There will be more protection for people who get caught out by rogue lenders who pretend to play by the rules but act like loan sharks. Enforcers now have the powers they need to crack down on the small minority of traders who treat consumers unfairly. Pressure sales techniques, unfair terms and conditions, extortionate interest rates or aggressive debt collection practices will not be tolerated". With changes coming to the legislation some 30 years after the initial legislation it is clear the Government is determined to continue the regulation of credit to consumers, which means those working in the credit industry have to be aware of the impact of the legislation on many aspects of debt recovery.

The Act lays down a comprehensive framework of rules which covers:

- the form and content of agreements with consumers;
- credit advertising;
- the method for calculating the annual percentage rate (APR) of total charge for credit;
- the procedures to be adopted in the event of default;
- termination of a Consumer Credit Act agreement;
- early settlement of an agreement; and
- the unfair relationships test between parties.

The Act also requires that all traders who make regulated agreements obtain licenses from the Office of Fair Trading (OFT). Credit brokers, debt advisors and others, may also require licenses. From October 2008, this licensing requirement extends to credit information/repair and debt information service providers. 2–14

Local trading standards departments and the OFT enforce the Act. The OFT also produces guidance about the Act and its regulations. For more information Practitioners can visit the department's comprehensive website *http://www.oft.gov.uk* and also contact local trading standards departments or the OFT directly.

History to the Consumer Credit Act 2006

The original Act was introduced in 1974 and is the one which most Practitioners working in the field of consumer credit are familiar with. However as with the entire area of debt recovery, the driver to review the Act due to the increasing amount of debt in the economy led to a Consumer Credit White Paper being published in December 2003. To implement the recommendations of this White Paper required primary legislation. After a thorough three year review the Government took these proposals forward in the Consumer Credit Act 2006 (CCA2006), which received Royal Assent on March 30, 2006. We can expect the new Act to be fully implemented by October 2008. 2–15

The implementation of the CCA2006 has been as follows:

2–16

First Commencement Order (SI 2006/2008)	The First Commencement Order under the new Act was made on June 10, 2006.	Schedule 1 of the order listed the powers coming into force on June 16, 2006 including • An administrative change to improve the OFT's processing of request from businesses to disapply the hirer's right to terminate hire agreements where this was in the hirer's interest. • Powers enabling the Secretary of State to make other secondary legislation, enabling the OFT to give general notices and defining a term "default sum". These powers prepared the way for the more substantive provisions in the Act which have been brought into force and have laid the foundations for the new consumer credit jurisdiction of the Financial Ombudsman Service (FOS). • Schedule 2 of the order included a power which came into being to extend the period that consumers have to respond to default notices from 7 to 14 days.

Second Commencement Order (SI 2007/123)	The Second Commencement Order was made on February 13, 2007	This introduced sections of the Act covering the following: • The new definition of "individual" for the purposes of the Consumer Credit Act 1974 and provisions relating to unfair relationships and related transitional, saving and repeal provisions in Schedules 3 and 4 of the Act which came into force April 6, 2007. • The bringing into force of s.8 of the 2007 Act, requires the OFT to prepare information sheets on arrears and defaults which came into force on January 6, 2007.
Third Commencement Order (SI 2007/3300)	This Order was made on November 22, 2007	It introduced all the remaining provisions in the Act apart from s.2 being removal of the financial limit which was introduced in March 2008 in the Fourth Commencement Order. In general, this Third Order enabled: • The OFT to publish guidance on fitness and the use of penalties. • The Ministry of Justice to take forward work on transferring Consumer Credit Appeals to the Tribunals Service—effective from April 6, 2008. • Introducing a licensing scheme from April 2008. • Introducing exemptions for high net worth individuals in business lending above £25,000 which came into force on April 6, 2008. • Creating post-contract transparency provisions which will come into force on October 1, 2008. • Creating two new licensing categories of business being debt administration and credit information services which will come into force on October 1, 2008.
Fourth Commencement Order (SI 2008/831)	This Order was made on March 20, 2008.	It introduced s.2 being the removal of the financial limit of £25,000 so that all agreements of whatever value are now regulated within the Act unless they come within one of the exemptions.
Statutory Instruments (SIs covering:	March 31, 2007.	These give full effect to a number of sections of the 2006 Act and these fall into three categories:

exemptions; post-contract transparency and licensing.		**Exemptions from regulation**—Sections 3 and 4 of the CCA2006. The Order specifies the conditions under which an agreement made with an individual of "high net worth" may be exempted from regulation and the form and content of the required statement of high net worth in relation to and the declaration by the individual. The Order also sets out the form and content of declarations by debtors or hirers where an agreement is wholly or predominantly for business purposes and the amount of credit provided under the agreement exceeds £25,000. **Post-contract information**—Regulations relating to ss.6, 7, 9, 10, 12, 14 and 17 of the CCA2006. These Regulations specify precisely what information must be included in statements and notices given to consumers by creditors and owners. The objective has been to balance the need to ensure that consumers are provided with relevant and clear information about the state of their credit account as set out in the 2006 Act, with the need to ensure that any burden on industry is not disproportionate. **Licensing issues**—Regulations relating to ss.34 and 35 of the CCA2006. These set out the maximum duration of a time-limited licence, and the periods for the payment of charges for indefinite licences.
Draft Legislative Reform (Consumer Credit) Order 2008	The draft Legislative Reform Order to amend the Consumer Credit Act 1974 was laid in Parliament on June 11, 2008	The draft Order proposes an exemption for buy-to-let lending, clarifies the position for the giving of statements for fixed-sum credit agreements and provides definitions of "payments" for the purpose of issuing notices of sums in arrears.

Consumer Credit—European Directive

The Consumer Credit Act implements the European Directive on Consumer Credit. The 1987 Directive on consumer credit established the Community framework for consumer credit with a view to promoting the setting-up of a common market for credit and establishing minimum Community rules to protect consumers. Following a review of the legislation, the Commission concluded that the 2–17

Directive no longer reflected the current situation on the consumer credit market and was in need of revision. In January 2008, the European Parliament reached an agreement on a compromise text with the Council following the political agreement reached in May 2007. A number of amendments were made by the Parliament. The text is expected to be formally adopted during Spring/Summer 2008, at which point each Member State will have two years to implement the Directive into national law. No doubt as a result Debt Recovery Practitioners will see domestic laws move forward again as a result of the directive being implemented.

Important milestones for debt recovery practitioners in the new legislation

The remaining paragraphs in the Consumer Credit Act set out the key changes to the Legislation.

2–18 The new definition of an "Individual" came into force on April 6, 2007 and amends s.189(1) of the 1974 Act. The removal of financial limits repealing s.8(1) and s.8(2) along with s.15(1)(c) and s.43(3)(a) of the 1974 Act have all been repealed and the new Act is now in force from April 6, 2008.

Exemptions relating to High Net Worth debtors and hirers inserts a new s.16A into the 1974 Act which came into force on April 6, 2008.

In relation to statements to be provided in relation to regulated agreements, s.6 of the new Act requires statements to be provided in relation to fixed-sum credit agreements. This is through a new s.77A being inserted into the 1974 Act which will come into force on October 1, 2008.

Businesses that require a Consumer Credit Act licence and extended powers of the OFT for dealing with businesses that do not have the appropriate licence, came into power on April 6, 2008.

2–19 The duties and powers of the Office of Fair Trading (OFT) came into force on April 6, 2008 with the Consumer Credit Appeals Tribunal coming in to force from April 6, 2008.

Finally, the Financial Ombudsman Service or (FOS) came into force on April 6, 2007.

In relation to regulated agreements a number of key changes have been introduced as the result of the Consumer Credit Act 1974 being amended and key changes are set out in the following paragraphs.

What is a regulated agreement?

2–20 The 1974 Consumer Credit Act provided protections and remedies for debtors and hirers under agreements that could be classed as "regulated agreements". An agreement is considered to be regulated for the purposes of the 1974 Act where the debtor or hirer is classed as an "Individual". There are in fact two types of regulated agreement as follows:

- Consumer Credit Agreement within the definition set out in s.8 of the 1974 Act; and
- A Consumer Hire Agreement within the definition set out in s.15 of the 1974 Act.

In both the definition of the "debtor" requires the debtor to be an "individual".

Why will there be a loss of protection for partnerships?

Up until now partnerships of however many individuals have been treated as an "individual" under the 1974 Act and so have enjoyed the protection and indeed the remedies available under the Act in the event of its default. **2–21**

The definition of "individual" is set out in s.189(1) of the 1974 Act as amended by s.1 of the 2006 Act.

As a result of these changes which were brought into force on April 6, 2007, it is no longer possible to include partnerships of more than three persons in the definition of "individual" and therefore loans to partnerships of more than three persons are no longer to be regulated by the 1974 Act (as amended).

This in itself is important in terms of debt recovery and subsequent enforcement of any judgment because such agreements are no longer regulated and therefore they can be treated as straightforward judgment debts for enforcement. The consequence of this is that they can transferred to the High Court for enforcement using execution against goods which means that High Court Enforcement Officers can seize partnership property, be it business equipment or stock or some other asset, and the services of county court bailiff will not be required.

Where the partnership consists of two or three people then the agreement will be viewed as a regulated agreement unless one of the exemptions, provided for by s.15 of the Consumer Credit Act 1974 as amended applies, or unless all the partners are limited companies. **2–22**

An agreement with an unincorporated association which is not a partnership and which does not consist entirely of limited companies will still be regarded as a regulated agreement irrespective of the number of persons in that unincorporated association unless the agreement is subject to one of the exemptions.

Is relief available to debtors under credit agreements which are not regulated?

2–23 Relief is available to debtors in these situations where the credit agreement is defined as an "extortionate credit bargain" dealt with under s.137–40 of the 1974 Act Such relief is only available to debtors who are "individuals".

The new unfair relationship provisions will replace the extortionate credit bargain provisions and will provide protection to individuals in respect of credit agreements by virtue of s.140(C)(1) which is to be inserted into the 1974 Act by virtue of s.21 of the Consumer Credit Act 2006.

Is there a financial limit for the value of the Consumer Credit Agreement?

2–24 As we can see from the various commencement orders that have been made, the existing financial limit under the 1974 Act, which set a ceiling of £25,000 for both Consumer Credit Agreements and for regulated Consumer Hire Agreements, has now been amended and in both types of agreement the section setting the ceiling of £25,000 have been repealed.

What is the effect of these financial limits being removed?

2–25 In relation to a Consumer Credit Agreement being one where the debtor is an individual this will now always be a regulated agreement unless it is found to be "exempt" under s.8(3) of the Consumer Credit Act 2006.

In relation to a Consumer Hire Agreement where the hirer is an individual as defined by s.189(1) of Consumer Credit Act 1974, this too will always be a regulated agreement unless it is found to be exempt under s.15(2) of the 1974 Act (as amended).

The removal of the limit will in fact have no effect if a lender varies and supplements an agreement on or before April 6, 2008 for the provision of credit over £25,000.

What exemptions apply under the new Act to a "High Net Worth" customer?

2–26 Provision is made in the new Act for an exemption for debtors and hirers of "High Net Worth". These will form a new category of exempt agreement and are designed to prevent a loss of business from wealthy debtors to offshore financial centres due to the formalities that will be required regardless of the value of the loan when the financial limit of £25,000 for regulated agreements is removed. To come within the definition of "High Net Worth" and therefore claim that the agreement is exempt the following provisions must apply:

Firstly, the debtor or hirer must be a natural person which in essence means that the debtor or hirer will be an individual. This in itself will make the agreement a regulated agreement. It should be noted that the definition of "Individual" in s.189(1) of the CCA 1974 (as amended) includes an unincorporated body of persons such as a sports club or social club.

Secondly, the agreement must include a declaration by the debtor or hirer that he agrees to forego the protection and remedies that would have been available to him if the agreement were a regulated agreement.

Thirdly, the debtor or hirer must have a net income value of £150,000 per annum or net assets of £500,000 through the whole of the year ending with the day on which the agreement is made [see s.16A(1) and (3)(c)]. For the purposes of valuing these assets this will not include the debtor's or hirer's residential property or other benefits such as pension or death in service values.

What are the formalities regarding the statement of "High Net Worth"?

Under s.16A(4)(b), the Secretary of State may make provisions by order as to the form content and signing of a statement of "High Net Worth" and the declaration to be made by the debtor or hirer that he agrees to forgo the protection afforded to him in relation to regulated agreements. In relation to such declaration the following must be present: 2–27

- the declaration must be set out in the agreement and be signed by the debtor or hirer;
- the debtor or hirer must be given time to read the "Statement of High Net Worth"—the statement should be completed and signed by the debtor or hirer;
- the statement must be completed and signed by the debtor or hirer;
- the Statement of High Net Worth must be "current", i.e. made during the year the agreement is made and for the purposes of calculating that year it is the period of one year ending with

the day on which the agreement is made, i.e. the previous 12 months;

- the debtor or hirer must provide proof that the criteria is satisfied by submitting accounts;
- there must be a High Net Worth statement for each debtor or hirer to ensure that each individual is exempt;
- the statement must be given voluntarily and the debtor or hirer cannot self-certify their net worth;
- the statement must be countersigned by the creditor/owner or an accountant that he is a member of a professional body—strict rules may prevent the use of the exemption;
- the lender must satisfy himself that each individual is of "High Net Worth" status;
- once the lender is satisfied that the criteria applies, an unregulated agreement can be presented to the debtor or hirer including the exemption in prescribed form, the form cannot be "freestanding";
- the debtor or hirer must then sign the appropriate exemption and the agreement as normal. The form and content of the prescribed form is set out in the Consumer Credit (Exempt Agreements) Order 2007; and
- agreements must be amended to include the exemption if the lender wishes to use it.

What exemption exists for business agreements exceeding the financial limit?

2–28 Interestingly, a Consumer Credit Agreement or Consumer Hire Agreement entered into by a debtor or hirer "wholly or predominantly" for the purposes of a business that he carries on, or intends to carry on, will now be exempt. By virtue of the new s.16(B) which is to be inserted into the CCA 2006 s.4, in the case of a credit agreement in which the creditor provides the debtor with credit exceeding £25,000, or in the case of a hire agreement the hirer is required to make payments exceeding £25,000.

If an agreement is found to be outside these financial limits it will be presumed to be entered into predominantly for the purposes of business either carried on or intended to be carried on by the debtor or hirer if it contains a declaration by the debtor or hirer to the effect that it is in fact entered into by the debtor or hirer wholly or predominantly for the purposes of such a business—see s.16B(2).

This presumption will, however, not apply if the creditor knew when the agreement was entered into, or had a reasonable cause to suspect, that the agreement was not entered into for the purpose of the debtor's business.

The creditor must therefore document the purpose of the loan and why it is believed to be for business purposes if he wishes the exemption to apply. The debtor must also sign the declaration contained within the agreement and that declaration must be in the prescribed format again set out in the Consumer Credit (Exempt Agreements) Order 2007. As yet the Office of Fair Trading have not provided a definition for "wholly or predominantly" and therefore, the onus remains on the lender to ensure that to achieve an exemption status, the loan or hire is indeed for business use. **2–29**

It should be noted that a credit agreement which is exempt by s.16B will nevertheless be subject to the unfair relationships provisions set out in ss.140A–140C in any event.

If a credit agreement provides the debtor with credit exceeding £25,000 or a hire agreement requires the hirer to make payments exceeding £25,000, it will be presumed to be entered into predominantly for the purposes of business carried on or intended to be carried on by the debtor or hirer.

This presumption will be confirmed by the fact the agreement contains a declaration by the debtor or hirer to the effect that the agreement is entered into by them wholly or predominantly for the purposes of their business (see s.16B(2) CCA 2006).

If such an agreement becomes exempt, in the event of default and subsequent judgment being entered into, a claimant can once again seek to enforce the agreement using the services of a High Court Enforcement Officer rather than relying on the public sector provision for enforcement through the county court. **2–30**

However, the presumption that the debtor is entering into the agreement wholly or predominantly for business purposes will not apply if the creditor knew that when the agreement was entered into he had reasonable cause to suspect that the agreement was not entered into for the purpose of the debtor's business.

What are the requirements in relation to "statements" that must be provided to debtors and hirers?

Under the new provisions of the 2006 Act in essence periodic statements must be provided to debtors and hirers under fixed-sum credit agreements and more information must be given to debtors and hirers in the prescribed form for "running-account" credit agreement statements. **2–31**

When must a statement be provided?

2–32 In the new s.77A for new forms of agreement there is a requirement to provide a statement within one year of the date of the agreement (plus 30 days which allows for the delivery of the statement). For existing agreements made prior to the new provisions then a statement must be provided within one year of this requirement which will come into force on October 1, 2008 again allowing 30 days for delivery.

Lenders must provide further statements within one year of the date of the last statement and no more than one year (again plus 30 days—6 month/12 months).

If the last day of the one-year period falls on a non-working day the one-year period is extended until the next working day which is then the end of the statement period due date. The 30-day delivery period starts on the end of the date the statement period becomes due.

Statements may be delivered, posted, or provided the debtor has agreed, they may be delivered to the debtor by being transmitted to a particular electronic address in a particular format transmitted to the address in that form an electronic transmission, such as email, must be in the form of an electronic communication that is capable of being stored for future reference in such a way that the information in it may be reproduced without change—see s.176A(1).

What are the practical implementation issues in relation to statements so far as existing agreements are concerned?

2–33 There are effectively two options. Firstly, the lender can release the first statement up to the date of the agreement and therefore the period of the first statement will be from October 1, 2008 until the date of the agreement. Following statements would then be required annually from the agreement date to be in line with the new agreements written after October 1, 2008.

Secondly, as a further option the lender can release a statement from the period of October 1 in batches. However, this could mean a lender would have to issue two annual statements.

What are the requirements of a statement for a fixed-sum credit agreement?

2–34 Regulations set out the form and content of the statement (see s.77A(2) inserted into the 1974 Act by virtue of s.6 of the CCA 2006).

Can the customer be charged for the provision of a statement?

The debtor is to have no liability to pay any sum in connection with the preparation or giving of a statement under the new section (see s.77A(3) inserted into the 1974 Act by virtue of s.6 of the CCA 2006). **2–35**

How is a statement to be "given" to the debtor?

Statements can be delivered, posted, or if the debtor has agreed, can be delivered to the debtor by being transmitted electronically. In fact the creditor is to "give" each statement which by virtue of s.189(1) means, "deliver or send by an appropriate method" and "appropriate method" meaning again by virtue of s.189(1) post or transmission in the form of an electronic communication in accordance with s.176A(1). **2–36**

An electronic transmission must be in a form of electronic communication which is capable of being stored for future reference in such a way the information can be reproduced without change at any stage.

How long does the obligation to send a statement continue?

Section 77A(4) provides there is an obligation on the lender to provide a statement until there is no sum payable under the agreement by the debtor or there is no sum which may become payable. As a result if the loan is paid or settled within one year the creditor need not give a statement or worry about the implications of these provisions under s.77A. **2–37**

Does the obligation to send a statement stop at judgment?

Unlike the obligation to send arrears notices the obligation to send a statement under this part of the Act does not stop at judgment being entered. **2–38**

What does "service by post" mean?

The Act requires that statements may be delivered or posted to the debtor and in relation to how to interpret this, reference is made to s.7 of the Interpretation Act 1978. This states that when an enactment authorises or requires any document to be served by post (whether **2–39** the expression "serve" or the expression "give" or "send" or any another expression is used), then unless there is a contrary intention which is apparent in the Act then service is deemed to be effected by properly addressing, pre-paying and posting a letter containing the documents. Unless the contrary is then proved, service is deemed to have been effected at the time at which the letter would have been delivered in the ordinary course of post.

What does "service by electronic transmission" mean?

2–40 Again for the purposes of ensuring that a statement is transmitted in accordance with s.176A then it is important to appreciate the following points:

- The person to whom the document is transmitted must agree that it will be delivered to him by being transmitted to a particular electronic address in a particular electronic form, i.e. the debtor must agree and give their email address.
- As a result of that agreement the statement must be transmitted to that address in the format agreed.
- The form in which the document is transmitted is such that any information in the document which is addressed to the person to whom the document is transmitted is capable of being stored for future reference for an appropriate period in a way which allows the information to be reproduced without change. For lenders this means that they must ensure that their electronic backup of email communication is sufficiently robust to ensure that such statements can be reproduced easily from archive. Whilst this may seem an obvious comment there have been examples in the past of mismanagement of data in electronic communications and therefore lenders need to ensure that these provisions are capable of being complied with through sound data management policies and procedures.

What is the presumption of delivery of an electronic transmission?

2–41 The document transmitted in accordance with subs.1 of s.176A must, unless the contrary is proved, be treated for the purposes of the Act as being delivered on the working day immediately following the day on which it was transmitted. The exception to this is under s.69 in which Notice of Cancellation by the debtor in respect of cancellable agreements means that it will be deemed to be served at the time of the transmission.

In this Section "electronic address" includes any number or address used for the purpose of receiving electronic communications for example by email, fax, etc. as appropriate.

What must statements in relation to fixed-sum credit agreements contain?

The content of statements provided in relation to fixed-sum credit agreements are contained in regs 3–12 and Sch.1 of the Consumer Credit (Information Requirements and Duration of Licences and Charges) Regulations 2007. Within Sch.1 of the 2007 Regulations the information to be provided and the form of wording to be included in statements in relation to fixed-sum credit agreements is set out. The Regulations can be found on the OFT website. **2–42**

What are the consequences of failing to comply with the sending of a statement?

In essence, the failure by a lender to send a statement outside the requirements of the Act will mean that any agreement cannot be enforced until the requirements are complied with. **2–43**

The debtor will be relieved of the following obligations:

- to pay interest for the period of non-compliance;
- to pay any default sum charged during the period of non-compliance; and
- to pay any sum charged after compliance but in relation to the event during non-compliance.

Creditors may also have to change their current calculations where interest is pre-computed at the outset (see s.77A(5)–(7)).

Are there any transitional arrangements in force?

At the time of producing this text in July 2008, it should be noted that the Government has said in relation to the transitional provisions for fixed-sum credit agreements that they see a "long term, but not open-ended transitional period lasting ten years". This should allow lenders, according to Government, "plenty of time" to input records **2–44** for loans lasting beyond this time into their systems, but would also mean that the majority of loans will have been completed. The transitional arrangements under the regulations therefore apply until September 30, 2017, but only apply to fixed-sum credit agreements.

What are the requirements for statements in relation to "running-account" credit agreements?

2–45 Many creditors will of course have sophisticated systems for the sending of statements on a monthly basis and debtors will of course be used to receiving and reading these documents in relation to their various regulated credit agreements.

If such a statement includes the demand for payment it must be given within one month after the end of the period to which it relates. If it does not include a demand for payment and the statement indicates that there is no credit or debit balance at the end of the period to which it relates, the statement must be given within 12 months of the end of that period.

If there has been no credit or debit balance on the account at any time during the period to which it relates, the statement is only required to be given within 12 months after the date of the first credit or debit balance on the account following the end of the period to which the statement relates.

In any other case the statement must be given within six months from the end of the period to which it relates.

These periods are prescribed by virtue of s.78(5) of the Consumer Credit Act 1974, Consumer Credit (Running-Account Credit Information) Regulations 1983 (SI 1983/1570) reg.3.

How can these statements be delivered to the debtor?

2–46 Running-account statements may be delivered, posted or, provided that the debtor has agreed transmitted to a particular electronic address in a particular electronic format and the same comments apply here as for fixed-sum agreements.

What are the effects of the debtor's failure to make payments under the new 2006 Act?

2–47 Under the new Act there is explicit provision for the Secretary of State to make regulations that require periodic statements in respect of a regulated running-account agreement to contain information in terms prescribed by the regulations about the consequences of the debtor's failure to make payments as required by the agreement.

As a result a new subsection, s.78(4A) was inserted into the 1974 Act by s.7(1) of the CCA 2006. This deals with the consequences of the debtor's failing to make payments as required by the agreement or only making payments of a description prescribed by the regulations, in circumstances again prescribed by the regulations. It is worth noting that the regulations apply regardless of when the agreement was made (see CCA 2006 Sch.3 para.3).

Statements will be required to contain warnings such as:

> **"Paying only your minimum repayment will substantially increase the amount that you must repay and the time that it takes to pay it. You may also incur additional charges, which may be added to your balance."**

And

> **"Failure to make your minimum repayment can mean that you are in breach of this credit agreement and could result in the creditor bringing legal proceedings against you. This could have a detrimental effect on your credit rating and affect your ability to borrow in future."**

These warning statements will be required to be in a prescribed format and must adhere to strict requirements to ensure they are displayed prominently in the statement itself. The Regulations even deal with the statement of the order and proportions of the statement. The statement itself must also include a dispute resolution statement to allow the debtor to refer it to the Financial Ombudsman Service (FOS) if he is dissatisfied.

The Regulations applicable to the new s.78(4A) are the Consumer Credit (Information Requirements and Duration of Licenses and Charges) Regulations 2007 Sch.2 regs 13–18 which again can be found on the BERR website or the OFT website.

It should be noted that the minimum payment statements do not apply to charge cards or overdrafts and the minimum payment statement only need to be included if minimum payments are required.

What is the procedure under the new Act if there are joint debtors?

Where there are two or more debtors under a regulated agreement, the general rule is that anything the creditor is required to do to the debtor must be done in relation to each of the debtors (s.185(1)(a)). **2–48**

Under s.7 of the new Act a new subs.(3) anticipates that where there is more than one debtor to whom credit is provided the debtor may provide a signed "dispensing notice" which will be given to the creditor so that the creditor is not obliged to provide a statement to that debtor. The notice would be operative when given to the creditor until revoked by a further notice given to the creditor by the debtor.

Such a dispensing notice would not be effective if it meant the debtor would not receive a statement. Any operative dispensing notice would cease to have effect if a debtor died. Also an operative dispensing notice would remain operative if the relevant earlier agreement was subsequently modified under some form of modifying agreement.

The question has to be in relation to this Section of the new Act as to how many debtors would really want to go to the time and trouble to prepare a "dispensing notice" or even have been advised on how to prepare a notice to prevent duplicate statements being issued? The answer is likely to be very few in practice.

What areas of protection does the new Act give for customers in default?

2–49 The new Act attempts to tackle the problem of over-indebtedness by ensuring that customers will be much better informed in future about the notices they receive with clear information and warnings about what happens should they be in arrears.

The British Credit Industry must be one of the most mature systems for the granting of credit in the world today and yet, despite this, many customers have failed to appreciate or ignored the dangers of over-indebtedness. Credit companies have in many instances taken advantage of the lack of interest in these formalities by the general public and the new Act attempts to ensure that the public are better informed about the risks of credit.

What is the purpose of information sheets?

2–50 Under s.86A(1) of the CCA 1974 which is inserted by CCA 2006 s.8, the OFT is required to prepare two forms of information sheet being for arrears and for default. Again the object of the exercise is to send these information sheets out with warning notices so again the public are informed of the consequences of not meeting their obligations under the agreement.

Details of the information sheets can be found on the BERR website or the OFT website.

The arrears information sheet must be sent at the same time as any arrears notice and the default information sheet must be sent at the same time as any default notice is sent to the debtor.

Creditors will have a responsibility to ensure that they adopt these sheets in their processes and that they are able to change them as the sheets are changed from time to time by the OFT.

The specification of the sheet is exacting and includes the following requirements: 2–51

- the information sheet must be self-standing and double-sided;
- if printed it cannot be altered in anyway;
- it is available for colour printing in either blue and gold or in black and white;
- a barcode and reference can be placed on the foot of the reverse page but not on the front; and
- the creditor can transfer the information from a PDF to an alternative format to facilitate printing but the requirements of the format and production of the sheets are stringent and therefore changes will be negligible.

What happens if a debtor says he has not received an information sheet?

Concerns were raised by the credit industry that one of the ways that debtors may try to avoid default charges, etc. was to claim they had not received the relevant "information sheet". The DTI response to this concern was dealt within an explanatory memorandum dated March 31, 2007 in which it was stated, "So far as customers' claims that an information sheet was not included are concerned, provided that lenders can demonstrate that their information systems are sufficiently robust and reliable as to ensure that information sheets are included with notices, and that the documentation as a whole is sent to the debtor's address which is last known to the creditor it would be for the debtor to prove that in his or her particular case those systems broke down". 2–52

What notices have to be given under fixed-sum credit and hire agreements?

Creditors will have to give periodic notices to customers who are in arrears under regulated fixed-sum credit agreements and regulated consumer hire agreements. 2–53

This will apply whenever:

- at least two payments have fallen due in relation to weekly payments; or
- for more frequent payments where at least four payments have fallen due; and
- the amount of the arrears equates to or exceeds two payments due (or for weekly or more frequent payments arrears equate to or exceed four payments).

At the time of preparing this text the definition of a "payment" is still subject to further consultation.

The arrears notice is not designed to cover other sums which are outstanding, i.e. default sums. For existing agreements in arrears as at October 1, 2008, the obligation to send an arrears notice commences after that date.

Arrears notices must be provided up until the debtor or hirer ceases to be in arrears or any court judgment is given in relation to the agreement under which a "sum" is required to be paid.

What guidance is to be given for new agreements?

2–54 For agreements falling into arrears after the regulations have come into force on October 1, 2008, where the creditor has not already terminated the agreement before the regulations come into force, and the agreement is then terminated and the entire balance becomes payable, this will be a sum due under the agreement.

If the debtor does not pay this sum he will be in arrears. He will then not cease to be in arrears for the purposes of s.86B(4)(a) until the balance is paid.

These facts should be reflected in the arrears notice sent to the debtor and it would also be open to the creditor to send an explanatory letter in addition to the requirement for notice to be sent.

If a court judgment were to be given in relation to the agreement and this included an obligation to pay the outstanding arrears (or any other sum) then under s.86B(4)(b) this would apply even if the obligation did not extend to the whole of the loan. The duty to send the arrears notice however would cease at the point of judgment for any sum.

2–55 If a payment plan were to be set up to avoid court proceedings s.86B(4)(a) would apply once the arrears, along with associated interest and default sums, had been cleared. If, however, the debtor went into arrears again a further duty to supply a notice would arise.

In relation to existing agreements if an agreement were to be terminated before October 1, 2008, and the entire balance became payable at that point, then under s.86B(1) there would be no requirement for an arrears notice to be sent as there would not be two or more payments falling due after the commencement of s.9 of the CCA 2006—Sch.3 para.6(2).

If, however, a payment plan was to be agreed prior to October 1, 2008 then the requirement under s.86B to send an arrears notice may be triggered once two or more payments fell due on or after October 1, 2008 if the accumulated arrears at that point were no less than the sum of the last two payments.

"Payments" for these purposes, as proposed to be defined by BERR in the Legislative Reform Order (LRO), would mean payments which the debtor is required to make under the agreed payment plan rather than the original contractual payments.

When does a debtor cease to be in arrears?

A debtor or hirer will cease to be in arrears when: 2–56

- no sum which he has ever failed to pay under the agreement when required is still owing;
- no default sum is still owing;
- no sum of interest is still owing; and
- no other sum of interest is still owing.

When does the default protection arrears notice for a fixed-sum credit and hire agreement need to be served?

Such a notice needs to be served within 14 days from the date on which the conditions are satisfied. Further notices may be required every six months until the debtor or hirer is no longer in arrears or there is a judgment or court Order. The notice must include the OFT arrears information sheet. 2–57

Notice must still be given even if the debtor ceases to be in arrears or judgment is given during that 14 day period.

There is to be no charge to the customer for the delivery of a notice which can be sent by personal delivery or through the postal system but not electronically. A transitional period is provided for in this context.

No requirement is specified as to the form and content of the arrears notice under s.86B but each notice must include a copy of the information sheet which is heavily specified.

What are the requirements for arrears notices under running-account credit agreements?

2–58 Creditors will have to give notices to debtors who are in arrears under regulated agreements for running-account credit, unless the agreement is defined as "non-commercial" or a "small agreement" (see s.86B(12)(b) inserted into the 1974 Act by CCA 2006 s.9).

The notice must include the OFT information sheet and the same rules apply that the notice will have to be given to the debtor unless there is a judgment debt or part of a judgment debt outstanding from him in relation to the agreement whenever:

- at least two payments have fallen due under the agreement;
- the last two payments to have fallen due have not been made; and
- the creditor has not already become obliged to give a notice under s.86C in relation to either of those two payments.

Again no requirement is specified in the new legislation as to the form and content of the notice except that it must include the arrears information sheet.

2–59 Once again the notice may be delivered or posted to the debtor or the debtor or hirer may agree to the notice being delivered to them in an electronic format as discussed above.

Once again the debtor or hirer has no liability to pay any sum due in connection with the preparation or giving of the arrears notice.

What are the consequences of failing to give an arrears notice?

2–60 If a creditor fails to give an arrears notice under s.86, the agreement will be unenforceable against the debtor or hirer during the period of "non-compliance". In addition, the debtor or hirer who would be released from the following liabilities:

- they would not be required to pay any interest calculated by reference to a period of non-compliance or to any part of the period of non-compliance;
- they would not be required to pay any default sum that would otherwise have become payable during the period of non-compliance; and
- nor would they be required to pay any default sum that would have become payable after the end of the period of non-

compliance in connection with the breach occurring during the period of non-compliance.

A period of non-compliance will begin on the day when the arrears notice should have been sent or will end on the day on which the notice is finally given.

What is the meaning of a "default sum" under the new Act?

By virtue of s.18 of the CCA 2006 the meaning of "default sum" when used in relation to a debtor or hirer under a regulated agreement is defined as, "any sum, other than interest, which is payable by the debtor or hirer in connection with the breach of an agreement by him". The expression is intended to include the cost of legal proceedings and court costs although it may not always be clear whether such costs are payable in connection with the breach of the agreement by the debtor or hirer. **2–61**

What notice must be given in relation to a default sum?

Under the new s.86E of the CCA 2006 inserted by virtue of s.12, creditors must give debtors and hirers notice of any default sums that become payable under the regulated agreement unless that agreement can be considered to be "non-commercial" or a "small agreement". **2–62**

Once again the notice of a default sum can be posted or it can be sent electronically if by agreement with the debtor. Again there should be no charge to the debtor or hirer for the preparation and sending of the notice.

What format does the default sum notice have to take?

Once again the notice must follow a prescribed form. It must state that it relates to a default sum and that it is given in compliance with the new Act. The notice must be dated and it must identify the agreement under which it is sent by giving a description of the agreement and the agreement number. The name, telephone number, postal address of the creditor or the employee of the creditor must be stated. In the notice itself the amount and nature of each default sum payable that has not been subject to previous notices must be stated along with a date that they became due. The date of the default sum must also be expressly set out. **2–63**

There must be a prescribed statement included in the notice confirming the notice will also cover default sums already notified in previous notices.

If interest is payable on the default sum then a prescribed "interest" statement for either fixed or variable interest along with the rate of interest to be charged must be included in the statement.

If the agreement does not provide for interest then it cannot be charged.

It is important to appreciate that the failure to give notice of a default sum renders the agreement unenforceable until the notice has been given and this is a strict requirement.

What are the new rules in relation to default notices?

2–64 The new requirement for notice of default sums is to be distinguished from the existing provisions of the Consumer Credit Act 1974 s.87 and 88 by which a creditor must give a default notice before becoming entitled as a result of any breach of a regulated agreement by debtor or hirer to terminate the agreement and demand earlier payment of any sum or recover possession of any goods or land or to treat any right conferred on the debtor or hirer by the agreement as terminated, restricted or deferred.

Section 88 of the 1974 Act is to be amended so as to increase the minimum length of a default notice from 7 to 14 days and that has been the position since October 1, 2006. Changes have also been made for the content of default notices.

From October 1, 2008 an arrears information sheet must be enclosed with any default notice.

What about time orders?

2–65 A "time order" is an order that may be made by the court under s.129 of the CCA 1974 which gives the debtor or hirer more time to pay any sum already owed under a regulated agreement or under a security for a regulated agreement. It can also give more time to remedy any breach of a regulated agreement other than the non-payment of the money.

The court, as a consequence of a time order, may vary the agreement by virtue of s.136 of the 1974 Act by, for example, reducing the rate at which interest may accrue on the sums owing or by extending the repayment term.

Under the existing provisions of the CCA 1974 the court can make a time order either of its own motion where the creditor or owner is applying for an Enforcement Order under s.127 of the 1974 Act or where the debtor brings an application after being served with the default notice under ss.76 of the 1974 Act.

Section 129 of the CCA 1974 is to be amended so as to enable a debtor or hirer to apply for a time order before the creditor takes any steps to enforce the agreement and even before the creditor has taken the step of giving a notice under ss.76, 87 or 98 of the Act.

In future a debtor or hirer will be able to apply for a time order when he has been served with an arrears notice under s.86B or s.86C [see above] by virtue of s.16 of the CCA 2006. This will be the position regardless of when the agreement was made. **2–66**

However, before a debtor can apply for a time order he must give the creditor at least 14 days' notice that he intends to make an application giving details of a payment proposal, [see s.129A(1) and (2) inserted into the 1974 Act by s.16(2) of the CCA 2006].

What notices are required to be served for interest after judgment?

Under the common law, contracts can provide for interest to be paid after judgment provided that a separate covenant is made for the payment of interest as opposed to the amount of the sum payable under the agreement (see *Economic Life Assurance Society v Usborne* [1902] A.C. 147, a case in which the merger of the right to interest in the judgment was avoided). **2–67**

In 1999, the OFT attempted to establish that the term providing for interest after judgment on a regulated consumer agreement was unfair and so not binding on the debtor by virtue of the unfair terms in consumer contracts Regulations 1994 (SI 1994/3159) (as was).

The situation was then reviewed by the House of Lords in a case of *Director General of Fair Trading v First National Bank Plc* [2000] 1 All E.R. 97. The House of Lords held that the term providing for interest after judgment unlikely to be considered "unfair" bases that a customer would have appreciated that interest would be payable.

However, the case raised concerns in relation to both existing regulations and county court procedure by failing to alert debtors of the fact that whilst they were paying off the judgment by instalments interest would be continuing to build on their account unless they had obtained a time order under ss.129 and 136 of the 1974 Act.

As a result of this in s.130A of the Consumer Credit Act 1974, which is to be inserted by virtue of s.17 of the CCA 2006, the new Act will: **2–68**

- require creditors to give debtors and hirers periodic notices of any post-judgment debt interest that they wish to recover; and

- enable Regulations to be made prescribing the form and contents of notices explaining the interest position.

The Regulations may be expected to require the inclusion of reminders about the court's powers under ss.129 and 136 of the CCA 1974.

The upshot of all this is that creditors will be required to give notice of any post-judgment contractual interest they wish to recover under s.130A, although this will only apply to regulated agreements.

2–69 Subsequent notices must be given at six monthly intervals. Notices must be given after judgment and there will be no timeline for the first statement (as set out elsewhere in the legislation) except that this must be served straightaway with the time order.

The creditor will not be able to recover interest for the period prior to the first notice and will not be able to recover interest for the period from the end of each six months to service of a repeat notice.

The debtor will not be liable to pay interest for the period for preparation of the notice of non-compliance.

Conclusion

2–70 As a result of this new legislation Debt Recovery Practitioners working in the field of consumer credit will have to ensure that their processes and procedures embrace the strict requirements of both the 1974 Act and the 2006 amending legislation.

In simple terms the new Act is all about ensuring that debtors and hirers are informed about their credit commitments and are reminded of the need to pay and pay in a timely manner so as not to continue to over-extend themselves with new credit agreements.

For sophisticated creditors the new Act will mean amending workflows and ensuring compliance with prescribed notices but computer systems will be the workhorses to ensure that this is done.

It will only be once all the formalities have been completed that the creditor is then in a position to make his claim for repayment of any debt under the consumer credit agreement being the sum outstanding in accordance with the Civil Procedure Rules. That area of consumer credit debt recovery is dealt with under Pt 7 by the issue of a claim in the county court. For more information on this see Chapters 5, 6, 7, 8 and 9.

2–71 Ultimately, the enforcement of a Consumer Credit Act agreement is only permissible in the county court (see Chapter 14) using the services of a county court bailiff, or by an attachment of earnings order or a third party debt order.

In addition to that many lenders and creditors will be reluctant to use the more robust approach of charging order although they may wish to secure their judgment against the debtor's property but certainly from there many creditors and lenders will be very reluctant to seek to enforce the charging order through an order for sale.

Ultimately the sanction for a lender or a creditor in the consumer area is some form of insolvency procedure but again taking customers up to this point of the debt recovery procedure is unlikely to be popular with the OFT.

Practitioners may also wish to consult Atkin's Court Forms Volume II(1) on the topic of Consumer Credit for precedents and further commentary.

Insolvency Act 1986 and Related Statutes

The insolvency area of legislation is complex and is driven by Government policy to tackle indebtedness and to rescue those on the brink of insolvency. 2–72

Debt Recovery Practitioners need to appreciate that any form of insolvency procedure is going to upset their strategy to recover the debt in full and so the skill to evaluate debt or types and which insolvency procedure might apply is going to be important in handling cases within a debt recovery team.

Put simply in an insolvency matrix we can start to consider how insolvency may impact on different types of debtors as follows:

2–73

Debtor Type	Insolvency Procedure Which May Apply	Legislative Reference
Individuals	Bankruptcy	Pt IX Insolvency Act 1986, Pt 6 Insolvency Rules 1986
	Individual Voluntary Arrangement	s.3 Insolvency Act 2000 (Approval procedure), Pt VIII Insolvency Act 1986, Pt 5 Insolvency Rules 1986
	Deed of Arrangement	Deed of Arrangement Act 1914, Deed of Arrangement Rules 1925
Sole Traders	Bankruptcy	Pt IX Insolvency Act 1986, Pt 6 Insolvency Rules 1986
	Individual Voluntary Arrangement	s.3 Insolvency Act 2000 (Approval procedure), Pt VIII Insolvency Act 1986, Pt 5 Insolvency Rules 1986
	Deed of Arrangement	Deed of Arrangement Act 1914, Deed of Arrangement Rules 1925

Debtor Type	Insolvency Procedure Which May Apply	Legislative Reference
Partnerships	Insolvent Partnerships Order	s.420 Insolvency Act 1986, Insolvent Partnership Order 1994, Insolvent Partnership Order 1986
Companies	Compulsory Winding Up	Pt 4 Insolvency Rules 1986, Pt IV Ch.VI Insolvency Act 1986
	Creditor's Voluntary Winding Up	s.96 Insolvency Act 1996, Pt IV Ch.IV Insolvency Act 1996, Pt 4 Insolvency Rules
	Member's Voluntary Liquidation	s.90 Insolvency Act 1986, Pt IV Ch.III Insolvency Act 1986
	Company Voluntary Arrangement	Pt 1 Insolvency Rules 1986
	Administration	Pt II Insolvency Act 1986, Pt 2 Insolvency Rules 1986
	Administrative Receivers	Pt III Insolvency Act 1986

2–74 Insolvent companies entering into liquidation in England & Wales and Scotland are dealt with under the Insolvency Act of 1986. Companies can either be the subject of a compulsory liquidation (winding-up) order obtained from the court by a creditor, shareholder or director, or alternatively pass a resolution themselves, subject to the approval of a creditors' meeting, that the company be wound up voluntarily (creditors voluntary liquidations). All such insolvencies are registered at Companies House and details will show in the insolvency notes to any such company. A company that is subject to either compulsory or voluntary winding up will be said to be "wound-up". A third type of winding-up, being members' voluntary liquidation, is not included in the official insolvency statistics for companies because it does not involve insolvency.

The Insolvency Act 1986 also introduced the procedures of company administration orders and company voluntary arrangements (CVAs). The administration procedure gives a period of time during which creditors are restrained from taking action and a court appointed administrator puts forward proposals to deal with the company's financial difficulties. The CVA procedure aids business by enabling a company in financial difficulty to come to a binding agreement with its creditors.

The Enterprise Act 2002 introduced revisions to the corporate administration procedures, replacing Pt II of the Insolvency Act 1986 with Sch.B1. These include the introduction of additional entry routes into administration that do not require the making of an administration order and a streamlined process for administrations whereby a company can in some circumstances be dissolved without recourse to liquidation.

The primary objective of administration (and of CVAs) is the rescue of the company as a going concern. These provisions came into force on September 15, 2003. Since the 2002 Act was introduced a number of streamlined administrations have subsequently been converted into creditors' voluntary liquidations.

Receivership appointments comprise administrative receivers **2–75** appointed under the 1986 Act and certain other receivership appointments, for example, under the Law of Property Act 1925. The provisions of the Enterprise Act 2002 under s.250 have made some changes to the procedures for administrative receivership.

Individual insolvencies in England and Wales are made up of bankruptcy orders and individual voluntary arrangements (IVAs). Insolvent individuals in England and Wales are dealt with mainly under the Insolvency Act 1986. A bankruptcy order is made on the petition of the debtor or one or more of his creditors when the court is satisfied that there is no prospect of the debt being paid.

There are also individual voluntary arrangements (IVAs) and deeds of arrangement (the latter under the Deeds of Arrangement Act 1914), which enable debtors to come to an agreement with their creditors. Changes to bankruptcy law in England and Wales introduced by the Enterprise Act 2002 came into force on April 1, 2004—the Act made no changes to the existing individual voluntary arrangement regime.

Under the Insolvency Act 1986 and the Insolvent Partnerships Order 1994, insolvent partnerships may be wound up as an unregistered company or administered following bankruptcy orders against the partners. Insolvent partnerships can also enter into administration or a voluntary arrangement.

The Insolvency Service website publishes regular updates on statistics for all the above types of insolvency and gives practical examples of what to do when faced with an insolvency situation. Debt Recovery Practitioners are encouraged to use this site, as an easy to use resource for all issues to do with the insolvency of any type of debtor they may come across in their department. The website can be found at *http://www.insolvency.gov.uk*.

Business Names Act 1985

It is important that both creditor and debtor businesses comply with **2–76** the Business Names Act but in relation to debtors it could become particularly useful when a Debt Recovery Practitioner is trying to establish who to sue to understand the nuances of the Act.

A business name is a name used by any person partnership or company for carrying on its business unless it is the same as their own name. It therefore applies to a company which trades under a name which is not its corporate name. For example, "XYZ Limited t/as "Bloggs Bakers". It also applies to a partnership which does not trade under the names of all the partners and it also applies to the individual who trades under a name which is not his or her surname.

If the Act applies then a business must comply with the disclosure rules which are particularly useful for Debt Recovery Practitioners. For example, if a Mr ABC Bloggs trades as "Bloggs Bakers" then the disclosure rules of the Business Names Act apply. These disclosure rules also apply to incorporated companies that trade in a different name, for example, "ABC Foods Limited trading as ABC Foods".

2–77 Incorporated companies must also comply with the disclosure rules as regulated by the Companies Acts. The disclosure rules apply to what must be said on company stationary about the company formation and are set out in the Companies' House Guidance Book "Company Formation".

In terms of the disclosure rules the information which must be disclosed about a business includes:

- the corporate name or the name of each partner or the individual person's name; and
- in relation to each person named an address at which documents can be served.

This information must be shown clearly in all places where the business carries on its business and where it deals with its customers or suppliers. It must also be shown on business letters and written orders for the supply of goods or services. The information must also be repeated on invoices and receipts and written demands for the payment of business debt.

2–78 As long as the details are "clearly legible" they can be handwritten or printed.

Disclosure rules require that the information about the business must be easily seen and read although it does not matter how the information is shown. Often on entering a business a Business Names Act notice will be in the reception or the front office. In larger organisations management may need to think carefully about the size of the notice and where it is displayed to ensure that all the customers and suppliers will see it. More than one notice is permissible.

2–79 If the business has more than 20 partners then not all the partners names need to be put on the business documents but there must an address given for the principal place of business so that a list of the full partners' names addresses can be inspected.

Failure to comply with the Business Names Act, which is important when dealing with debtor businesses, is that they commit a criminal offence.

In addition we will see in Chapter 5 that changes to the CPR 2007 now require a partnership to respond to a request for information within 14 days when served with a "partnership and membership statement".

The Communications Act 2003

Sections 128–131 of the Communications Act 2003 brings a series **2–80**
of requirements for organisations collecting debt using automated calling systems.

As many of us have experienced abandoned calls create problems when an automatic dialler continues to call a telephone number repeatedly with little or no human intervention. This Act addressed this issue with severe consequences for anyone who does not manage their telephone system adequately.

Abandoned calls must now be below 3 per cent of total calls for any 24-hour period for each telephone campaign run by an organisation and records must be kept to demonstrate compliance with these requirements. On the Ofcom website in June 2007 it was stated that "the problem with silent and abandoned calls remains a priority. Ofcom has further decided to extend its programme of monitoring and enforcement for a further six month period."

Non-compliance with Ofcom regulations is severe. The maximum financial penalty which can be imposed is a £50,000 fine for persistent misuse of an electronic communications network. Operation Managers and IT Managers working in debt recovery need to be very aware of this legislation and ensure they implement robust policies and procedures to manage abandoned call rates to ensure compliance along with detailed record keeping.

Office of fair trading debt collection guidance

The Office of Fair Trading is becoming increasingly important as a **2–81**
regulator of debt collection practice in England and Wales. At the heart of its advice it is a requirement for debt collectors to deal fairly with the public where they are in the position of being a debtor. The guidance is aimed at all Consumer Credit licence holders and applies to the collection of debt once an account is in default. The full guidance can be downloaded from the OFT website at: *http://www.oft.gov.uk/advice_and_resources/resource_base/legal/cca/debt-collection.*

In December 2006 the OFT published findings with review into how initial guidance given in 2003 has changed the behaviour of debt collectors and raised awareness of good practice. The findings were that the guidance could be viewed as a success in terms of its contents and that awareness has increased among collectors of debts, individual debtors and consumer advisers and as a result there has been positive changes in industry behaviour but there was more to be done in improving levels of compliance.

Consumer advice organisations said that the most serious practices such as threats of violence to debtors had reduced. The main complaints by consumers remained in relation to threatening statements from companies being contacted at unreasonable times and firms failing to investigate disputed debts. A common complaint revolved around the theme of court action being threatened but then not describing the process correctly in any form of communication. This will be dealt with later in this book in terms of how to ensure letters and telephone calls do comply with OFT guidance.

2–82 Positive changes in industry behaviour were found to include the creation of dedicated complaint handling units, the revision of standard letters where they have the potential to mislead or be perceived as threatening and the cessation of anonymous telemessages to contact debtors.

The OFT's review found that 17 per cent of those licensed to collect debts had attracted complaints from debtors between April 2004 and August 2006 and the OFT had taken action against those collecting debts in a 101 cases. Indeed in the same period the OFT investigated 262 licensees for alleged breaches of guidance and issued notices to 9 licensed debt collectors, three of which retained their licenses and 6 surrendered their Consumer Credit Act licence altogether.

The OFT took informal action against 92 organisations and in 77 of those cases advice or warning letters from the OFT secured immediate compliance.

2–83 Since the Guidance was issued 14 licensees have agreed with the OFT following intervention to revise standard letters and the OFT received commitments from four licensees, including a major high street financial institution and a major UK utilities company, to stop sending anonymous telemessages to debtors. With the Credit Services Association estimating there are around 500 debt collection businesses in the UK of which only 200 are members of the CSA engaging in debt collection worth £5 billion of the credit industry, the OFT have a long way to go in terms of cracking down inappropriate and threatening behaviour in the collection of debt.

In essence the Guidance deals with the following areas:

In relation to communications the OFT guidance states it is unfair to communicate in whatever form with consumers in an unclear, inaccurate or misleading manner. A list of examples of such unfair practices are stated in the OFT report including using official looking documents intended or likely to mislead debtors as per their status, for example documents made to resemble a court claim.

Nor is it acceptable to misrepresent one's authority or legal position and indeed it is stated that debtors must not be deceived by the creditor's misrepresenting their authority and/or legal position. An example of this might include falsely implying or stating that the failure to pay a debt is a criminal offence or that criminal proceedings will be brought. **2–84**

OFT guidance also deals with the possibility of physical or psychological harassment of debtors. This used to be dealt with under s.40 of the Administration of Justice Act 1970 but now, although that Act is still in being, the OFT guidance in fact probably has more teeth in terms of ensuring compliance from those collecting debt and therefore ensuring that harassment is eradicated.

Examples of harassment under the guidance included contacting debtors at unreasonable times and unreasonable intervals or acting in a way to embarrass the debtor either deliberately or through lack of care, for example, failing to put correspondence for the debtor's attention in a sealed envelope and putting it straight into a letterbox thereby running the risk that it could be read by third parties.

Dealings with debtors are not to be deceitful or unfair which might include contacting the debtors directly and bypassing their appointed representatives or failing to refer on to the creditor reasonable offers to pay by instalments. **2–85**

In relation to charging for debt collection OFT guidance is that charges should not be levied unfairly with examples of unfair practices including claiming collection costs from the debtor in the absence of any expressed contractual term or other legal provisions or implying unreasonable charges which are not based on actual and necessary costs.

- In relation to debt collection visits those visiting debtors must not act in an unclear or threatening manner which might include visiting a debtor when it is known that they are vulnerable or entering the debtor's property uninvited.
- In relation to statute-barred debt the OFT do concede that if a creditor has been in regular contact with the debtor before the debt is statute-barred then it is not considered unfair to continue to attempt to recover the debt even though legal proceedings are no longer possible. However it is unfair to mislead debtors as to their rights and obligations. For example falsely stating or implying that a debt is still legally recoverable and relying on consumer's not knowing the relevant legal provisions that the debt has in fact become statute-barred.

The OFT guidance also sets out a checklist for advisers in order that they can complain about a Consumer Credit Act licence holder.

With the number of interventions being made by the OFT against the licence holders and it being a requirement that the collection of debt requires a licence to be held, clearly licence holders must review their processes and procedures to ensure they are complying with the OFT guidance.

The Common Financial Statement

2–86 Pioneered by the Money Advice Trust and the British Bankers' Association, the Common Financial Statement (CFS) was devised to standardise the way money advisers and creditors communicate with each other about repayment offers from debtors. The CFS introduced a streamline process so that repayment offers can be dealt with more quickly and seeks to introduce a partnership approach between money advisers and creditors.

The commitment of the British Bankers' Association members to support the CFS is reflected in the Banking Code. Further information about the Current Financial Statement and how it may impact on the process of certain types of debt recovery practice can be found at *http://www.moneyadvicetrust.org*.

Mental health guidelines

2–87 The Money Advice Trust (see website above) introduced a series of guidelines for debtors found to be suffering from mental health problems. Clearly in telephone collections and field visits there is the opportunity to speak to a debtor and perhaps through a field visit, see their situation at first hand. These guidelines for the first time give Debt Recovery Practitioners an opportunity, when faced with the most vulnerable, suffering some of the most difficult problems in relation to understanding that they are in debt, the opportunity to act responsibly on the advice of health professionals in their dealings with the public. Debt Recovery Practitioners are encouraged to read and review these guidelines not only for mental health problems but then to think about other issues which can be found in a debt recovery department including serious health issues, bereavement, redundancy and severe poverty. All of these social issues require, when the time is right, a sympathetic and human response to the plight of the debtor.

Civil Procedure Rules

2–88 Compliance with the Civil Procedure Rules is going to be a day to day occurrence for the Debt Recovery Practitioner and throughout the rest of this book there will be numerous references to the rules to ensure that procedurally the Debt Recovery Practitioner is in compliance. In 1999 when the new Rules were introduced the spirit of litigation in England and Wales changed from being "practitioner led" to being "court led". As a result, the court is now in control of litigation and certainly once the defence is filed and a case is allocated to track, which will be seen in later Chapters, the court takes a clear management role in moving the case through the procedure to trial.

With that in mind Practitioners need to be aware of Pt 1 of the rules in relation to the overriding objective, and Pt 3 being the court's case management powers. Time and time again in proceedings these rules will be used by district judges and by the parties themselves to ensure that they are complying, not just with the spirit of the rules, contained in CPR Pt 1.

So far as the overriding objective is concerned this should be very much viewed as "a compass" by which the court and the parties should approach litigation and debt recovery proceedings.

Rule 1.1 puts it succinctly that the rules are there to deal with a case justly and so far as practicable that includes ensuring that the parties are all on an equal footing, that expense is saved, that the case is dealt with in ways which are proportionate to the amount of money involved and the importance of the case, along with the complexities of the issues, and of course the financial position of each party is to be taken on board. The court will also look to deal with the cases expeditiously and as fairly as possible and allot to it the appropriate share of court's resources including time whilst taking into account the many hundreds and thousands of cases which have to go through the court system each year.

2–89 The court must seek to give effect to the overriding objective under CPR 1.2 when exercising any of the powers given to it by the rules or when interpreting any rule then the court will have regard to this requirement.

Under CPR 1.3 it is not just the court that has to pay close attention to the CPR as there is a requirement on the parties themselves to assist the court wherever possible.

Perhaps the biggest change which was introduced in 1999 is now the court's duty to manage cases which is enshrined in CPR 1.4.

Under the terms of that rule the court must further the overriding objective by actively managing cases before it, and active case management includes encouraging the parties to cooperate with each other and also to identify the issues at an early stage. Pre-1999 the game of litigation was about keeping the cards up the sleeves for as long as possible and ambushing the other side with new evidence late in the day. Under the terms of the CPR this is no longer possible. The court will take a very active role in deciding which issues need full investigation and trial, and disposing summarily of others and we will see later on in this book how the court has power under CPR 3.4 to strike out a statement of case in certain circumstances.

2–90 The court must of course decide what issues need to be resolved and can encourage the parties to deal with their disputes through alternative dispute resolution procedures.

If the court can, it will help the parties to settle the whole or part of any claim. The court is very cost conscious, and in taking any particular course of action it will look at the cost of what it is proposing. It will also look to deal with as many aspects of the case as it can on any occasion when the case comes before the court. So an application may start off on one footing by the applicant only to find the district judge is looking at a whole raft of other issues. In its role of keeper of the purse the court will look to see if it can deal with the case without the parties needing to attend court and therefore saving costs. It will look to use technology to reduce costs in the form of video and telephone conferences and it will always be looking for opportunities to give directions to ensure that a case proceeds to trial quickly and efficiently.

In addition to the spirit of the overriding objective, the court has clear general powers of management under CPR 3. The court has power under r.3.3 to make orders of its own initiative. It is worth Practitioners using r.3.3 where it can to encourage the court to review a case and if necessary to make an application which might seem slightly unusual but is pragmatic. Debt Recovery Practitioners should never be unwilling to assist the court by giving their opinion and experience to the court in terms of how to move a case forward. The district judge will be looking to experienced Practitioners to assist the court where possible particularly when the suggestion assists the court in meeting the spirit of the overriding objective.

Special rules for Debt Recovery Practitioners in a Solicitors Office

2–91 In accordance with the Solicitors Code of Conduct, solicitors need to be aware that they need provide clients with full a "client care" letter at the outset of their instructions.

Rule 2 of the Code provides details as to the nature of the information to be provided to the client at the outset and covers:

- the solicitor's terms of business;

- the name of the solicitor or Practitioner who will have conduct of their case;
- details of the solicitor's complaints procedure;
- details as to the likely costs involved in pursuing the case on behalf of the client; and
- confirm the steps to be taken by the solicitor in pursuing the client's case.

There is then an ongoing obligation upon the solicitor to ensure that the client is kept fully informed as to developments in their case as the matter progresses. This includes providing the client with regular updates and statements regarding the position on costs being incurred.

Whilst Practitioners within a DCA will not necessarily be solicitors, and therefore not governed by the Solicitors' Code of Conduct, as a matter of good practice it would be advisable for them to have a similar procedure in place in order to ensure that new clients are provided with the above information. **2–92**

As well as the above considerations, Practitioners now also need to be aware of the money laundering regulations which exist and ensure that they have the proper procedures in place to comply.

Whilst, technically, litigation is not "relevant business" for the purpose of the Money Laundering regulations, again, as a matter of best practice it is advisable for both solicitors and Practitioners to have systems in place to comply with the requirements of the regulations.

This is particularly relevant in the debt recovery arena, as it has been known in the past for debt recovery to be used as a mechanism to "launder" money. The parties to the claim, are involved in the litigation for no other reason than to launder the money by ensuring that payment of the "debt" is dealt with through either one party's solicitors or the court.

As most solicitors' practices deal with "relevant business" areas as well as litigation, they will already have in place the necessary systems to ensure compliance with the regulations. DCAs however, are only going to be concerned with the area of litigation and should therefore ensure that they create the necessary systems for their clients. **2–93**

Whether within a solicitors' practice, or a DCA, Practitioners should ensure that they complete the necessary identity checks in respect of new clients at the outset of the instructions. This involves obtaining proof of identity in respect of individual clients and corporate clients.

With individual clients, the proof needs to be twofold and confirm not only the individual's identity but also place of residence. With corporate clients, the identity of the company/firm/partnership needs to be established, as well as then confirming the identity of the individual from the company/firm/partnership who is providing the instructions.

The corporate identity can readily be checked by electronic means by conducting on-line searches at Companies House, Law Society, etc. depending upon the nature of the business.

2–94 The money laundering regulations require a report to be made to the Serious Organised Crimes Agency (SOCA) if there is any suspicion of money being connected with the proceeds of crime.

Therefore, Practitioners should ensure that they not only have a procedure and system in place for the checking of clients identities at the outset of instructions, but that they also have a system in place for the reporting of any suspicious cases to SOCA. Solicitors are required to have appointed Money Laundering Reporting Officers within their firms for this purpose; DCAs would be advised to put in place similar arrangements.

Chapter 3

Know Your Contract, Know Your Debtor, Know Your Remedy

Introductory Comments

In the first two chapters of this book we have looked at the recovery process from a credit management point of view and then the regulatory environment in which Practitioners operate. We now move into areas which, if not checked prior to legal action being commenced, can cause difficultly both in the litigation arena and when it comes to the enforcement of any resulting judgment. The three key areas of this chapter being knowing the debtor, knowing the terms of the contract and then understanding the remedy that is available may seem obvious, but they remain the cornerstones of a successful debt recovery action or in a larger organisation, a debt recovery operation. Big or small, these cornerstones have to be understood and processes must be put in place to ensure that the action or actions to be commenced are going to be viable and ultimately successful. We will now look at these three cornerstones and the issues they create as part of this chapter. **3–01**

Know Your Contract

The Debt Recovery Practitioner must make time to fully understand the basis of a claim against the debtor and by that an understanding of the terms of the contract between the parties must be achieved. **3–02**

When a supplier agrees to sell to a customer then he or she is entering into a contract which has legal consequences even if that agreement is only verbal. To prevent misunderstandings and as a safeguard should legal action become necessary creditors would be well advised to ask customers to sign a written contract or order confirmation at the outset of the relationship and before goods are dispatched or services are performed (see Chapter 1 for further details of pre-contract considerations).

The strategy is very simple, it is the creditor's terms and conditions which should take precedence over any terms and conditions of business of the customer or the would be debtor. In the event of a dispute, it is the creditor's terms and conditions which should form the basis of a contract and if the customer has signed those terms and conditions without trying to introduce their own, it will be these terms and conditions on which any contractual claim is based.

What can go wrong?

3–03 Often in debt recovery the documentation on which the contract is based will come almost too late to the Debt Recovery Practitioner who is being asked to take action against the would be defendant. In debt recovery instructions, it is important to ask for sight of any contractual documentation such as it is. Many creditors will have their standard terms and conditions printed on the reverse of their invoices. They can be disappointed when told that by the stage of an invoice being issued it is usually too late for them to be introducing their contract terms into the contract. In such a situation and in the absence of the creditor's contractual terms, it may be that the contract will actually be regulated by the general law and not on the creditor's terms at all, or worse still, the other party's conditions govern the contract. Or there may be a finding that there is no contract at all because there has never been a true meeting of minds and the intention to create legal relations. In fact the documentation as it is between the parties ends in a draw with neither party's terms and conditions taking precedence. This is referred to as the "battle of the forms" and is dealt with below.

How can contracts come into being?

3–04 Contracts can come into place quite informally and Debt Recovery Practitioners need to be aware of this. It follows that once there is an offer and that offer is accepted, which is then supported by valuable consideration, and there is an intention on the part of the parties to create legal relations, a contract comes into being. So contracts can be made by telephone, fax or email and of course verbally, although verbal contracts should be avoided wherever possible. Where orders are to be placed by telephone, fax or email the client should always add a statement that such agreement will be subject to the creditor's standard terms and conditions of business. Indeed documentation to that effect must follow through the entire sales process so by the time the contract is made it is subject to the creditor's terms and conditions of business wherever possible.

Where formal offer and acceptance documents are used, it is important to ensure the other party's documents do not become the leading set of terms and conditions. If these are put forward, the creditor should send them back with an acknowledgement of the order and his own terms and conditions of business. The client, on receipt of an order from a customer respond by sending an acknowledgement of that order in duplicate incorporating the standard terms and asking the customer to sign and return one copy making it clear that the customer's order will not be actioned until that copy has been received.

Even if this cannot be done, all orders should be acknowledged by sending the acknowledgement of order form incorporating the creditor's terms.

Whilst the customer may say nothing in response to this and although silence does not constitute consent, if a customer raises no objection and then goes on to accept the goods or services, he will have difficulty at a later stage in disputing that the creditor's terms applied.

However, creditors should be advised that if contract terms contain an onerous provision, the court may not enforce that provision unless adequately drawn to the attention of the other party (see *Interfoto Picture Library Limited v Stiletto Visual Programmes Limited* [1998] 1 All E.R. 348).

What is the effect of the "battle of the forms" on any contract?

It has to be remembered that the court will strive to find there is a **3–05**
contract between the parties as was the case in *Butler Machine Tool Co v Ex-Cell-O Corporation (England) Limited* [1979] 1 All E.R. 965 where effectively the "last to shoot" won in terms of documentation being incorporated into the contract. However, the more recent case of *(1) Hertford Foods Limited (2) TSB Commercial Finance Limited v Lidl UK GMBH* [2001] EWCA Civ 938 found that the circumstances of the parties' negotiations was such, that the only reasonable conclusion to draw was that neither of their respective sets of terms and conditions had been incorporated into the contract between them.

As a result, it followed that there was no force majeure provision upon which the claimant could rely to excuse its non-performance of the contract. The court held that as neither party's terms and conditions applied to the agreement, the agreement itself was to be governed by the general law.

In general law, there is no concept of a "force majeure" and therefore the provision upon which *Hertford* had intended to rely to excuse its non-performance of a contract did not apply. *Hertford* was therefore in clear breach of the contract and *Lidl*.

Looked at another way, if *Hertford's* terms and conditions had been found to have been incorporated into the contract then those terms and conditions would have allowed it to rely upon its force majeure clause and to recover the amount due under the contract despite its non-supply of tinned corn beef. However, as the clause was found not to have been incorporated into the contract, *Hertford* could not rely on its clause and were therefore not entitled to recover the outstanding sum which was £156,000.

What about international contracts?

3–06 Legal implications of doing business abroad and outside of England and Wales can no longer be overlooked and Debt Recovery Practitioners have to anticipate what will be the impact of trying to collect debt outside of the courts of England and Wales. The contract itself can start to anticipate the international dimension of any agreement in the following ways:

- The contract can include a "choice of law" clause—this prescribes the law by which disputes arising under the contract will be decided. It does not of itself dictate which court is to have jurisdiction over such disputes as the two are entirely separate issues, and it is by no means unknown for the courts of one country to try a dispute by reference to the laws of another.
- If English law is chosen to govern a contract, it will be a factor which will influence the English courts in deciding whether or not to take the point on jurisdiction over a foreigner. The absence of a choice of law clause will result in the court having to decide which law the parties have intended to apply. As well as being time-consuming and expensive, this can have unsatisfactory results and it is best avoided by ensuring that the international dimension is anticipated and drafted for in the actual contract.
- Submission to jurisdiction—by such a clause a foreigner agrees to have any dispute relating to the contract tried in a court other than his own jurisdiction. It may be quicker and cheaper in a simple debt case to sue the foreigner in his own country where he has his assets, rather than to sue him in England and Wales and then attempt to enforce the judgment abroad (see Chapter 16 for Enforcements of Judgments in Foreign Jurisdictions).

At this juncture, it is worth a Debt Recovery Practitioner thinking seriously about the profile of the debtor and how in the event of default the contract on which the claim is based is going to be litigated and enforced. There are certainly a number of collection organisations which will attempt to collect debt without the need to litigate in a foreign jurisdiction; again working on a no-win no-fee basis and the most reputable of these will be Members of the Credit Services Association (see *http://www.csa-uk.org.uk*).

Knowing Your Debtor

It is absolutely vital in debt recovery procedures to identify the type of debtor that is about to be sued and to ensure that proceedings are issued in the proper capacity to avoid, on the one hand the proceedings being struck out, or more likely, to prevent an enforceable judgment being obtained which leaves the creditor without the real remedy of payment. **3–07**

In essence this goes back to the familiar saying of ensuring the debtor is not a "man of straw". When a choice is made to issue proceedings it is important to anticipate, and indeed to build, strategies to ensure that the debtor is going to be able to pay. If that fundamental question cannot be answered with any certainty either the client creditor must be put on notice of this fact or litigation should be avoided with some other method of recovery coming in its place.

Too often in debt recovery operations there is little attention paid to the capacity of the would be defendant to pay which does lead to proceedings being struck out or worse still thousands of unenforceable judgments being obtained against people who cannot be found, have no assets, or worse still, never existed in the first place.

At this stage we need to view debtors as defendants in legal proceedings and of course in doing so we categorise them into different types of "legal person" to determine which rules apply to which group.

3–08

Type of Defendant	Rules that apply
Individuals and Sole Traders	Debtors who are individuals should be sued in their known forenames along with their surnames and title, be it Mr, Mrs, Miss or Ms or any other title which they use such as Dr. (see CPR Practice Directions 16.2.6b). The Practice Direction requires the full unabbreviated name of the individual to be included in the proceedings. In the case of a sole trader the trading name must also be added to the proceedings. Under CPR Sch.1 RSC Order 81 r.9 an individual carrying on a business within the jurisdiction in the name or style other than his own name may be sued in his own name followed by the words

Type of Defendant	Rules that apply
	"Trading as [the business name]" or in the business name followed by the words "[a trading name]". The question that a claimant must consider therefore is how have they verified the name of the would be defendant and of course the best source of information for this will be through a credit application form which in turn has been verified by an external source such as a credit reference agency report. The identity of a sole trader and his or her trading style can of course be verified by the same means but also perhaps by a Business Names Act notice hanging in the trading premises of the would be defendant.
Partnerships	Identifying the partners within a firm can be a tricky area within debt recovery and Practitioners should take care when they identify that the would-be defendant is a firm of partners. The partnership is defined by s.1 (1) Partnership Act 1890 as "The relationships existing between persons carrying on a business in common with a view of making a profit". As such a partnership is made up of its members and has no separate legal personality as is the case of a limited liability company. In the 42nd set of amendments of Civil Procedure Rules introduced in October 2006 the age old problem of identifying the correct entity to sue when dealing with a partnership or firm started to be resolved. A new rule was inserted into CPR Pt 7 at para.7.2A along with an accompanying Practice Direction introducing procedures to be followed when claims are issued against a partnership within the jurisdiction. The Practice Direction itself at CPR PD7 para.5 sets out the procedures where claims are to be brought against two or more persons who were partners and carried on partnership business within the jurisdiction at the time the debt arose. CPR PD7 para.5A.2 defines "partners" as persons claim to be entitled as partners and persons alleged to be partners. Where the partnership has a name then unless inappropriate to do so claims must be brought against the name under which the partnership carried on business at the time the cause of action arose (see CPR PD7 para.5A.3). However, in CPR PD7 para.5B.1 a new term "partnership membership statement" is introduced into the CPR. This is a written statement of the names and last known places of residence of all persons who were partners in the partnership at the time the debt arose. Under para.5B.2 if the partners are requested to provide a copy of the partnership membership statement by any party to the claim, i.e. the creditor, then the partners must do so within 14 days of receipt

Type of Defendant	Rules that apply
	of the request. In that request the party seeking a copy of the partnership membership statement must specify the date when the relevant "cause of action accrued" which of course in debt recovery is the date when the debt became due. The new amendments not only deal with partners but also with sole traders. Under CPR PD7 para.5C.1 where a claim is brought against an individual and that individual carries on business within the jurisdiction (but although he need not be within the jurisdiction) and that business is carried on in his own name ("the business name") which is the classic case of a sole trader then the claim may be brought against the business name as if it were the name of a partnership. This means that the requirements of the Business Names Act 1985 are now being enforced so that disclosure of information has to be made. Reference to the Business Names Act was set out in Chapter 2 but for ease of reference the sections which involve disclosure of name and particularly relevant in debt recovery proceedings are as follows: Section 1 Persons subject to the Act Section 4 Disclosure required of persons using business name Section 5 Civil remedies for breach of Section 4 in relation to the disclosure of name
Limited Liability Partnership	Limited Liability Partnerships or LLPs were introduced by the Limited Liability Partnerships Act 2000. Such a partnership is a corporate body which does have a separate and distinct legal personality which is separate from the members. An LLP can be sued in its corporate name which must end with the words "Limited Liability Partnership" or LLP. If the LLP has a registered office in Wales it must use the Welsh term of "PAC".
Companies	Limited Liability Companies by the very nature are designed to limit the liability of the shareholders and directors and as such care must be taken at the outset of granting credit to companies to ensure that they are of substance and can, if sued, be worth the effort. A company registered under the Companies Act can be sued in its registered name (see *Foss v Harbottle* (1843) 2 HARE 461). However, companies become easier targets for debt recovery in as much that the information about the company is in the public domain and can be easily checked. A basic Webcheck can be carried out at Companies House at no cost, to establish that the company does legally exist. Such a search will also establish the registered office of a company and confirm that it is still solvent. This search can be enhanced through a credit reference agency search for even more information about the company including its directors, its accounts, and its credit rating.

Type of Defendant	Rules that apply
	A frustrating point for Practitioners is that, should a company be dissolved, then it cannot be sued, although it is possible to apply to restore the company to the register under s.653 of the Companies Act 1985. However, there may be little point in restoring a company to the register to chase a debt and then find there are no assets on which to enforce against. It is also worth understanding whether the company to be the target of litigation has associated companies linked with it and to ensure that the correct trading style of the company is checked on the basis of the contract that was made. A trap for Practitioners is to believe that company ABC Limited should be sued when in fact it is ABC Services Limited who should have been the target of litigation. In such an instance, the debtor company can avoid liability. The setting up of a new company it is possible that individuals who may become directors or shareholders, will enter into contracts for goods and services. Of course a seasoned Financial Director, Managing Director or Credit Manager would be wary of such contracts and take personal guarantees in some shape or form to ensure that new directors and/or shareholders were made personally liable in the event of default. However, a company is not bound by such contracts which are aimed to be entered into on its behalf before it becomes incorporated. Contracts made at the time when the company has not yet been formed mean that the person proposing to act for the company or as agent for it may be made personally liable for that contract. Companies also have to be very aware that by s.349 the Companies Act 1985, every company must have its name mentioned in legible characters in all business letters of the company, all notices and other official publications, and all Bills of Exchange, Promissory Notes, endorsements, cheques and orders for money or goods purporting to be signed by or on behalf of the company. A breach of these conditions renders the company liable to a fine and more importantly by s.349(4) of the Companies Act 1985, if an officer of a company or a person on its behalf signs or authorises to be signed, on behalf of the company, any bill of exchange, promissory note, endorsement, cheque or order for money or goods in which the company's name is not mentioned, he is personally liable to the holder of the bill of exchange, promissory note, cheque, or order for money or goods to the amount of that instrument. Debt Recovery Practitioners should always therefore check through the documentation to see if any paperwork issued by the company has been issued in compliance with the legislation. Any breach of that legislation will make the individual who signed personally liable.

Type of Defendant	Rules that apply
	Of course the question then has to be whether that individual is worth suing but it does give another avenue to pursue in the event of default. This scenario also assists where an order for goods is placed but no reference is made to the fact that the order is placed on behalf of a limited company. A director who has put himself in that situation can assert that he or she has no liability as the order was placed by the limited company. Section 349(4) of the Companies Act 1985 makes it quite clear that the person who places the order for goods without disclosing the company's name in full (which will include the fact it is a limited company) is personally liable for payment in respect of that order. In the case of *Contex Drouzhba Limited v Wiseman* [2007]EWCA Civ 1201 the Court of Appeal found Mr Wiseman liable for an agreement he had signed on behalf of his company promising it would pay for goods ordered in the future. Mr Wiseman did in fact know his company was insolvent and there was no prospect of any injection of capital. Interestingly, the claimant decided to sue Mr Wiseman personally under the tort of deceit and the court found for the claimant. It was held that in signing the agreement on behalf of the company Mr Wiseman was making an implied representation that the company had the capacity to meet its obligations. This was untrue and Mr Wiseman was found to be personally liable for that deceit in that he knew the true position. Mr Wiseman submitted that he had signed the document on behalf of the company and not in his personal capacity. However, the court held that where a director is effectively the mind of the company as in the case of Mr Wiseman, and in the document he signed he made a fraudulent representation using his knowledge, it was clear that even if the company would be liable for the deceit carried out by its director, the director had a personal liability for his own fraud. The logic of this case will not apply to every claim against a director but where the director is in effective control of the debtor company and signs an order for goods or services knowing that the company is insolvent there is now a good chance that the claim may be made against him personally.
Unincorporated associations and clubs	Unincorporated associations (or clubs) have no separate legal personality and so generally cannot be sued in their own name (see *Campbell v Thompson* [1953] Q. B. 445). If the club is a limited company the usual rules will apply however, and if two or more proprietors of the club could be said to be a partnership they may be sued under the partnership provisions. Therefore generally unincorporated associations cannot be construed as a limited company or a partnership and therefore one or more

Type of Defendant	Rules that apply
	members of the club will have to be sued as representative of that club with the heading "[name of the members] on behalf of all the members of the [name of the unincorporated association/club] on [date that the debt became due]" (see CPR 19.6).
Crown, government and local government.	Civil proceedings against the Crown must be instituted against the appropriate authorised government department or, if there is no appropriate government department, or if there is any doubt as to who to be sued, the defendant becomes the Attorney General (see Crown Proceedings Act 1947 s.17(3)). In the CPR at Practice Direction 19a a list of authorised government departments with the name and address for services is set out. In relation to local councils in England and Wales these must be sued under their titles and name of their areas (see Local Government Act 1972 ss.2 and 8).
Foreign State	A foreign state cannot be sued in a court in the United Kingdom unless it has submitted to the jurisdiction of the domestic courts. Or the case falls within one of the following categories: • A commercial transaction contract to be performed in the United Kingdom. • A contract of employment. • VAT and customs duties. • Some admiralty proceedings (see State Immunity Act 1978). • A claim for personal injury and/or damage to property. • Proceedings in relation to patents or trademarks.

Tips on locating the "Gone Away" debtor

3–08.1 It is a fact of life in debt recovery departments that a number of debtors will just not be at the address where it is said they would be, or the creditor thought they would be, and indeed debtors do move from place to place. So a Debt Recovery Practitioner has to have a number of processes to be able to trace debtors and establish and verify their correct address for proceedings to be issued and for enforcement action to be taken later on.

Since the introduction of the World Wide Web and the growth of tools on the web to be able to assist a Debt Recovery Practitioner, there are now a number of sites which can be used to help find "Gone Aways". The Matrix of Information Resources provides a starting point for a Practitioner to build his or her own set of resources but it is important to remember that all the information contained on the web is in the public domain and so any such search for information is likely to be lawful. In Chapter 2 references to breach of data protection were mentioned under s.55 Data Protection Act. Whatever process is used for checking and verifying information it must be compliant with the terms of that legislation.

If searches on the web draw a blank in terms of being able to find a debtor then the Debt Recovery Practitioner has the option to choose a reputable tracing agent to carry out further enquiries.

A search of the Association of British Investigators at *http://www.theabi.org.uk* will list members who are considered reputable tracing agents. However, even if choosing a member from the ABI a prudent Debt Recovery Practitioner will ensure that the tracing agency has notified its activities to the Information Commissioner's Office by checking the Information Commissioner's Office's website and that its process are compliant with the Data Protection Act (see Chapter 2). In a recent report the Information Commissioner outlined his concerns on the trade in personal data in this report entitled "what Price Privacy–The Unlawful Trade in Confidential Personal Information" set out on the ICO website at *http://www.ico.gov.uk*. It makes for sombre reading in relation to action taken against tracing agents for the illegal trade in personal data.

What is the position regarding deceased debtors?

Where the debtor has died but the Debt Recovery Practitioner has **3–08.2**
to consider whether this was during the course of proceedings or before it.

It is possible for the proceedings to be brought against a debtor who dies before the proceedings are issued. In this situation the claim should be brought against the "Personal Representatives of …". The claimant must then within four months of the issue of the claim apply to the court for it to appoint the Personal Representatives for the sole purpose of the proceedings, if indeed, none have stepped forward and been appointed. If the claimant knows the names of the Personal Representatives their names can be included in the initial claim as "Joe Bloggs and Fred Bloggs" the Personal Representatives of Mary Bloggs".

In the event that there are no Personal Representatives then the claim must be brought against the "Estate of …". Again, within four months of the issue of the claim the claimant must apply to the court for an order appointing a person to represent the deceased's estate.

In the event the debtor dies during the course of the proceedings it is likely that court will simply order that the Personal Representatives be joined to the action and essentially they will take the place of the debtor and the claim will continue as it would have done had the debtor not died. In the event there are no Personal Representatives of the debtor then the court may order any other person with an interest in the deceased's estate to be given notice. It is possible that the action will continue without any Personal Representative of the deceased debtor, or the court may appoint someone to act as the deceased debtor's Personal Representative for the sole purpose of the proceedings.

What is the position regarding debtors outside England and Wales?

3–08.3 Debt Recovery Practitioners are increasingly having to take account of the fact that debtors will fall outside of the jurisdiction of the courts of England and Wales and need to have remedies and avenues open to them in pursuing debts outside of their usual jurisdiction. A credit policy should include a policy to handle default for countries outside England and Wales so that there is no hiatus in the momentum to collect the debt.

The Civil Procedure Rules do in fact define the jurisdiction of the Courts of England and Wales at CPR r.2.3 to include. "England and Wales and any part of the territorial waters of the United Kingdom adjoining England and Wales".

However, to avoid any confusion the following areas are NOT within the jurisdiction of the English and Welsh Courts and these are as follows:

- Any of the Channel Islands
- Isle of Man
- Northern Ireland
- Scotland
- Eire

However, the Isle of Wight and the Scilly Isles are included within the definition of r.2.3. In building a policy it is suggested that for each foreign jurisdiction where the creditor is likely to have debtors the following matrix is set out below:

Collection Strategy		Legal Process			Enforcement Process	
Country	Collection Agent	CPR Rule for Service	Documents Required	Time Allowed for Service	Reciprocal Enforcement Treaty	Enforcement Procedure

Collection Strategy		Legal Process			Enforcement Process	
France	ABC Globe Collections	CPR 6—s. III	See Rules for detail	21 days	CPR Pt 74	See Judicial Network in Civil and Commercial (Matters—France)

A useful website link for litigating and enforcing elsewhere in Europe is set out at *http://www.ec.europa.eu/civiljustice/*. The Enforcement of Judgment section will take you to an enforcement fact sheet for each country in the EU.

In addition to understanding how to litigate claims for unpaid debts where the customer lives abroad a Debt Recovery Practitioner also needs to have an understanding of how to enforce judgments outside England and Wales in different parts of the UK, Europe and further afield. In Chapter 16 in this book the requirements of CPR Pt 74 will be dealt with in an easy-to-read format.

Know Your Remedy

Debt recovery needs a strategic approach. With the increased cost of **3–09**
litigation and claimants having tighter budgets to use for litigation and enforcement expenditure, a strategy to sue those who can pay as opposed to suing everybody is the smart way to work.

Of course knowing the remedy and anticipating what may be required comes through experience along with knowledge of the client's requirements, the rules on what is permitted under the Civil Procedure Rules and Insolvency Rules and ultimately, how to use these in combination to achieve a positive cash result. It should never be forgotten that the ultimate aim of a Debt Recovery Practitioner is to recover cash and achieving an unenforceable judgment is not a success so far as the client is concerned.

Debt Recovery Practitioners should be encouraged to have a wide view of any file or case that comes to them for recovery or indeed any portfolio made up of any number of debts which is sent to them for collection. Whether it be one debt or multiple debts the approach involves analysing the client's records and files and looking at what information is available about the debtor, reading notes of conversations and correspondence which had been recorded in relation to the debtor's accounts and assessing how many accounts have telephone numbers, mortgage information, employment details, etc. which ultimately will have a bearing on the ultimate strategy for the recovery of the debt.

Unfortunately there are still Practitioners who rush to issue claims in the county court only to find when it comes to enforcement they have no strategy and the client is left with a bill to pay and no money recovered.

3–10 For Debt Recovery Practitioners operating in a solicitor's environment one has to ask if such an approach is in the "best interest of the client" particularly if the debtor is found to be subsequently insolvent or, even worse, where there was no hope of paying even the fixed cost of litigation let alone the outstanding judgment debt, costs and interest.

The problem of litigating without hope of recovery can be avoided by some simple risk management within the debt recovery department and at the outset of instructions for a new client or indeed for any particular debt.

Whether a single debt or a multiple portfolio processes can be developed to assess and categorise the judgment debtor's situation and this can then be streamlined into a matrix to handle different types of debtors with different types of assets.

The table below which we will call the "Enforcement Matrix" categorises debtors and uses some of the approach in the "Know your Debtor" section of this chapter.

3–11 The matrix identifies the type of debtor and then begins to anticipate what type of premises that debtor may reside in or trade from. The issue of type of premises is important because in relation to a domestic address the use of a bailiff or a High Court Enforcement Officer (see Chapter 14) will be of limited effect due to the current rules on rights of entry into private houses. Again, Debt Recovery Practitioners just from their own experience of running their home and business can then anticipate what possible types of assets each type of debtor may have, and as a result of that, it is possible then to anticipate the type of enforcement action that would be likely if a debtor profile fits the type of address and the type of assets, so that the outcome for enforcement is known.

Of course it is hoped that enforcement will not be necessary, but what it does mean is that all the way through the debt recovery process in conversations and correspondence with debtors, the Debt Recovery Practitioner has a clear path and indeed, is able to point out to the debtor the action that will be taken against him, her or it in the event of continued default.

So far as the Office of Fair Trading guidelines are concerned (see Chapter 2) this is important because the debtor is being told about the consequences of continued default, which is also in accordance with the Civil Procedure Rules and therefore it is difficult for the debtor to argue at any point in time that he was not told what would happen in the event that he did not pay.

3–12

Type of Debtor	Type of Premises	Possible types of assets	Type of Enforcement
Individual	Domestic address where the debtor may be viewed as a consumer of goods and service whether or not regulated under the CCA 1974 (as amended)—for sole trader see below.	Goods—ranging from the family car to goods inside the premises such as state of the art television set, home entertainment system, antiques, jewellery, but consider carefully items which are exempt from seizure by virtue of s.99 Sch.7 of the Courts Act 2003.	Execution against goods using county court bailiff and/or High Court Enforcement Officer.
		Equity in home	Charging Order—see CPR Pt 73
		Employment	Attachment of Earnings—CPR Sch.2, CCR Order 27
		Bank account	Third Party Debt Order—CPR Pt 72
		Pension/Life Policies	Appointment of a Receiver—CPR Pt 69
		Not sure what assets the debtor has	Order to Obtain Information—CPR Pt 71—focussing on the income and expenditure and other assets of the debtor as per the record of examination questionnaire set out in Form EX140.
		Benefit payments	The Debt Recovery Practitioner must be realistic about how any resulting claim can be enforced if there is evidence that a debtor is in receipt of state benefits.
Sole Trader	Domestic—as above	Goods—as above	Execution—as above.

Type of Debtor	Type of Premises	Possible types of assets	Type of Enforcement
		Equity in home	Charging Order—as above
		Bank account	Third Party Debt Order—as above
		Pensions/Life Policies	Appointment of Receiver—as above
		Not sure what assets the sole trader may have	Order to Obtain Information—as above—this time focussing on the accounts for the sole trader business including the sales ledger where the debtor may be owed money along with other financial information to draw conclusions on what assets may be available.
Sole Trader	Commercial	Goods–In this situation we are looking at the goods available against the judgment debtor in his business property such as stock, plants and machinery, business equipment.	Execution against goods—here a county court bailiff or a High Court Enforcement Officer is not prevented from forcing entry to a commercial property to levy execution and ultimately to remove goods for sale in the event of non-payment.
		Equity in property	Charging Order—as above
		Bank account or debts owed to the business Not sure what assets the sole trader business has	Third Party Debt Order—as above Order to Obtain Information—as above—again focussing on the accounts for the business—as above.
Partner	Domestic	Goods—as above	Execution against goods—as above
		Equity in home	Charging Order—as above
		Bank account/debts owed to the business	Third Party Debt Order—as above

Type of Debtor	Type of Premises	Possible types of assets	Type of Enforcement
		Not sure what assets the partner has	Order to Obtain Information—as above—focussing on accounts for the business—as above
Partner	Commercial	Goods—as above	Execution against goods—as above
		Equity in property	Charging Order—as above
		Bank account/debts owed to the business	Third Party Debt Order—as above
		Not sure what assets the partner has	Order to Obtain Information—as above—focussing on sales ledger and other assets and liabilities
Company	Domestic	Goods	Execution against goods—the issue here to resolve is the goods the company's goods or do they belong to the director personally and can the director be made personally liable for the company's debt?
		Equity in director's home—if company owns the property	Charging Order—as above—here the check needs to be whether the property is owned by the company or whether it is owned by the director personally and again whether the director can be made personally liable for the company's debt.
		Director's salary	Attachment of Earnings—as above—if the company director can be found personally liable for the company's debt then the salary can be attached.
		Bank account/debts owed to the company	Third Party Debt Order—as above

Type of Debtor	Type of Premises	Possible types of assets	Type of Enforcement
		Not sure what assets the company owns	Order to Obtain Information—involving an officer of the company—with that officer completing form EX141 which focuses on the assets and liabilities of the debtor company.
Company	Commercial	Goods—This will include stock, plants and machinery, business equipment within the company's premises.	Execution against goods—the issue to watch for here is that the correct company is to be sued and judgment is to be taken against the correct company's name.
		Equity in commercial property	Charging Order—again the same issue occurs in that the correct company must be sued and own the property and searches should be carried out before litigation is commenced.
		Bank account/debts owed to the company	Third Party Debt Order—as above.
		Not sure what assets the company owns	Order to Obtain Information—again a cross examination of the company's directors should take place and the com pany's directors should be required to bring the company's books to the hearing to verify whatever is said. The other approach is to seek to wind up the debtor company on the basis that it meets one of the grounds for insolvency although see Chapter 18 on the limitations in relation to this course of action.

The Debtor has tendered part payment in full and final settlement—what should be the response?

3–13 It is often the case in debt recovery proceedings that a debtor will offer a part payment in full and final settlement of the outstanding debt. Debt Recovery Practitioners need to be aware on how to deal with such offers commercially, again using the enforcement matrix detailed above. Debt Recovery Practitioners will have to weigh up whether the offer in full and final settlement is going to be better than ultimately the amount that may be recovered by way of litigation and the enforcement of any resulting judgment.

In law the contractual position of an offer of part payment in full and final settlement has been reviewed in two cases. In the case of *Re-Select Move* (1995) All E.R. 531 the debtor made a promise to pay the debt by instalments as to full and final settlement of the outstanding balance and tendered its first cheque. The creditor accepted the cheque and paid it into the bank but then sued for the balance outstanding. *Select Move* argued that there was a new contract for the debt to be paid by instalments. However, the court held that there was no new contract for instalments as no fresh consideration had passed and the contract could not be enforced. As such the debtor was found not to have entered into a new contract and was liable under the original contract for the full amount of the debt outstanding.

In 2001 the case of *Inland Revenue Commissioners v Fry* (2001) STC 1715 involved the payment by a taxpayer Mrs Fry of £10,000 to the Inland Revenue in settlement of her tax bill of £113,000. Her husband had sent the cheque in full and final settlement and the accompanying letter from the debtor to the Revenue stated that by the presentation of the cheque the Revenue would be deemed to have accepted Mrs Fry's offer in full payment of the outstanding tax bill.

The Revenue's evidence was that the procedure within its post room was for all cheques received in the post to be separated from correspondence and immediately presented for payment. The accompanying correspondence was only then passed to the appropriate caseworker and had the letter and cheques stayed together it was likely that the offer enclosed with the letter would have been found to be unacceptable and either the cheque would have been treated as part payment or the debtor would have had his money back. The taxpayer, Mrs Fry, contended that as the cheque had been banked there was a binding compromise on the Revenue. The House of Lords however held differently. They said that for any contract to come into existence there has to be a meeting of minds—a basic of contract law. The Revenue had banked Mr Fry's cheque without any knowledge of the offer being made and the circumstances were such that there could not have been any active acceptance of that offer. If the matter failed to be dealt with on the basis of what a reasonable person would think, the court could not consider that because of the Revenue's internal procedures the mere banking of Mr Fry's cheque would be an acceptable binding offer.

What action should be taken in response to a payment in full and final settlement?

3–14 Relying on the case of *Fry* and indeed the case of *Re-Select Move* it is clear that a cheque tendered in full and final settlement of an outstanding debt which has been banked without fresh consideration and without a meeting of minds cannot form the basis of a binding compromise.

Of course debtors try to make payments in full and final settlement all the time in debt recovery and a creditor will be minded to bank that cheque in partial settlement to the outstanding sum. If this course of action is to be taken, the debtor must be advised immediately that the sum is not accepted in full and final settlement and the cheque is only accepted in part payment. If there is any doubt as to whether a fresh consideration and a meeting of minds could be construed or implied into the contract then the creditor should return the payment. Commercially, of course, this could be unpalatable.

If the debtor intimates that a cheque must only be presented if an offer is accepted, there is a likelihood that a court would say there had been a meeting of minds, although of course, there will be no fresh consideration as was required in the *Re-Select Move* case. Ideally the letter going out to the debtor should clearly state that any offer of payment will result in monies being banked, but such monies will not be accepted in full and final settlement and will only be allocated to the outstanding balance as a partial payment. This line of approach should be taken all the way through debt recovery so that a creditor is always in the driving seat in terms of any offers that are made by debtors.

What steps can be taken to prevent a Debtor from dissipating assets?

3–15 If there is concern that a defendant or judgment debtor (as they may become) will dissipate the assets which are believed to be available to satisfy the judgment debt then the Court has the power under its "Interim Remedies" provisions found at CPR Pt 25 to make a broad range of orders to preserve the position and protect a party from another's attempt to dissipate assets.

An order for detention, custody or preservation may be made in relation to property which may become the subject matter of subsequent proceedings under CPR Pt 25.1(1)(c).

A "Freezing Injunction" (formerly known as a *Mareva injunction*) under CPR Pt 25.1(1)(f) and (g) provides power to the court to restrain a party from removing from the jurisdiction assets located within the jurisdiction or restraining a party from dealing with any assets whether in the jurisdiction.

The following table is designed to highlight key issues surrounding the use of Freezing Orders as one of the remedies which a Debt Recovery Practitioner may use as part of this section: 3–16

Can the claimant use a Freezing Order if there is no intention to issue proceedings?	The court has no jurisdiction to grant a freezing injunction in circumstances where the applicant has no intention of issuing proceedings immediately or almost immediately (see *Fourie v Roux and others* [2004] EWHC 2260).
Can a claimant make the application without notice to the defendant?	Yes, for obvious reasons, in the first instance the application for a freezing injunction is made without notice to a Judge (see Practice Direction 2B (Allocation of Cases to Levels of Judiciary)).
What is the approach to take in framing the applicant's application to the court?	It is important to ensure that the application for a freezing order is framed to result in minimum interference with the respondent's rights. The purpose of the freezing order is not to punish the respondent but to protect the applicant (see *Flightwise Travel Service Ltd v Gill* [2003] EWHC 3082.
How does the applicant demonstrate to the court that assets are "at risk"?	It is not necessary to establish that the respondent is likely to act with the object of putting his assets beyond reach. Instead what has to be shown is that there is, without the freezing order being made, "a real risk that a judgment or award in favour of the claimants would go unsatisfied" (see *Ninemia Maritime Corporation v Trave Schiffahrtsgesellschaft mbh and Co KG* [1984] 1 All E.R. 398.
Can a respondent be permitted to trade despite a freezing order being made?	A respondent can be permitted to carry on trading, by making payments of invoices in the course of trading which may result in any judgment or award becoming unsatisfied wholly or partially had it not been for the trading and the payment of invoices (see *TTMI Ltd of England v ASM Shipping Ltd of India* [2005] EWHC 2666 (Comm)). The applicant should be aware of this and look to deal with this within the application.
How strong does the "real risk" have to be in convincing the court to make the order?	Something more than a "real risk" that the judgment will go unsatisfied is required. The purpose of the injunction is to ensure that the Court's judgment is not rendered valueless "by an unjustifiable disposal of assets" (see *Ketchum International Plc*

	v Group Public Relations Holdings Ltd [1997] 1 W.L.R. 4, CA).
Can a freezing order be made in county court proceedings?	The power of county courts to grant freezing injunctions is restricted by the county court Remedies Regulations 1991 made under the county courts Act 1984, s.38 (as amended in 1990). The general rule is that a county court *may not* grant a freezing injunction. However, exemption from this restriction is enjoyed by nominated circuit judges sitting in Patent county courts and Mercantile courts and by High Court judges sitting as judges for any county court District. It should be noted that a county court can grant a freezing order in the circumstances listed in reg.3(3) of the 1991 Regulations where a freezing order is necessary for the purpose of making an order for the preservation, custody or detention of property which forms or may form the subject matter of proceedings (i.e. where the property is subject to a proprietary claim), and in aid of execution of a judgment or order made in proceedings in a county court to preserve assets until execution can be levied upon them.
Can a county court revoke a High Court freezing order?	A county court may not vary or revoke a freezing order granted by the High Court but may vary the freezing order where all the parties are agreed on the terms of the variation (see reg.3(1) and(4)(b) of the 1991 Regulations).

3–17 Preliminary steps

Can the High Court assist the County Court in the granting of a freezing order?	Article 3 of the High Court and County Courts Jurisdiction Order 1991 provides for the High Court to have jurisdiction to hear an application for a freezing order made in the course of or in anticipation of proceedings in a county court where a county court may not, by virtue of regulations under s.38(3)(b) of the County Courts Act 1984 grant the relief. The High Court therefore has jurisdiction to grant freezing orders incidental to and in support of county court proceedings. In *Schmidt v Wong (Practice Note)* [2005] 1 EWCA Civ 1506, [2006] 1 All E.R. 677 the Court of Appeal explained that

	in order to invoke the High Court's assistance a claimant in county court proceedings would have to make an application to the High Court in accordance with CPR Pt 23 by issuing the application at the Royal Courts of Justice or the appropriate District Registry and paying the higher court fee. The application would then be made returnable before a Judge. In the body of the application there should appear an explanation along the following lines: "This application is being made in the course of [in anticipation of] proceedings in the county court pursuant to Article 3 of the High Court and County Courts Jurisdiction Order 1991. The county court has no jurisdiction to grant the relief sought by reason of Regulation 3(1) of the County Court Remedies Regulations 1991." NOTE: The High Court's assistance should not to be invoked by issuing a claim form in the High Court for the freezing order. This is because any freezing order which is then made can be extracted from the claim to which it relates and be treated as a free-standing remedy.
How is a Freezing Order Applied for?	The forms of injunction available in both the High Court and county courts are set out in the note to CPR Pt 25 in the White Book Service at 25.1.13. The application for a freezing order is made on an application notice in accordance with the provisions of CPR 23 (General rules about applications for Court orders) as modified by the provisions of Practice Direction (Interim Injunctions) and the accompanying Practice Direction. The modifications are substantial. Applications for freezing orders must be supported by written evidence in the form of affidavit (Practice Direction (Interim Injunctions), para.3.1). The claimant should depose to objective facts from which it may be inferred that the defendant is likely to move assets or dissipate them. Unsupported statements or expressions of fear have little weight (see *O'Regan v Iambic Productions* (1989) 139 N.L.J. 1378 (1998) and *Rosen v Rose* [2003] EWHC 309 (QB) January 27, 2003). Great care should be taken in the presentation of evidence to the court so that the court can see, not only whether the applicant has a good arguable case, but also whether there is a real risk of dissipation of assets (as outlined above). A freezing order should not be granted unless the applicant has established an appropriately strong case

	showing, amongst other things, that the respondent owns the assets concerned or has some interest in them. It is for the applicant to make out his case.
How should the applicant deal with issues of the respondent's "dishonesty"?	Where the applicant believes that the respondent has been dishonest, the court should scrutinise with care whether what is alleged in this respect and do these allegations really justify the inference that the respondent is likely to dissipate assets unless restricted (see *Thane Investments Ltd v Tomlinson* [2003] EWCA Civ 1272, July 29, 2003, CA).
What must the applicant's evidence show on the issue of making the application without notice?	Where an application is made without notice to the respondent, the applicant's evidence must state why notice was not given [Practice Direction (Interim Injunctions) para.3.4]. It is essential that the respondent is entitled to a proper opportunity to present his case at the with notice hearing. He therefore has to be supplied with all the evidence on which the applicant is going to rely (see *Flightwise Travel Service Ltd v Gill* [2003] EWHC 3082 (Ch), *The Times*, December 5, 2003 (Neuberger J.))
Can the Court Vary or Revoke a Freezing Order? **What is the Sanction for Failing to Obey the Freezing Order?**	The court can vary or revoke a freezing order (r.3.1(7)) and a person who is not a party to the terms of the order but who is directly affected by such injunction may apply to have it set aside or varied (40.9). A person who disobeys a freezing order may be dealt with by contempt proceedings [Practice Direction (Judgments and Orders), para.9.1]. A party's contempt is not a complete bar to an application for a variation of the terms of a freezing order but in such circumstances, the court should exercise its discretion in the best interests of justice (see *Federal Bank of the Middle East v Hadkinson,* 1999 EWCA 1232.

Chapter 4

Recovering the Cost of Debt Recovery through the Courts

Introductory Comments

Recovering debts through the courts has a cost attached and creditors are going to want to ensure that as far as possible they recover the cost of using the court system to pay for their debt recovery. 4–01

Before a creditor even gets into the arena of issuing a letter before action and preparing a claim there are steps that can be taken at the outset of a customer relationship to alleviate the cost of recovery.

It is possible to include terms at the outset of a contractual relationship with a customer which expressly state that in the event of default of payment the cost of recovery will be borne by the customer. Of course this is a very general statement but creditors and those advising them need to consider the commercial reality that to recover a debt costs the creditor money.

It may be said that that cost is the creditor's problem but more and more we are seeing that the cost of recovery in certain industries such as local government, and utility services, means that the cost of default and recovering debts is falling on the rest of the customer population who do pay.

Of course much depends on the industry sector, regulation, and the basis of the contractual relationship but the fact is it is not unlawful to charge the customer for the cost of recovery. 4–02

The amount of debt in the UK economy stands at a staggering £1.4 trillion or in figures £1,400,000,000,000,000,000 (source: *http://www.bbc.co.uk*). So perhaps the time has come for businesses to grasp the nettle of how to recoup the cost of recovery from their customers who can pay, and creating processes and systems for those who can't.

What collection costs should be anticipated by a contractual term for their recovery?

4–03 Some thought needs to be given as to what the costs of recovery are likely to entail. In the stages before a Letter Before Claim is sent, there may be the cost of field visits by in-house recovery officers, or external field agents. There may be tracing costs to establish an address and of course there will be the cost of commission on any debt which is collected. If these types of costs are to be recoverable from the debtor then any contractual arrangement needs to anticipate these to ensure they can be added on to the final amount that is to be collected. It is also important to ensure that any cost passed on to the debtor is lawful and has actually been incurred and can pass external scrutiny whether it be by the court, or by perhaps a regulator.

Any such clause must be well drafted and written to fit in with existing contractual position. Taking advice from commercial lawyers on how to write such a clause, and indeed perhaps to review the existing terms and conditions of business as a whole is always a worthwhile exercise. Commercial lawyers will have access to the most recent precedents covering the entire spectrum of business activity and will draft according to the nature of the creditor's business. Of course in the recovery of certain types of debts, such as banking, finance, consumer credit, local government, utilities such contracts are highly regulated and so the end result may be that despite the desire to recoup costs the fact remains it is impossible to pass on pre-legal costs on to defaulting customers.

That then leaves the issue of recouping the costs of recovery once the Letter Before Claim is sent to the debtor. From this point on the situation starts to change. Below is a table which sets out the likely expenses that a creditor would incur in the recovery of a debt from the time the debt becomes due and in outline how could these costs can be recovered:

4–04

Typical Costs of Recovering a Debt	Recoverable Through Express Provision in a Contract	Recoverable Through a Court Claim
PRE LEGAL ARENA		
Tracing costs of finding a debtor	Only if expressly provided in the contract	Not recoverable without supporting contract provision
Commission charged by third party to collect a debt	Only if expressly provided in the contract	Not recoverable without supporting contract provision

Typical Costs of Recovering a Debt	Recoverable Through Express Provision in a Contract	Recoverable Through a Court Claim
Credit or Debit Card Charges	Only if expressly provided in the contract.	Not recoverable without supporting contract provision.
Field Agent Visits	Only if expressly provided in the contract.	Not recoverable without supporting contract provision.
Cost of Telephone Collection	Only if expressly provided in the contract.	Not recoverable without supporting contract provision.
Collection Letters	Only if expressly provided in the contract.	Not recoverable without supporting contract provision.
Letter Before Claim	Only if expressly provided in the contract.	Not recoverable without supporting contract provision.
Court Fees including issue fee for claim/enforcement applications/allocation questionnaire	May be included in the contract with the customer.	Recoverable as part of a successful claim.
LEGAL ARENA		
Fixed Solicitors Costs—as allowed under the CPR Fees Orders	May be expressly included in the contract with the customer.	Recoverable as part of a successful claim.
Interest—In a Pre-Legal Environment	Should be provided for expressly in the contract at a commercial rate.	Statutory interest under s. 69 of the County Courts Act 1984 or s.35A of Supreme Court Act 1981 provide for interest from date of debt becoming due.
Interest—From Issue of Claim to Judgment	Again for certainty contract may confirm statutory position.	Statutory interest under above sections continues to run.
Interest—After Judgment	Contract should specify post judgment interest position.	Interest on judgment debts over £5000 continues to run in the county court. For sums over £600 interest will only run from date of transfer at judgment rate if judgment can be transferred to the High Court. For sums under £600 interest will not continue to run on a county court judgment unless expressly allowed.

Typical Costs of Recovering a Debt	Recoverable Through Express Provision in a Contract	Recoverable Through a Court Claim
Late Payment of Commercial Debts (Interest) Act 1998	No need for specific provision in contract. Interest and compensation costs can be added to the claim for the debt.	Recoverable as part of a successful claim—need to be included in Particulars of Claim.

It can be seen from the above table that a large amount of resource can be spent in the pre-legal arena in attempting to collect a debt without that cost being recoverable from the debtor unless it is made part of the contract. Again creditors in certain sectors will have to consider how feasible such an approach will be particularly in the light of the OFT's Guidance on Debt Collection, and the campaign in recent months to review the cost of banking charges.

4–05 One of the benefits of going to the courts to recover the debt is that the cost of collection becomes recoverable from the debtor as part of the claim. However, there is a catch to this. When talking about fixed costs, interest and fees all being recoverable from the debtor, they still have to end up in the bank account of the creditor as cash. Practitioners should not lose sight of that fact, particularly when working in a third party collection business as many claims are issued where no money is ever recovered although a fee is paid to the solicitor on the issue of the claim.

Research indicates that both solicitors and Debt Collection Agencies (or DCAs) are likely to charge a commission on monies recovered by using their letters and telephone calls to collect a debt in the first instance. Solicitors are able to make a charge based on a commission basis up to the issue of proceedings but their professional conduct rules (see Solicitors' Code of Conduct 2007) prevents solicitors then from working on a "no collection, no fee" basis unless they have a particular kind of fee arrangement in place called a "Conditional Fee Arrangement".

Collection agencies have no such obstacles. However, as they are not regulated to take a step in legal proceedings, unlike their solicitor counterparts, DCAs cannot issue proceedings in the name of the client and have to outsource the litigation steps to a firm of solicitors who may be linked exclusively to the DCA, or who may be working as a practice on behalf of many clients, one of which is the DCA. The trade association for the debt collection industry is the Credit Services Association (CSA) and more information about DCAs can be found on the CSA website at *http://www.csa-uk.com*.

In practical terms this means that the collection of debt by letter/telephone/field visit can be carried out by DCAs and solicitors on a "no collect, no fee" basis with contingency fees being charged usually in the form of commission.

For solicitors this pre-legal arena is viewed as "non-contentious" business and the Solicitors' Code of Conduct allows contingency fees to be charged. Depending on the age of the debt and the complexity of the situation, contingency based commissions can range from anything between 5 per cent and 20 per cent of the monies recovered. The older the debt or the more complex the recovery process needed then the commission rates are likely to rise. **4–06**

Of course for the creditor client this means that if the debt can be collected they will be charged a commission on monies collected, in the absence of any express provision with the debtor to add that commission to the outstanding debt. Regardless of the amount of resource used by the DCA or solicitor to collect the debt, the client will usually be charged nothing or only agreed disbursements in the absence of a full or partial collection.

When the debt recovery process moves to the legal arena, the first step is always to send the Letter Before Claim. The letter is sent by a solicitor business, and usually there is a fixed price for the sending of the letter. There are a large number of good quality law firms who offer this service and they can be found through the Law Society's website at *http://www.lawsociety.org.uk*.

Solicitors will add in additional services to prompt the debtor to pay. More and more solicitors are using pre-legal telephone collections to collect the debt without resorting to legal action which of course is within the spirit of the overriding objective of the CPR. This work is also still viewed as non-contentious, and as such if a collection is made the solicitor can charge commission on a recovery.

However, once the claim is issued at the court, the way that a solicitor charges will need to change to be compliant with the Solicitors' Code of Conduct 2007. Under r.2.04 it is expressly forbidden for the solicitor to charge a contingency fee for work done in prosecuting ... any contentious proceedings before a court of England and Wales except as permitted by statute or the common law. "Contentious proceedings" are defined by s.28 of the Solicitors' Act 1974 as "business done, in or for the purpose of proceedings begun before a court". **4–07**

As a result a contingency fee paid to a solicitor before the issue of the claim is lawful. If a contingency fee is sought to be charged once proceedings have begun then the agreement itself is unlawful and unenforceable since the work done both before and after the start of proceedings will be assessable by the court on a contentious fee basis.

However, the approach taken by the bodies which regulate litigation and how litigation services are to be charged for is changing. The Courts and Legal Services Act 1990 provided under s.58 and 58A for "Conditional Fee Arrangements" (CFA) to be available and in many areas of litigation these are now common. A CFA is an agreement under which the solicitor receives no payment (or less than normal payment) if the case is lost, but normal or higher payment if the client is successful. This might be seen as a "no win, no fee" agreement, but as we have already seen contingency fees are not allowed to be charged. Instead a CFA should be seen as an agreement for the client to pay a fee based on the solicitor's usual hourly charging rates with a fee payable on success as a percentage increase in the hourly charging rate up to a maximum of 100 per cent. The important point to note is that the fee is not based on the solicitor receiving any proportion of money recovered by the client which of course would be on a contingency basis.

The requirements of a CFA agreement are technical and expert advice should be sought if one is contemplated. In straightforward debt recovery matters they might be seen as "a sledgehammer to crack a nut" when solicitors will normally charge the fixed costs (see below) allowed by the court along perhaps with an agreement by the client to pay an additional sum on a "solicitor and client" cost basis.

4–08 CFAs come into the picture when a debt recovery claim becomes a defended matter and solicitors then have to handle the response to the debtor's defence and or counterclaim (see Chapter 8). At this point the solicitor's original terms of business with the creditor client should enable the solicitor to change his or her charging basis to hourly rates although more innovative solicitors are even looking to charge fixed rates for defended actions. No doubt as competition in the solicitor's market increases over the coming years as a result of the Legal Services Act 2007 more solicitors will find more and more ways to attract clients into their debt recovery services with more innovative and lawful charging schemes.

Of course the real problem with litigation for parties is not so much about the arrangement with one's own solicitor on what needs to be paid, at least that should be outlined at the first stage of taking instructions and through the requirements of the Solicitors' Code of Conduct to inform the client on costs from the outset.

The problem comes in anticipating what will be the downside if the litigation is lost and the losing party has to pay not only his own solicitor's legal bill, but the other sides as well. This is dealt with in Chapter 8 in looking at defended claims.

Of course the skill of the Debt Recovery Practitioner will be to ensure that cases are only litigated where the client has a high percentage chance of winning and clients do not waste time and money on hopeless cases.

Can the "late payment" legislation help in compensating a creditor to collect a debt?

4–09 The answer is "yes". Although there is no data available it seems anecdotally that the use of the compensation provisions within the late payment legislation are under-utilised by creditors when collecting commercial debts. Full information about the late payment legislation is set out on *http://www.payontime.co.uk* website which has up-to-date tools for both dealing with the credit management issues but also working out what late payment compensation and interest is payable on any particular matter. It is a useful site for Debt Recovery Practitioners to have in their "favourites" on their internet browser.

Compensation is permitted under the Act and works out as:

£0 to £999	£40 compensation fee
£1,000 to £9,999.99	£70 compensation fee
£10,000 plus	£100 compensation fee

Although perhaps not a large amount of money in commercial terms, for a business which has a high number of debtors who consistently pay late, this amount of compensation can mount up and indeed no doubt can be used to fund a litigation and credit control function within a business.

What are the "fixed costs" allowed under the Civil Procedure Rules in debt recovery actions?

In essence, fixed costs are those which are allowed by the court under the Rules in respect of each stage of the debt recovery process. **4–10**

Fixed costs have to be distinguished from court fees. Court fees are payable to Her Majesty's Courts Service and are the income which the Court Service generates to finance the running of the courts in England and Wales. Fixed costs are a different issue altogether.

Under CPR Pt 45 the rules provide for the amount to be allowed in respect of the solicitor's charges to which CPR Pt 45.1 applies.

CPR 45.1 therefore applies where:

- the claim is for a specified sum of money and the value of that claim exceeds £25.00; and
- where judgment in default has been obtained under r.12.4(1); or
- or judgment on admission is obtained under r.14.4(3); or
- judgment on admission on part of the claim is obtained under r.14.5(6); or
- where summary judgment is given under CPR Pt 24; or

- the court has made an order to strike out the defence under r.3.4(2)(a) where no reasonable grounds for defending the claim have been disclosed; or
- where a judgment creditor has taken steps under Pt 70 to 73 to enforce the judgment or order.

There are other aspects to r.45.1 but they do not involve a debt recovery action and therefore are outside the scope of this book. In addition to the costs set out in r.45.1 the rule also expressly allows for the appropriate court fee to be allowed at CPR 45.1(3).

4–11 A debt recovery system should keep these costs and fees in the setup files so they can be changed when the Rules change. Up-to-date fees can be checked at *http://www.courtservice.gov.uk/* and sometimes changes on fees can come in very quickly so systems which notify you when fees are about to be increased by being on mailing lists or subscribing to a resource which will notify the subscriber of changes in fees.

It should be remembered that if proceedings are issued in the Claims Production Centre (CPC) or the County Court Bulk Centre (CCBC) then court fees are reduced. The costs for both these forums however are the same. The most recent fee order came into force on May 1, 2008 and is the Civil Proceedings Fees Order 2008.

4–12 As to the amount for fixed costs these are set out in the Reference Tables accompanying CPR Pt 45 and can be summarised as follows:

Table 1—Deals with fixed costs on the commencement of a claim for the recovery of money.

Table 3—Deals with the fixed costs on the entry of judgments in a claim for the recovery of money.

Table 4—Deals with various miscellaneous fixed costs including personal service by a party, which includes the preparation of the certificate of service or for preparing service by an alternative means.

Table 5—Deals with costs in relation to enforcement matters where an award is to be enforced under a court order.

By combining fees and costs a Practitioner can explain to a client the likely cost of a debt recovery matter as a total cost before any amount is recoverable from the debtor. Depending on the agreement for debt recovery services, a client may be required to fund these amounts, or make a payment on account. It will all depend on how the debt recovery business structures its commercial arrangements.

What level of investment needs to be made by a debt recovery client in an action?

The tables below show the way in which fees and costs build up over the course of a debt recovery action. They can be useful to explain to clients how the costs and fee have to be paid as part of the investment in recovering the debt and how those costs can be offset by any monies paid by the debtor/defendant. **4–13**

As mentioned earlier it is important to remember from the client's point of view that fixed costs are just paper figures until the money is actually paid by the debtor.

When we look at the cost of issuing a county court claim this is the sort of matrix that can be built to appreciate the real investment by the creditor in taking legal action:

Table 1

Value of Claim based on amount of outstanding loan and other charges including interest	**Court Fee***	**Fixed Cost***	**Default Judgment Cost***	**Cost of Achieving Judgment**	**Solicitor/Own Client Charges**—Some Solicitors charge additional fees to their client on top of solicitors costs regardless of outcome or on a contingency basis. **Unrecoverable on a Default Judgment**
Up to £300	30.00	50.00	22.00	102.00	Value to be determined
£300.01–£500	45.00	50.00	22.00	117.00	Value to be determined
£500.01–£1,000	65.00	70.00	22.00	157.00	Value to be determined
£1,000.01–£1,500	75.00	80.00	22.00	177.00	Value to be determined
£1,500.01–£3,000	85.00	80.00	22.00	187.00	Value to be determined
£3,000.01–£5,000	108.00	80.00	22.00	210.00	Value to be determined
£5,000.01–£15,000	225.00	100.00	30.00	355.00	Value to be determined
£15,000.01–£50,000	360.00	100.00	30.00	490.00	Value to be determined
£50,000–£100,000	630.00	100.00	30.00	760.00	Value to be determined
£100,00.01–£150,000	810.00	100.00	30.00	940.00	Value to be determined
£150,000.01–£200,000	990.00	100.00	30.00	1120.00	Value to be determined

Value of Claim based on amount of outstanding loan and other charges including interest	**Court Fee***	**Fixed Cost***	**Default Judgment Cost***	**Cost of Achieving Judgment**	**Solicitor/Own Client Charges**—Some Solicitors charge additional fees to their client on top of solicitors costs regardless of outcome or on a contingency basis. **Unrecoverable on a Default Judgment**
£200,000.01–£250,000	1170.00	100.00	30.00	1300.00	Value to be determined
£250,000.01–£300,000	1350.00	100.00	30.00	1480.00	Value to be determined
Over £300,000 or for an unlimited amount	1530.00	100.00	30.00	1660.00	Value to be determined

*** Fees and costs marked with an asterisk are only recoverable if the debtor pays at a point within the debt recovery process after the claim is issued**

To this table we can add additional matrices which show the cost involved in taking a claim beyond judgment and into the enforcement arena.

Table 2

Value of Claim based on amount of outstanding loan and other charges including interest	**Court Fee***	**Fixed Cost***	**Default Judgment Cost***	**Cost of Achieving Judgment**	**Fee of Enforcing Judgment Warrant**	**Total Cost of Enforcing by way of Warrant of Execution**
Up to £300	30.00	50.00	22.00	102.00	35.00	137.00
					55.00	157.00
£300.01–£500	45.00	50.00	22.00	117.00	55.00	172.00
£500.01–£1,000	65.00	70.00	22.00	157.00	55.00	212.00
£1,000.01–£1,500	75.00	80.00	22.00	177.00	55.00	232.00
£1,500.01–£3,000	85.00	80.00	22.00	187.00	55.00	242.00
£3,000.01–£5,000	108.00	80.00	22.00	210.00	55.00	265.00
£5,000.01–£15,000	225.00	100.00	30.00	355.00	55.00	410.00

Value of Claim based on amount of outstanding loan and other charges including interest	Court Fee*	Fixed Cost*	Default Judgment Cost*	Cost of Achieving Judgment	Fee of Enforcing Judgment Warrant	Total Cost of Enforcing by way of Warrant of Execution
£15,000.01–£50,000	360.00	100.00	30.00	490.00	55.00	545.00
£50,000–£100,000	630.00	100.00	30.00	760.00	55.00	815.00
£100,00.01–£150,000	810.00	100.00	30.00	940.00	55.00	995.00
£150,000.01–£200,000	990.00	100.00	30.00	1120.00	55.00	1175.00
£200,000.01–£250,000	1170.00	100.00	30.00	1300.00	55.00	1355.00
£250,000.01–£300,000	1350.00	100.00	30.00	1480.00	55.00	1535.00
Over £300,000 or for an unlimited amount	1530.00	100.00	30.00	1660.00	55.00	1715.00

If the judgment is over £600.00 it can be transferred to the High Court provided it is not a Consumer Credit Act Agreement which in effect means the total cost of starting litigation in the county court and transferring to the High Court increases. However, an allowance for the costs of execution in the sum of £101.75 is recoverable on each successful matter as is interest at 8 per cent per annum from date of transfer of the county court judgment.

Table 3

Value of Claim based on amount of outstanding loan and other charges including interest	Court Fee*	Fixed Cost*	Default Judgment Cost*	Cost of Achieving Judgment	Fees of Transferring to the High Court	Total Cost of Enforcing by way of Writ of FiFa
Up to £300	30.00	50.00	22.00	102.00		N/A
						N/A
£300.01–£500	45.00	50.00	22.00	117.00	50.00*	167.00
£500.01–£1,000	65.00	70.00	22.00	157.00	50.00	207.00

Value of Claim based on amount of outstanding loan and other charges including interest	Court Fee*	Fixed Cost*	Default Judgment Cost*	Cost of Achieving Judgment	Fees of Transferring to the High Court	Total Cost of Enforcing by way of Writ of FiFa
£1,000.01–£1,500	75.00	80.00	22.00	177.00	50.00	227.00
£1,500.01–£3,000	85.00	80.00	22.00	187.00	50.00	237.00
£3,000.01–£5,000	108.00	80.00	22.00	210.00	50.00	260.00
£5,000.01–£15,000	225.00	100.00	30.00	355.00	50.00	405.00
£15,000.01–£50,000	360.00	100.00	30.00	490.00	50.00	540.00
£50,000–£100,000	630.00	100.00	30.00	760.00	50.00	810.00
£100,00.01–£150,000	810.00	100.00	30.00	940.00	50.00	990.00
£150,000.01–£200,000	990.00	100.00	30.00	1120.00	50.00	1170.00
£200,000.01–£250,000	1170.00	100.00	30.00	1300.00	50.00	1350.00
£250,000.01–£300,000	1350.00	100.00	30.00	1480.00	50.00	1530.00
Over £300,000 or for an unlimited amount	1530.00	100.00	30.00	1660.00		

The same approach can be taken to evaluate the cost of an attachment of earnings application.

Table 4

Value of Claim based on amount of outstanding loan and other charges including interest	Court Fee*	Fixed Cost*	Default Judgment Cost*	Cost of Achieving Judgment	Fee of Attachment of Earnings	Process Servers Fees to Serve Order (incl VAT)	Total Cost of Enforcing by way of Attachment of Earnings
Up to £300	30.00	50.00	22.00	102.00	65.00	76.38	243.38

Value of Claim based on amount of outstanding loan and other charges including interest	Court Fee*	Fixed Cost*	Default Judgment Cost*	Cost of Achieving Judgment	Fee of Attachment of Earnings	Process Servers Fees to Serve Order (incl VAT)	Total Cost of Enforcing by way of Attachment of Earnings
£300.01–£500	45.00	50.00	22.00	117.00	65.00	76.38	258.38
£500.01–£1,000	65.00	70.00	22.00	157.00	65.00	76.38	298.38
£1,000.01–£1,500	75.00	80.00	22.00	177.00	65.00	76.38	318.38
£1,500.01–£3,000.	85.00	80.00	22.00	187.00	65.00	76.38	328.38
£3,000.01–£5,000	108.00	80.00	22.00	210.00	65.00	76.38	351.38
£5,000.01–£15,000	225.00	100.00	30.00	355.00	65.00	76.38	496.38
£15,000.01–£50,000	360.00	100.00	30.00	490.00	65.00	76.38	631.38
£50,000–£100,000	630.00	100.00	30.00	760.00	65.00	76.38	901.38
£100,00.01–£150,000	810.00	100.00	30.00	940.00	65.00	76.38	1081.38
£150,000.01–£200,000	990.00	100.00	30.00	1120.00	65.00	76.38	1261.38
£200,000.01–£250,000	1170.00	100.00	30.00	1300.00	65.00	76.38	1441.38
£250,000.01–£300,000	1350.00	100.00	30.00	1480.00	65.00	76.38	1621.38
Over £300,000 or for an unlimited amount	1530.00	100.00	30.00	1660.00	65.00	76.38	1801.38

Alternatively one can look at charging orders as a way to enforce any county court judgment although the table below does not include the cost of enforcing the charging order by an Order for Sale under CPR Pt 73. Again this will be an additional cost.

Table 5

Value of Claim based on amount of outstanding loan and other charges including interest	Court Fee*	Fixed Cost*	Default Judgment Cost*	Cost of Achieving Judgment	Fee on issuing Charging Order	Disbursements payable– HMLR Fee + Office Copy Entries	Total Cost of Enforcing by way of Charging Order
Up to £300	30.00	50.00	22.00	102.00	55.00	43.00	200.00
£300.01–£500	45.00	50.00	22.00	117.00	55.00	43.00	215.00
£500.01–£1,000	65.00	70.00	22.00	157.00	55.00	43.00	255.00
£1,000.01–£1,500	75.00	80.00	22.00	177.00	55.00	43.00	275.00
£1,500.01–£3,000	85.00	80.00	22.00	187.00	55.00	43.00	285.00
£3,000.01–£5,000	108.00	80.00	22.00	210.00	55.00	43.00	308.00
£5,000.01–£15,000	225.00	100.00	30.00	355.00	55.00	43.00	453.00
£15,000.01–£50,000	360.00	100.00	30.00	490.00	55.00	43.00	588.00
£50,000–£100,000	630.00	100.00	30.00	760.00	55.00	43.00	858.00
£100,00.01–£150,000	810.00	100.00	30.00	940.00	55.00	43.00	1038.00
£150,000.01–£200,000	990.00	100.00	30.00	1120.00	55.00	43.00	1218.00
£200,000.01–£250,000	1170.00	100.00	30.00	1300.00	55.00	43.00	1398.00
£250,000.01–£300,000	1350.00	100.00	30.00	1480.00	55.00	43.00	1578.00
Over £300,000 or for an unlimited amount	1530.00	100.00	30.00	1660.00	55.00	43.00	1758.00

So by building matrices in this way clients can understand the cost involved in moving through a debt recovery action.

How does this calculation work in practice?

Finally the way to view the costs of a debt recovery action might be as follows: 4–14

1. Calculate the debt value to be recovered through the court;
2. For commercial debt matters add late payment interest and collection charges on to business-to-business type debt as provided under the legislation;
3. Calculate interest at 8 per cent per annum from the date the debt arose or use late payment interest if appropriate, so that the debt carries interest at the best statutory or contractual rate;
4. Calculate the fee the creditor will have to pay to the court to process the issue of the claim;
5. Add to the claim the fixed costs which can be added with VAT to pay for legal representation referred to as "solicitor's costs";
6. Add further fixed costs plus VAT for any judgment entered on the creditor's behalf;
7. Total up the initial outlay by the creditor to collect the debt being the amount in 4, 5 and 6 of this calculation;
8. Offset against this total amount the amount recoverable from the debtor as provided under CPR 45.1;
9. If enforcement becomes necessary add an additional charge to cover the management fee for enforcement of the judgment;
10. Add to this total cost the cost of any court fee for issuing an enforcement application;
11. Set against this the amount of recoverable costs from the debtor;
12. Assuming the debtor pays all the recoverable costs the bottom-line investment by the creditor to recover the debt should be as little as possible!

How should a supplier be chosen?

Readers of this book may well be looking for answers on how to 4–15 choose a third party to assist in the collection of their debt. A question might be, which is best—DCA or solicitor's firm? In truth both types of third party have their strengths. The distinction between them is blurring and is likely to blur further as the market for legal services is de-regulated as a result of the Legal Services Act 2007.

What is clear is that the relationship between a creditor who wants his/her/its money back from the court system needs to be supported by a pro-active and incisive debt recovery process. Gone are the days when suppliers could issue claims without any thought as to the cost of litigation, or enforcement. Creditors are becoming more sophisticated in their own collection processes and can benchmark external services by measuring the cost of recovery and the actual amount of cash recovered.

Of course solicitors currently hold the trump card in terms of being able to do the litigation part of the process but in time that may change, and DCAs are looking at how they can operate their own litigation departments.

Either way suppliers and clients should be looking at the cash collection results and the cost/benefit of using any particular approach to see what works for them and their particular business.

Finally any service which is offered has to be professional and comply with all the areas of regulation set out in Chapter 2. Creditors should be looking for a provider of a quality service which keeps them on the right side of the law.

Chapter 5

Preparing a Debt Recovery Claim

Introductory Comments

In Chapter 1 of this book credit management as the prelude to debt recovery was explored and in many ways this chapter picks up on the process outlined in Chapter 1 as the debt moves from the collection environment, where the credit management systems handle a customer in default, to this stage of the process where the previous stage has been exhausted and the customer now needs to understand that the creditor is looking to recover the debt via legal action. **5–01**

Some of the ideas put forward in Chapter 1 involving well-written and presented collection letters, structured telephone calls and if necessary field visits, which should be followed through into the legal arena. The need not be duplicated, but whatever is said from this point on needs to compliment what has gone before. A review of the credit management process into which the legal process dovetails sends a signal to a defendant that the creditor knows what it is doing in relation to its recovery process.

Chapter 2 of this book also reviews the regulatory environment in which debt is recovered and again those themes must play a part in how the debt recovery process through the courts is continued in the process of litigation. So creditors need to be aware of the Office of Fair Trading guidelines in relation to debt collection, they need to be aware of the Data Protection Act, to ensure that data is processed fairly and properly in accordance with the eight principles of the Data Protection Act and they need to be aware of issues such as limitation, and to ensure that the formalities of the Consumer Credit Act, where working in the regulated arena, are all dealt with.

In addition to all of what has gone before in Chapters 1 and 2, it is important that the creditor has a profile of the defendant who is to be the subject of litigation through its debt recovery procedures, has reviewed the terms of any contract and has in mind the ultimate strategy for the remedy which will be pursued in the event that the defendant does not respond to the litigation process, i.e. that the creditor has a strategy for enforcement of any resulting judgment should that become necessary.

5–02 Finally, we have reviewed in Chapter 4 the fees and costs connected with debt recovery. The creditor's computer system will no doubt handle these or the creditor will be using, perhaps, the Money Claims Online system to be able to recover the debt through the litigation process. This aspect of debt recovery is in many ways set by the computer itself. Of course the Debt Recovery Practitioner must understand what fees and fixed costs can be charged and must understand which types of interest can also be added to the debt in the recovery process. We will look at that in this chapter.

In the section of this book headed "Casestudy" there is a fully worked example of a debt recovery action together with a full set of completed court forms. The story is a simple one involving non-payment of an invoice with characters that readers of a certain age will recognise. The casestudy has been used to train new recruits into the world of debt recovery and has been found to be a fun and useful way to get to grips with some of the more difficult concepts in debt recovery.

What action should be taken on receipt of a debt recovery instruction?

5–03 Whether a Debt Recovery Practitioner is working in a small debt recovery practice or a larger operation a process should be put in place to handle instructions and to take a "checklist approach" to the recovery path of any particular debt or debts.

Debt recovery is often seen as the poor relation of commercial litigation but, be that as it may, debt recovery through the courts is still litigation and therefore, despite perhaps a lower value in some cases, the Civil Procedure Rules still apply and must be adhered to so it is important that Practitioners prepare themselves and their caseload in a systematic way.

Are there special conduct rules for solicitors?

5–04 Solicitors need to be very aware when conducting any form of litigation that they comply with their professional conduct rules. This is underlined in the case of *Pilbrow v Pearless De Rougemont & Co* [1999] 3 All E.R. 355. In this case the client told the receptionist that he wanted to see a solicitor about a family law matter and thereafter was referred to someone who, unbeknown to him, was not a solicitor. It appears the referral by the receptionist was competently done but even so the Court of Appeal held that the defendant, i.e. the client who had not paid for the service, was not liable to pay for those services as the claimants being the solicitors had failed to perform their contract to provide legal services by a solicitor. Similarly a solicitor may also find himself guilty of negligence if he fails to consider at the outset of a case whether the client is eligible for legal aid (see *David Truex v Kitchin* [2007] EWCA Civ 618).

In more complex litigation matters it is possible that the solicitor will need to interview the client and allow the client to tell his or her story as to the events which have led to a claim being made. In debt recovery this is less likely and unless the client is a "litigant in person" instructions are likely to come by email, spreadsheet, telephone call or some other form of automated process and therefore in these situations the solicitor, or the solicitor's team, may not have the opportunity to discuss with the client individual cases for the recovery of debts. In some ways the fact that the debt arrived in a more automated fashion means that the strategies for the collection of that debt need to be thought through more carefully to ensure that any debt that arrives and is to be recovered through the solicitor's office is done so in a consistent and strategic way.

What initial approach should a Debt Recovery Practitioner take in relation to client's instructions?

Whether the client is sitting in the office or the debt is coming via a spreadsheet with multiple debts to collect there are some basic areas which always need to be understood by a Practitioner. The table below offers a summary of these: **5–05**

Motive	At the outset the Debt Recovery Practitioner needs to appreciate the client's motive for wanting to recover the debt through the courts. In debt collection Practitioners need to understand that more often than not this will mean actually collecting the cash, and not just winning a defended claim or achieving a default judgment, which then becomes unenforceable through lack of strategic thinking. In debt recovery this is perhaps one of the most challenging aspects for Practitioners to ensure that they make it clear to clients or users of their systems, that it is not always going to be possible to recover the cash and what the fallback position will be in the event that full recovery or partial recovery is not possible. Getting the client to understand the frustrations with the enforcement system particularly is something that Practitioners should outline at the outset of either a one-off instruction or in taking a client with multiple debts.

Identifying The Correct Parties	This always needs to be double checked. We have discussed in Chapter 3 the need to "Know your Debtor" but Practioners also need to know your client. Making basic checks about the identity of the client and who was the contracting party is going to be vital again, whether it is a one-off debt to collect or a multiple portfolio and one should not just assume that the client's knowledge of the situation is correct. The Practitioner should make enquiry using both credit referencing systems, the internet and Companies House to ensure that the claim is to be issued in the correct form and in the correct legal person.
Understanding the chronology	Ideally, and where possible, the client should be asked to outline his or her understanding of the chronology that led to the debt being owed. This may come from computerised notes on the client's system or in a more complex recovery case the client is asked to provide a statement perhaps by sitting down in front of the Debt Recovery Practitioner and rehearsing the facts that led to the position where a Letter Before Claim is now necessary. Although in debt recovery actions this time may not be chargeable it may become so if it is part of the outline retainer to the client, and in any event, it is never wasted if subsequently a witness statement is required somewhere down the line particularly if there are issues where a potential defence is anticipated and services.
Identifying issues	The Debt Recovery Practitioner at this stage is going to have to identify the basis of the claim and in debt recovery terms that is usually going to be non-payment of an invoice for the supply of goods and materials.
Using the overriding objective as "a compass"	We have seen through Chapters 2 and 3 that litigating to recover a debt is seen as a last resort. However should a dispute arise or be disclosed then the matter will be reviewed judicially by the judge through his or her case management powers and the overriding objective be applied wherever the court feels it is necessary to do so. The client should be made aware of the court's wide powers at the outset of litigation.
Answering the client's questions	The client wants to know generally speaking how much the debt recovery process is going to cost and for that reference should be made to in Chapter 4. The client is also going to want to know how much he or she is going to get back from the debt recovery process which of course by the time judgment has been obtained will include fixed costs and interest. Again this needs to be explained to the client. Finally the client is going to want to know how long the debt recovery process is going to take and generally speak ing a Debt Recovery Practitioner can do this without too much difficulty in relation to a default action, although

	once a defence comes in that timetable changes. The client needs to understand the various tracks the claim could go down based on its value. It is always best to explain this all to the client or to have standard literature or website pages where the client can view information sheets. Some suppliers of debt recovery services go even further and allow the client to track the progress of their claim online and of course this is the way forward for debt recovery business so the client can see progress for themselves.

What evidence needs to be collated in relation to a debt recovery action?

Often the evidence will be simple in a debt recovery action and will 5–06 involve the paper trail relating to the debt being the outstanding invoice or invoices, any purchase order, delivery notes and communications relating to the supply of goods and services.

From the outset of the litigation process the client must be made aware of the nature of the disclosure obligations and that if he is aware a document exists which undermines his or her or its own case it is important that this is disclosed immediately.

Debt Recovery Practitioners also need to give some thought as to how they will retrieve all the relevant documents and often clients will resist disclosing documentation on the basis it is too difficult. Again the Debt Recovery Practitioner must coax and cajole the client to ensure that the evidence of a debt is in place before litigation begins to avoid some nasty cost consequences arising down the line if evidence is not disclosed or subsequently is undermined by the opponent's documentary records.

At this stage it is also worth considering whether experts need to 5–07 be instructed to provide evidence; or at least located. There may also be witnesses who need to be interviewed in relation to how the service was performed or how goods were supplied. Inspecting and photographing property in more complex cases is also going to be necessary and certainly should not be ignored simply because the claim is seen as simple debt recovery. Again, Practitioners should view each claim as if it were a full blown litigation action where cost consequences could lie against the client.

Even in a multiple debt recovery operation perhaps in a particular industry sector or due to the profile of defendant, the evidence which is required, the requirements on disclosure, witnesses, and the types of response to be received by the debtor should all be anticipated as part of a systematic approach to the recovery of the debt in that operation.

Does a pre-action protocol apply to a debt recovery action?

5–08 Protocols were introduced in the Civil Procedure Rules in 1999 to minimise the delay and expense of litigation. They are required to give each side sufficient and timely details of the case and to put cards on the table in relation to any outstanding issues.

Pre-action protocols at the moment do not apply to debt recovery, but in the absence of a fully drafted protocol the rules require that the parties act in the spirit as if a protocol did exist, so where no approved protocol exists the court will expect the parties to "follow a reasonable procedure", suitable to their particular circumstances, which is intended to avoid litigation.

The procedure should not be regarded as a prelude to inevitable litigation. It should normally include: (a) the claimant writing to give details of the claim; (b) the defendant acknowledging the claim promptly; (c) the defendant giving within a reasonable time a detailed written response; and (d) the parties conducting genuine and reasonable negotiations with a view to settling the claim economically and without court proceedings Pre-Action Protocol's Practice Direction (para.4.2).

The seven key elements to protocol are therefore as follows:

1. Content of the Letter Before Claim;
2. Timetable for acknowledgment and response from the defendant;
3. Content of the defendant's response;
4. Instruction of experts;
5. Disclosure of documents;
6. Negotiations in alternative dispute resolution; and
7. Costs.

What should a standard Letter Before Claim for debt recovery include?

5–09 As debt recovery has no approved pre-action protocol it is important that the Letter Before Claim sets out concisely the legal and factual basis of the claim for the outstanding debt so that the prospective defendant can investigate it without requiring extensive further information.

The claimant should ask for a prompt acknowledgment of the letter usually within seven days of the debt recovery actions (although various industry sectors will have either less or more time given) followed by a full written response within a reasonable period.

The Letter Before Claim should state that in the absence of a full response court proceedings will be issued. The prospective defendant's attention should be drawn to the court's powers to impose sanctions for failure to comply with the Practice Direction and where possible and feasible a copy of the Practice Direction should be enclosed if the prospective defendant is likely to be unrepresented Pre-Action Protocols P.D. (see para.4.3).

What response should a Creditor/Claimant expect from a Debtor/Defendant?

Again, in the absence of an approved protocol the defendant/debtor's letter of response should identify which of the prospective claimant's contentions, i.e. non-payment of the debt, is accepted and which are disputed. Where there is dispute then the prospective defendant is going to have to give reasons. **5–10**

At this stage in the book we will move to calling the debtor the "defendant" as in litigation terms that is the correct term to use and by this stage of the recovery process with no payment in sight the debtor is about to become a defendant to the proceedings.

Do documents need to be disclosed at the pre-action stage?

The Protocols Practice Direction provides that the Letter Before Claim should enclose copies of essential documents relied on and ask the prospective defendant for the disclosure of any key documents that the prospective defendant can supply. In debt recovery this is going to be unlikely and probably unworkable but that is the strict wording of the Practice Direction. The defendant's letter of response should therefore enclose copies of these essential documents which are relied on along with copies of any documents requested by the prospective claimant or an explanation as to why they cannot be disclosed. **5–11**

In the event that the defendant/debtor denies liability for the debt he should send with his response letter any documents in his possession which verify the issues identified in the Letter of Claim.

Are experts required in debt recovery actions?

Often in debt recovery the appointment of experts is going to be a rare occurrence as opposed to say the personal injury area of litigation where experts are going to be necessary in virtually every case. **5–12**

If the client is anxious to know from the outset that he will win his claim because the value of the claim is important or it establishes an important principle then an expert in a particular field may be necessary. Of course the pre-action protocol encourages parties to select joint experts although the report of the expert will still belong to the party that instructs the expert.

The cost of an expert report from an agreed expert appointed jointly will usually be paid for by the instructing party and if the client has relevant insurance cover it may be that the cost of appointing the expert will be covered by the term of the policy.

What reference should be given to negotiations in alternative dispute resolution as part of a debt recovery action?

5–13 The Protocols Practice Direction provides that letters of claim and responses thereto should give details of any form of Alternative Dispute Resolution (ADR) that the parties may be prepared to engage in. Again in a complex debt recovery issue referral to some form of ADR procedure may be more suitable particularly in the area of debt recovery in the construction industry and related trades.

Indeed at para.5 of the Construction and Engineering Disputes Protocol the parties are required to arrange a pre-action meeting as soon as possible after the receipt of the defendant's letter of response so that the parties can identify the main issues, and try to resolve those disagreements as best as possible.

How should the Letter Before Claim in a debt action be worded to meet the requirements of the Protocol?

5–14 At the time of writing this book there is no pre-action Protocol for debt claims although one is always threatened by various policy-makers and so Debt Recovery Practitioners should be aware of the Protocols Practice Direction on the basis that at any time such a protocol may be introduced.

The Protocols Practice Direction specifically deals with the area of where no Protocol exists at para.4 by stating that in cases not covered by any approved protocol the court expects the parties to comply with the requirements of the overriding objective in CPR Pt 1.1 and in particular at para.(2)(a) (b) and (c) so as to act reasonably in exchanging information and documents relevant to the claim and generally in trying to avoid the necessity of starting proceedings.

As a result of this and the outline of a suggested timetable for pre-action behaviour put forward in the Protocols Practice Direction, Practitioners should tailor their Letter Before Claim as follows: **5–15**

- The letter should identify the claimant and the prospective defendant as has been referred to earlier in this book.
- The letter should outline the basis on which the debt arose, referring to the contract and evidenced by say the invoice which should, where possible and feasible, be enclosed with the Letter Before Claim to ensure that the prospective defendant cannot not argue that he has never received a copy.
- The Letter Before Claim should state the principle amount owing.
- An indication should be given as to when the principle amount should have been paid, i.e. the due date of the invoice.
- A statement of the aggregate amount claimed should also be given.
- The date by which the principle sum must be paid in order to avoid a claim must be clearly set out for the prospective defendant to see and adhere to.
- The method for making payment to the claimant should be stipulated in the letter. Often in an automated process this is still not done and yet it is one of the easiest ways to encourage the defendant to pay. So if payment is to be made by cheque, postal order, direct debit or standing order this needs to be set out but also if the claimant is able to take payment by credit or debit card then the details of how to do this should be set out including any website where payment can be made.
- A warning on the costs and interest penalties if the letter is ignored should be clearly set out although the letter must comply with the OFT Guidelines referred to in Chapter 2 to ensure any threat of costs is accurate and appropriate.
- A contact number or email address to enable queries to be resolved prior to litigation being commenced is highly valuable and indeed a requirement of pre-action behaviour anticipated in the Protocols Practice Direction.
- For good measure the Letter Before Claim may go on to say that the prospective defendant might wish to take independent legal advice and in so doing that the Letter Before Claim should be passed to his advisers immediately.

5–16 The Protocols Practice Direction recommends the defendant should reply within a reasonable time which, within debt recovery, is usually seen as seven days in a business to business debt recovery action. However, other sectors will have longer periods and so Practitioners need to gauge what is an acceptable time for response in their area of debt recovery business.

As is good litigation practice the date for the response to the letter should be given as a calendar date, not for example, "seven days from the date of postmark" or "seven days from the date of this letter" which can be misunderstood. Practitioners should leave no room for ambiguity in this area.

The claimant should remember that at some point in the future the Letter Before Claim and its enclosures may well come before a District Judge who will look to ensure that the Protocols Practice Direction has been complied with. A well-worded, clear and properly drawn Letter Before Claim will assist the claimant should that happen and will confirm to the court that the overriding objective set out in CPR Pt 1 has been followed in terms of spirit and practice.

How should a claimant respond to a prospective defendant who replies to the Letter Before Claim?

5–17 If a prospective defendant replies positively with a proposal for payment of the debt, arrangements will need to be made to take payment and this should be made as easy as possible.

If the prospective defendant does outline a dispute then the claimant again needs to take this onboard and investigate those matters before the claim is issued on the basis they may be able to resolve these issues without the need of litigation.

A claimant who attempts to pursue the recovery of a debt, having been made aware of the existence of a dispute, without looking to resolve that dispute, is likely to be viewed by the court at any future point in time of failing to comply with the Rules and also may well find that the OFT Guidance has also not been followed. The court can deal with such non-compliance by way of an unfavourable costs order, and a serious and persistent breach of the OFT Guidance may leave a question mark hanging over the renewal of a creditor's organisation's Consumer Credit Act Licence.

What happens at the end of any period given in a Letter Before Claim for payment to be made?

5–18 In the absence of any payment or response from the prospective defendant, after a proper Letter Before Claim has been sent, setting out all the information mentioned above, the claimant can go on to issue proceedings on the basis it has done everything that is expected of him/her, or it, has so far as the Protocols Practice Direction is concerned.

Does action need to be taken to preserve assets?

In Chapter 3 of this book we have already, under the "Know your Remedy" section, dealt with the possibility of seeking a Freezing Order to prevent the prospective defendant dissipating any assets which are believed to be ultimately enforceable against following any judgment that may become available. **5–19**

It should also be remembered that under the Torts (Interference with Goods) Act 1977 s.4, the High Court may order delivery up of goods which are, or may become, the subject matter of proceedings for wrongful interference with goods. This power may be exercised before proceedings have been commenced.

If it is thought that assets may be dissipated after commencement of proceedings, the party may apply for an order for the detention, custody or preservation of any property which is the subject matter of the action itself or as to which any question may arise. For example in 1977 in the case of *Mobil Oil Kenya Limited v East African Airlines Limited* Parker J. ordered the defendant company not to fly a Boeing 707 from Heathrow.

A shrewd Debt Recovery Practitioner will, particularly in a high value case where the client is particularly anxious, develop 360 degree vision to ensure that from the start of proceedings, throughout the proceedings, and into the enforcement arena, an eye is kept on the available assets and the behaviour of the prospective defendant to ensure that at the end of litigation there is something to enforce against.

If an alarm bell rings as to any action that the defendant might take to try and defeat the claim by removing assets, selling them or disposing of them in someway Practitioners are well advised to take action, or at least advise the client of the availability of action, in writing so that even if it is felt that this is uneconomic to pursue it was raised with the client at the outset or as soon as any concerns become apparent.

What should a debt recovery claim form contain?

CPR 16.2 sets out the requirements for a claim form which are straightforward and can be listed as follows: **5–20**

- The claim form must contain a concise statement of the nature of the claim and the basis on which the debt is said to be owing. Practitioners usually choose a standard set of particulars from a precedent bank although the emergence of the popular

Money Claims Online system (see Chapter 6) has made the art of drafting full particulars of claim rather an outdated skill and in any event most particulars are stored within the database of the leading brands of debt recovery software.

- For purists, reference should be made to one of the leading precedent textbooks, such as, *Atkin's Courts* Forms or Butterworths' *County Court Precedents*. Interestingly, if a statement of case exceeds 25 pages (excluding schedules) an appropriate short summary must also be filed and served, as prescribed by the accompanying Practice Direction to CPR Pt 16. In a debt recovery action this is unlikely, but one never knows if a matter is particularly complex.
- The remedy which the claimant seeks from the court must also be set out in the claim form. Again, in simple terms this means the payment of the outstanding debt together with claims for interest and costs. The court may grant any remedy to which the claimant is entitled even if that remedy is not specified in the claim form itself but again this is unlikely in a debt recovery action.
- A statement of value must be set out in the claim form in accordance with CPR 16.3 and more details about this are set out below.
- A statement of the interest accrued on the debt must be included in the claim form. The claims of various types of interest in a debt recovery action are dealt with later in this book. For the purposes of a statement of value interest is however excluded from that calculation (see CPR 16.3(6)(a)(i)).

5–21 The practice direction at para.13 requires "other matters" to be included which can be summarised as follows:

- The claim form must include an address at which the claimant "resides or carries on business". This paragraph applies even though the claimants' address for service is the business address of his solicitor.
- Where the defendant is an individual the claimant should (if he is able to do so) include in the claim form an address at which the defendant's solicitors have agreed to accept service on the defendant's behalf.
- Any address which is provided for the purpose of complying with the rules should include a postcode unless the court makes an order to the contrary. Postcode information may be obtained from *http://www.royalmail.com* or the Royal Mail

Address Management Guide and is available freely on the internet which means there are no excuses for not complying with this part of the rule!

- The postcode information does become important if the claim form does not show a full address for the parties where the claimant and defendant reside or carry on business. In this circumstance, the claim form can be issued but it will be retained by the court and will not be served until the claimant has supplied the full address including the necessary postcode or the court has dispensed with the requirement to do so. To avoid time being wasted in making an application to dispense with the need for the postcode it is easier to comply with the rule and ensure the postcode is included.
- Paragraph 2.6 of the Practice Direction to CPR Pt 16 goes on to state that the claim form must be headed with the title of the proceedings including the full name of each party. "Full Name" is defined where it is known as follows:

Individual Person	The full unabbreviated name and title by which he or she is known.
Individual carrying on business in a name other than his or her own name	The full unabbreviated name of the individual together with the title by which he is known and the full trading name (for example using the case study in the Appendix Tom Good trading as Good Food and Manure).
A partnership (other than a Limited Liability Partnership (LLP))	Where partners have been sued in the name of the partnership, the full name by which the partnership is known together with the words "(A Firm)" or Where partners are being sued as individuals the full unabbreviated name of each partner and the title by which he or she is known.
Company or Limited Liability Partnership registered in England and Wales	The full registered name including the suffix (Plc, Limited, LLP, etc.) as required.
Any other company or corporation	The full name by which it is known including the suffix where appropriate.

In civil proceedings against the Crown, (the Crown is defined in CPR r.66.1(2)), a claim form must also include:

- the name of the government departments and offices of the Crown concerned; and
- brief details of the circumstances in which it is alleged that the liability of the Crown arose.

Do the particulars of claim have to be served with the claim form?

5–22 The simple answer is "No" as CPR 16.4 anticipates that if particulars of claim are not included or are not served with the claim form, the claimant must state on the claim form that the particulars of claim will follow within prescribed time limits. In fact the claimant has three choices when serving the claim form which include:

- serving the claim form with the particulars of claim contained within the form—where the particulars are usually held in a computer database or are very simple these can be accommodated in the space provided on the claim form;
- serving the claim form accompanied by separately prepared particulars of claim where the particulars are more complicated and will not fit in the space provided so that they have to be set out in a separate document; or
- serving a claim form followed by separate particulars of claim within 14 days after service of the claim form (see CPR 7.4)—in which case the claim form must contain a statement to that effect (see CPR 16.2(2)). This will usually happen where the claimant wants to verify the information with the client or some other source and takes the extra 14-day period to finalise the particulars of claim.

Examples of a claim form prepared on the basis of 1 and 2 above are set out in the case study area of the Appendix at page 446.

In accordance with the accompanying Practice Direction to CPR Pt 16 at para.3.8, particulars of claim served separately from the claim form must also contain:

- the name of the court in which the claim is proceeding;
- the claim number;
- the title of the proceedings; and
- the claimant's address for service.

Does the claim form have to include the claimant's address?

5–23 Paragraph 2.2 of CPR PD 16 requires that even if the address for service is the claimant's solicitor's address, the claim form must nevertheless include the residence or business address of the claimant. In a legal practice this will have been checked and verified at the start of the client relationship as part of the set up of the client's file. In an in-house debt recovery operation, the claim form should be checked to ensure the business address of the claimant is stated accurately and from time to time it does no harm to check basic information held in computer systems to ensure that matters such as postcodes, etc. are still up-to-date.

How is the statement of value calculated as a requirement of CPR Part 16?

As mentioned above, one of the requirements of a statement of case is that a "statement of value" is included in the claim form. Essentially the rule applies in every debt recovery claim if the claimant is making a claim for money. The claimant must therefore state the amount of money which is being claimed and whether he expects to recover: **5–24**

- not more than £5,000;
- more than £5,000 but not more than £15,000;
- more than £15,000; or
- if he cannot confirm the amount, that he cannot say how much he expects to recover

If the value of the debt to be recovered is in excess of £15,000 then the claim for the debt may be issued in the High Court but it must state that the claimant expects to recover more than £15,000. This is because debt claims can only be commenced in the High Court if the statement of value exceeds this threshold figure. To issue in the High Court without a clear belief that this sum will be recovered could lead to the claimant being penalised on costs.

How is the statement of value calculated?

When calculating how much a claimant expects to recover, the amount of costs and interest must be disregarded and cannot be included in the value. Counterclaims and claims for a "set-off" must also be disregarded in calculating the figure for the statement of value. **5–25**

Whenever the statement of value is given in the claim form this will not fetter the court in its decision-making process to give judgment for the amount which it finds the claimant is entitled to and it is possible that this should be explained if the client is unfamiliar with debt recovery proceedings.

How should a claim be put concisely as a requirement of CPR 16?

5–26 Under CPR 16.4 a claimant must state the facts upon which he/she or it relies so the defendant understands the allegations which are made against him/her or it. Whilst the claimant is not limited to stating only the material facts upon which he relies there is the requirement nevertheless to be concise. Indeed any material which is viewed as an abuse of the court's process or is otherwise likely to obstruct the just disposal of the proceedings can be struck out either upon application by the defendant or by the court on its own initiative (CPR r.3.4).

The accompanying Practice Direction also permits a party to:

- refer to any point of law (see para.13.3(1));
- name any witness (see para.13.3(2)); and
- attach a copy of any document considered necessary which may include an expert's report (see para.13.3(3)).

When and how can a claim for interest be included in a debt recovery action?

5–27 CPR 16.4 is the starting point for looking at when and how interest can be claimed in a debt recovery action. It is important that the Practitioner appreciates all the nuances of interest as the rules are complex, perhaps, unnecessarily so. The following paragraphs deal with the areas of the rules in relation to how interest should be claimed and this should be set out in the statement of case.

What are the statutory powers to award interest on debts?

5–28 The powers of courts to award interest on debts is derived from and regulated by s.35A of the Supreme Court Act 1981 in relation to claims commenced in the High Court and s.69 of the county courts Act 1984 in relation to claims commenced in the county court.

The power to award interest is discretionary and this should not be forgotten by Debt Recovery Practitioners. In either court the exercise of that power is subject to the provisions of the CPR. Practitioners should be aware that case law which precedes the CPR insofar as it relates to these two important statutory provisions is fully applicable and effective even if it predates the introduction of the CPR in 1999, which means the discretion lives on and parties who are found to have acted unreasonably may well find their claim to interest is reduced or removed by the court.

How must the claim for statutory interest be set out in the claim form?

CPR 16.4(1)(b) and (2) require a claimant to state that he is claiming interest and, if that claim is made, then the basis of the claim. 5–29

When seeking interest the claimant must state in its claim whether it is claiming interest under the terms of contract or under an enactment and identify the legislation or if on some other basis, then the basis of the claim and the right to claim interest.

In a debt recovery action the claim for payment should also state:

- the percentage rate at which interest is claimed;
- the date from which interest is claimed;
- the date to which interest is calculated, which cannot be later than the date the claim form is issued;
- the total amount of interest claimed to the date of the calculation; and
- the daily rate at which interest continues to accrue after that date.

The interest calculation will need to be verified by a Statement of Truth, which is dealt with later in this chapter. 5–30

An example of how to work out interest without a computer is set out in the Appendix.

When does the claim for statutory interest take effect?

Under s.35A(1) of the Supreme Court Act 1982 and s.69(1) of the County Courts Act 1984 interest can only be awarded on debts from the date of issue of the claim form (see *I M Properties Plc v Cape and Dalgleish (a firm)* [1998] 3 All E.R. 203, 457, CA). However interest may be awarded if the debt is paid after the start of proceedings (see *Edmunds v Lloyd Italico e L'Ancora Cia di Assicurazioni e Riassicurazioni SpA* [1986] 2 All E.R. 249). 5–31

What is the position if a debt is paid after the start of proceedings but before judgment?

Both statutory provisions, being s.35A(3) of the Supreme Court Act 1982 and the County Courts Act 1984 s.69(3), expressly provide that the court does have the power to award interest in respect 5–32 of a debt paid after the proceedings have commenced but before judgment.

What is the position if the debt is paid after judgment?

5–33 In this situation there are again are another set of rules and reference is made to Chapter 10 of this book in relation to the post-judgment position in relation to interest.

Does a delay in issuing proceedings have an effect on the claim for interest?

5–34 Practitioners are reminded that a claim for statutory interest is discretionary and therefore if there is a delay in issuing proceedings and/or on entering judgment, the court has the power to award interest for less than a full period ie between the start of the action and the date of payment, if it is found that there has been an unjustifiable delay by the claimant (see *McDermid v Nash Dredging and Reclamation Co Ltd* [1986] 2 All E.R. 676, CA).

What rate of interest can be claimed under the statutory provisions?

5–35 Under s.35A(1) of the Supreme Court Act 1982 and s.69(1) of the County Courts Act 1984, the court can award interest at such rate as the court thinks fit or as the rules of court may provide. If the interest is claimed without specifying the rate, it may be awarded at whatever rate the court thinks fit.

There are however advantages in specifying the same rate as is payable on judgments, which is currently set at 8 per cent per annum and has been the case since 1993. This is because where the substantive claim is for the recovery of a specified sum and the claim for interest is then limited to the judgment rate, then the rules of the court permit default judgment to be entered for interest on top of the specified sum (see CPR 12.6). If the claim for interest is left open-ended then the claimant must make an application to the court for any higher rate of interest to be awarded (see CPR 12.6(1)).

So by specifying the rate and keeping it in line with the judgment rate the claimant saves himself from further application and can enter judgment that much more quickly.

What happens if the claim for interest involves a "commercial claim"?

Leaving aside for a moment the Late Payment of Commercial Debts (Interest) Act 1998, then both s.35A(1) of the Supreme Court Act 1981 and s.69(1) of the County Courts Act 1984 do provide the court with an option to choose a rate at either 1 per cent, 2 per cent or 3 per cent over base lending rate for interest on a commercial claim. A commercial claim is defined as a claim by a business. The court may also discount that rate by any tax advantage which non-payment has given the creditor (see *Tate & Lyle Food and Distribution Ltd v Greater London Council* [1981] 3 All E.R. 716). **5–36**

In a commercial claim by a small business the claimant's claim for interest may be awarded under s.35A at 3 per cent over base rate because of the relatively higher cost of their borrowing (see *Jaura v Ahmed* [2002] EWCA Civ 210).

Where the creditor has been indemnified by credit insurers who have rights of subrogation against the defendant and can therefore step into the shoes of the creditors to pursue the claim for the debt, the mitigation of loss due to insurance must be left out of the account (see *H Cousins & Co Ltd v D & C Carriers Ltd* [1971] 1 All EH 55, CA and the more recent case of *Shearson Lehman Hutton Inc v Maclaine Watson & Co Ltd* (No. 2) [1990] 3 All E.R. 723).

How is interest calculated under the Late Payment of Commercial Debts (Interest) Act 1998?

This relatively recent Act confers a statutory right to claim interest on the Late Payment of Commercial Debts (which is defined and set out below) and therefore in relation to any debt to which the Act applies the operation of s.35A of the Supreme Court Act 1981 is excluded by subs.(4). For a straightforward guide to the legislation visit the Better Payment Practice Group website at *http://www.payontime.co.uk*. **5–37**

Since the arrival of the Act on to the statute books there have been five commencement orders. To navigate the rules, Practitioners need to be clear about the date of the debt and then see which commencement order was in place to then see if they can make use of the terms of the Act. Of course the more time which elapses between the commencement dates and dates on which Practitioners are collecting debts, then this in time will no longer be a consideration because more than six years will have passed, and most debts will be caught by the Limitation Act provisions (see Chapter 2).

The website for the Better Payment Practice Group has a useful tool where by a series of questions are asked and then depending on the answers the website will confirm if Late Payment interest can be charged and if so at what rate—see *http://www.payontime.co.uk*. The website also provides free resources such as continually updating free guides to the legislation which can be downloaded by Practitioners.

5–38 In 2002 late payment penalties were introduced alongside the interest provisions which are recoverable under a statutory implied term in contracts made on or after August 7, 2002.

As a result the penalty rate is £40 on a debt of up to £1,000, £70 on a debt of up to £10,000 and £100 on a debt of £10,000 or more (see SI 2002/1674) and s.5A of the Act. A precedent for claiming interest under the Late Payment of Commercial Debts (Interest) Act (1998) is provided in Volume 8(3) of Atkins' Court Forms at page 77.

Can both statutory interest and late payment interest be claimed?

5–39 The short answer is "No". A claimant is only able to claim one type of interest in a claim (or a defendant allowed to claim one type of interest in a counterclaim). The claimant must make a choice as to which type of interest is to be pursued.

Of course it may be that the contract itself provides for only one type of interest to be claimed which may be higher than the statutory provisions.

How should the particulars of claim be drafted?

5–40 One of the most difficult areas for Practitioners perhaps working outside of a solicitor's office to grasp in debt recovery is the appropriate wording of the particulars of claim which of course under CPR Pt 16 is the area of the claim form in which the "nature of the claim" is set out.

However, help is at hand through various precedent banks and indeed in most debt recovery software, precedents for the claims will be already preloaded.

In the Appendix to this book the wording for potential claims which could be met in a debt recovery action due set out as follows:

- Claim for goods supplied and delivered;
- Claim for goods supplied and fitted;
- Claim for supply of professional services;
- Claim for for storage charges and work done;
- Claim for retailer loan;
- Claim for personal loan; and
- Claim for a dishonoured cheque.

If the claim involves a debt in a foreign currency the claim must set out:

- that the claim is for payment in a specified foreign currency;
- the payment is to be made in that currency;
- the sterling equivalent of the sum to be claimed at the date of the claim; and
- the source of the exchange rate relied on to calculate the sterling equivalent.

In addition where a claim is based upon an *oral* agreement, the Particulars of Claim must set out the contractual words used and state by whom, to whom, when and where they were spoken (see CPR PD 16 para.7.4). **5–41**

Where a contract is based upon an agreement involving conduct such as a trading relationship where goods are continually being delivered, the Particulars of Claim must specify the conduct relied upon and state by whom, when and where the acts constituting the conduct were done (see CPR PD 16 para.7.5).

Over time Practitioners tend to build their own libraries of precedents and leading texts such as Aktin's Court Forms will supply the more unusual precedents and more websites are appearing where Particulars of Claim are offered as free resources.

What is the importance of the Statement of Truth in a Debt Recovery Action?

The Statement of Truth should be seen by Practitioners as a fundamental step in the debt recovery process. **5–42**

This is dealt with extensively under CPR Pt 22. The statement verifies the contents of the document and confirms that the person signing has an "honest belief" in its contents. The words "honest belief" are not to be taken lightly.

At the time of its introduction the rule was viewed with concern by some Practitioners as to how it could be complied with and what would be the consequences for an advisor signing such a Statement if it was subsequently found that the client did not have an "honest belief" in what had been included in the document.

Over the years Practitioners have developed processes to ensure that the requirements of Pt 22 are complied with and can be shown and demonstrated to the court to have been complied with should the District Judge ask for further information.

It is important that Debt Recovery Practitioners do establish and check and review the process for the signing of the Statement of Truth **5–43** because the consequences of signing something which is found later not to be true are severe and can be avoided if simple checks are put in place at the outset of litigation.

CPR 22.1(1) specifies the documents which must be verified by a Statement of Truth the first one of which is the statement of case (see CPR 22.1(1)(a)).

The aim of the rule is not only that proceedings should be taken more seriously by the parties, but that they also state the facts simply and concisely rather than making an elaborate play on the technicality of pleas as used to be the case in old fashioned litigation before the introduction of the Civil Procedure Rules (see CPR 22.1.2).

The Statement of Truth itself should be worded in such a way that it can be sensibly verified by a client and understood by a *defendant*. In certain circumstances the Statement of Truth can itself be used as evidence of the matters it contains.

Which documents must be verified by a Statement of Truth?

5–44 CPR Pt 22 requires that certain documents must be verified by Statement of Truth and these include the statement of case which is defined in CPR 2.3(1) as a claim form, particulars of claim where these are not included in a claim form, defence, Pt 20 claim, or reply to defence along with further information given to the court by way of further evidence and in witness statements.

The requirement for documents to be verified by Statement of Truth also extends to any amendment of a statement of case which is dealt with in Chapter 9.

An application notice (see CPR Pt 23) if verified by a Statement of Truth may itself stand as evidence in support of that application.

In essence therefore it is essential that all documents which are to be relied on as part of a statement of case in whatever format should contain a Statement of Truth to ensure they comply with CPR Pt 22 in any event. It will do no harm to verify everything in accordance with the rule!

Who can sign a Statement of Truth?

5–45 The accompanying Practice Direction to CPR Pt 22 sets out detailed provisions in relation to who can sign a Statement of Truth be it the claimant or the claimant's legal representative (see CPR PD para.3).

Interestingly in-house lawyers such as counsel, solicitors or legal executives are not "legal representative" as defined in CPR 2.3(1) and strictly speaking a person in that capacity will sign the document as an employee of the party rather than as the legal representative of the party.

Where a party is legally represented, the legal representative will sign the Statement of Truth on behalf of the party. If this is the case, the statement refers to the client's belief in that the client has *an honest belief* in what is put forward. It is not the legal representative's belief (see CPR PD para.3.7).

Where the legal representative signs the Statement of Truth then his or her signature will be taken by the court as a statement that before signing the document he or she has explained to the client that he or she is confirming the client's belief that the facts stated in the document are true (see para.3.8(2)) and before signing, the legal representative has informed the client of the possible consequences to the client if it should subsequently be found that the client did not have an honest belief in the truth of those facts (see para.3.8(3)).

The table below sets out these rules in a simple format: 5–46

Partnerships	The Statement of Truth should be signed by a partner or person having control or management of the partnership business.
Companies or Corporations	The Statement of Truth should be signed by a Director, Treasurer, Secretary, Chief Executive, Manager or other Officer, Mayor, Chairman or Town Clerk. A "Manager" is defined as a person holding a senior position who has personal knowledge of the facts or is responsible for those who do have personal knowledge of the facts.
In-house legal representative	As stated above an in-house legal representative may sign a Statement of Truth but if they are not a solicitor, barrister or other authorised litigator they may not sign unless they are a Manager and a person therefore holding a senior position.

What safeguards can be adopted for signing a Statement of Truth in a debt recovery department?

As mentioned above, it is important that Debt Recovery Practitioners 5–47
have a clear process for the signing and recording of how a Statement

of Truth is completed on any claim or number of claims which are issued in the court.

For Practitioners dealing with day-to-day debt recovery in a busy department this will be a structured process. There needs to be a system in place whereby if there are multiple debts to be issued as part of the claim process, and the Practitioner is signing the Statement of Truth as a legal representative, then the client checks at the last possible moment that the balances are correct along with the persons to be sued. Undoubtedly, this means a check has to be made in the client's account system as to the outstanding balance as close as possible to the claim being issued ideally same day and after the day's posting of money recovered has been completed.

For Practitioners who have just a one-off case of debt recovery then the procedure may be slightly less pressurised in terms of timing but again as close as possible to the issue of the claim the client should be asked to sign a form confirming that they have the honest belief in the statement put forward in terms of the defendant's details and also the balance outstanding on the account.

All approvals and instructions from the clients in this regard should of course be noted on the file in the debt recovery system or filing system should these be required by the court at a later time.

5–48 Clients need to be reminded that the signing of a Statement of Truth is not a casual procedure. In debt recovery it is vital that the most up-to-date balance is recorded and this requires the accounting systems of the client to ensure that all credits and payments have been posted to the account so that the balance which is relied upon is the most up-to-date. In a busy department it is possible that if this procedure is not in place payments will be missed and therefore a claim form could inaccurately state the balance outstanding at the date the claim is issued. This inaccuracy should be avoided at all costs.

It is also important for recording purposes that the Debt Recovery Practitioner can show that the consequences of signing a Statement of Truth with inaccurate information has been pointed out to the client and what that means in terms of being found in contempt of court.

What is the penalty for making a false statement?

5–49 CPR 32.14(1) provides that proceedings for contempt can be issued against a person who makes or causes to be made a false statement in any document which is verified by a Statement of Truth without an honest belief in the truth of that document.

Needless to say, if a legal representative is in any doubt as to the client's honest belief in the facts put forward in a Statement of Truth then the client should be invited to sign the Statement of Truth not the legal representative.Where a party alleges that a Statement of Truth is false, the party must refer that allegation to the court dealing with the claim in which the Statement of Truth has been made.

5–50 The court may then exercise any of its powers under the rules or initiate steps to consider if there has been a contempt of court and where it is found that there is contempt to then punish accordingly. The Practice Direction to RSC Order 52 (Sch.1) and CCR Order 29 (Sch.2) makes provisions where committal to prison is a possibility if contempt is subsequently proved. Alternatively it may direct that the party making the allegation, if there is false statement, refers the matter to the Attorney General for a request for him to consider whether he wishes to bring proceedings for contempt of court. The Practice Direction at para.28.2 goes on to explain how the application to the Attorney General should be made.

Clearly to avoid such severity of Penalty Debt Recovery Practitioners must ensure that their processes and procedures avoid any suggestion that the statement is found to be anything less than an honest belief. If there is doubt as to this or the client's accuracy of information then the client should be invited to sign as ultimately it will be the client who takes the risk.

How is a Statement of Truth to be worded?

5–51 The form of Statement of Truth is actually set out in the Practice Direction to CPR Pt 22 at para.2.

In verifying a statement of case at para.2.1 the Statement of Truth will read:

> "[I believe] [the (claimant or as the case may be) believes] that the facts stated in this (name document being verified) are true."

Where the form of Statement of Truth is a witness statement as opposed to a statement of case then the form is "I believe that the facts stated in this witness statement are true" (see para.2.2 of the CPR PD 22).

5–52 If the Statement of Truth is contained in a separate document, the document containing the Statement of Truth must be headed with a title of the proceedings and the claim number (see CPR PD 22 para.2.3). The document being verified should be identified in a Statement of Truth as follows:

> Claim form: "The claim form issued on [date]",
> Particulars of claim: "The particulars of claim issued on [date]",
> Statement of case: "The [defence, or as the case may be] served on the [name of party] on [date]",

CPR PD 22 para.1 details the documents to be verified by Statement of Truth which includes the statement of case.

5–53 In relation to CPR PD 22 para.3 as to who may sign a Statement of Truth, the following points need to be noted:

- If the client is a managing agent who manages property or investments for a party, they cannot sign a Statement of Truth. It can only be signed by the party or by the legal representative of the party concerned.
- Where the proceedings involve a trust and some or all of the trustees comprise a single party then one or some or all of the trustees comprising that party may sign the Statement of Truth as well as the legal representative of the trustees concerned.
- In relation to insurers and the Motor Insurers Bureau if an insurer has a financial interest in the claim involving its insured then if the insured is the party the insurer may sign a Statement of Truth in a statement of case for the insured party. The Claims Manager employed by the insurer responsible for handling the insurance claim or managing the staff handling the claim may sign the Statement of Truth for the insurer. The position of the Motor Insurers Bureau is similar.
- Where the Statement of Truth is to be signed on behalf of a company then paras 3.4 and 3.5 of the Practice Direction apply in as much that the Statement of Truth must be signed by a person holding a senior position in the company or corporation be it a Director, Treasurer, Secretary, Chief Executive, Manager or other Officer. The word Manager will be construed in the context of the phrase "a person therefore holding a senior position". The court can consider the size of the company and the size of the nature of the claim. The court would expect the Manager signing the Statement of Truth to have personal knowledge of the content of the document or to be responsible for double managing those who have knowledge of the content of the document.
- Where the company is considered to be a small company it may not have a Manager apart from Directors who actually hold a senior position. A large company conversely will have many such managers.
- In relation to in-house legal representatives, this has already been discussed above and is defined in CPR r.2.3(1) although the definition is strict it may of course be that the person who needs to sign can be construed as a Manager and therefore able to sign a statement on behalf of the company in that capacity instead.

What happens if the party cannot read or sign the document to be verified by the Statement of Truth?

The Rules do provide for this occurrence and in a debt recovery scenario where the claimant is found to be unable to read or sign a document, then, under CPR PD 22 para.3A, a certificate can be made by an authorised person and that person must be the one who is able to administer oaths and take affidavits. The authorised person must certify that the document to be signed has been read to the person signing it and that that person has appeared to understand the document and approved its content as accurate and that the declaration of truth has also been read to that person who in turn appears to understand the declaration and the consequences of making a false declaration. As a result of all that the person has signed or made his mark in the presence of the authorised person. The formal certificate as provided under this section of the Rules is set at Annex 1 to the Practice Direction to CPR PD 22. **5–54**

What happens if the statement of case is not verified by a Statement of Truth?

Under CPR PD 22 para.4 if the case is not verified by a Statement of Truth then the statement of case will remain effective unless it is struck out but a party cannot rely on the contents of the statement of case as evidence until it has been verified by the necessary Statement of Truth. **5–55**

Any party may apply to the court for an order but unless, within the period as specified by the court, the statement of case is verified by the service of the Statement of Truth then the statement of case will be struck out.

The usual order for costs on such an application and as referred to in para.4.2 of CPR PD 22 will be that the costs be paid by the party who has failed to verify the statement of case in any event and immediately.

Can a claim be issued on a future debt?

Under CPR Pt 7 the course of action must have accrued *before* the issue of proceedings. This is illustrated by a claim in respect of instalments due under a contract. The claim or the instalments must have fallen due before the date of issue as was discussed in the case of *Eshelby v Federated European Bank Ltd* [1932] 1 K.B. 254. **5–56**

Who may issue the claim form?

5–57 The claim form is a formal document and as such may not be issued by any person other than the claimant or by a person who has a right to conduct litigation in accordance with s.28 of the Courts and Legal Services Act 1990. To act without the right to conduct litigation is a criminal offence and a contempt of court (see *Paragon Finance v Noueri* [2001] EWCA Civ 1402).

Can a claim form be issued against a defendant who is bankrupt or in liquidation?

5–58 A claim may not be issued or proceeded with against a company in administration or in liquidation or against an undischarged bankrupt without the permission of the court (see ss.11 (3), 130(2) and 285(3) of the Insolvency Act 1986).

An application for permission should be made to the Company's Court or the court where the insolvency proceedings are pending.

Permission to sue cannot be granted retrospectively (see *Re Taylor* [2006] EWHC 3029).

For Debt Recovery Practitioners this means that a process should be in place in the department to ensure that as part of the pre-claim issue process a check is made to ensure that the proposed defendant is not insolvent. For companies this can be done through the Companies House web check service. For individuals or sole traders and partners this can be done through the Insolvency Service website using the Individual Insolvency Register Search which is a useful tool for Debt Recovery Practitioners. Simply by entering the defendant's name or trading style it can quickly be established whether there is any form of insolvency against a would be defendant who is not a limited company.

Does a Company have to act by a Solicitor?

5–59 Under CPR 48.6 (6) a "litigant in person" is defined under para.(a) as a company or other corporation which is acting without a legal representative". As a result, a company does not need to act by a solicitor when issuing its claim (see also *R. H. Tomlinson (Trowbridge) Ltd v Secretary of State for the Environment* [1999] 4 E.R. (D) 870).

In that case it was in fact a transitional case between the old rules in which a company would have had to be represented by a solicitor and the new CPR. It was accepted in the decision that the new CPR would have allowed the company to act without a solicitor but the timing of the case meant that the old rules applied.

In fact the CPR goes even further and just for completeness, and particularly when advising company directors at the outset, it is also possible by virtue of CPR 39.6 and the accompaying Practice Direction CPR PD 39A para.5 or a company or other corporation to be represented at any trials provided an employee has been authorised by the company or corporation to appear at the trial on its behalf and the court also gives the necessary permission. More details on this appear in Chapter 8.

How does the issue of claim in relation to a Consumer Credit Act agreement differ to the standard rules for issue of a claim?

Actions under the Consumer Credit Act are dealt with under CPR **5–60**
7.9 and the accompanying Practice Direction. For certain types of Consumer Credit Act claims the court has to give a fixed date for hearing as soon as the claim is issued. A separate Practice Direction being PD 7B supplements the rule at 7.9 by specifying the location of the particular county court where actions must be started and stating that the court will fix the hearing date when the claim form is issued along with prescribing the format of the particulars of claim.

In relation to debt recovery procedures therefore the special practice direction in relation to Consumer Credit Act procedures is to do expressly with the following sections:

Section 141	Claim by the creditor to enforce regulated agreement relating to goods, etc.
Section 129	Claim by debtor or hirer for a time order.
Section 90	Creditor's claim for an order for recovery of protected goods.
Section 92	Creditor's or owner's claim to enter premises to take possession of goods.
Section 140B(2)(a)	Debtor's or Surety's application for an order relating to an unfair relationship.
Section 139(1)(a)	Debtor's claim for a credit agreement to be reopened as extortionate.
Various sections	In relation to creditor's or owner's claim for court order to enforce a regulated agreement relating to goods or money where the court is required to take particular action as set out in the practice direction.

However, the Practice Direction does not apply to a claim made by a creditor under s.141 of the Act to enforce the regulated agreement where the agreement relates only to money. The Practice Direction expressly states that such a claim must be started by the issue of a Pt 7 claim form (see CPR PD 7 3.3).

For more detailed information on structuring claims under the Act reference should be made to Atkin's Court Forms Volume II(1) Consumer Credit.

Is it necessary to litigate outside England and Wales?

5–61 Before starting to even think about litigating outside of the home jurisdiction of England and Wales Debt Recovery Practitioners should consider the possibility of collecting debt by telephone and personal visit. There are an increasing number of organisations who can help with this. The Credit Services Association which can be found at *http://www.csa.uk.org* has members across the world and many of these who act on a "no-collection, no-fee" basis. A Debt Recovery Practitioner would do well to consider whether collection by one of these methods might be more appropriate before launching into litigation. There are also firms of debt recovery solicitors in England and Wales who are themselves building a niche practice in the collection of firm debt both by telephone and by creating their own network of agents outside of the home jurisdiction. Again a conversation with one of these firms which can easily be found using the internet may be preferable to launching into litigation overseas.

However, if the value of the debt is large and the client is anxious to secure the position litigation may be the only way forward and in that case knowledge of the rules and understanding of the rules for service outside of the home jurisdiction is going to be necessary.

Through this book we will look at issues in debt recovery that have a foreign element and as we do so we will split the geography between countries within the European Union (EU) and those outside it. The table below provides a resource for Practitioners to use on how to go about recovering debt where the defendant is based in or outside of the EU.

5–62

EU Countries	• All EU countries are governed by a jurisdictional code created by Council Regulation 44/2001 (The Regulation). EU countries include: Austria, Belgium, Bulgaria, Cyprus, Czech Republic, Denmark, Estonia, Finland, France, Germany, Greece, Hungary, Ireland, Italy, Latvia, Lithuania, Luxembourg, Malta, Netherlands, Poland, Portugal, Romania, Slovakia, Slovenia, Spain, Sweden, United Kingdom.

	• In addition as a result of a similar jurisdictional code called "The Lugano Convention" Norway, Switzerland and Iceland are incorporated into English law by virtue of the Civil Jurisdiction and Judgments Act 1982 (CJJA1982) • Between the various parts of the UK s.16 of CJJA1982 also governs the jurisdiction between Scotland, Northern Ireland and England and Wales. • The Defendant must be sued in his local jurisdiction. • For an individual this means his or her place of domicile. • For a company it means its statutory seat/central place of administration/principal office of business. • The Regulation allows courts of member states to have jurisdiction, where the contract was performed. For the sale of goods this means where the goods were delivered or should have been delivered and for supply of services it means the State where the services were provided or should have been provided. • If the contract contains a "jurisdiction clause" stating that the dispute must be resolved in a particular State then unless both parties agree to waive the clause proceedings must take place in the stipulated country regardless of the defendant's domicile or where the contract was to be performed. • If the defendant takes any step in the proceedings such as filing a defence he will be taken to have submitted to the jurisdiction of the English courts.
Countries Outside the EU	• Remember if the defendant can be served in England and Wales while being present in this country—even if just changing planes at Heathrow—then this will be considered good service and proceedings can continue in this jurisdiction. • The defendant could object if it is considered the English and Welsh courts are not the most convenient. • If a basis to serve in England and Wales cannot be found permission will be needed to serve outside the jurisdiction—see Chapter 6.

As the subject of international litigation is a specialist area further reference should be made to standard textbooks on private international law such as Dicey and Morris.

Chapter 6

Issuing a Debt Recovery Claim

Introductory Comments

In this chapter the focus will be how to issue the claim form and from there how to make sure that the claim form is properly served. The service of court documents is extremely technical and whilst in debt recovery this may seem, once again, a straightforward procedure, the fact is that Debt Recovery Practitioners are having to be more adventurous in how they litigate beyond England and Wales and therefore have to have an understanding of the rules for service outside of their home jurisdiction. **6–01**

In which court should the completed claim form be issued?

On the Courts Service website there is a useful tool called "HMCSCourtfinder". This website includes the court's address and facilities, opening hours, contact details and information on how to get to the court—all of which can be very useful to have to hand if the Practitioner needs to be in contact with the court. **6–02**

In the "courtfinder" tool there are a number of searches that can be made to establish which courts have jurisdiction. In the case of doubt the Practitioner should contact the court using the telephone number provided to confirm jurisdiction before proceedings are issued.

In which forum can a debt recovery claim be issued?

The simple rule here is that the county court has unlimited jurisdiction in most contract cases (see County Courts Act 1984 s.15(1)). The only exception to this, as far as a Debt Recovery Practitioner is **6–03** concerned, is that the jurisdiction of the county court does not stretch to handle an Order for Sale application under CPR Pt 73 over the sum of £30,000 (see county courts Act 1984 s.23 and the County Courts Jurisdiction Order 1981). This means that any such application will have to be transferred to the High Court where the value of the sum to be recovered is over £30,000.

The jurisdiction of the High Court itself was changed in 1999. Up until that time it had been possible to issue a debt claim in the High Court for over £600, but on the introduction of the Civil Procedure Rules on April 26, 1999 the new threshold was set at £15,000. The downside of this change for practitioners has been losing the swift action taken by Master's in debt claims and again for those Practitioners with claims over a certain value, and a certain level of complexity.

Which court should be used?

6–04 However, only in exceptional cases will a debt recovery claim be started in the High Court and in any event the threshold for issuing a claim in the High Court is £15,000 which puts most practitioners off from using this forum. Usually claims are started in the county court.

Which court office should be chosen by the claimant?

6–05 There is generally no restriction on which court is chosen for the claimant to start proceedings.

Most claimants will want to issue out of the court office which is known to them or is convenient to their office.

However, there are some types of claim where the freedom to issue is restricted. Consumer credit claims for example must be issued in accordance with the necessary Rule and Practice Direction although money claims under consumer credit legislation can be issued under CPR Pt 7 and no special Practice Direction applies.

6–06 It is also worth considering that claims for the recovery of money may at some point be transferred to the "defendant's home court". Instances where this can happen include:

- where the defendant applies to set aside or vary a default judgment pursuant to CPR 13.4; or
- where the judge is required to determine the time and rate of payment of a judgment obtained after a CPR Pt 14 admission has been filed; or
- a defence is filed.

The "defendant's home court" is the county court or High Court (if a claim is proceeding in that forum) for the district in which the defendant resides or carries on business.

Where there are two defendants who have different home courts then the rules provide that if the defendant who filed the defence first is an individual then the proceedings will be transferred to his home court. It should be noted that automatic transfer can only occur once in each set of proceedings.

Can the parties agree to start proceedings in a particular court?

This question was answered in the case of *Snookes v Jani-King* (GB) Ltd [2006] EWHC 289, where the parties had agreed the term of the contract that "... any proceedings arising out of, or in connection with this agreement shall, be brought in a court of competent jurisdiction in London". 6–07

The claimant subsequently issued proceedings in the Swansea District Registry of the High Court and it was held that the term of the agreement was binding on the parties and as such the court set aside the claim form as clearly Swansea was not same as a court of competent jurisdiction in London.

At what point are proceedings commenced?

Legal proceedings for the recovery of a debt are actually started when the court issues the claim form which is dated (see CPR Pt 7.2). If the claim form is received by the court office on an earlier date the claim is actually "brought" for the purpose of the Limitation Act 1980 at that point in time. 6–08

The court should record when the claim form is received by date-stamping it on any part of the claim form itself or on any letter that accompanies the claim form.

Where claims for the recovery of debt are on the very edge of the limitation period it is always sensible to ensure that the paperwork is taken to the court personally and issued over the counter with the necessary receipt being given just in case the court cannot immediately process the documentation and the limitation period expires.

Which forums are available to issue a debt claim?

There are in fact a number of choices available to a Debt Recovery Practitioner in issuing a claim for the recovery of debt under Pt 7 6–09 of the CPR which coincides with the need by Her Majesty's Courts Service to handle the debt recovery process within the courts as efficiently as possible and to free up judicial time for more complex cases.

In effect there are five choices listed in the table below:

1. The claimant can issue in the local county court	Practitioners get to know their local court, the staff, the District Judges and they feel comfortable doing business in their local court forum. This choice is dealt with above and complies with the Rules on where to start proceedings contained within Practice Direction 7.2 of CPR. The benefit of starting the claim in the claimant's local county court is going to be the knowledge of the local staff and systems and indeed of the judiciary and the ability to attend the court for hearings and to resolve matters generally.
2. The claimant can issue proceedings in the Debtor's local county court	As mentioned above there are rules on automatic transfer of proceedings in the event that a defence is filed or the debtor makes an application to vary or set aside a judgment and it may be the claimant wishes to save time by anticipating that event and issuing in the "Defendant's home court". Again this is subject to the rules regarding where to start proceedings as set out in Practice Direction 7.2.
3. The claimant may issue in the Claims Production Centre (CPC)	The Claims Production Centre is co-located in Northampton with the County Court Bulk Centre (see option 4 below). This unit together with CCBC has been set up by Her Majesty's Courts Service specifically to deal with straightforward debt recovery business which in the main will be undefended. Certain claimants such as utility companies, banks, finance houses and mail order firms have a need to issue hundreds if not thousands of claims in any one batch. The Production Centre came into existence in 1989 specifically to handle this bulk business. The claimants or their legal representatives prepare the documents for issue in the usual way but these are submitted electronically to the CPC. A single Statement of Truth accompanies each batch of claim forms so Practitioners are encouraged to be aware of the points made in Chapter 5 on the requirements of CPR Pt 22 and the Statement of Truth. The CPC will issue each claim form on behalf of the named county court and notify the county court when it has been issued. The value of any one claim cannot exceed £100,000 and the CPC cannot be used to issue High Court claims or claims against more than one defendant. Permission must be obtained to use the CPC which can easily be done by applying in writing to the Court Manager. Each user

	must agree to comply with the Code of Practice that forms part of the accompanying practice direction for this area of court business.
4. The claimant can issue in the County Court Bulk Centre (CCBC)	Court users have the opportunity to use the CCBC which provides for further streamlining of bulk debt claims. Claims are issued through the CCBC in the name of Northampton County Court and where a valid defence is filed the CCBC will serve a copy on the claimant who has 28 days to consider their response. An allocation questionnaire is only sent to a claimant in a CCBC case where the claimant confirms he wishes to proceed towards a defended action. In this situation where the defendant is an individual, the claim will be transferred to the defendant's local County Court under the automatic transfer provisions. If the defendant is a business the claim will either be transferred to the claimant's solicitor's local court or where the claimant is not represented to the claimant's local court. Both the CPC and CCBC have their own Practice Direction being PD 7C of the CPR. More information can be found about the County Court Bulk Centre and the Claims Production Centre at Her Majesty's Courts Service website.
5. The claimant can use Money Claims Online (MCOL)	Perhaps one of the most innovative measures to come out of changes to debt recovery procedure in recent years has been the Money Claims Online system (MCOL). It is now possible for individuals, businesses and government departments to issue their claims for fixed amounts of less than £100,000 using the online MCOL system. The approach has its own rule under CPR 7.12 and Practice Direction 7E. The website can be found at *http://www.hmcourts-service.gov.uk/onlineservices/mcol/index.htm* A claim cannot be against more than two defendants using the MCOL system. Each defendant must have an address for service in England and Wales. MCOL can only be used for debt recovery claims. The claimant will need to have a valid credit or debit card in order to pay the court fees. All MCOL claims are issued in the name of Northampton County Court to take advantage of the court's existing technology. The MCOL procedure differs from the usual Pt 7 procedure in that the particulars of claim cannot exceed 1,080 characters including spaces and punctuation. The MCOL screen does have a character counter to help claimants ensure they stay within the allotted space. However, improvements to MCOL are planned throughout 2009. So far as the Statement of Truth provisions are concerned these are provided for in the Practice Direction

	Once all the information required by the system is completed through a series of easy to read pages and the online the court fee is paid the system will display the claim number. MCOL then submits the claim to Northampton County Court who will issue the claim and arrange to serve the claim form and response pack on the defendant.

What is the process for issuing paperwork at the local county court?

6–10 If the decision is made to issue the claim at the local county court or the defendant's home court then the claimant will need to send the claim form and particulars of claim to the court in triplicate to the court for issue.

The court will then issue the claim and allocate it a claim number. Court staff will seal all three copies of the claim form and return one copy to the claimant for his or her file, retain one copy for the court file or system and serve the third copy on the defendant. If the claimant believes the defendant is going to try and avoid receiving the claim form and that service therefore may be evaded, the claimant can request the claim form is returned to the claimant so that the claimant can make arrangements for personal service.

If, as is usual in a debt recovery claim, the court arranges for service of the documentation then it will simply send the papers to the defendant using first class post. If the claimant believes the defendant will return the papers to the court indicating that the defendant has "gone away" then again it is advisable for the claimant to request the papers are returned to the claimant to make arrangements for "personal service" which is explained below. The claimant may be able to claim slightly increased fixed costs on the claim form if arranging personal service although these will not completely cover the expense of instructing a process server. However, it will save the potential cost of a successful claim by the defendant later on in the proceedings who may try to set aside any judgment on the grounds he did not receive the claim form. Personal service avoids that application getting off the ground.

When does the claimant have to serve the claim form?

6–11 Ideally the court is going to serve the claim form. This will be done using ordinary first class post. The court will give notice to the claimant on prescribed form N205A that service has been effected and this form will also include the date of deemed service. This date then needs to be added to the claimant's debt recovery system to calculate the date when judgment can be entered. If after posting the claim form to the address given it is returned to the court, the claimant will receive a notice to that effect from the court (see CPR 6.17).

If the claimant wants to take control of having the claim form served the claimant should attend at the court in which he wishes to issue the claim and have it issued and then take it away along with the necessary response pack for the defendant.

Alternatively a Practitioner can send the claim form into the court and ask for it to be issued and then returned to him for service. However, the covering letter accompanying such a request must make it clear what the court is being asked to do.

What address must be used for service?

Under CPR 6.6 the party's address for service is going to be the one in which all documents are served either by post, DX, fax, email or other electronic means. The court will usually serve the claim form by the "post" method of service but Practitioners need to be aware of the other types of service and when these may need to be utilised. **6–12**

The address must be within the jurisdiction although the rules provide for service out of the jurisdiction is dealt with later in this chapter.

The claimant gives an address for service on the claim form and where the claimant is represented by a solicitor then the solicitor's business address will be given as the claimant's address for service (see CPR 6.7).

A party who resides or carries on business within the jurisdiction who is not represented by a solicitor must give his residence or place of business as the address for service.

Where a defendant has no solicitor acting for him and has not given any address for service, then service can be achieved by posting the documents, or serving the defendant personally to one of the five places specified by CPR r.6.9(2) which are as follows: **6–13**

1. to an individual person by serving the same at the person's usual or last known residence;
2. to a proprietor of business who can be served at his usual or last known residence or at his place of business or last known place of business;
3. to an individual who is being sued as a firm documents can be served at the usual or last known residence or at the principal or last known place of business of the firm; limited liability partnerships are served by using the principal office of the partnership or any place of business within the jurisdiction which has a red connection with the claim;

4. to a corporation incorporated in England and Wales documents can be served at the company's principal office or at any place within the jurisdiction where the corporation carries on its activities and which has a real connection to the claim; and

5. to a company registered in England and Wales it can be served at the company's principal office or any place of business within the jurisdiction which has a real connection with the claim.

The rule helpfully sets out a comprehensive table at para. CPR 6.9(2).

What happens if service occurs where the party no longer resides or carries on business?

6–14 This is often an important area for Debt Recovery Practitioners because debtors, be they individuals, sole traders, partners, or companies will often have "gone away". Shrewd Practitioners will also know that it is easy for documents served on defendants to be put back into the Royal Mail system with an indication given by the person at the address that the addressee is "no longer at the address", "gone away", "not known", etc. There is nothing to indicate on the envelope that the reason for the return of mail has not be given by the debtor in person and this has to be factored in to the decision on how to ensure service is achieved. Often the debtor's address will have been verified by a credit search, or a tracing agent's report but care must be taken to appreciate how that data has been gathered. Pre-sue visits are one of the surest ways of assessing whether a party is at the address before proceedings are issued, with enquiries being made with the occupant at the alleged address, neighbours or local businesses or the postman. Of course all such enquiries have to be carried out in accordance with the principles of the Data Protection Act (see Chapter 2).

Be that as it may it is important to note that service will be achieved if documents are posted to one of the places specified above and will be viewed as valid service even if the defendant no longer resides at that address, carries on business from that address, or even if it is the solicitor's address and the solicitor no longer carries on business at that address or has been disinstructed. Reference is made to (CPR 6.9(1).

The definition of a person's "usual ... residence" as stated above has been looked at by the courts. In the case of *Lexi Holdings Plc v Shaid Luqman and Others* [2007] EWHC 1508 (Ch) it was held that service could not be effected at the home address of one of the parties when the party to be served was in prison and the party serving the document knew that fact. Again Practitioners should check on taking instructions where the address for service for the defendant has come from.

What constitutes a person's "last known residence"?

This is a very important point for Practitioners because one of the big hurdles in successfully suing any defendant, particularly where it has not been able to establish the most recent address, is to be able to serve at the "last known residence". 6–15

There are three approaches to this problem:

- a narrow approach which considers only the knowledge of the party serving the document or his agents;
- a wider view which considers the knowledge available to the general public whether or not it was known to the party serving the document or his agents; or
- a middle view which considers the actual knowledge of the party serving or his agents but which also imputes into their knowledge steps which they could have taken to check the address.

In the case of *Mersey Docks Property Holdings Ltd and Others v Kilgour* [2004] EWHC 1638 (rcc) the phrase "last known place of business" as set out in CPR 6.5(6) was held to mean *the last place of business known to the claimant*. In this case the defendant was a professional architect and searches could have been made through the RIBA or through Yellow Pages as to where his practice was located. The failure by the claimant to search the RIBA Directory to produce an address for the defendant should have prompted the claimants to make further enquiries. As a result it was found that the defendant had not been validly served with a claim form.Under the new CPR Pt 6 a claimant must take reasonable steps to ascertain the address of the defendant's current residence or place of business (see CPR 6.9(3)).

What are the standard methods of service in a debt recovery action?

In civil litigation there are essentially five standard forms of service 6–16
which are listed below. Throughout a debt recovery action issues

about service will crop up although practitioners do rely on the court system to achieve service. However, from time to time a practitioner is going to have to arrange service by another method and so the table below sets out a summary of the methods allowed by the Rules and the requirements of each one:

The five methods of service within the Rules are:

1. Personal service in accordance with CPR 6.5.
2. A method of postal service including first class post, document exchange (DX) or since the monopoly of the Royal Mail has been dismantled any other postal system which provides for next date delivery (see CPR 6.3 (1)(b).
3. Leaving the claim form at a place set out in CPR 6.7, 6.8 or 6.9 — which are now under the updated Rules a far more comprehensive code of where to serve.
4. Using a fax or other means of electronic communication in accordance with Practice Direction A to the updated CPR Pt 6.
5. Any other method of service authorised by the court under 6.15.

6–17

Method of Service	Points to Note
What does personal service mean?	Personal service mentioned in 3. above is dealt with under r.6.5 of the CPR and a document is said to be served personally on an individual by "leaving it with" that individual. For this purpose solicitors often employ enquiry agents or process servers to ensure that the document is left with the person to be served. The server should hand the document to the person and tell him what it contains. If the person will not take the document the server should explain what the document contains and leave it as near as possible in that person's possession. It is in fact sufficient for the document to be dropped at the feet of the person to be served. Where a partnership is being sued in the firm's name then personal service is effected by leaving the document with any one of the partners in the firm. In accordance with the Rules it appears that personal service should be at the partner's residence or on him at the firm's principal place of business. To avoid any ambiguity it is sensible to always serve a partner at his home or at the partnership's trading address. Of course where the partnership has more than one place of business one has to consider what constitutes the "principal

Method of Service	Points to Note
	office". The headed notepaper of the firm might confirm this, or it may be defined as where any central administration is carried out on behalf of the firm. Whoever is being served must also be handed a notice in Form N218 stating whether he is being served as a partner or as a person having control or management of the partnership business or as both. A process server should be instructed to explain this notice to whoever is being served. In relation to a company or other type of corporation then personal service means serving the person holding a "senior position". In respect of a company that is going to mean the Director, Treasurer, Secretary, Chief Executive, Manager or other Officer and for a corporation which is not a registered company such as the Local Authority it will include a Mayor, Chairman, President, Town Clerk or other similar Officer.
How is postal service effected?	Under r.6.3(1)(b) service by post is only effective if first class post is used or an alternative service method is used which provides for delivery *on the next working day*. The Rules do not permit service by second class post except where the party to be served is a registered company. So for companies registered under the Companies Act 1985 s.725, the restriction on using first class post is relaxed and any document can be served on the company registered under the Act whether or not by first class post or recorded delivery or registered post. Except for service on registered companies, under r.6.2(1)(b) postal service does not include recorded delivery or registered post even though these may seem more certain in terms of proving that service has been effected. Under CPR 6.32(1)(c) provision is also made for a document to be served by leaving it at a "place of service". This method of service is a variation on service by post. Instead of using a postman to deliver the document to the recipient's address the party serving the document takes the document there himself or employs another agent to do so for example a courier or enquiry agent.
How is service by Document Exchange effected?	The Document Exchange or DX is a private postal service used by many businesses and professions including most solicitors. Each member of the Document Exchange has a unique box number which is located at the DX office nearest to their business. Letters and parcels delivered to that DX box or any DX box in the country will be delivered within 24 hours which means as required by the Rules service is effected on the next working day (see CPR 6 PD A paras 2.1 and 3.1).

Method of Service	Points to Note
	Service by DX is permitted if the party to be served includes his DX number in his address for service or on his solicitor's notepaper. In the event that the DX member later becomes unwilling or unable to accept service by DX he can prevent that by informing other parties in writing or by altering his notepaper to say "service by DX is not accepted". Where service takes place by DX again the irrebuttable presumption that service has been effected once the document enters the DX is made.
How is service by fax effected?	Under CPR 6 PD A para.4.1, service by fax can only be effective if the party to be served or his legal representative has indicated a willingness to accept service by fax and the fax number to which the document is sent is published. The publication of a fax number on a solicitor's notepaper will be taken as notice of that willingness to accept service by this method, as will the inclusion of the fax number in a statement of case, acknowledgement of service or similar document. However the inclusion of a fax number on the notepaper of a party to be served (as opposed to the legal representatives) must be accompanied by an express indication of their willingness to accept service by fax which may be either by letter or by including the fax number in the statement of case, acknowledgement or similar document. For a recent example of the need for written notification to be given of the intention to deliver service by fax see *Hart Investments Ltd v Fidler* [2006] EWHC 2857. Service of a claim form by fax takes place when the document is delivered even though it is not stated on the document to be faxed "by way of service" and no response pack is served with it (see *Asia Pacific (HK) Ltd v Hanjin Shipping Co Ltd* [2005] EWHC 2443).
How is service by email and other electronic means established?	Again under CPR 6 PD A para.4.1, service can only be effected by email or other similar electronic means if the party to be served or his legal representative has indicated a willingness to be served as such and has stated the email address or other electronic identification to which documents may be sent. It is important to note the inclusion of the email address or electronic identification in a statement of claim, acknowledgement of service or similar document does constitute such notice. Nor does the inclusion of an email address on the notepaper of the party or his legal representatives by itself authorise service by email. Assuming that a party has expressly authorised service by email then the party seeking to serve any document should clarify with his opponent whether this is limited in any way such as

Method of Service	Points to Note
	the file format in which the document is to be sent, the maximum size of attachments that may be received and indeed the email address to which service will be accepted (see CPR 6 PD para.3.2). Once the document is served by email it is not necessary to follow it up with a hardcopy by either post or fax although it may be worthwhile to do this if there is likely to be any argument about whether service was effected.

How is service on a company effected?

CPR Pt 6 provides for service on companies incorporations including foreign companies if they have an address for service in the UK or authorise a solicitor to accept service or indeed have a place of business in the UK. CPR 6.3(2) provides the mechanism for service of documents on companies by reference to s.725 of the Companies Act 1985 which states: 6–18

(1) A document may be served on a company by leaving it at, or sending it by post to, the company's registered office;

(2) where a company registered in Scotland carries on business in England and Wales, the process of any court in England and Wales may be served on the company by leaving it at, or sending it by post to, the company's principal place of business in England and Wales, addressed to the manager or other head officer in England and Wales of the company;

(3) where process is served on a company under subsection (2), the person issuing out the process shall send a copy of it by post to the company's registered office.

For service on overseas companies the provisions of s.695 of the Companies Act 1985 apply which states: 6–19

(1) Any process or notice required to be served on an overseas company is sufficiently served if addressed to any person whose name has been delivered to the registrar under preceding sections in this Part and left at or sent by post to the address which has been so delivered.

(2) However—

(a) where such a company makes default in delivering to the registrar the name and address of a person resident in

Great Britain who is authorised to accept on behalf of the company service of process or notices, or

(b) if at any time all the persons whose names and addresses have been so delivered are dead or have ceased so to reside, or refuse to accept service on the company's behalf, or for any reason cannot be served, a document may be served on the company by leaving it at, or sending it by post to, any place of business established by the company in Great Britain.

In relation to s.725 it is fairly standard practice in debt recovery proceedings to leave a document or send it by post to the company's registered office as provided in paragraph 1 of s.725 above.

6–20 Where a company registered in Scotland carries on business in England and Wales the process of any court in England and Wales may be served on the company by leaving it or posting it to the company's principal place of business in England and Wales and addressing the document to the manager or other lead officer in England and Wales of the company. If a document is served in this way then the person issuing the process must send a copy to the company's registered office as provided in s.725(2) and (3) of the Companies Act as set out above.

In relation to overseas companies there are two ways in which they can be served with documents. Where an overseas company has a place of business in Great Britain then s.695 of the Companies Act 1985 provides for service on a named person as an address registered with the Registrar of Companies at that address.

Under s.695A which was inserted in 1992 by the Overseas Companies and Credit and Financial Institutions (Branch Disclosure) Regulations 1992, SI 1992/3179, service of documents is provided where there is a British branch of the company registered under Sch.21A, para.1 of the Act for any limited company incorporated abroad where the subject matter of the claim is in respect of the carrying on of the business at the branch. This latter form of service was held valid in the case of *Saab v Saudi American Bank* [1998] 4 All E.R. 382.

What is the effect of defective service on a company?

6–21 Fortunately, defective service on a company is a curable irregularity following the decision in *Singh (Santosh Kumari) v Atombrook Limited* [1989] 1 All E.R. 385.

How is "place of business" defined?

Under s.725 of the Companies Act 1985 any document can be served on a company registered under the Act by leaving it, or sending it, by post to the registered office of the company even if it is not its "place of business". **6–22**

A place of business however for the purpose of service of documents under the Companies Act 1985 involving a foreign company means a degree of permanence. An address with which the company has no more than a "transient or irregular connection" is not sufficient for either the Companies Act or the Rules to create an acceptable place of business (see *Laka Group v Al Jazeera Satellite Channel* [2003] EWCA Civ 781).

What method of postage should be used in serving a company?

It has been said earlier that in relation to a company it is immaterial whether the claim is served by first class post, second class post, recorded delivery or registered post. Delivery will be presumed "in the ordinary course of post" provided there is proof of proper addressing, prepaying and posting (by virtue of s.7 of the Interpretation Act 1978). **6–23**

The presumed date of service depends upon the class of post used.

How should proceedings be served on the crown?

Service in compliance with CPR 6.10 is important not least because the court must be satisfied as to proper service on the appropriate defendant in proceedings against the Crown before judgment in default can be obtained. The Rules state at CPR 12.4(4) that in civil proceedings against the Crown a request for default judgment must be considered by a Master or district judge, who must be satisfied that the claim form and particulars of claim have been properly served on the Crown in accordance with s.18 of the Crown Proceedings Act 1947 and the Rule at 6.5.(8). **6–24**

What is the procedure if the documents are duly served on a member of the armed forces?

The accompanying practice direction to CPR Pt 6 at para.5 along with the Annex to the practice directions sets out the detailed requirements for serving documents on members of HM Forces and the United States Air Force. **6–25**

What is the position if the defendant is outside the jurisdiction?

6–26 As was said at the start of this chapter, not every defendant is going to be conveniently situated within the jurisdiction of England and Wales. Practitioners need to have strategies to cope with these types of recovery situation.

The sort of problem that can arise was set out in the case of *Fairmays (formerly Palmer Cowen) (a firm) v Palmer* [2006] EWHC 96. In that case the defendant had been residing in England up until May 2003 but had left to live in Addis Ababa in Ethiopia. He was working on a three year consultancy contract in Ethiopia. In July 2003 he wrote to the claimant saying that he was working abroad and no longer living at his former address in England. The court held that at the time the proceedings were issued it was not open to a court to conclude the proceedings issued for service within the jurisdiction could properly be served because at the time of deemed service the defendant was physically out of the jurisdiction. It was acknowledged that this created potential difficulties for a claimant seeking to serve proceedings on a defendant for whom they did not have an address for service, but whom they suspected (in this case the defendant had let the claimant know he was going to be out of the country) might be abroad. It was suggested in the case note to *Fairmays* that those difficulties could be met by the issue of concurrent proceedings for service abroad in respect of which an order for alternative service on a last known address of the defendant within the jurisdiction could be obtained. The decision in *Fairmays* can be contrasted with the decision in the case of *Kamali v City & Country Properties Limited* [2006] EWCA Civ 1879. In this case the claimant was served at his place of business in England, but he was temporarily out of the jurisdiction at the time. The Court of Appeal held that the service was valid on the basis there had been no notification that the defendant would be abroad as there had been in the *Fairmays* case. The court held that the fact that Kamali had been out of the jurisdiction at the time of service was not of itself a good reason for setting aside the default judgment.

However as a result of the new Pt 6, service of the claim form and other documents out of the jurisdiction is dealt with in Pt IV of CPR Pt 6.

When will the claim form and particulars of claim be considered to have been served?

6–27 After either the court has dealt with the service of the claim form or whether one of the other methods of service has been used, a timetable begins to run from the time service has been effected.

CPR 6.14 sets out when service will be deemed to have taken effect depending upon the method of service used. Again Practitioners will generally rely on service by post being carried out by the court, and the deemed date of service being calculated in accordance with information coming back from the court which will be input into the debt recovery system.

Under the new CPR Pt 6, "deemed service" is calculated on taking place on the second business day after completion of the relevant step under CPR 7.5(1). That rule states that, where the claim form is to be served within the jurisdiction, the claimant must "complete the step required" before midnight on the calendar day four months after the date of issue on the claim form.

Rule 7.5(1) contains a table setting out the "step" to be completed according to the method of service which is provided in r.6.3 as follows:

Personal service in accordance with CPR 6.5	The step needs to be completed by following the requirements of r.6.5(3)
A method of postal service including first class post, document exchange (DX) or since the monopoly of The Royal Mail has been dismantled any other postal system which provides for next day delivery (see CPR 6.3(1)(b)	Posting, leaving with, delivering to or collection by the relevant service provider
Leaving the claim form at a place set out in CPR 6.7, 6.8 OR 6.9—which are now under the updated Rules a far more comprehensive code of where to serve	Delivering or leaving the document at the relevant place set out in the various Rules
Using fax or other means of electronic communication in accordance with Practice Direction A to the updated CPR Pt 6	Completing the transmission of the fax or sending the email or other electronic transmission—and for certainty ensuring there is a record that the transmission has been sent successfully or received at the other end
Any other method of service authorized by the court under r.6.15	Completing the steps as authorised by the Court.

As the court usually sends the claim form out in a debt recovery action by first class post then service will be deemed to have taken place on the second day after the claim form and the accompanying paperwork was posted. **6–28**

Where the court serves the claim form then it must send the claimant a notice which includes the date of deemed service under CPR 6.7. It is this date that must be noted on to the Debt Recovery Practitioner's system to allow for the system to calculate the first available day when judgment can be entered.

If the claimant arranges service personally then the claimant must follow the new requirements of CPR 6.17(2) which includes certifying the date of service in accordance with the details set out in r.6.17(3)(b).

A claimant must now file a certificate of service within 21 days of service of the particulars of claim unless all the defendants to the proceedings have filed acknowledgements of service within that time. A claimant cannot obtain judgment in default under CPR Pt 12 unless a certificate of service has been filed. The accompanying Practice Direction to CPR Pt 6 stipulates at para.7.1 that a claimant when filing a certificate of service does not also have to file either a further copy of the claim form, or a further copy of the particulars of claim where these documents have already been filed with the court.

Does service have to be through one of the above methods?

6–29 The short answer is no. If a claimant believes that attempting service upon the other party by one of the methods indicated in the section above is not going to be effective the claimant can take steps to effect service by another means such as advertising in the local press. The claimant must demonstrate to the court that "there is good reason to authorise service by a method not permitted by these rules" (see CPR 6.15).

If the application for alternative service is successful then any order must specify the method of service to be used and the date when the document will be deemed to be served.

The case of *Albon v Naza Motor Trading SDN BHD (No.2)* [2007] EWHC 327 reviewed in what situation the court would be minded to make an order allowing alternative service. The case referred to the need for the court to have in mind the overriding objective and whether the making of such an order would enable the court to deal with the case justly. Previous decisions had viewed "good reasons" for allowing alternative methods of service to include cases where the defendant was evading service or had become untraceable. Under changes to the CPR these scenarios do not create a problem if the claimant follows the requirement CPR 6.9(3) and (4).

The situations in which Practitioners are therefore going to rely on alternative methods of service are going to be rare but should it be needed the provision is catered for within the rules.

Does service have to take place at a certain time?

6–30 There is no actual restriction in the rules as to when a document may be served. In fact it may be served at any time of a day or night and contrary perhaps to popular belief can also be served on Sunday or Christmas Day or any other bank holiday.

In CPR 6.2 the meanings a "bank holiday" and "business day" are clearly defined and follow the defınctions set out in the former Rules of Service. Deemed service is dealt with in CPR 6.14 and the new rule provides the mechanism for fixing the deemed day of service for the claim form.

The deemed day is arrived at by omitting from the calculation the days which are non business days being Saturday or Sunday, and the bank holidays of Christmas Day and Good Friday (see CPR 6.2 and then by calculating when the step for service needs to be completed. **6–31**

As far as the Debt Recovery Practitioner concerned the need to arrange for the court to serve the claim form is the safest route and personal service or alternative means of service should only be considered for some reason where there is going to be a problem in relation to a prospective application by a defendant to try and set aside judgment for effective service.

Can defective service be validated retrospectively?

It is possible to correct mis-service using para.(2) of CPR 6.15; this is being seen as a "new and novel" provision which has been designed to remedy what were thought to be defects in the previous law. Under the old r.6.8 the court could not order that mis-service should stand as good service at the time at which it was effected. **6–32**

The new Rule states that the court may order that "steps already taken to bring the claim form to the attention of the defendant by an alternative method or at an alternative place" amounts to good service. This provision may therefore allow a claimant to escape the serious consequences if service could not be established by another method which of course becomes an acute problem if the limitation period has expired.

Can a contract agree a special method for service of the claim form?

Some contracts may specify that the service of the claim form must be made in a particular way. **6–33**

CPR 6.11 provides that where this is set out in the contract then the claim form will be deemed to be served on the defendant if served by the method specified in the contract provided the claim form is issued only in respect of a claim under that contract.

A typical clause in a contract would be for service upon a nominated firm of solicitors in England or Wales.

Is it possible to have an ad hoc agreement for service between the parties?

6–34 This situation was the subject of the case of *Kenneth Allison Ltd v AE Limehouse & Co* [1992] 2 AC 105. In that case proceedings were issued against a firm of chartered accountants. Papers were served at the firm's principal place of business on a personal assistant who immediately before service was authorised to accept service by one of the partners who was in another part of the building. The service was held to be effective even though this was not one of the methods permitted by the then rules of court. There was no personal service on the partner which would have been the normal method nor could the personal assistant be said to have been a person in control of the business which again is mentioned in the rules. Despite the rules being stretched in this sort of scenario such a method of service is risky and should be avoided in debt recovery proceedings where the standard methods of service should anticipate and cope with any situation that a Debt Recovery Practitioner may come across.

What about service on an agent for a principal who is overseas?

6–35 CPR 6.12 anticipates this situation and if a principal resides and carries on business out of the jurisdiction but enters into a contract with a claimant by or through an agent who resides or carries on business within the jurisdiction then the court may order service of the claim form on that agent.

To enable the court to make such an order the claimant must apply to the court for its permission with supporting evidence dealing with the following:

- give full details of the contract including details of the fact it was entered into within the jurisdiction by an Agent who was also acting within the jurisdiction;
- confirm that the Principal is, and was at the time of the contract, out of the jurisdiction;
- give reasons as to why service out of the jurisdiction cannot be achieved—service cross-border is now a far more routine matter than it was say ten years ago; and
- confirm at the time of the application the Agent's authority had not been terminated and he was still the appointed Agent of his Principal.

If the court is minded to make such an order it must state the period within which the defendant must respond to the particulars of claim (see CPR 6.12(3)).

When should a certificate of service be used?

A claimant who serves the claim form personally must also file at court a certificate of service in Form N215. This is the most usual reason why a certificate of service is required. In doing so the claimant is complying with CPR 6.17(2)(a) which requires a certificate to be filed within 21 days of service of the particulars of claim (see CPR 6.17(2)(a)). **6–36**

Must the court notify the claimant of postal service?

Under Rule 6.18 where a document is served by the court and served by post and that document is returned to the court then the court must send notification to the party who requested service stating that the document has been returned. Debt Recovery Practitioners need to watch out for this and ensure they have a process to immediately begin to arrange service by one of the other methods as no further action will be taken by the court. Also in Rule 6.19 where the court baliff is required to the serve the claim form and if unable to do so the court will send a notification to the claimant. **6–37**

Does the claim form and particulars of claim need to be served in a certain timeframe?

The simple answer is yes, the claim form must be served on the debtor within four months of the date of issue (see CPR 7.5(2)). **6–38**

There may be a number of reasons why a claimant does not wish to immediately serve either the claim form and/or the particulars of claim on the defendant following the issue of the claim itself. It is acceptable for a claimant to delay serving the papers once issued but a diary note must be made to ensure that service is arranged within four months of the issue of the claim form. In calculating this four-month period the claimant should consider the deemed service period and make sure that they allow sufficient time for service. For example if the four-month period expires on Wednesday, August 16 there is no point in sending the papers to the defendant in the post on 16th as service will not be deemed to have taken place until Friday, August 18 which is outside the four-month time limit.

Unless this time limit is on the very edge of the limitation period (see Chapter 2) then the risk to the claimant is that they will have to issue proceedings again and pay a further fee. If the time period is on the edge of the limitation period the claimant risks losing the right to bring a claim at all. Clearly, calculating and diarising time limits is an important function of the Debt Recovery Practitioner and at every stage the client should be warned about delays and what information is needed to ensure that papers, once issued, are served promptly.

Can the time for service be extended after the four-month period?

6–39 In accordance with CPR 7.6 it is possible to make an application to the court to seek an extension of time for service of the claim form and/or the particulars of claim. The application should be made using form N244 and should set out the reasons why a service has not been possible within the four-month period and explaining what steps have already been taken to effect service and indicate the period of extension to be sought.

What is the situation if the defendant lives outside the jurisdiction of England and Wales—is it still a four-month period to serve?

6–40 Under CPR 7.5(3) the period of time for service of the claim form outside the jurisdiction is extended from four to six months.

It should be noted that the rules with regards to the method of service of claim forms out of the jurisdiction are provided for under CPR Rule 6 part IV.

How does limitation effect the issue of a claim and subsequent service of proceedings?

6–41 As mentioned above when pursuing a debt recovery claim arising out of a simple contractual dispute then the limitation period is six years from the date the course of action arose or in simple terms when the debt became due. Failure to issue within the limitation period will mean the claim will be statute-barred and rather than pursuing a claim on behalf of the claimant, the solicitor acting for the claimant may well be on the end of a professional negligence claim!

When must particulars of claim be served if separate to the claim form?

Unless the court orders otherwise particulars of claim which are separate to the claim form must be served no later than the latest time for the serving of the claim form. Provided that the claim form has been served in the time required by CPR 7.4 being the four month window, the court has a general discretion to extend the time for service of the particulars of claim and the very narrow restrictions under CPR 7.6 in relation to extending time for service of a claim form do not apply (see *Totty v Snowden* [2001] EWCA Civ 1415). **6–42**

An extension of time for service of particulars is not an ideal situation and a Debt Recovery Practitioners should ensure that particulars are served with the claim form itself.

What is the situation if the court fails to serve?

Where the court fails to serve due to a mistake or neglect, an extension may be granted (see *Cranfield v Bridgegrove Limited* [2003] EWCA Civ 656). **6–43**

Can the parties agree to extend time for service of the claim form?

It is possible for the parties to agree an extension of time for service of the claim form pursuant to CPR 2.11 which will require a "written agreement between the parties". **6–44**

There is no express provision in CPR 7.5 or indeed CPR 7.6 which actually excludes the availability of CPR 2.11 in these circumstances.

Again it is unlikely in a debt recovery action that such an agreement will be necessary or contemplated but should it be required the Rules do permit it.

What is the situation where the debtor is overseas?

The easiest way to consider this issue is to separate EU countries from non-EU countries. The table below separates the two areas: **6–45**

EU Countries (as at August 2008) being: Austria Belgium Bulgaria Cyprus Czech Republic Denmark Estonia Finland France Germany Greece Hungary Ireland Italy Latvia Lithuania Luxembourg Malta Netherlands Poland Portugal Romania Slovakia Slovenia Spain Sweden United Kingdom	• No special permission is required to serve a defendant who is based in another part of the United Kingdom be it Scotland, Northern Ireland or another EU country provided the court has jurisdiction under Council Regulation 44/2001. • The claim form must state the grounds on which the claimant is entitled to serve the claim form outside of the jurisdiction. The form of words to use is set out in the accompanying Practice Direction 6B. • The time for responding to the claim form will usually be extended to 21 days. • Rules 6.40 make special provision for the methods of service when the claim form needs to be served outside of the jurisdiction.
Non-EU Countries	• The claimant will need to obtain permission to serve proceedings on a defendant outside the EU. • Practitioners should look for an English or Welsh address for service to avoid having to take this step—perhaps the defendant company has solicitors instructed within the jurisdiction. • Rule 6.36 sets out the grounds for seeking the necessary permission. • Application for permission to serve outside the jurisdiction is made without notice and on supporting evidence. • If allowed then time for service will be extended.

Chapter 7

Handling the Debtor's Response to the Claim

Introductory Comments

In this chapter we will look at the responses that can be made to a claim issued and served upon a debtor. 7–01

In many ways the Debt Recovery Practitioner will be hoping that there will be no response to the claim and the claim can move immediately to default judgment. We will look at that scenario in this chapter.

However, there are a number of responses which must be anticipated by the Debt Recovery Practitioner and once again systems must be in place to handle each one, particularly in a busy department where responses from debtors may even fall into trends or patterns.

The areas that we will therefore look at include:

1. Acknowledgment of service of the claim by the debtor (see the section below headed "**Acknowledgement of Service**").
2. An admission by the debtor that the debt is due either in full or in part (see the section below headed "**Admission**").
3. Any defence which the debtor may file with or without a counterclaim (see the section below headed "**Defence**").
4. An offer made under the CPR Pt 36 (see the section below headed "**Part 36 Offer**").
5. And finally, where there is no response how a default judgment will be entered and the implications of this (see the section below headed "**No Response**").

What is sent to the defendant by the court when a claim form is served?

7–02 Usually, in debt recovery cases it will be for the court to serve the claim form, although we have looked at earlier in this book, the fact that because service could not be achieved the court has returned the documents to the claimant for service but by and large it will be left to the court to carryout the service of the claim form. As standard procedure the defendant will also receive a response pack from the court containing the following forms:

- an acknowledgement of service form on Form N9;
- an admission form on Form N9A; and
- a defence and counterclaim form on Form N9B.

The debtor then must consider how he/she/it wishes to respond to the claim, if at all, and as a result of that various consequences flow which will be dealt with in this chapter.

What would be the best advice to the debtor on receiving the claim form and response pack?

7–03 A debtor served with a claim form and response pack should ideally read through the claim form and check that the information is correct. The claim form will of course set out the details of the nature of the claim in the particulars as well as claims for interest and costs. It has to be accepted that in this day and age legal advice for debtors is not always readily available except for those who can afford it. Therefore, the debtor may well try to deal with the claim form and its response in person or take it to an advice centre for them to advise on the way to respond.

In business to business debt it is likely that the proprietors of an incorporated business or the directors of an incorporated business would seek proper legal advice from their advisors, be it their solicitor or their accountants, on how to respond to a claim form, but again this cannot be said with any certainty and therefore claimants need to anticipate that the sophistication of a response from defendants may be often lacking.

In some ways of course this may help the claimant but in other ways bearing in mind the overriding objective set out in Pt 1 of the CPR should the case proceed to a defended hearing or an application to set aside or vary any final judgment, the judge may consider there is an inequality between the parties which the court may be prepared to look at. Debt Recovery Practitioners should therefore ensure that they have systems in the office, particularly in debt recovery, whereby they are able to speak with debtors in person, handle offers, talk through any responses that are made and generally open up communication to encourage debtors to pay rather than taking, perhaps, the age-old litigious approach where they are expecting the other side to be legally represented.

The claimant should also anticipate that if the particulars of claim are not correct or the party sued is not correct, the defendant can apply to make applications for either the claim to be dismissed or for summary judgment in accordance with CPR Pt 24, which will be dealt with in Chapter 9. CPR Pt 24.2 sets out the grounds upon which the court may consider granting summary judgment. Where the claimant has sued the wrong defendant it is likely that summary judgment would be granted in accordance with CPR 24.2 (a)(i), as the claimant has no real prospect of succeeding in the claim in that they have sued the wrong person.

Acknowledgment of Service

What can a claimant expect to receive when the defendant returns a signed Acknowledgment of Service Form on Form N9?

A defendant will complete an Acknowledgment of Service Form if he/she/it is unable to file a defence within the period allowed by the rules, which is a 14 day window from the date of deemed service of the particulars of claim and claim form (see CPR 15.4). Alternatively the defendant may wish to dispute the court's jurisdiction (see CPR 10.1(3)). **7–04**

How is the period for filing the Acknowledgment of Service to be calculated?

The claim form and the accompanying response pack will be served by the court on the debtor as we have seen from Chapter 6. The forms will have been sent by first class post and the claim form will therefore be deemed to have been served on the debtor two days after it was posted in accordance with CPR Pt 6 in relation to deemed service. The 14 day window is calculated from the date of deemed service. **7–05**

If for some reason the claimant has decided to serve the documents personally without relying on the court to achieve service then, depending on the method of service, the deemed day of service will need to be calculated and a 21 day window for acknowledging service will run from that deemed day of service. Again reference is made to the various methods of service discussed in Chapter 6.

Can the defendant make an application to extend time for service?

7–06 Rule CPR 10.3 provides that where a defendant has failed to serve an Acknowledgment of Services Form or indeed a defence within the time limits prescribed and the claimant then seeks judgment in default, the defendant will require the court's permission to serve an Acknowledgement of Service or defence out of time. Whether that permission will be granted is a matter within the court's discretion under CPR 3.1(2)(a), but the discretion will normally be exercised in favour of extending time as discussed in the case of *Coll v Tattum* [2002] 03 LS Gaz R 26.

Is a longer period allowed for acknowledging service?

7–07 The period for acknowledging service where a claim has been served outside England and Wales is now dealt with in the form of CPR Part and the accompanying Practice Direction B and reference is made to the relevant rule being 6.35 which sets out the period for responding to a claim form where permission was not required for service of the same out of the jurisdiction.

CPR 6.35 makes a clear distinction between service of the claim form on a defendant in Scotland or Northern Ireland (see CPR 6.35(2)), a defendant who is in a Convention territory (as defined in CPR 6.31(h)) within Europe or a Member State, or service on a defendant in a Convention territory outside Europe and finally service on a defendant "elsewhere".

Under para.6.1 of that Practice Direction the period within which a defendant must file an acknowledgement of service, or file or serve an admission or defence is calculated in accordance with rr.6.3, 6.4 or 6.5 as appropriate.

A table set out in the Practice Direction B to CPR Pt 6 gives the various periods for the countries throughout all the regions mentioned in the Rules.

What options are available to the defendant in completing the Acknowledgment of Service Form?

7–08 There are three boxes on the Acknowledgement of Service Form and the debtor will need to choose which box is appropriate as the response to the claim. These can be summarised as follows:

Debtor ticks "I intend to defend all of this claim"	The debtor will tick this box if he does not agree with any aspect of the claimant's claim against him and denies that he/she/it owes the claimant any money at all.
The debtor ticks "I intend to defend part of this claim"	The debtor will tick this box if he/she/it owes the claimant some of the money which is the subject of the claim but perhaps not the full amount as set out in the particulars and will therefore tick this box to indicate that part of the debt is disputed.
The debtor ticks "I intend to contest jurisdiction"	The debtor will tick this box if he/she feels the proceedings had been issued in a wrong court or indeed the wrong country and therefore calls in to question the court's jurisdiction.

Once the debtor has ticked the relevant box the form must be completed with the defendant's address for service following the Rules in CPR 6.5.

Who should sign the Acknowledgement of Service?

The Acknowledgement of Service Form should be signed by the defendant or his legal representative who has been instructed to accept service on his behalf. If a solicitor signs the Acknowledgement then the address for service must be the solicitor's business address. For the definition of "legal representative" reference should be made to CPR 2.3. 7–09

In the accompanying Practice Direction to CPR Pt 10 at para.4 it confirms that not only must the documents by signed by the defendant or his legal representative but where the defendant is a company or other corporation then the person to sign must hold a senior position and state the position that he holds (see CPR PD 10 para.4.3).

A senior position is defined under para.1 of para.4.3 being in respect of a registered company or corporation as a Director, Treasurer, Secretary, Chief Executive, Manager or other officer of the company; and (2) in respect of a corporation which is not a registered company such as a local authority then the additional persons include a Mayor, Chairman, President, Town Clerk or similar officer of that corporation.

Where the claim is brought against a partnership then service must be acknowledged in the name of the partnership on behalf of all the persons who are partners at the time when the debt arose and the Acknowledgement of Service may be signed by any of those partners, or by any person authorised to sign the Acknowledgment of Service on behalf of the partners (see CPR PD (10) para.4.4).

Can the acknowledgement of service be amended or withdrawn?

7–10 Under CPR PD 10 para.5.4 an Acknowledgment of Service can only be amended or withdrawn with the permission of the court and an application for permission under para.5.4 must be made in accordance with Pt 23 (see Chapter 9 of this book) supported by accompanying evidence.

Who sends the acknowledgement of service to the claimant?

7–11 Where the defendant files the Acknowledgement of Service in response to a debt claim (being a claim under CPR Pt 7) then it is provided in CPR 10.4 that the responsibility is for the court to notify the claimant in writing that the Acknowledgment has been served.

Why would a defendant wish to dispute the court's jurisdiction?

7–12 The defendant may wish to dispute the court's jurisdiction because he is a resident outside of the jurisdiction and contends the permission to serve was incorrectly obtained and as we have seen from Chapter 6 there are special rules when the defendant is known to be outside the jurisdiction in relation to the service of the claim form.

The defendant may also contend that England and Wales is not the appropriate place for the matter to be tried even though he is within the jurisdiction, or he contends that the claim is governed by an arbitration agreement.

As to what further steps the defendant may take in relation to one of these contentions, reference should be made to CPR Pt 11 which deals with the rule for the procedure to be followed when the court's jurisdiction is disputed.

What are the consequences of a defendant who fails to acknowledge service?

7–13 Under CPR 10.2 if a defendant fails to acknowledge service within the period specified in Rule 10.3 and also fails to file a defence in accordance with Pt 15 of the Rules or serve or file an admission in accordance with the Pt 14 of the Rules then the claimant is going to be able to obtain default judgment in accordance with Pt 12 provided the necessary criteria is fulfilled.

What is the situation if no defence is subsequently filed?

If the defendant files an Acknowledgment of Service the claimant will then diarise his system and wait for the defence to arrive. It is possible, however, that the defendant will not subsequently file a defence. 7–14

It may be that for some reason the claimant does not apply for default judgment under Pt 12 of the Rules or seek summary judgment and in that case Rule 15.11 provides the claim to be automatically stayed for six months after the end of the period allowed for filing a defence.

If either party then wishes to bring the action back to life they must apply to the court for the stay to be lifted before the proceedings can continue.

Admission

How should a claimant tackle an admission?

An Admission from the defendant is a response generally that they accept something needs to be done about getting the debt resolved. There is a skill to reading the information contained in an Admission and drawing conclusions from it on the defendant's position in line with the enforcement matrix outlined in Chapter 1. 7–15

So, for example, if a defendant indicates he or she is working in the Admission form this should be a clear indicator to the claimant that in the event of default, any judgment could be enforced using the Attachment of Earnings procedure (see Chapter 15).

CPR Pt 14 deals with the various types of admission that a claimant can expect to receive in a debt recovery action. The form for admission Form N9 will have been served on the defendant with the response pack and the particulars of claim and a party may make an admission in writing in any document.

Admissions can also be made prior to the commencement of proceedings but unless that admission is repeated in accordance with the requirements of CPR Pt 14 then the first admission pre-action is simply going to be evidence for an application under CPR Pt 24 in an application for summary judgment.

At this point in the book we are dealing with admissions made once the claim and the response pack have been served.

Of course the purpose of Pt 14 is to allow the defendant to admit the claim as early as possible and to take advantage of the provisions in relation to allowing time for payment (see CPR 14.9).

It should also be noted that in accordance with CPR 16.5 (5) a failure by a defendant to deal with an allegation in the particulars of claim may in certain circumstances amount to an admission.

What is the situation if the defendant admits all of the claim?

7–16 If the defendant returns the admission form which will usually be in Form N9A, (although note above that it does not have to be on this form), but it must be "in writing", indicating how much of the claim is admitted, the claimant should check whether it is the full amount of the claim or only a specific sum which is being admitted.

Where it is the full amount the debtor may propose to pay the debt by instalments and therefore it is important that the financial information as set out on Form N9A as to the debtor's income and expenditure and other assets is completed to enable the claimant to make a fair assessment of whether the defendant's offer is reasonable and acceptable.

If the claimant evaluates the defendant's response and considers it to be acceptable then the claimant may request judgment to be entered for the amount which has been admitted under CPR 14.4(3).

Does the defendant have to file the admission within a specific time period?

7–17 Under the CPR Pt 14.2 where the defendant is returning the admission form then he must file it within 14 days of service of the particulars of claim (see CPR 14.2 (1)).

Provided that the claimant has not requested judgment in default it is also possible for the defendant to file the admission outside of the 14 day period referred to above and for it to be taken as having been filed within that period (CPR 14.2(3) and CPR 14.2 (4)).

Does the claimant have to accept an offer to repay the debt by instalments?

7–18 Although Form N9A provides the opportunity for the defendant to put forward an offer to pay the debt off by instalments. There is no requirement under the rules for the claimant to accept that offer.

If the claimant is minded to accept the debtor's offer then the claimant can request the judgment to be entered in the usual way indicating that the judgment debt will be paid by instalments on or before a specified future date. The court will then draw the judgment accordingly. If the claimant does not accept the proposal to pay by instalments it must file a notice at the court (see CPR 14.10 (2)).

On receipt of the claimant's notice the court will then enter judgment for the amount admitted by the debtor to be paid at the time or at a rate to be determined by the court (see CPR 14.10 (4)).

A defendant who wants time to pay under the CPR 14.9 must, in compliance with CPR PD 14 para.2.2, complete the statement of means contained in the admission form as fully as possible. If details are incomplete the court may, on its own initiative, make an order requiring details to be given and the claimant should always draw the court's attention to any defects in the statement of means form and ask the defendant to give the necessary information. **7–19**

It is important to remember that if the admission was made under Rule 14.4 the admission form would have been received by the claimant directly from the defendant and if the claimant feels the information is inadequate he should send a copy to the court and ask it to direct that the defendant completes the form fully with all the relevant information.

How does the court determine whether the defendant's payment proposals are acceptable?

This involves the "determination of rate of payment procedure" which is contained in CPR 14.10 to 14.12. It is something that Debt Recovery Practitioners are encouraged to understand. **7–20**

Claimants must of course take a realistic view of the weekly or monthly amount the defendant is offering to pay, particularly when taking a strategic view of the litigation and debt recovery process and coming to an assessment that there are likely to be little or no assets at the end of the litigation in which to enforce against. An offer of £20 a week or £80 a month is going to be better than trying to remove a vehicle which is worth nothing except scrap value.

If the defendant asks for time to pay and has completed their details of means the claimant should consider whether the offer is reasonable based on the information on Form N9A along with any other information they have about the defendant's general lifestyle and assets.

Consideration should be given to the time it would take to clear the debt. In many cases defendants will supply figures that are a combination of weekly, monthly or even quarterly payments. It is vital that these are converted into the frequency of the income of the defendant. If a defendant is paid monthly all expenses should be converted to monthly figures providing an accurate figure of an average monthly income and expenditure. The hint here is to convert weekly figures to monthly by multiplying them by 4.33 not just by 4.

7–21 Where no offer of payment is made on a full admission. If the defendant admits the claim but makes no offer of payment the claimant should apply for judgment on Form N205A or N225 with an order for payment of the unpaid balance of the claim forthwith.

What is the process for accepting the defendant's offer?

7–22 If the claimant accepts the offer the claimant should complete the bottom part of Form N205A being a notice of issue (specified amount) or Form N225 being a "request for judgment and reply to admission (specified amount)" in the terms of the offer and send the form to the court. The defendant should be notified that the offer has been accepted by the claimant directly.

What is the position if the offer of the payment is found to be unacceptable?

7–23 There may be grounds for the claimant refusing the offer of the defendant based on the fact that the stated income does not coincide with findings, not only what the debtor says it has to pay, but also on the claimant's own experience of running a household or running a business. The Debt Recovery Practioner should think about what they pay for their own gas and electricity and utility bills along with what it costs to run a vehicle and travel to and from work. If this raises a doubt it needs to be investigated. Practitioners should also look for details of unnecessary or inflated expenditure for socialising or excessive utility or other bills.

7–24 Practitioners should also contact the defendant by telephone and question and clarify any figures provided before applying to the court. The objective of such a phone call is to get the defendant to make an increased offer of payment. If the defendant agrees to make an increased offer then claimant should obtain their written consent which can then be sent to the court and acted upon.

How does the court determine whether the debtor's payment proposals are acceptable?

7–25 For debts under £50,000 the determination as to the offer made by the defendant can be made by a court officer without the need for a hearing and this can cause claimants to express some disquiet at the orders which are made (see CPR 14.11).

For debts over £50,000, the determination will need to be made by a Judge (see CPR 14.12). This may be done with or without a hearing.

If it is to be done by way of a hearing then the matter must be transferred to the debtor's local court. Where the determination has been made by a court officer there is the opportunity for a claimant or a defendant to make an application to the court for re-determination under CPR 14.3(1) but that application must be made within fourteen days of service of the determination upon the party who wants to have the decision re-determined (see CPR 14.13(2)). 7–26

How does a claimant evaluate if the defendant's proposal is acceptable?

If the defendant has admitted the debt owed to the claimant then the claimant should consider the information provided within the admission form (see above). 7–27

It is common for a debtor to declare not only their own income and expenditure but also that of their partners' and other members of their family who have an income. For the purposes of the claim and considering any offer that is put forward it is in fact only the income and expenditure of the debtor which is relevant as the debt can only be recovered from them and not their partner.

What should the claimant do if the debtor has not completed the admission form properly?

If this is the case the claimant should request further information from the debtor where there are gaps in the information given. If the debtor has provided information where the figures appear unusual or unrealistic, the claimant is entitled to request copies of documentation to support the information provided in the admission form. It is of course in the debtor's own interest to be as cooperative and comprehensive as possible in providing this information as it increases the possibility that the claimant will accept the proposals put forward and the debtor will have time to pay. 7–28

Can an admission be withdrawn?

Under CPR PD 14 para.7.2 the court has a discretion to permit the withdrawal of an admission. 7–29

If the court wishes to take this course of action it will have to have regard to all the circumstances of the case including those set out in para.7.2.

The court will not allow the withdrawal of an admission made under a mistake where this would cause serious prejudice to a claimant who has relied on the admission.

What happens if the admission of liability is made before an action is brought?

7–30 An admission made before proceedings are commenced does not come within the ambit of Pt 14 of the CPR and the party to an action does not require the court's permission under CPR 14.1(5) to withdraw an admission of liability made before the action started (see *Sowerby v Charlton* [2005] EWCA Civ 1610).

Can any order that has been made be varied?

7–31 Either party may apply for an order to be varied (see CPR PD 14 para.6(1)) where circumstances change and that change may include a failure to pay an instalment.

What is the situation if an instalment is missed?

7–32 There is no actual provision in CPR 14.4(4) that if an instalment is missed then the whole judgment becomes payable immediately. However, such a term is likely to be incorporated into any order under either CPR Sch.2 CCR Ord 22 r.10 in relation to variation of a judgment or under CPR Sch.1 RSC Ord 47 r.1.

Flowcharts

7–33 Flowcharts explaining how admissions operate in a simple process are set out in the flowcharts section of the Appendix.

Defence

How should the defendant defend his position in the claim?

7–34 If the debtor returns the Acknowledgment of Service within 14 days he/she/it has a total of 28 days from the date of service of the claim form to file a defence. As part of the response pack sent to the defendant by the court there will be a defence and counterclaim form (Form N9B).

If the defendant intends to defend the claim and/or make a counterclaim against the claimant this is the form which will need to be completed.

As with particulars of claim if the defence is likely to be lengthy and will not fit into the space provided on Form N9B then the defendant can prepare the defence on a separate document which will need to be headed with the name of the court, claim number, details of the parties and the defence in detail.

The preparation of the defence in response to a debt recovery claim is dealt with in Chapter 8 of this book.

Does the claimant have to give the defendant more time to complete a defence?

As you will have seen above it is possible that the defendant will seek 7–35 to agree with the claimant or their solicitor to an extension of time to file a defence which is permitted under CPR 15.5(1). If agreed, an extension of time under this rule can be given for up to a further 28 days.

If that extension of time is agreed the defendant must notify the court in writing of the agreed extension period under CPR 15.5(2).

If the claimant does not want to agree to give an extension then they should be prepared for the defendant to make an application to court on Form N244 for an extension to be given. In making that application the defendant will need to set out the reasons why he/she/it seeks an extension of time along with an indication as to when he/she/it will be able to file the necessary form of defence.

How should the defendant complete a defence?

The first section of Form N9B requires the defendant to indicate how 7–36 much of the claim he/she/it intends to defend.

The defendant will need to tick the box indicating whether he/she/it intends to defend:

- all of the claim; or
- a specific amount and in so doing must complete the box detailing the amount which it is intended to defend.

The defendant will also need to complete Pt 2 of Form N9B. If the defendant is intending to defend the claim because he had already paid the debt to the claimant he needs to tick the "Yes" box and provide details of the amount paid and the date or dates when payments were made. The defendant should also elaborate with further information in that box as to evidence confirming payment has been made, so that this can be readily reviewed by the claimant and if necessary the claimant can check their own facts as to the situation.

Finally, the defendant will need to complete the body of the defence in Pt 3 of Form N9B.

What must a defence contain?

7–37 The requirements of a defence are set out under CPR 16.5. In the defence the defendant must state:

- which of the allegations in the particulars of claim he/she/it denies;
- which allegations he/she/it is unable to admit or deny and which he requires the claimant to prove; and
- which allegations he/she/it admits.

If the defendant denies an allegation under CPR 16.5(2) he/she/it must state his reasons for doing so, and if he/she/it intends to put forward a different version of the events given by the claimant, then he/she/it will need to state his own version of those events.

Of course it is at this juncture that the different versions of how the debt has come to be owed and why payment has not been made may begin to surface although ideally these should have been identified in the pre-action arena rather than at this stage. However, it is inevitable that for some cases it is only the issue of the claim form which is going to bring forward any response from an intransigent defendant.

The defendant's defence will need to deal with each allegation which has been made in the claim form itself. A defendant who fails to deal with an allegation, but who sets out in his defence the nature of his case in relation to the issue to which the allegation is relevant, will be taken as that meaning that the allegation needs to be proved (see CPR 16(3)(b)).

7–38 If the defendant disputes the claimant's statement of value then under CPR 16.3 he/she/it will have to state why he/she/it had disputed it and give his own statement of value of the claim which could have repercussions in terms of allocation to the various tracks for defended litigation which we will look out in Chapter 8.

If the defendant is defending the claim in a representative capacity, perhaps as a personal representative, then he/she/it will need to state what that capacity is (see CPR 16.5(7)).

At this stage if the defendant has not filed an Acknowledgment of Service under Pt 10 of the rules then he/she/it will now need to give his address for service (as required by Pt 6 of the rules).

Once again the defence must be verified by a Statement of Truth as required by Pt 22 of the rules and dealt with in Chapter 5 of this book. The defendant's address for service must be within the jurisdiction (see r.6.5).

How should the claimant respond if the defendant makes a counterclaim?

In debt recovery Practitioners need to be aware of the possibility for a counterclaim being received from the defendant as a response to the claim being served. 7–39

If the defendant wishes to make a counterclaim he/she/it will need to complete Pt 4 of Form N9B. The part of the rules which deals with counterclaims is CPR Pt 20.

Under CPR 20.4(1) the defendant may make a counterclaim against the claimant by filing particulars of the counterclaim.

The counterclaim can be made against the claimant without the court's permission if the defendant files it with his defence or at any other time with the court's permission.

CPR 20 PD2.1 provides details as to the contents of the application when seeking permission to file a counterclaim.

It is important to remember that the counterclaim must comply with the requirements of CPR Pt 22 as to the signing of the Statements of Truth which will verify the contents of the counterclaim.

Does the claimant need to reply to the defence?

Under CPR 16.7.1 the filing of a reply is actually an optional step and the claimant need only to do this if he/she/it wishes to allege facts which were not included in the original particulars of claim in response to the points raised by the defendant in their defence. 7–40

If the claimant does decide to file a reply then this must be done with their allocation questionnaire and it must be served on the parties at the same time (see CPR 15.8 dealing with the "Reply to Defence" and r.26.3(6) which requires the parties to file allocation questionnaires and specifies the period for doing so).

As with all other documents included in the "Statements of Case", the reply must be verified by a Statement of Truth in accordance to the CPR Pt 22.

Important tactical note for claimants!

7–41 If the defendant has filed a counterclaim in response to the claimant's claim for the outstanding debt then the claimant must take action to file their own defence to that counterclaim to prevent the defendant being able to enter judgment in default against the claimant!

Under Rule 15.3 if a defendant fails to file a defence the claimant may obtain judgment in default and the same rule applies in the event that the claimant fails to file a defence to the counterclaim.

If the claimant wishes to file both a reply and a defence to counterclaim then these should form one document with the defence to counterclaim following on from the reply (see CPR 15.8.3).

What tactical action should a claimant take on receipt of a defence from the defendant?

7–42 Throughout litigation the issue uppermost in most Practitioners' minds is the questions of costs. If a defence is particularly weak then consideration should be given to either encouraging the court to exercise its powers under CPR Pt 3.4 to strike out the defendant's statement of case on the basis that it discloses no reasonable grounds for defending the claim, or worse still is an abuse of the court's process, or there has been a failure to comply with a Rule Practice Direction or court order.

There is anecdotal evidence that this rule is used far too infrequently by court staff and as a result claimants therefore have to make an application under CPR Pt 24 for summary judgment to enable the defence to be struck out.

If the defence and/or counterclaim shows some element of merit and there is a real possibility that the defendant will be successful at a trial then serious consideration needs to be given to continue with the litigation, as there is an increased risk regarding costs which may be awarded against an unsuccessful claimant. Of course as a result of a clear pre-action process any potential defence should have been unearthed well before the claim was issued. If, for a variety of reasons, the facts do not emerge until after the litigation has been commenced and if a situation arises where there is clearly going to be a problem in winning a case, any client needs to be told sooner rather than later.

The issue of costs in debt recovery, and indeed in litigation generally, can become paralysing to both Practitioners and to the parties they represent. Even in small claims issues, it can become a vexed question, particularly where, although there is supposed to be no provision for costs to be awarded by the court, a party who has been considered to have acted improperly during the course of proceedings can find themselves on the wrong end of a costs order.

The stakes grow higher where claims are over £5,000 and could be allocated to either the fast track or the multi-track. Here there is a real risk of costs being awarded against the losing party and those costs being higher than the actual value of the claim which is in dispute. Practitioners should never lose sight of the economic down side of debt recovery litigation on behalf of their client. All the time Practitioners should be focusing on the value of the claim and what assets may be available to enforce that claim against the defendant in the event a judgment is obtained, whether it be by default or whether it be by a full trial. 7–43

It is very easy to lose sight of this, particularly with the client who is determined to have their "day in court". A responsible Practitioner will continually remind the client of the possibility of the costs order being awarded against him/her and seek to quantify what the cost of an unfavourable award might be. It is one thing to say that "costs may be awarded against you" but it is another to say costs may be awarded against you as much as £20,000. This will certainly help the client to focus on whether or not it is worth pursuing the claim.

As to the issue of what costs might be awarded then reference is made to Chapter 4 of this book and to other leading texts the subject of litigation and costs.

Part 36 Offer

How should the claimant respond to any offer from the defendant?

Simply put, the claimant needs to decide whether or not to accept or reject the offer. 7–44

However, the way in which the rejection or acceptance is communicated to the defendant is critical.

The claimant has 21 days after service of the defendant's offer to accept the offer put forward. The response must be in writing and filed at court as well as being served on the defendant, or their solicitor.

Following the written acceptance being filed and served by the claimant, proceedings are stayed. The defendant must arrange for payment to be made to the claimant within 14 days, together with the claimant's costs as appropriate up to the relevant period, with the claimant paying the defendant's costs from the expiry of the relevant period up to the date of acceptance of the offer.

Flow charts

In the Appendix there are a series of flowcharts which show various scenarios relating to Pt 36 offers which are easy to follow. Practitioners 7–45 can use these to check where they are in proceedings and the consequences of accepting or rejecting an offer in a debt recovery case.

What are the practical consequences of accepting a Part 36 offer?

7–46 In the forefront of either the claimant or the defendant's mind when accepting a Pt 36 offer is the question of balancing the value of the claim, against the offer put forward, and against the cost of continuing with the litigation to trial.

As above, once a Pt 36 offer is accepted it has the effect of staying the proceedings, therefore there needs to be no further preparation for trial, by either party. As the offer will have taken into account the question of costs up to the point that the offer is made, acceptance of the offer also means that the question of the cost of the litigation is crystallised and consequently both parties are in the position of knowing how much the claim has actually "cost" them.

Effect of Part 36 offer at trial

7–47 Where a claimant achieves judgment at the trial which is more advantageous than the offer put forward by the defendant, the claimant will be viewed as having been justified in not accepting the Pt 36 offer beforehand. In this situation the defendant will therefore have to pay the amount of the judgment plus interest and also the claimant's costs on the standard basis (for an explanation of "standard basis" see later in this Chapter). Interest on those costs will normally only be payable from the date of judgment.

Where the amount awarded at trial is exactly the same or less than the defendant's Pt 36 offer the court is likely to make a "split costs" order under the CPR 36.14(2) unless it considers it is unjust to do so.

In determining whether the claimant has been awarded more or less than the amount of the defendant's offer a "like with like comparison" has to be made.

Where the claimant has made a claim for an amount of money judgment will be for the capital sum plus interest awarded at the trial using the judge's discretion. Usually interest will run from the date the debt arose to the judgment given at the end of the trial, or subsequently if judgment is reserved.

7–48 In the case of *Blackham v Entrepose* UK [2004] EWCA Civ 1109 which was reported in *The Times* on September 28 in that year, Brooke L.J. said that in his judgment to decide whether the claimant had achieved a more advantageous position than the Pt 36 offer he would need to compare "like with like".

If in that case the defendants had offered say £39,000 plus £1,000 of interest calculated up to the last day when the claimant could have accepted the offer but the claimant only received at trial £38,800 plus £950 interest up to that date then he could not have been said to have bettered the Pt 36 offer because he would only have achieved £39,750 as opposed to the defendant's offer which including interest was £40,000. "Like with like" comparisons can be calculated by doing the following:

(a) Interest should be calculated on what would have accrued on the sum awarded by the judge from the date interest became payable up to the last day of acceptance of the Pt 36 offer, i.e. the end of the relevant period; 7–49

(b) Then add the figure in (a) to the amount of the judgment; and

(c) If the figure in (b) is equal to or less than the amount offered by the defendant then the claimant has failed to obtain a judgment which is more advantageous than this Pt 36 offer and CPR 36.14(24) will apply.

What is a split costs order?

If CPR 36.14(2) applies then the rule provides that the court will, unless it considers it unfair, order that the defendant is entitled to: 7–50

- his costs from the date on which the relevant period expired; and
- interest on those costs.

As it is usual for the losing party to pay the winning party's costs then in a split costs order the claimant becomes the winner of the proceedings having secured a judgment for the defendant to pay him a sum of money but as he has not been awarded more than the defendant's Pt 36 offer he loses because he should have accepted that offer and by failing to do so since the relevant period has expired he has wasted the time and money both for the defendant and the court.

The effect of CPR 36.14(2) is that:

- the defendant pays the claimant's costs from when those costs first were incurred until the relevant period expired which is 7–51 usually the 21 day period unless it has been extended by an agreement in writing as part of the offer;

- the defendant will not pay the claimant any interest on those costs and those costs should be agreed by the parties or they will be assessed by the court on a standard basis; and
- the claimant pays the defendant's cost from expiry of the relevant period usually day 22 from the date of the offer being made until judgment. These can be expensive! This is the period when the litigation may well have accelerated up in preparation for trial. So these costs, where possible, should be agreed by the parties or again these in turn will be assessed by the court on a standard basis. Worse still for the claimant, the claimant is responsible for interest on those costs from when each item is incurred. Unfortunately, the rule is silent on how much interest is payable. The Court of Appeal in the case of *Bim Kemi AB v Blackburn Chemicals* [2003] EWCA Civ 889 offered some guidance on the point as to when it might be appropriate to award interest on costs before judgment. In that case the court indicated that an award of 1 per cent above base rate would usually be the appropriate rate of interest.

All of these points may therefore be summarised in a simple table as follows:

Outcome at Trial	**Expected Cost Order—As always subject to the Court's discretion**
Claimant awarded more than defendant's offer so claimant beat defendant's Pt 36 offer.	Seek and expect to be awarded costs of the claim to be paid by the defendant on the standard basis.
Claimant awarded the same or less than defendant's offer so claimant fails to beat defendant's Pt 36 offer.	Here the court will make a split costs order as set out above and the defendant will be ordered to pay the claimant's costs on a standard basis up to the date of the last day of the relevant period. From the day after the relevant period the claimant will be ordered to pay the defendant's costs on a standard basis until judgment plus interest on those costs.
Claimant fails to beat the defendant's offer at trial.	Result at trial [see losers at trial]. The claimant will be ordered to pay the defendant's costs of defending the claim on a standard basis plus interest on costs incurred from day after relevant period to judgment.

What are the issues in relation to the secrecy of the Part 36 offer?

Except in very limited circumstances a Pt 36 offer should not be revealed to the trial judge until all questions of liability and quantum have been dealt with. **7–52**

In the case of *Garratt v Saxby* [2004] EWCA Civ 341, the Court of Appeal indicated that it is for the judge to decide whether the disclosure of any offer made a fair trial possible, or indeed whether justice would be better served by the judge withdrawing from the case.

A judge in exercising that discretion was entitled to take into account additional time, cost and difficulty involved for all concerned if the hearing were to be aborted as a result of the disclosure.

Tactical considerations

Litigation at this stage is often a game of bluff and so Part 36 offers can be used by litigants and their advisers to exert pressure where the merits of a claim or a defence are weak or create the environment for sensible discussions to take place because the risk on cost for both parties can be overwhelming. **7–53**

As a case proceeds towards trial it can become uneconomic when hourly rates start to be applied in the preparation of the case for trial. Hourly rates of a £150 to £200 can soon begin to eat into a party's budget and indeed the value of the amount which is in dispute can pale into insignificance when compared against the costs that each party is running up in maintaining their positions.

In some senses it is not just the issue on costs, it is the time and the stress and strain that litigation can take on parties themselves.

Interestingly where a defendant does not accept a claimant's Pt 36 offer and the claimant equals or beats his offer at trial the defendant will be liable to pay the cost not only of himself but also the claimant. This contrasts quite sharply with the position of a claimant who fails to equal or beat his own offer but will usually be found to be in no worse position than if this offer had not been made. The upshot of this is that there is no apparent downside for a claimant in making an offer, but the defendant will be placed under a considerable pressure just by making a reasonable proposal.

Tactically, it is therefore sensible for a claimant to make an offer as soon as there is enough information to judge the amount of what that offer should be and in both parties' interest to make any offer prior to proceedings being issued.

On whom should the Part 36 offer be served?

7–54 Under CPR PD 36 para.1.2 of Pt 36, Notice of Exceptions or Notice of Withdrawal or change of terms where parties legally represented must be served on a legal representative.

Is there duty to co-operate under the rules?

7–55 Under CPR 36.8 the parties are obliged by virtue of CPR 1.3 and CPR 1.4 to cooperate and this obligation extends to explaining any procedural points they intend to take see *Hertsmere Primary Care Trust v Estate of Balasubramanium Rabindra-Anandh* [2005] 3 All E.R. 274.

What does "costs on the standard basis" mean?

7–56 If agreement cannot be reached as to the amount of costs before any hearing then under CPR 36.10 costs will be assessed in accordance to CPR 44.4 and 44.5 and the test of proportionality applies to the costs and the cost officer must take into account the conduct of the parties.

Such an assessment will have to be commenced within three months of service of the notice of acceptance in accordance with CPR 47.7.

If the sum offered in acceptance is within the small claims limit the court may, as a matter of discretion, order the payment of no more than the costs which would have been awarded if the case had proceeded on the small claims track (see *E Ivor Hughes Educational Foundation v Leach* [2005] All E.R. (D) 127 (JUN).

How is a stay lifted when a Part 36 offer is accepted?

7–57 Under CPR Pt 36.11 if a Pt 36 offer is accepted then the claim will be stayed by virtue of CPR 36.11(1).

In the context of Pt 36 offers, "stayed" does not mean that the proceedings are temporarily put to sleep, but indicates that the case is effectively over, but for the assessment of costs and any subsequent enforcement proceedings.

The question then arises as to when the court would be prepared to lift the stay. In doing so a court would have to have regard to the overriding objective and to the same principles which applys on whether to set aside a consent order. It should be noted that the court will not lift the stay simply because the offeror has failed to satisfy the terms of the Pt 36 offer.

No Response

What happens if the defendant does not respond to the claimant's claim?

In debt recovery actions the majority of all claims issued result in a default judgment. Literally this means a judgment is entered in the default of the defendant doing anything to prevent Judgment being entered against him/her/it. Judgment will be entered by the claimant completing the usual practice form on Form N255. 7–58

Depending on the forum in which the claim has been issued this is either going to be as follows:

- the form being completed on the computer system and sent to the local county court where the claim is proceeding;
- in the CPC by judgment being entered, in the CCBC via file being sent to the court for judgment to be entered electronically; and
- in relation to Money Claim Online the claimant seeking judgment through the automated system.

However, in whichever way judgment in default is entered, the requirements are strict and under the rules any judgment incorrectly obtained must be set aside irrespective of the lack of merit of any defence (see CPR 13.2).

When can judgment in default not be obtained?

If there is a hearing of the defendant's application to strike out the claimant's statement of case under CPR r.3, or an application for summary judgment is pending under Pt 24, then the claimant cannot obtain judgment in default. 7–59

What is the position where the defendant is resident outside of the jurisdiction?

If the defendant is outside of the jurisdiction and for purposes of enforcement abroad a judgment based on merits is required then instead of seeking default judgment under CPR Pt 12 a claimant would best be advised to make an application for summary judgment under CPR Pt 24 to ensure that final judgment is going to be recognised by the foreign court. 7–60

What happens if judgment in default is not entered?

7–61 As mentioned earlier where judgment in default is not entered then the claim will be stayed under the provisions of CPR r.15.11 where the defendant fails to acknowledge service or file a defence and the claimant allows six months or more to pass before taking any further action.

What is the meaning of "default judgment"?

7–62 Under the CPR "default judgment" means a judgment obtained without a trial where a defendant has failed to file an acknowledgement of service or has failed to file a defence (see Pt 10 and Pt 15 of the CPR respectively in relation to those two areas).

Must a certificate of service be filed?

7–63 Where the claimant has served the claim form personally he cannot obtain default judgment unless he has filed a certificate of service in Form N215. Where the court has served the claim form there is no such requirement.

When in a debt recovery action would an application be needed?

7–64 An application will be necessary under CPR Pt 23 (see Chapter 9 of this book) where a default judgment is sought against the defendant who is served outside of the jurisdiction or who resides within the jurisdiction but is domiciled in Scotland, Northern Ireland or any other conventional regulation territory or against a state. The application must be supported by evidence and will be contained in the particulars of claim where verified by a Statement of Truth or in the notice of application itself but again verified by a Statement of Truth. In both cases the evidence will be admissible as evidence for hearings other than a trial.

Is default judgment available against the crown?

7–65 Default judgment is only available against the Crown after it has been considered by a Master or district judge.

Judicial consideration needs to be given as to whether the claim has been properly served. Section 18 of the Crown Proceedings Act

1947 and r.6.5(8) of the CPR include strict requirements for service of process on government departments. A list of who to serve is reproduced as an Annex to the Practice Direction to Pt 66 of the CPR.

How is judgment entered against more than one defendant?

The procedure for obtaining judgment in default against more than one defendant is set out in CPR 12.8. 7–66

Is judgment in default possible for "costs only"?

Provision is made within the rules to obtain a judgment in default for costs only under CPR 12.9. 7–67

What can the claimant specify in relation to default judgment?

Under CPR 12.5(1) a claimant can specify the date for payment of the judgment and the instalments, if any, which he is prepared to accept. 7–68

In effect, the claimant can invite the defendant to pay by a particular date or to pay by instalments but in the absence of such an invitation the judgment will be payable forthwith.

If the defendant wishes to respond with proposals for the date he wants to make payment or the rate of instalments he wishes to make then he can apply to vary the judgment under CPR Part 13.

How is interest calculated on a default judgment?

Interest is dealt with under CPR 12.6 (see para.12.7 for the procedure for deciding the amount of interest). 7–69

Rule 12.6 provides for the claimant to be allowed to claim an amount of interest provided he has complied with the conditions set out in Rule 12.6(1) which includes ensuring that the claim for interest is properly pleaded in the statement of case.

The rate of interest is the rate applicable to judgment debts when the claim form is issued. The rate of interest on judgment debts has not so far changed since 1993.

If that rate were to subsequently decrease from the current rate of 8 per cent the claimant would still be entitled to the previous higher rate if that was available at the time of issue but again it will be open to the defendant to have the amount varied.

7–70 If the rate of interest were to increase it would be up to the claimant to enter judgment for the amount of his money claim and to apply separately for the court to decide the amount of interest that could be awarded (see CPR 12.10).

If the contract under which the debt is made provides for a rate of interest higher than the rate applicable to judgment debts the claimant must apply for interest to be assessed under the court order by virtue of CPR 12.7.

Interestingly, the rule itself does not allow the claimant to abandon that higher rate of interest so as to be entitled to a default judgment so claimants have to think carefully about whether they wish to claim that higher rate at the outset of their claim and then take more time to have the interest assessed at the end when default judgment is due or simply to stay with the statutory provision for interest so that there is no hold up when it comes to entering judgment.

What is the procedure for obtaining a default judgment for costs only?

7–71 If the claimant wishes to obtain a default judgment for costs only then he will use the particular part of CPR 12 at CPR 12.9 which provides for this situation.

If the claim is for fixed costs this can be applied for by filing the necessary request but if it is the other type of costs then an application must be made in accordance with Pt 23. Where an application is made then judgment will be made with the amount to be decided on by the court.

What is the position where there are two or more defendants?

7–72 If a claim against one defendant can be dealt with separately from the claim against the other or others, then it is possible to enter default judgment against one defendant and the claimant can continue with proceedings against the other defendant. However, if the claim against the defaulting defendant cannot be dealt with separately from the claim against the others then the court will not enter default judgment and it will have to be dealt with by way of an application at the same time it disposes of the claims against the other defendant(s).

How can a default judgment be set aside?

CPR Pt 13 of the rules sets out the procedure where an application is to be made to set aside or vary judgments entered in default of either acknowledgement of service or in default of defence. 7–73

The situation occurs because the majority of judgments are obtained just by simply filing the request on the appropriate form. The merits of the claim have never been anywhere near a judge, or any form of judicial decision-making, and so when a defendant decides that he wants to apply to vary or set aside the judgment this procedure under Pt 13 is the mechanism for doing so.

When must a court set aside a default judgment?

The court will be required to set aside the default judgment when it was wrongly entered for one or more of the following reasons: 7–74

- the judgment was obtained prematurely, i.e. before the time of acknowledgment of service and/or the time for serving a defence had expired—with a computer system this is unlikely to happen;
- the judgment was obtained after the defendant had applied to have the particulars of claim struck out under CPR 3.4 or the claim summarily dismissed under CPR Pt 24 and before the application had been disposed of;
- judgment had been obtained even though the whole claim including interest and cost had already been paid or satisfied; or
- in, relation to a money judgment, it had been obtained after the defendant had filed or served an admission with a request for time to pay.

Under CPR 13.2 all these circumstances give rise to the opportunity for the judgment to be set aside or varied.

However, where judgment is to be set aside it is not unusual for the court to insist on certain conditions being met from the defendant and also for costs to be awarded against a claimant.

The defendant who wishes to apply to set aside judgment is going to need to act quickly and certainly a failure to do so will be looked at by the court in whether or not to exercise its discretion (see CPR 13.3(2)). 7–75

However, claimants should not simply rely on a delay by the defendant to make an application as a certainty the application will be rejected, as was the case in *National Westminster Bank Plc v Bowles* [2005] EWHC 182 Q.B.

What is the test for a successful application to set aside?

7–76 Under CPR 13.3(1)(a) if the defendant can show that there is a "real prospect of success" in defending the claim (which is similar to the test under the application for summary judgment under CPR Pt 24) then the application may succeed.

However, the burden of proof falls on the defendant to show that he has a real prospect of success rather than just a "fanciful" one.

In the case of *Royal Brompton Hospital NHS Trust v Hammond* [2001] BLR 297, 317, the Court of Appeal held that, in looking for the standards for the court to apply in such an application, it was not the balance of probabilities test which would be needed at trial, but instead, whether the evidence could be reasonably be expected to be available at the trial as to whether the application should be successful.

There have been a series of cases on the point and in the case of *ED & F Man Liquid Products Ltd v Patel* [2003] EWCA Civ 472 it was held that the defence relied on must carry some degree of conviction.

Tactically, if any claimants want to get to default judgment as quickly as possible then they should set their system so that default judgment is entered immediately on the date the judgment is available. If met with a set aside application the defence should be carefully evaluated, certainly the defendant is in a weaker position by allowing default judgment to be entered against it than it was had it served its defence within the proper timescale as provided prior to judgment being entered.

What is the position if there is an issue on service of the judgment?

7–77 If proceedings were served in accordance with the CPR Part 6 then the fact the defendant had no knowledge of the claim before judgment in default was entered is not in itself a sufficiently good reason for setting the judgment aside (see *Akram v Adam* [2005] 1 All E.R. 741).

In this case the defendant's usual or last known address was a room in a house in which the claimant, his landlord also lived. The claim form was correctly posted to the house thereby raising the irrebuttable presumption of deemed service. The claimant later obtained judgment in his absence and it was held on appeal the defendant was not entitled to have that judgment set aside. This was done on the basis that in all the circumstances it was found the defendant had no real prospect of successfully defending the claim and simply setting the judgment aside because he apparently had failed to receive prior notice of the claim would have been pointless.

However, if it is found that the service of the judgment was "irregular" the Court of Appeal in the case of *Nelson v Clearsprings (Management Limited)* [2006] EWCA Civ 1252, indicated that the following steps would need to be taken:

(1) if the defendant could show he had not been served or not deemed to have been served with the claim form at all then he would normally be entitled to an order setting the judgment aside and to his costs in making the application;

(2) if, when the claimant is served with the application to set aside by the defendant he believes he can show the defendant has no real prospect of successfully defending the claim then he can apply to the court for an order dispensing the service of the claim form under CPR 24.4(1) and apply forthwith for summary judgment and for summary judgment on his claim;

(3) if such an application by the defendant and costs application by the claimant are made, the court should make an order as it considers just; and

(4) if the claimant can show the defendant has been guilty of "inexcusable delay" since learning the judgment has been entered against him but not taking any action to set aside then the court would be entitled to make no order on the defendant's application for that reason. The judgment would then stand perhaps subject to any direction by the court whether in relation to statutory interest due on the judgment or otherwise.

In the case of *Messer Griesheim GmbH v Goyal MG Gases Pvt Ltd* [2006] EWHC 79, the claimant did apply successfully to set aside its default judgment but at the same time was granted summary judgment on the same claim for the same amount. It did so because although the summary judgment would be enforceable in India against the defendant company, the default judgment would not. The defendant was an Indian Company with no, or at least no known, assets in England and Wales or anywhere else in the world except in India.

What conditions might the court impose in setting aside default judgment?

7–78 Under CPR 3.1(3) the court may make any order setting aside judgment subject to various conditions.

Will the application be transferred?

7–79 The application to set aside default judgment will lead to an automatic transfer of the claim to the defendant's home court if not already being dealt with at that court. (See CPR 13.4 which applies where the claim is for a specified sum of money and is not in a specialist list and the defendant is an individual and the claim has not been automatically transferred to his home court.)

Rule 13.6 states that in cases where the claimant has abandoned a claim for certain remedies in order to obtain a default judgment on request in accordance with 12.4(3).

Chapter 8

Managing a Defended Claim

Introductory Comments

In a debt recovery department a Practitioner is looking to get default judgment as quickly as possible. However, there is a need for debt recovery departments to be able to anticipate and handle defended actions and to be able to keep the client informed of what is happening in relation to a case which moves from being a straightforward debt claim to a more complicated piece of litigation. Before the CPR there was a tendency for Debt Recovery Practitioners to stay away from defended matters and perhaps pass them to colleagues in the litigation department or perhaps, for more complex claims, to pass them to counsel. Times have moved on and there are litigants in person being able to handle their own small claims and being encouraged to do so through the CPR. There is a need for Debt Recovery Practitioners to handle confidently defended actions when they come across them. 8–01

With that in mind this chapter will outline the key steps through a defended action on the small claims, fast track and multi-track although for complex claims readers are encouraged to check the rules thoroughly and go to one of the leading texts be it the *White Book* or the *Green Book*.

In the case study to this book the parties Tom and Margot have prepared and filed their claim, defence and counterclaim and the case study documentation deals with the key documents needed to deal with the small claims track which have been completed. These appear in the Appendix.

How should a claimant respond to an allocation questionnaire being sent?

The allocation questionnaire will be sent to all parties to the claim and is the first stage in the court's case management process. In the 8–02

Practice Direction accompanying CPR Pt 26 in relation to case management, the rules actually draw the party's attention to the overriding objective defined in CPR 1.1 and the duty of the court to further that objective by actually managing cases (see CPR 1.4).

There is also the requirement of the parties to help further that objective (see CPR 1.3). The allocation questionnaire referred to in Pt 26 of the rules will be in Form N149 and the court will use the information provided by the parties in the questionnaire to ensure that the claim is then allocated to the correct track within the county court procedure or High Court arena to progress the claim to trial.

Do the parties have to fill in the questionnaire?

8–03 The parties need to complete and return the questionnaire to the court by the date specified. Failure to do so will mean that the court will make whatever order it sees fit, which is likely to be an "unless order" stating that unless the questionnaire is filed by a specified date then the claim/defence will be struck out (see CPR 26.5(5)). Under the Practice Direction to CPR Pt 26 there is also a requirement that an estimate of costs is filed and served when the application questionnaire is filled out by a party to a claim which is outside the limits of the small claims track, i.e. the value of the claim is £5,000 or above. The requirement is to comply with s.6 of the Costs Practice Direction supplementing the CPR Pt 43 to 48.

Compliance with that obligation will be made if a party files and serves a statement showing the figures for base costs incurred and to be incurred which, if successful, he expects to recover from the other party. The estimate should also show an itemised breakdown of how it is calculated and separate the amount for profit cost, disbursements and VAT. Ideally, it should be in the same illustrated form as Precedent H in the schedule to the Costs Practice Direction. For Debt Recovery Practitioners this means being very aware of how a defended matter is going to be charged and, as part of the overall structure of the debt recovery department, Practitioners should have access to a cost draftsmen who is an expert in legal costs and who should be available to assist either on a case by case basis for the production of such an estimate or has reviewed the cost of the department as a whole and set up templates for Practitioners to use.

How is the allocation questionnaire to be served?

8–04 The same rules regarding service and deemed service mentioned in Chapter 6 will apply to the service of the allocation questionnaire by the court.

Can the parties agree a different time for filing the allocation questionnaire?

The answer here is no. Unlike other timetable dates set by the court it is not possible for the parties to agree a variation between themselves for the filing of the allocation questionnaire (see CPR 26.3(6A)). **8–05**

When will the court send the allocation questionnaire where there are two or more defendants?

Where there are two or more defendants and at least one of them has filed the defence the court will serve the allocation questionnaire under the CPR 26.3(1) when all the defendants have filed the defence, or when the period for the filing of the last defence has expired, depending on which comes first. **8–06**

Will proceedings be transferred to the defendant's home court?

Proceedings are automatically transferred to the defendant's home court (as defined under CPR 2.3) when a defence is filed because, in a debt recovery matter, the rules on automatic transfer will apply. **8–07**

As the claim will be for the specified amount of money it is likely it will have been commenced in a court which is not the defendant's home court, it is likely that the defendant will be an individual and for the purposes of this rule the claim must not have been transferred either on application to set aside or vary a default judgment under CPR 13.4 or to deal with the determination of rate of payment by a judge under CPR 14.12. **8–08**

Do special rules apply in relation to the service of the allocation questionnaire at the Production Centre?

Reference should be made to the CPR 7.10 and the accompanying Practice Direction CPR PD 7C. **8–09**

At para.5.2(1) of the Practice Direction the filing of the defence will mean that the court officer at the centre will send a notice to the claimant seeking notification within 28 days of whether the claimant wishes to proceed. If the claimant (referred to in the Practice Direction as "centre user") does not notify the officer within the time specified in the notice that he wishes the claim to proceed, the claim will be stayed and the court will notify the parties.

If, however, the claimant wishes to proceed then the proceedings will not be transferred to the defendant's home court until the claimant notifies the court officer that he wishes the claim to continue.

In outline how should the allocation questionnaire be completed?

8–10 The claimant should consider whether or not a stay of proceedings is needed to allow the parties an opportunity of trying to resolve the claim through negotiation with the other party or seek alternative dispute resolution (see CPR 26.4(1)).

The CPR 26.4(2) does not provide for the claim to be stayed if both parties make a request to the court. The court also may stay the proceedings if it considers it is appropriate to do so. In that instance it is therefore possible for there to be a stay of the proceedings even if only one party requests the stay.

If a stay is requested, or the court makes one of its own motion, then the stay will normally be for a period of one month. However, it is possible for the court to stay the proceedings for any period, or to extend the stay for a further month once the original stay has expired.

It should, however, be noted that the court will not continue to stay the claim indefinitely. If a party requires an extension to the original one month period it will need to be able to demonstrate to the court that a real effort has been made in trying to resolve the matter within the initial period and that there is a realistic prospect of the matter being resolved within any extended period.

Can the claimant choose the location of the trial?

8–11 The answer to this is that within reason, yes the location of the trial can be chosen by the claimant. Normally, however, it will take place at the defendant's home court (see definition of defendant's home court at CPR 2.3) as the proceedings will have been transferred to that court once the defence is filed.

However, if there is a particular reason why the trial should take place in another court then the claimant should indicate that in Part B of the allocation questionnaire response. It may be that a claimant has difficulties in travelling to a court, or that certain facilities need to be available at the court, such as one of the parties is disabled or has a disabled witness and these facilities are not available at the allocated court house.

If the reasons are set out for why the trial should take place at somewhere other than the defendant's home court then these will be considered and the court will make it's decision.

Usually, the claim will remain with the existing court and it would be simply transferred so far as the trial hearing is concerned.

How does the protocol practice direction affect this stage of debt recovery proceedings?

As discussed in Chapter 5 the pre-action protocols are essentially a set of "guidelines" as to how a matter should be handled prior to proceedings being issued. **8–12**

At the allocation stage a party has to indicate whether or not the matter is subject to a pre-action protocol and, if so, confirm that it has complied with that protocol. As debt recovery proceedings are themselves not subject to a specific pre-action protocol, a party must indicate whether or not it has exchanged information and documents with the other party so as to try and settle the dispute.

By this stage of the debt recovery matter it would be hoped that details of the debt or debts outstanding and supporting documentation would have gone across to the defendant who will have had an opportunity to respond. Any response and, resulting queries would have been dealt with so that the parties in completing the allocation questionnaire can say that, so far as possible, they have exchanged information and documents to comply with the requirement.

How should the case management information part of the allocation questionnaire be completed?

In completing this part of the allocation questionnaire it is important to remember that it will be used to allocate the case to one of the three tracks, be it small claims, fast track or multi-track and that track will then has its own set of rules and Practice Directions on how the matter will be treated going forward. **8–13**

The Debt Recovery Practitioner must ensure that accurate information as to the value of the claim (see Chapter 5 in relation to "statement of value") is given so that the case is allocated to the correct track and that suitable directions will then be given to progress the claim. If this section is not completed or completed incorrectly then the claim will be allocated to the wrong track. Difficulties then begin to arise regarding the progress of the claim to trial. It is also important to bear in mind that a party who completes this information recklessly may be penalised on costs by the court

How should the section "applications" be completed?

8–14 If a party intends to make an application, for example for summary judgment, or to amend the proceedings, then this should be indicated on the form in this part of the form. If any application has already been made then details should be provided as to what the application was for and if a hearing date has already been given then this should be stated.

If a party is intending to make an application it should indicate what the application is for and include a copy of the application notice on Form N244 with the completed allocation questionnaire. This should then be returned to the court with the appropriate fee. Details of fees for applications can be located on the court service website at *http://www.hmcourts-service.gov.uk/infoabout/fees/county.htm*.

What information should be given about witnesses on the allocation questionnaire?

8–15 The parties are required to provide details of witnesses who they intend to rely on in support of their claim. So far as the case study is concerned this would mean Tom providing details of other customers in the way that they have interacted with him.

In response Margot would include witnesses who saw the alleged damage to her rose bushes and perhaps was present when she asked Tom whether the manure was the right type to put on her rose garden!

How should the issue of experts be dealt with in debt recovery actions?

8–16 The Debt Recovery Practitioner would have made some early decisions well before proceedings were issued about the use of experts and if there is already an expert's report then it has to be indicated in the allocation questionnaire. As no pre-action protocol is in place then there is an expectation by the court on both parties that they would have gathered evidence *before* issuing proceedings.

To consider at this stage whether expert evidence is required when completing the allocation questionnaire is far too late in the day as it should have been one of the first matters to be considered at the outset of instructions of the claim being made.

It should also be noted that there is no provision for expert evidence within the small claims track procedure.

The three tracks how do they apply to debt recovery actions?

The statement of value in the claim will be the starting point on how a claim is to be allocated for trial. 8–17

In simple terms the three tracks are as follows:

Small claims track	Value of claim up to £5,000
Fast track claim	Value of claim between £5,000 to £15,000
Multi-track claim	Value of claim exceeding £15,000

How is a low value claim with complex issues dealt with?

If a Debt Recovery Practitioner considers that the small claims track procedure (see below) is not suitable as the forum to try the claim a request can be made that the case to be allocated to one of the other tracks. A justification as to why it should be allocated to a higher track is going to be needed as well as reasons why it is not suitable for the small claims procedure. It could be that the value of the claim, although below £5,000, has resulted in complex issues to be considered and expert evidence is needed. However, track allocation is one of the cornerstones in the changes to the CPR which occurred in 1999 and a case will not be taken off track easily, so a Debt Recovery Practitioner is going to have to work hard to justify a change in the track. Allocating a case to the wrong track without good reason can result in penalties being awarded by the court in respect of costs. 8–18

Can a hearing be postponed?

In a busy debt recovery department there may only be a few people who can actually deal with defended matters and so occasionally a date is going to be given for a trial and the person needed is not going to be in the office. 8–19

If this happens then the Practitioner needs to consider how long the actual trial is going to last and whether the person handling the case or indeed any of the witnesses in fact will not be able to attend court on that day.

Anticipating the length of a trial is always something of an art and comes really from experience. It is important to bear in mind that every witness that is called will need to give evidence in chief and be cross-examined and possibly re-examined and this is where a formal court day of five hours can be eaten up. So if a Practitioner thinks that a trial is going to take 5 hours or 10 hours or 15 hours, be that one, two or three days then they need to indicate that on the allocation questionnaire.

Is a request for directions needed?

8–20 The court will prefer the parties to try and agree directions between them.

In small claims matters the court will normally give standard directions once the allocation questionnaire has been filed, as to how it wishes to deal with the issue of witness evidence and the disclosure of documents. These standard directions will go on to include the disclosure of any documentation which either party intends to rely on at trial, together with the exchange of witness statements and the time table for this.

For cases allocated to both the fast track and multi-track then more detailed directions will be needed which will relate to issues such as witness evidence and disclosure documents along with other issues pertinent to the individual case. A Practitioner can expect a far more detailed set of directions in relation to these two higher tracks with specific dates for completion of each direction being included.

Wherever possible, these directions again should be agreed between the parties but if a party has not been able to agree directions then a list should be attached to the allocation of questionnaire asking the court to make those directions as part of the overall case management of the claim.

If the other side file their own suggested list of directions the court will then consider both lists before making a final order as to what directions it is prepared to make. It has to be remembered that the issue of directions relating to the claim is now very much with the court and the judge.

Parties can expect that if they filed their own request for directions the court may list the matter for hearing and require all parties to attend so those directions can be agreed before it makes its final order.

Is a statement of invoice required in relation to costs?

8–21 In relation to small claims then there is no need to provide details of costs as there is no entitlement to recover costs in small claims; although see the notes on the small claims track below.

It has been mentioned above that for cases which are to be allocated to one of the higher tracks then a cost assessment would be required in accordance with the necessary Practice Direction.

In trying to provide that estimate a Practitioner should have consideration to the amount of work which is going to be needed to prepare for trial such as:

- how many witnesses are going to be called, how long it would take to prove their evidence and prepare their witness statement;
- whether experts are going to be needed and again how long it will take to instruct them and then for them to prepare their reports and consider the outcomes of those reports in consultation with the client;
- pick carefully the number of documents which will need to be collated and paginated for the court bundle and consider a realistic estimate for the time taken to prepare a list of documents which can be very time consuming;
- the Practitioner should also consider whether counsel should be instructed and if so how long it would take to prepare instructions to counsel perhaps to advise on both the evidence and to attend the hearing to represent the claimant and whether a conference will be needed with the counsel and if so how long that will take.

One can see from the list above that that the hours spent in preparing a case for trial can soon add up. Ideally, in a defended scenario there will be some form of time recording where, even if the full cost of the time taken to prepare the trial cannot be passed on to the client, then at least the cost of preparing for trial is known.

As mentioned earlier instructing a professional Costs Draftsman to prepare a detailed statement of cost is a sensible option at this stage for either an individual case or as a part of an overall process in a busy department. Details of costs draftsmen can be found at *http://www.alcd.org.uk/.htm*.

What other information might be required?

Practitioners need to use their initiative to consider whether there **8–22**
is any further information that is going to be required in effectively briefing the court on the extent of handling the defended claim. If there are other issues to consider then details should be put on the final page of the allocation questionnaire. This part of the form is there to be used to raise genuine issues affecting the management of the claim.

What are the three tracks?

8–23 As mentioned earlier within the civil court system there are three track systems to handle claims which are:

- the small claims track;
- the fast track; and
- multi track.

The claim will be allocated to one of these tracks depending on a number of factors, the starting point of which is the statement of value that was put in the original claim form and the amount which was included on the allocation questionnaire.

We will now look at these three tracks as follows:

Small claims track

8–24 Under CPR 26.6 so far as debt recovery is concerned then the small claims track is a normal track for a claim which has a financial value of not more than £5,000. There are some exceptions to this but they are outside the scope of this work.

Where a claim is originally above £5,000 so far as the statement of value is concerned but before allocation the defendant makes an admission reducing the claim to an amount which is beneath the limit then the track reverts back to the small claims track (see CPR PD 26 para.7.4(4)).

CPR Part 27 deals entirely with the small claims track procedure, and is the guiding part of the CPR dealing with the process through the county court.

So far as the issues mentioned above are concerned it is worth noting as follows:

- **Experts**—No experts can be used in a small claims track without leave (see CPR 27.5).
- **Legal representation**—A party may be represented by a Lay Representative provided that party is present throughout (see CPR PD 27 para.3.1 and 3.2). Practitioners will perhaps be pleased to know that the conduct of the hearing is informal and the court has a very wide discretion as to how that hearing should be conducted. This does mean that where a defendant is without legal representation the district judge will often be more flexible in how the defendant prepares and offers his evidence to the court than perhaps a legally qualified representative might be allowed to do.

- **Costs**—Costs, including the cost of any appea, are limited by CPR 27.4 although, if by consent a case with a financial value above £5,000 and below £15,000 was allocated for the small claims track for expediency, then the "no costs court rule" in CPR 27.14(5) will not apply.

It should be noted in small claims matters that the although the court may not order a party to pay a sum to another party in respect of its costs fees and expenses, there is provision under CPR 27.14(2)(g) that the court may decide to impose a costs order by summarily assessing costs to be paid by a party who has behaved unreasonably. **8–25**

In debt recovery matters this can happen and so an understanding of what "behaved unreasonably" means is needed. Types of behaviour which might provoke the court to make an order in these terms includes the making of unnecessary applications, failing to comply with directions or orders, refusing to negotiate, causing late adjournments of the hearing, or deliberately misstating the value of a claim so as to cause it to be allocated to the small claims track instead of to the fast track in order to avoid the subsequent liability on costs.

- **Appeal**—The CPR Pt 52 applies to appeals in small claims but with modifications to reduce cost (see CPR PD 52 para.5.8). This now means following the revocation of previous rules CPR 27.12 and 27.13 that permission to appeal in a small claims track matter is now required and reference should be made to CPR Pt 52 in relation to appeals.
- **Final Remedy**—It should be noted that although a case might be allocated to the small claims track that does not mean the court's jurisdiction is fettered in any final remedy that it can make. Under CPR 27.3 the court has, as said earlier, a very wide jurisdiction which includes granting a judgment for any sum and any final remedy which it could have granted had the claim been allocated to the multi-track. For example in a small claims track the court may award interest of any amount, it may grant an injunction but its power to award costs is restricted.
- **Directions**—The court will give standard directions and fix a date for the final hearing as provided in CPR 27.4 and standard directions means that each party must, at least 14 days before the date fixed for the final hearing, file and serve on every other party copies of all documents, including expert's reports, on which they intend to rely along with other standard directions set out in the relevant Practice Direction to Pt 27.

Usually, the court will give directions without any hearing particularly if the claim only requires those standard directions. Under CPR **8–26**

27.7 the court does have power to add, vary or revoke directions. In CPR PD 27 para.10 at Appendix B the standard directions of a small claim case are set out and at Appendix C there is a set of special directions.

- **Experts**—Permission will be required in a small claims track to rely on expert evidence and that application should be made under CPR 27.6(1)(a) or a request should be made in box D in the allocation questionnaire.
- **Preliminary hearing**—The court may hold a preliminary hearing for the consideration of the claim but only if it considers special directions are needed or it appears that the party must attend the court to understand what to do with any special directions. If a preliminary hearing is felt to be needed the court must give at least 14 days notice of the date of the hearing (see CPR 27.6(3)).

The court may also treat the preliminary hearing as the final hearing if the parties agree. It may also hold a preliminary hearing if it is minded to dispose of the claim on the basis that one or more of the parties has no real prospect of success at the final hearing or it wants to strike out a statement of case or part of a statement on the basis it discloses there are no reasonable grounds for bringing the claim (see CPR 3.4).

- **Conduct of hearing**—At a small claims hearing, a party has the right to be represented by a "Lay Representative". A company just as much as an individual has the right to be represented by a Lay Representative, and CPR 39.6 in relation to representation at hearings by companies does not apply to small claims and nothing in CPR PD 27 para.3.2(4) dilutes the right of a company to have a Lay Representative (see *Sunrule Limited v Avinue Limited* (2003) EWCA Civ 1942).

8–27 The court can adopt any method of proceeding at a hearing that it considers to be fair and hearings are informal. As a result the strict rules on evidence do not apply and the court does not even need to take evidence on oath. The court may also limit cross-examination.

- **Non-Attendance**—If a party does not attend the final hearing it must: give notice to the court at least seven days before the hearing date that it will not attend has served on the other party at least seven days before the hearing any documents which it has filed at court it has requested the court to decide the claim in its absence confirmed compliance with both giving written notice to the court and confirmation that documents have been served the court will take into account the party's statement of case and any other documents it has filed and served when it then decides the claim (see CPR 27.9(1)).

If a claimant, however, does not attend the hearing and give the notice referred to at least seven days before the hearing date that it will not be attending, then the court may strike out the claim (see CPR 27.9(2)).

If a defendant does not attend the hearing or give the necessary notice at least seven days in advance that it will not be attending and the claimant does attend the hearing or give the notice referred to at least seven days before that it will not be there, the court may decide the claim on the basis of the evidence of the claimant alone. In the situation that neither party attends or gives notice, the court may strike out the claim or any defence and counterclaim. That said, under CPR 27.10 the matter may be disposed of without a hearing if all the parties agree. **8–28**

- **Setting aside judgment or rehearing**—If a party does not attend court at the hearing of the claim and did not give the relevant notice under CPR 27.9(1) there is provision under CPR 27.11(1) for the party to apply for an order that any judgment be set aside and the claim re-heard.

However, that application needs to be made not more than 14 days after the date on which notice of judgment was served on the party and the court can only grant an application under CPR 27.11(2) if the applicant:

- had a good reason for not attending or being represented at the hearing or giving the written notice required; and
- has a reasonable prospect of success at any hearing.

If the court is convinced that there should be a re-hearing or the judgment set side, then the court will fix a new date for the hearing of the claim and that must take place immediately after the hearing of the application to set the judgment aside and this may be dealt with by the judge who set aside the judgment.

However, a party cannot apply to have judgment set aside under this rule if the court dealt with the claim without a hearing under CPR 27.10. **8–29**

- **Evidence**—Helpfully the Practice Direction to Pt 27 sets out in Appendix A the information and documentation the court needs in particular types of case, which includes building disputes, repairs, goods sold and similar contractual claims. The following type of documentation is required as follows:

- Any written contract;
- Photographs;
- Any plans;
- A list of works complained of;
- A list of any outstanding works;
- Any relevant estimate invoice or receipt including any relating to repairs to each of the defects;
- Invoices for work done or goods supplied;
- Estimates of work to be completed; and
- Evaluation of the work done to date

What is the position on costs if the claim is allocated to another track?

8–30 If a claim is allocated to another track then the rule on small claims track costs under CPR 27.14 will no longer apply after the claim has been allocated and fast track or multi track costs will apply from the date of reallocation.

Fast Track

8–31 For claims of the value between £5,000 to £15,000 then the normal track will be the fast track which is dealt with entirely under its own part of the rules being CPR Pt 28.

When the court receives the allocation questionnaire if it decides that the value of the claim means the case must be allocated to this track it will then provide detailed case management directions on the progress of the claim. These directions will provide details of what the parties need to do as well as the timetable for when they need to be done by (see CPR 28.2).

8–32 Fast track cases are designed to move quickly to trial and the intention is that there should be no more than 30 weeks from the time the claim is allocated to this track to the time of the final hearing (see CPR 28.2(4)).

Interestingly, the trial for matters allocated to this track should not be expected to last for more than one day and any oral expert evidence must be limited to one expert per party (see CPR 28.3.5).

To enable the court to assess the issues in a fast track case it will hold a case management conference at which all the parties will be expected to set out the directions that they want but have not yet sought on the allocation questionnaire. This ensures that the court deals with its duty to deal with as many issues as possible on one occasion (see CPR 1.4(2)(i)).

Such a conference may take place by telephone if arranged in accordance with the directions set out at para.6.5 of CPR PD 23 or with the pilot scheme set under CPR PD 23B. Alternatively it may be done with the use of written submissions in accordance with CPR PD 28.

At the time of the case management conference the court will fix the trial date or period not to exceed three weeks within which the trial is to take place. 8–33

Before listing a claim for trial the court will send the parties a pre-trial checklist and this will be sent out not more than eight weeks before the trial, date or the beginning of the trial date period.

The court will give the parties at least three weeks notice of the day of the trial, unless in acceptable circumstances the court directs that shorter notice is to be given.

It should be noted the courts power to award trial costs is limited in accordance with CPR Pt 46 and in particular CPR 26.2.

Directions

In a fast track case disclosure is going to be more formalised and directions will deal with this. The court may make an order for disclosure of documents and the disclosure can be limited or dispensed with altogether. When the case is allocated to the fast track the court will give directions for the management of the case along with a timetable. In fast track cases courts also start to plan the date for the actual trial itself which is generally referred to as the "trial window" (see CPR PD 28 para.7.1(2)). 8–34

Costs

Costs are fixed in a fast track case will be limited as follows: 8–35

Value of the claim	Amount of fast track trial cost which court may award
Up to £3,000	£350
More than £3,000 but not more than £10,000	£500
More than £10,000	£750

It should be noted that under CPR 46.3 the court can award a higher level of costs but these are not limitless and the circumstances in which they will be awarded are restricted.

As discussed in Chapter 7 in relation to fast track cases where Pt 36 offers are made then the limits on costs will be another factor to take into account. In the event that a party is served with a Pt 36 offer, they will have to consider carefully whether in the event of losing the proceedings they can afford to pay costs limited to the meagre amount set out above.

It is also possible for a court to award costs against a party even if they are successful where it finds that a party has acted inappropriately during the course of proceedings and failed to comply with any orders or where it has pursued vexatious litigation. This is unlikely in a debt recovery matter but one should be aware of it.

Case management timetables

8–36 In a fast track case if a party wishes to vary a date which has been fixed by the court for either, the return of its pre-trial checklist the trial itself, or the trial window, then an application will have to be made to the court.

Any of these dates cannot be varied simply by the parties looking to agree a variation (as was the case pre-1999) if the variation upsets the date of the return of the pre-trial checklist, the trial date or the trial window.

Pre-trial checklist (aka "listing questionnaire")

8–37 The pre-trial checklist or, as is known by Practitioners, the listing questionnaire, will be sent out by the court for completion and must be returned by the parties on the date specified. The court may not send the listing questionnaire if it considers the claim can proceed to trial without it. Filing the listing questionnaire must not be more than eight weeks before the trial date or the beginning of the trial window. Again, in a debt recovery department these dates need to be diarised and warning systems put in place to ensure that at least a sensible buffer period is created so that it gives time for compliance.

In the event that a party does not file a listing questionnaire then an "Unless Order" will be made which will require the listing questionnaire to be filed within seven days of service of the order otherwise the party can expect the claim, defence, or any counterclaim, to be struck out without further order of the court.

If one party files a listing questionnaire but the other party does not, or a party has failed to give all the relevant information, or the court considers that a hearing is necessary to enable it to decide what further directions are needed for trial, then it may give those directions as it thinks appropriate.

Experts

The continuing duty of the parties is to assist the court and to cooperate with each other when fixing the trial date to ensure that all the relevant material and evidence is available including expert evidence. **8–38**

Giving directions

These will be given by the trial judge completing a tick box form and the parties can assist the court by completing this form and agreeing before the case management conference what is required. The form provides a large space at the end headed "other directions" for the parties to add in non-standard directions without the need for a formal application under CPR Pt 23. The most common "standard directions" are set out in the Appendix to the CPR PD 28 and include the following: **8–39**

- Further statements of case;
- Request for further information;
- Disclosure of documents;
- Witnesses of fact;
- Expert evidence;
- Questions to expert;
- Request for information;
- Documents to be filed with the pre-trial checklists;
- Dates for filing pre-trial checklist and the trial; and
- Directions following filing of pre-trial checklist in relation to expert evidence.

In relation to directions following the filing of the pre-trial checklist the directions will include matters relating to expert evidence, the trial timetable itself, the trial bundle and directions on settlement if this is achieved before the hearing.

Trial timetable

8–40 The court sets the timetable in consultation with the parties (see CPR 39.4) and the likely trial timetables may be along the following lines:

Disclosure	–	4 weeks
Exchange of witness statements	–	10 weeks
Exchange of experts' reports	–	14 weeks
Sending of pre-trial checklists (listing questionnaires) by the court	–	20 weeks
Filing of completed pre-trial checklists	–	22 weeks
hearing	–	30 weeks

The above periods will run from the date of notice of allocation (see CPR PD 28 para.3).

The all important accompanying Practice Direction to Pt 28 also deals with the following matters in relation to fast track:

Variation of directions	–	CPR PD 28 paragraph 4
The consequences of failing to deal with case management directions	–	CPR PD 28 paragraph 5
Requirements as to the pre-trial checklists (listing questionnaires)	–	CPR PD 28 paragraph 6
The trial itself	–	CPR PD 28 paragraph 8

Multi-track trials

8–41 Multi-track is for cases above £15,000 in value, or claims for lower value where the trial is likely to last for more than one day or oral expert evidence will not be limited to one per party.

As with other tracks the multi-track has its own dedicated Civil Procedure Rule being Pt 29.

It should be noted that the High Court deals only with multi-track claims and by virtue of CPR PD 7A para.2.1 a claim may not be started in the High Court unless the value of the claim is more than £15,000. Multi-track cases can of course be started in the county court which has unlimited jurisdiction.

Practitioners may be concerned about this particularly if a claim is started in the High Court but then it is subsequently found that it should not have been. In such a case the claim itself is not a nullity. The position can be regularised by the application of CPR 3.10 which deals with the consequences of failure to comply with the rule or Practice Direction. The claim is preserved and consequently the error is corrected by the transfer of the claim to the appropriate county court.

How does multi-track differ from fast track and small claims track?

In essence multi-track cases give the court the ability to deal with claims of widely differing values and complexity and also allow them to manage the case according to its particular needs (see CPR PD 29 para.3.2). **8–42**

As with fast track, on allocation to the multi-track, the court will give its directions for the management of the case and set a timetable. However, unlike fast track it will not automatically set a trial date or a trial period.

And as an alternative to giving directions the court may fix a "case management conference" or a pre-trial review or both. The court will then fix the trial date or the trial window as soon as it can.

What is a case management conference?

A case management conference is in fact a hearing which can be conducted by telephone by virtue of CPR PD 23 para.6.5 or by written submission and which takes place before the pre-trial checklist stage. It is a forum for the parties to meet with the procedural judge to deal with all the necessary decisions for the contractual management of the case. **8–43**

What is a pre-trial review?

This is generally a directions hearing after the case management conference (see CPR 29.7) and applies to multi-track cases. It gives the court an opportunity to give fund directions and set the trial time table. **8–44**

How are multi-tracks dealt with in the various divisions of a High Court?

Practitioners should make themselves aware of the differing guides published by each division of the High Court including the Queen's **8–45**

Bench Division, Chancery Division, Commercial Court and Specialist Proceedings where, although unlikely in debt recovery matters, proceedings under Pt 49 of the rules and CPR Pt 57 to 63 have their own specific Practice Directions.

The most likely arena in which a Debt Recovery Practitioner is to find him or herself will be the Queen's Bench Division or the Chancery Division.

What are the requirements for legal representation in a multi-track case?

8–46 Where a party is legally represented in the proceedings then a representative with sufficient knowledge of the case and authority to make decisions must attend the hearing (see CPR 29.3(2)). It is not acceptable for an agent to be instructed to attend who is not likely to have sufficient authority to make decisions or who is unfamiliar with the facts of the case.

What sanctions apply in the event that a case management timetable is not adhered to?

8–47 Practitioners should pay close attention to CPR 29.3.3 which sets out the sanctions which can be imposed upon a party who fails to keep to the case management timetable in a multi-track matter.

What costs are recoverable in a multi-track case?

8–48 As with fast track, the successful party will be entitled to recover costs but these are not fixed as they are in fast track. The party should provide a statement of costs which will either be approved or amended by the court and ultimately the court may order the successful party is entitled to recover costs "to be assessed if not agreed".

8–49 The cost of a full multi-track case should not be underestimated. Parties should try to agree the amount of any costs ordered to be paid in the event they are unable to reach agreement the successful party will arrange for a costs draftsman to prepare a detailed bill of costs for application to be made to the court for detailed assessment.

If an application for detailed assessment is made then that in itself is another process whereby the matter will be listed for hearing, the sole purpose of which will be to consider the amount of costs claimed by the successful party on a item by item basis. The court will make its assessment as to what is reasonable or acceptable which in turn will result in an order stipulating the amount that the losing party must pay.

In effect a detailed assessment procedure is the court deciding what is fair and reasonable in relation to paying the losing parties' costs.

How should disclosure of documents be tackled in debt recovery actions?

Disclosure as a step in proceedings cuts across all three tracks of the Civil Procedure Rules and relates to documents which are to be relied upon by the parties to an action in a defended matter. We saw at the outset of this book that documents which are to be relied upon by the claimant as evidence that the debt is outstanding should be disclosed as soon as possible. **8–50**

In dealing with a defended matter then, the rules require the existence of documents to be relied upon to be disclosed to the other party before the actual trial. CPR 31 is the part of the rules dealing entirely with the question of disclosure and what constitutes a "document".

Under CPR 31.2 the definition of disclosure is given as a party disclosing a document by stating "the document exists or has existed". It is important however to note that this rule does not apply to claims allocated as small claims track (see CPR 31.1(2)), but even so in a small claims matter it is still necessary to gather up the documentary evidence if one is trying to pursue a debt to ensure that important evidence can be disclosed to the court even on an informal basis.

What constitutes a "document"?

It is important to understand the definition of "document" within the rules. The Debt Recovery Practitioner needs to understand it does not simply mean a paper document such as an invoice or delivery note but extends to include anything upon which information is recorded (see CPR 31.4). **8–51**

In debt recovery terms this can include computer records, emails, or terms and conditions on a website.

So this means that Practitioners need to think very carefully about just how far disclosure will have to be taken to ensure that everything is included. The best approach is to encourage the claimants to hand-over absolutely everything and then for the Practitioner to decide what needs to be used to comply with the rules. There is nothing worse than something coming out of the "woodwork" which dilutes or in worst case scenario completely demolishes the claimant's claim for the debt.

How standard is "standard disclosure"?

8–52 When providing standard disclosure a party will complete Form N265 indicating the enquiries they have made to locate the documents they are disclosing and providing a detailed list of the actual documents to be disclosed. However, CPR 31.8 extends the duty to disclose documents which are no longer physically in the possession of the party, but which once were controlled by the party making the disclosure, so in a debt recovery action these might include paperwork that has been given to the defendant on delivery such as copies of delivery notes, certificates of completion etc. Both the original and the copy document must be disclosed.

Are there any documents which need not be disclosed?

8–53 There are documents which a party can object to the other party seeing, although they will need to give a reason for this objection. The most common is the issue of "privilege" in which documents which could be the subject of disclosure actually relate to correspondence passing between the party and his or her legal representative. Such documents are "privileged" and CPR 31.3.13 provides further detailed information regarding this type of privilege status and how it should be used in proceedings.

Is there an ongoing obligation to provide disclosure?

8–54 Clients should be reminded at the outset of any legal proceedings that there is an ongoing obligation to disclose documents which both support their case but also which could have an adverse effect (see CPR 31.6(b)(i)).

Parties should be aware that although there is a timetable in which disclosure is placed amongst the court's directions in the run up to a trial, the ongoing obligation is that parties must disclose any document which comes into their possession after disclosure has been given and must provide disclosure to the other party (see CPR 31.11).

How can the other party be made to disclose a specific document?

8–55 If a party wants the other party to disclose a particular document or a party wants the other party to carry out a specific search for documents then an application can be made to the court for specific disclosure under CPR 31.12.

The application should be made using Form N244 and the nature of the disclosure which is sought should be specified in the application.

Can documents be disclosed pre-action?

In more complex debt recovery cases it may be necessary to seek disclosure from the other party of any documents before proceedings start. This can be particularly useful if there are documents which need to be seen in order to assess the viability of the litigation itself. However, the court will only grant such an order if both the applicant and the respondent of the application are likely to become parties to the proceedings (see CPR 31.16(3)). **8–56**

Once documents have been disclosed what happens next?

The direction for disclosure goes hand in hand with the direction for inspection. **8–57**

Disclosure requires the parties to provide the list of documents they are disclosing and there is then a procedure for copies of the actual documents to be provided through the next step which is "inspection of documents".

CPR 31.15 provides details with regards to the procedure to be followed by the parties when requesting inspection of documents.

Not all documents will be required to be copied and inspected as there will be an amount of duplication between both parties' lists.

However, if a party wants to see and inspect documents then the inspection needs to take place not more than seven days after the request has been made (see CPR 31.15(B)).

How is witness evidence dealt with by the court?

After disclosure of documents comes the next stage in terms of preparing evidence and there is a requirement under CPR 32.4(2) for the parties to provide witness statements. These give the detailed evidence of the witnesses who are to be called and is basically a chronology of that evidence. The exchange of witness statements again avoids any surprises at trial. **8–58**

The art of preparing a witness statement is to simply tell the story and, in the claimant's case, to ensure the story is in the right order and is verified by documentation as the chronology unfolds.

The court will also provide a date by which witness evidence is to be exchanged as part of the directions order and that statement will stand as a witness's evidence in chief at the final hearing (see CPR 32.5(2)). The statement therefore needs to be comprehensive and contains all the evidence and information which the witness will bring to the trial.

Where possible the witness statement should be in plain English and in the witness's own words. Practitioners who have the time and inclination would do well to read some of Lord Denning's judgments where His Lordship often giving judgment rehearsed the facts of the case before him simply by telling the story in a manner that the most complex of cases became easy to follow as the chronology unfolded.

The consequences of failing to exchange a witness statement with the other party are that it cannot be used as evidence at trial without the permission of the court. Clearly that is a hurdle that a party would not wish to have to jump at the trial itself and therefore preparation and anticipation of which witnesses are to be called in the evidence as needed should be all part of the pre-action process in planning consequences should a defence be made to any claim.

Can other points be raised at trial in addition to the witness statement?

8–59 If other points need to be raised at trial then a supplementary statement should be prepared with all the additional information and the other party should be asked to agree the additional evidence being produced at trial.

If the other party will not give their consent to this additional information being available at trial then an application will need to be made to the court for permission to produce the additional evidence. This application should be made at the start of the trial itself if there is no opportunity to do so sooner although preferably it should be a standalone application well in advance of the trial date. A Practitioner would not wish to be in front of a district judge trying to make this application on a trial date when there is a time clock running for the time allotted for the trial and the trial judge can see time being eaten up in dealing with an application that really should have been anticipated some time ago. However, in certain circumstances this will be unavoidable and if the information comes late in the day then this should be pointed out to the trial judge.

It has to be said that without the permission of the court a party will not be able to use any witness evidence which has not been disclosed prior to the trial.

How should the witness statement be set out?

There are certain points to bear in mind when producing a statement. **8–60**

The heading of the statement should be the same as the heading for any other type of document filed at court setting out the details regarding the parties, the court and the claim number (see CPR PD 32.17).

In addition in accordance with the Practice Direction when setting out a witness statement the following information should be included in the top right hand corner of the front page of the statement including:

- the description of the party on whose behalf a statement is being filed, i.e. claimant or defendant;
- the initials and surname of the witness;
- the number of the statement in relation to that witness, i.e. 1st, 2nd or 3rd;
- the identifying initials and number of each exhibit referred to; and
- the date the statement was made.

The witness statement should state the following information in the opening paragraph: **8–61**

- the name of the deponent of the statement being his or her full name;
- the address of the deponent—if the statement is provided by the deponent in connection with business such as a solicitor's office then the business address for the deponent will be sufficient along with his or her position such as Debt Recovery Manager;
- if the occupation is not stated as above then the occupation of the deponent such as Manager, Chief Executive, Director; and
- whether the deponent is a party to the proceedings or an employee of the party.

Reference should be made to CPR PD 32.18 in relation to the form and content of the statement.

It is imperative to check that the statement is signed in accordance with the requirements of CPR Pt 22 where a statement of truth will be needed for each witness statement. As set out in Chapter 5 there are stringent requirements for the signing of a statement of truth, and the consequences of signing one where there is not an honest belief in its contents have already been rehearsed.

Does the witness still need to give oral evidence at trial?

8–62 Even though a comprehensive witness statement will have been prepared there is still a requirement for oral evidence to be given at trial. In effect the witness statement will stand as evidence in chief, i.e. primary evidence, and it is therefore essential the statement is comprehensive. The witness will be cross-examined on the statement by the defendant or the defendant's legal representative or counsel. It is therefore important that in a complex debt recovery matter that the implications of cross examination are understood as trying to answer gaps in a witness statement in cross examination can be, to say the least, uncomfortable.

If the witness statement is put into evidence as part of the trial bundle and it is decided not to call that witness to give oral evidence then the statement can be used as hearsay evidence. Even if the party who prepared the statement decides not to put it into evidence it still could be put in by the other party anyway so this too needs to be anticipated as well (see CPR 32.5(5)).

How should witnesses be prepared for trial?

8–63 In preparing for trial it should not be overlooked that some witnesses have never even been inside a court room and that therefore, confronted with the enormity of having to give evidence, this can make people nervous and therefore their evidence seem less compelling. Practitioners should prepare witnesses for what it will mean to give evidence in terms of giving evidence on oath, standing in the witness box, addressing the judge and the other parties, including the legal representatives for the opponent, generally encouraging the witness to simply tell their story and be clear in their mind about the chronology of events and the documentary evidence which makes up the basis of the claim.

A Practitioner cannot tell the witness what to say but it can be explained to them how they will be required to give their evidence and the procedure for cross-examination. It is always possible to take a witness to have a look around the court before the actual trial so they are familiar with the building and therefore less intimidated on the day.

Supporting and encouraging witnesses is all part of the Debt

Recovery Practitioner's role in their preparation for trial and is not something that should be left for the last minute if one wants to get the best evidence possible from the witness on the day.

What happens if a document has been destroyed or lost which is required for disclosure purposes?

As said above each party is required by CPR 31.10(4) to identify documents which are no longer in their control and to say what has happened to them. Documents which have been lost or destroyed will need to be accompanied by a statement with an explanation as to what has happened to the document. In a straightforward debt recovery case such a statement may be sufficient but if they are critical to the nature of the claim contained in a party's statement of case then that statement and explanation may be found to be lacking. **8–64**

What happens if the document required is in the control of a third party?

If the document which is needed to be disclosed is in the control of a third party application may be made under CPR 31.17 for the third party to disclose the document and in the event that this is not forthcoming a witness statement be issued in accordance with CPR 34.2(4) and (5). **8–65**

Is there any limit to the amount of standard disclosure that can be made?

Standard disclosure as set out in CPR 31.6 means there is a limit to how much needs to be disclosed. **8–66**

Certainly a party does not need to try and speculate what documents could come about by way of disclosure and inspection. Conversely a party is under a continuing obligation to provide disclosure in accordance with CPR 31.11.

If expert evidence is directed to be exchanged what type of evidence might be required?

In debt recovery proceedings the likelihood of experts being appointed is relatively rare but even so Practitioners should be aware of the requirements of CPR Pt 35. Although expert evidence will only be **8–67** required to resolve the claim in relation to the debt should ordinary witness evidence not be sufficient. If an expert is required attention is drawn to the requirements of CPR Pt 35.3 in that experts have an overriding duty to the court regardless of who they are instructed by.

Expert evidence should be given in writing unless the court orders otherwise as required by CPR 35.5. It is possible for the expert to give evidence orally at the trial in the same way as an ordinary witness. But in a fast track claim oral evidence by an expert will only be allowed if the court considers it to be in the interests of justice to do so.

It is also possible to put written questions to experts under r.37.5 written questions about his report. However those questions may only be put to the expert once and must be within 28 days of service of the expert's report. The purpose in asking the question in a written form is to seek clarification of the report and once the answer is given by the expert it is treated as part of his report.

When can a party claim a document is "privileged"?

8–68 The Debt Recovery Practitioner needs to be aware when a document will be privileged. Privilege involves protecting confidential communications, and the relevant part of the CPR here is CPR 31.15.

The area of privilege is specialist and the reader is advised to consult a heavyweight litigation manual as to the ramifications of it but some examples of privilege include:

- Communications between a solicitor and other lawyers or other professionals acting for the client;
- Instructions and Brief to Counsel;
- Opinions and drafts prepared by counsel; and

8–69 However, privilege will not extend to cover documents obtained for the purpose of litigation if they came into existence before litigation was contemplated, which may well be the situation in debt recovery where there are various processes in train before litigation becomes necessary to recover the debt.

Litigation has been defined as contemplated for the purpose of litigation privilege if it is said to be "reasonably in prospect" and that becomes the matter of fact in each case as to whether litigation was reasonably in prospect at the time of the communication in question (see *United States of America v Philip Morris Inc* (2004) EWCA Civ 330 (2004), *The Times*—April 16).

What happens if a privileged document is inadvertently disclosed or inspected?

Documents may from time to time be included in witness statements or other documentation within the litigation process and this is specifically dealt with in CPR 31.20 in which a document may not be used without the court's permission. 8–70

The area has been subject to a large amount of case law and it is accepted that the pre-CPR case law, i.e. before 1999 remains relevant but is always of course subject to the overriding objective in CPR Pt 1 and the recognition that that privilege is a substantive and fundamental right.

So where privilege documents are inadvertently disclosed in circumstances where the party to whom the disclosure is made must have known that a mistake has occurred and the document has been disclosed then the copy must be returned and the court will even intervene and restrain by injunction the use of information contained in or derived from privileged documents which have been inadvertently disclosed.

However, inadvertently disclosed documents may be used if it was reasonable for the party to whom they were disclosed to believe they were disclosed intentionally.

To avoid issues around disclosure of documents whether privileged or not care must be taken in the litigation environment in handling documentation. It is very easy to copy everything and then find it has ended up in the opponent's hands. It is very easy to send the other side privileged information by mistake by putting the wrong contents in an envelope. Seasoned Practitioners at some point in their careers, perhaps very early on, may have been on the receiving end of a principal's wrath when these situations have occurred. It is therefore vitally important that documentation is handled carefully and is managed with thoroughness of record keeping. It is always a good idea to start trial bundles running very early in the litigation process and paginating them and categorising them so that privileged documents are in fact kept to one side. 8–71

In a busy department a system must be built to handle this type of scenario particularly in debt recovery matters where information is privileged by virtue of the type of debt that is being collected and to give the other side an opportunity to see privileged information would be catastrophic to the successful outcome of the claim.

What is diplomatic privilege?

Embassy documents are protected by absolute privilege and such privilege may be claimed even though the defendant's personal 8–72 diplomatic immunity has been waived. Debts against foreign states therefore have to be considered carefully and the commercial activities of foreign states have to be separated from their diplomatic immunity situation. This is an issue that should be sorted out at the start of the trading relationship and not when it comes to litigating an unpaid debt involving a foreign embassy.

How should the parties respond to the receipt of a listing questionnaire?

8–73 Also known as a pre-trial checklist form N170 is the "listing questionnaire" and as the name suggests it is the court's way of checking the status of the proceedings by all parties before the trial. This enables the court to ensure that all parties are ready to proceed with the trial and clearly it is another important step in a defended action case.

How should the listing questionnaire be completed?

8–74 The completion of a listing questionnaire should be approached in the same way as the allocation questionnaire and should be dealt with section by section.

This includes:

Step towards trial	Action to be taken
Confirm directions have been complied with	It is important that all the directions which have been given by the court, standard or otherwise, have been completed before the matter proceeds to trial. A party should indicate on the listing questionnaire whether or not directions have been completed. If directions have not been completed then the party must state which ones are still outstanding and when it is anticipated compliance will take place. If directions are still outstanding it will be necessary for a party to apply on form N244 together with the draft order requesting a revised directions timetable as can be seen earlier in the chapter the timetable in the progression towards trial cannot be varied without the agreement of the court.
Witnesses	A party should provide details of the number of witnesses it is intending to rely on at trial. It is particularly important if the number has changed since the allocation questionnaire was completed.

Step towards trial	Action to be taken
Experts	Again if the number of experts has changed this must be noted on the listing questionnaire. It should be borne in mind that the purpose behind the questionnaire is to assess party's readiness for trial and for the court to be able to case manage each claim to ensure it is properly listed for trial with the correct time estimate and slot being given in the trial window.
Legal representation	A party should provide details of who will be representing the party at the trial and this is the final opportunity to provide details of dates to avoid. If necessary, checks should be made with counsel's clerk, if they are representing the party at the hearing, to ensure their availability as counsel's own diary can change due to the listing of other cases. Failure to advise the court at this stage of changes and dates to avoid, leaves the Practitioner open to the risk of the matter being listed when the legal representative is not available.
Trial details	A party is given the opportunity of confirming the information previously provided in the allocation questionnaire or revising it regarding the timeframe for the trial.
Fee on filing listing questionnaire	It is only the claimant who has to pay the fee when lodging the questionnaire. Fees can be found on the Court Service website at *http://www.hmcourts-ervice.gov.uk/courtfinder/forms/ex50.pdf*
Practice directions	Practice directions dealing with the filing of the listing question for claims in both multi-track and fast track claims in CPR PD 28.6 and 28.8 respectively.

Disclosure has been given, witness statements exchanged and the listing questionnaire filed—is there anything else to do before the trial?

Having got to this stage the next thing to consider is the preparation of the trial bundles although a good Debt Recovery Practitioner will have been collating documentation from first receiving instructions to collect the debt but this does take the management of documentation to the next level. The trial bundle is the bundle of documents containing all the relevant documents applicable to the case (see the definition of "document" given above which will be needed for reference purposes during the trial). 8–75

CPR Pt 39.5 deals with what is required in the trial bundle and basically this includes:

- Documents required by any relevant Practice Direction;
- Any court Orders made in the proceedings; and
- Document set out in the accompanying Practice Direction to CPR Pt 39 at para.3.2 which will include:

  - the claim form and all statements of case;
  - the case summary and/or chronology of the case where appropriate;
  - requests for further information and responses to those requests;
  - all witness statements to be relied on as evidence;
  - expert's reports and responses to them;
  - any order giving directions in the conduct of the trial; and
  - any other necessary documents.

Whose responsibility is it to prepare the trial bundle?

8–76 In accordance with CPR Pt 39.5(2) it falls to the claimant to arrange for the preparation of the trial bundle.

The bundle itself must be prepared not more than seven and not less than three days before the start of the trial and if the claimant is not legally represented and the defendant is, then the defendant's legal representative should prepare the trial bundle.

How should the trial bundle be presented?

8–77 CPR PD 39 para.3 gives detailed instructions on how to prepare a trial bundle.

In essence the bundle itself must be prepared in a chronological and logical order with paginated pages and an index describing each document on the front. If the number of pages exceeds a hundred then the bundle must be divided at relevant intervals.

Good bundles are well presented by a hole punched in the right place and putting matching binders with labels on the side. If they need to be indexed inside they are done so properly with proper labels being printed.

Some of the best bundles to be prepared are by taking them to a specialist legal copy shop who are well used to preparing bundles and can prepare them quickly and inexpensively rather than tying up staff from the department standing by the photocopier for hours on end. The most efficient way to prepare a bundle is to get one master copy ready properly paginated and prepared in accordance with the rules of a Practice Direction and then take it off to the local specialist legal copy shop. Legastat in Carey Street, London, WC2 does an excellent job in preparing bundles for court.

Sufficient copies of the bundle will have to be prepared for all the parties and that includes copies to use by the judge and the witnesses at trial. Judges can become very irritated if the bundle is poorly presented and not well paginated. There is nothing worse than trying to flick through numbers of pages trying to find the document which is being referred to and a party will not endear themselves to the Bench if they do not take the necessary time and attention to this particular aspect of preparation for trial.

What should happen on the day of the trial?

Debt Recovery Practitioners must make themselves available and **8–78** aware that a debt recovery claim could be settled at anytime. They should have instructions from their client (if they are solicitors) on what they are prepared to accept should a late new offer or an offer made "at the court door" be made.

It is not unusual for the offer to be made just as the parties are about to sit down in the courtroom. Often on the morning of a hearing the issues of cost will become overwhelming for clients and their advisors and everyone will just want to settle the case.

However, if that is not the case and the trial is to continue then there are some areas of etiquette which we feel this book ought to touch on in preparing Debt Recovery Practitioners for what they can expect.

On entering the court which will be open court it is best to bow to the Bench even if the judge is not there and take one place at the bench either with counsel or on the front bench if presenting oneself. It is always a good idea to have some form of note taker where possible such as a junior with you so that a note of what said and how it is said can be taken throughout the day. The judge will enter the courtroom and all parties must rise. Once the judge sits down he will invite the parties to sit down. The way to address the judge in the county court is to call a male judge "Sir" or a female judge "Madam". In the High Court the judge should be addressed as "My Lord" or "My Lady".

In the county court a Circuit Judge should be addressed as "Your Honour".

Hearings in a Small Claims court are fairly informal but in the fast **8–79** track where a case will last the whole day the typical programme will be:

Judges reading time	– 30 minutes
Opening statement	– 10 minutes
Cross examination and re-examination of claimant's witnesses	– 90 minutes
Cross examination and re-examination of defendant's witnesses	– 90 minutes
Defendant's closing statement	– 15 minutes
Claimant's closing statement	– 15 minutes
Judge preparing and delivering judgment	– 30 minutes
Some reassessment of cost	– 20 minutes

The claimant's advocate will usually open proceedings by making opening submissions outlining the facts and indicating areas of dispute with any legal principles involved being highlighted. Only the essential parts of the statement of case should be referred to. The defendant's advocate may then be invited to address the court and after that the first witness of the claimant will be called. It is customary although not required in the rules to call the claimant first. Other witnesses will take the oath or make a solemn affirmation.

As mentioned above unless ordered otherwise the witness statement of any witness stands as the evidence in chief of that witness and therefore the witness will then be cross-examined by the defendant's advocate and if necessary re-examined by the claimant's advocate.

Normally the judge will give judgment at the end of the trial although it is possible for the judge to reserve his judgment to allow him time to prepare his judgment in chambers. Once judgment is given by the judge it is the court's responsibility to draw up the order unless the court orders otherwise (see CPR 40.3(1)). It is hoped that the claimant has succeeded in winning the case and judgment is given in favour of the Debt Recovery Practitioner.

What happens once the order is drawn?

8–80 If judgment has been entered against the defendant then the judgment or order can be enforced in the same way as any other judgment if the defendant fails to comply with the terms or the order.

For example, if the order is worded "judgment to be entered on behalf of the claimant in the sum of £5,000.26 payable by the defendant within 14 days of the date of this order" and the defendant then fails to pay £5,000.26 within the fourteen days the claimant can commence enforcement action against the defendant on day 15.

What happens if a settlement can be achieved before trial?

If a settlement can be achieved before trial which will no doubt deal with the issue of the payment of the debt and any costs attached and interest available then the parties should draw up Consent Order up which is often done on a piece of file notepaper outside the court which can be signed by both of them and sealed by the court to bring the proceedings to an end. **8–81**

A well organised Practitioner will actually take a draft form of order, if only, in terms of the heading to the court which can be used to prepare a handwritten order to hand to the judge in the event that a settlement can be achieved.

CPR 40.6 provides directions in detail as to the procedure to be followed in the event the parties to a claim agree to terms and it is important that the order contains the following information.

- it must be drawn up in the terms agreed;
- it must be expressed to be "By Consent"; and
- it must be signed by the legal representative acting for the party or by the parties themselves if they are litigants in person.

Can a claim be discontinued anytime?

A party may discontinue all or any part of a claim anytime subject to instances where the permission of a court is required which include whether it is an undertaking, injunction, interim payment or more than one claimant. **8–82**

The general rule is that the party discontinuing will be liable for the costs of the proceedings although the court does retain its discretion to make an alternative order.

There is no provision however for the withdrawal of a defence. If a defendant does not wish to continue to defend the claim then this needs to be dealt with by the filing of an admission on which the claimant can then enter judgment.

The part of the rules dealing with discontinuance is under CPR Pt 38.

The discontinued rule does not apply to claims allocated to small claims track although it does have application prior to the case being allocated to the track. Further, discontinuance would be a factor for the court to consider in whether a party had behaved unreasonably along which it could therefore make an order for costs in accordance with CPR 27.14(2)(d).

And finally ...

8–83 CPR Part 39 and its accompanying Practice Direction at CPR PD 39(a) deals with various issues in relating to failure to attend a trial, the representation of companies at trial, the recording of proceedings, etc.

Issues within this Practice Direction which may affect debt recovery involve the following:

Welsh language provisions—Guidance for listing of civil cases where the Welsh language is to be used and which originates from courts in North Wales will be found at CPR PD 39 WEL.

Lay Advisor—A litigant in person will be allowed to have the assistance of a Lay Advisor or "McKenzie Friend" where proceedings go ahead in open court or in chambers except if proceedings are in private or if the judge is satisfied that in the interests of justice the litigant in person does not need to have such assistance (see *R v Bow County Court Ex p. Pelling* (1999) 4 All E.R. 751).

The discretion to grant rights of audience to individuals who do not meet the stringent requirements of the Courts and Legal Services Act 1990, will only be exercised in exceptional circumstances.

8–84 McKenzie Friends are allowed so as to further the interests of justice by achieving a level playing field between the parties and ensuring a fair hearing Debt Recovery Practitioners need to be aware that this issue can crop up from time to time where the defendant is without legal representation.

Failure to attend trail—The fact that the claimant is not present but his legal representatives are was held in the case of *Rouse v Freeman* (2002) *The Times*, January 8 not to be a reason for the judge to exercise his discretion to strike out a claim.

If the discretion is exercised so as a claim or fundamental part of a statement of case is struck out for failure to attend then an application should be made under CPR Pt 23 to reverse the position. That application needs to be made promptly.

8–85 Debt Recovery Practitioners should be aware that even if a defendant fails to attend trial but sends a message requesting an adjournment but the court is minded to hear the case and give judgment, the defendant does have a cause to apply to set judgment aside. This does happen from time to time.

Recording of proceedings—Parties should be aware that any hearing whether in the High Court or County court the proceedings will be tape recorded unless the judge directs otherwise.

It is not open to a party or member of a public to use unofficial recording equipment in the court without the judge's permission and to do so can constitute contempt.

Any party or person under CPR PD 39A para.6 may then require a transcript of the recording which will require the payment of a fee through one of the recognised transcription companies.

Where judgment is given and evidence is complex requiring a transcript is often a sensible course of action particularly in relation to the giving of any judgment. 8–86

Change of Solicitor—CPR Pt 42 of the rules deals with the procedure in relation to change of Solicitor.

In accordance with CPR Pt 6 whether or not a solicitor's business address is the address of service is dependent on whether that solicitor is acting for the party to be served.

CPR Pt 42 states that when a party has provided the business address of his solicitor as his address for service he will be treated as acting for that party. And that address for service will remain the address of service until a notice of change in accordance with the rule is filed.

If a new solicitor is appointed then he will file and serve a notice of change. 8–87

Under CPR 42.3 where a solicitor ceases to act for a party and an order will be required, this will not have effect until it is served on the party. An application should be made in the ordinary way in accordance with CPR Pt 23.

Solicitors must of course have regards to the requirements of their professional conduct rules when terminating a retainer on behalf of a client as this can only be done in certain circumstances and reference should be made to the Code of Conduct and particularly r.2.

Chapter 9

Tactical Applications in Debt Recovery

Introductory Comments

So far in this book we have looked at the road to achieving judgment either through judgment by default or judgment following a hearing and whatever track is applicable to the case. In many ways Debt Recovery Practitioners look to get from A to B in the most straightforward of routes and at the least possible cost but inevitably there are going to be times when having more "tools in a toolbox" is going to be essential to win a case or at least to call the bluff of the other side as a tactical move. **9–01**

It was said in the foundations of the CPR that the courts will not be used by macho lawyers and whilst this is a laudable aim, the fact is that applications do become necessary to keep a case on track and ultimately to win it. As far as the claimant is concerned he/she/it is of course only interested in winning back their money. That is the cut and thrust of debt recovery and so knowing when to make a tactical strike in one of the following applications is going to be important.

This chapter is therefore going to deal with:

- Striking out a statement of case;
- Seeking Summary Judgment;
- How to deal with accidental slips and omissions;
- Handling applications to set aside or vary a judgement; and
- Amendments to statement of case.

We will now look at each of these scenarios from the Debt Recovery Practitioner's point of view who is seeking to win his or her case on behalf of the client.

Striking out a statement of case

9–02 Often in debt recovery proceedings a defence is received from the defendant which has no merit or is poorly constructed. There are examples given in CPR PD 3.4 at para.1.4 and 1.6 as to when a claim or a defence might be struck out on the basis they disclose no reasonable grounds for bringing or defending the action.

If a party believes that his opponent's case has no real prospect of success on the facts or the matter is bound to fail because of a point of law that party may apply under r.3.4 for the case to be struck out.

The difference between the rule here under 3.4 and Pt 24 of the rules for summary judgment is that the court is deciding on its own initiative to make the order.

Where a court proposes to make such an order based on its own view and assessment of the case it may give the person likely to be affected by the order an opportunity to make representations to the court. In doing so it must specify the time and the manner in which those representations must be made (see CPR r.3.3(2)). If the court is then to hold a hearing to hear those representations it must give each party likely to be affected by the order at least three days' notice of the hearing. However, the court still has the power to make an order without hearing representations.

9–03 As one might expect a party adversely affected by such an order may apply to have it varied or set aside (see CPR Rule 3.3(5)) and the court's order will contain a statement on the rights of a party to make such an application to have the order set aside or varied.

If the court does strike out a statement of case on its own initiative as it considers the claim to be totally without merit the court order will record that fact and the court must consider at this stage whether it is appropriate to make a Civil Restraint Order which basically prevents a party on taking any step in the proceedings without first obtaining the permission of the judge identified in the order or to prevent further proceedings being brought at all.

As such in debt recovery if a court officer receives a document purporting to be a defence for filing and considers it may fall within the ambit of CPR r.3.4(2)(a) or CPR r.3.4(2)(b) he may consult a judge under the Practice Direction at para.3.1 accompanying r.3.

Basically, the court is deciding that the statement of case, i.e. the defence discloses no reasonable grounds for defending the claim or that the defence is an abuse of the court's process or is likely to obstruct the just disposal of the proceedings.

9–04 The judge may then on his own initiative make an order striking out the defence or he may order the defendant has an extension of time to serve a proper defence (see CPR PD 3 para.3.2)). As said above, he may order that there is a hearing in which the defendant can be present to make further representations.

Of course judges are very mindful of their needs to satisfy the requirements of the overriding objective to deal with cases justly. Therefore one cannot assume that even though a defence appears to a seasoned Debt Recovery Practitioner to be nothing more than a sham, judges will go out of their way to assist, particularly litigants in person, to comply with the rules. So a judge may order the defendant to provide further information about his defence or to clarify pursuant to CPR r.18.1 in requesting more information. However that order may include a provision that if the defendant fails to provide that information his defence will be struck out.

If met with such an order, this does not limit the claimant's right to continue to make an application against the defendant for summary judgment which is dealt with below.

Of course an application to seek to vary or set aside such an order is going to cost the defendant money, although where defendants are not assisted with legal representation there is no cost other than their time at court and, therefore sometimes it is the claimant who has to pay for legal advice to counter or progress such an application whilst it costs the defendant nothing in terms of hard cash.

The point to remember is that if the application to set aside or vary **9–05** the order made is unsuccessful there is a strong risk that the court will make a costs order against the applicant particularly where there is seen to be an abuse of process. However, this too has to be considered carefully because a costs order against someone who is worth nothing is worth nothing to the person who has the benefit of the order! It is one thing to say you have a costs order against the party but does it mean you will be able to enforce it and get it paid? This is something that needs to constantly be underlined to the paying client. A piece of paper confirming one has an order against the defendant for payment of this, that and the other, will only be any good if the defendant has the means to pay or can be forced to pay through further enforcement proceedings. Of course if the reader has taken on the spirit of this book then these issues will have been considered well before the claim was actually issued.

The general rule is that the unsuccessful party will pay the costs of the successful party although the court always has a discretion to make a different order by virtue of CPR 44.3(2).

Tactically, the claimant can bring a single application for both summary judgment under CPR Pt 24 and to strike out under CPR Pt 3.4 and this is provided for under CPR PD 3 para.1.7.

There are, however, advantages to including an application CPR r.3.4 compared to a full summary judgment hearing and that is that CPR 3.4 applies to cases of non-compliance with a rule, Practice Direction or court order which may be easier to demonstrate to the court and the procedure itself has less procedural requirements than the procedure for summary judgment.

9–07 The difference between CPR r.3.4 and a summary judgment application was considered by the Court of Appeal in the *Independents' Advantage Insurance Co Ltd v Cook* [2003] EWCA Civ 1103. In that case the claim concerned the liability of an accountancy firm for losses as a consequence of relying on allegedly misleading financial statements and the court held that this should proceed to trial because the relevant area of law was a developing one and on the pleaded facts the case was at the margin of existing decisions as to whether or not it should be struck out.

The procedure for making the application is governed by Pt 23 of the rules and the application notice will be on the Form N244 (a form which Debt Recovery Practitioners will get to know and love!).

The application notice itself should identify the grounds the application is made on and whether the claimant he is seeking to strike out the defence or counterclaim.

Whatever part of the statement of case the application relates to this must be clearly identified in the application notice.

As always the statement of truth must be signed by the applicant his or her solicitor or litigation friend and where the applicant is a registered company then the statement of truth will be signed by the appropriate officer of the company (see Chapter 5 on the rules relating to this important step in any proceedings).

9–08 The evidence in support of the application may be as simple as the applicant pointing to the statement of case to establish the grounds for striking out and CPR PD 3 para.5.2 confirms that applications may be made without the need to serve additional evidence. If additional facts need to be proved this will have to be in the form of written evidence on the form itself (in the box provided at Question 10) or by preparing a witness statement or affidavit. The decision to give additional evidence by way of affidavit may mean that the additional costs of making it may not be allowed, i.e. the oath fee.

As always the evidence must be verified by a statement of truth and to be a more credible statement it would be better if it was made by the claimant directly and not the legal representative of the claimant. Parties should be careful not to produce so much evidence that the application becomes unsuitable for summary determination by the court.

A draft order should also be prepared which will usually be appended to the application when filed at court and served on the opposing party by the court. If the case is proceeding in one of the specialist courts then the applicant should consult the relevant court guide for additional requirements such as the Queen's Bench guide or the Chancery Division guide.

Once the application has been prepared it must be filed at court and the appropriate court fee must be paid. For information on fees for "on notice" applications reference should be made to the Civil

Proceedings Fees Order 2008. As said throughout this book these fees are likely to change on a yearly basis and therefore practitioners are directed to the website at *http://www.hmcourts-service.gov.uk/courtfinder/forms/ex50.pdf*, where up-to-date fees from the Court Service are maintained.

Once filed, the application notice, together with evidence in support, and the draft order if attached to the application should be served on every respondent. The application notice should be served as soon as practicable after it is filed by virtue of CPR 27.7(1).

Although the application notice will be filed at court it will be **9–09** the responsibility of the applicant to actually arrange service of the application and the draft order appended to it. Reference should be made to Pt 6 as to arrangements for service. If a defendant is legally represented then service by fax or email subject to the rules will probably be sufficient.

Where the defendant is not legally represented then Practitioners need to consider carefully, bearing in mind this application is to strike out the defence and to avoid any suggestion thereafter that the notice was not properly served, on how best to serve it and to ensure it is brought to the attention of the defendant without perhaps relying on the deemed service provisions.

In preparing for the hearing a bundle will need to be prepared and it is the responsibility of the applicant's solicitor to prepare the bundle for the hearing. We saw in Chapter 8 the importance of preparing a neat and well organised bundle and it is no less a thing to prepare a bundle for an application than when it is for a full trial.

The bundle should therefore contain the pleadings to date served by both parties, the application notice itself and the parties' evidence in support of their respective positions. The draft order should be included along with an index and always a chronology to assist the court. The chronology should be agreed with the other side as again this can cut down a lot of judicial time in trying to get the series of events in the correct order. It is always best if the parties can agree the contents of the bundle and again if the bundle is needed quickly then it is always best to outsource the printing and pagination of this to a specialist legal copying service.

There is nothing worse than going to court and having a district **9–10** judge not follow the chronology of the application simply because nobody has taken time and trouble to prepare the bundle properly.

Once the bundle is prepared it should be lodged at court not less than three and not more than seven days before the hearing.

Rule 2.8 states the meaning of "clear days".

Depending on whether the application is to be made in the county court or the High Court reference should be made to the specialist court guides particularly for Queen's Bench Division Commercial Court and Chancery Division.

9–11 If the application to strike out the opponent's statement of case is a critical one, which may well be the case in a valuable debt recovery action, it is likely that counsel will have been instructed to review the merits of the case and to be the advocate on the day to put these points to the court. It should be noted that if the application itself is likely to take more than one hour then a skeleton argument should normally be prepared and counsel will assist in the preparation of this. Skeleton arguments themselves must be filed at court and served on all other parties prior to the hearing and in practice this is usually done the day before. It will usually be the party's solicitors who arrange for skeleton arguments to be simultaneously exchanged once they have been finalised by their respective counsel. Again, Practitioners are encouraged to check the relevant court guide for guidance on whether a skeleton argument is required but again Practitioners are reminded not to fall into the trap of producing such complex argument that the judge determines that the case is unsuitable for summary determination.

In preparing for the hearing it is likely that a costs order will be assessed summarily and therefore the parties are obliged to file and serve a schedule of costs that they will seek in the event of their success at least 24 hours before the hearing. This statement should follow as closely as possible Form N260 and must be signed by the party or his legal representative. Again, it will be taken from the notes on the file or the system and it is worth having it reviewed by a cost draftsman where there are significant costs incurred in preparation for the hearing. A failure to serve the necessary schedule will be taken into account by the court when deciding what order it should make.

Once prepared the schedule should be filed at court and served on the other party as soon as possible.

The title of the action, the number of hours spent on a particular task and the hourly rate of a solicitor performing a task need to be input. The total boxes will be calculated automatically the form must then be printed out and signed by the party's solicitor, any reference to cost draftsman should be taken out.

A copy of the form can be found at:

http://www.hmcourts-service.gov.u k/docs/guidanceappendix3.pdf.

9–12 Ideally and as always under the CPR, if the parties can agree terms prior to the hearing this is going to save time and costs. In a debt recovery action the tactic of applying to strike out a case may bring to the surface underlying issues which were not previously seen or it may be that the other side capitulates and agrees to make a payment.

A copy of any consent order signed by each of the party's representatives, be it counsel, the solicitor for the applicant, or a person with authority to bind each of the parties, such as a director should be lodged at court together with a copy for each party. The consent order that will then be drawn by the court and sealed and copies of the order will be sent to the applicant's solicitors who will then need to serve these on the respondent.

If an agreement is reached but it is too late to vacate the hearing the parties should still attend the court and, to inform the court of the consent order and its terms. A letter from the solicitor for any party not attending indicating agreement to the consent order should be obtained and shown to the court.

The court will take account of the party's conduct in reaching agreement at such a late stage when considering the position and its order on costs.

If consent cannot be reached then interim applications are generally heard by a district judge in the county court or a Master in the High Court.

Either the district judge or Master will consider the application and **9–13** the evidence in support. The merits of the application will be considered to see whether they satisfy the requirements set out in CPR 3.4. A decision will then be made whether to strike out the statement of case either in whole or in part in the applicant's favour or whether to make some alternative order. It is also possible that the judge will simply decide to dismiss the application.

As this is a hearing which is likely to last less than a day it would be usual for the court to summarily assess the amount of costs which will need to be paid to the successful party. As a general rule, and as we have said throughout this book, a costs order will be made in favour of the successful party.

In making its decision the court will consider the costs summary as filed by the losing party, and hear submissions from counsel where instructed, before it reaches a decision as to the amount of costs recoverable from the losing party. That party has 14 days to satisfy the costs order unless the court imposes a different time limit under the terms of CPR 44.8.

There is also a requirement under CPR 44.2 that where the representative of the paying party is not in court then the solicitor representing that party must within seven days of the hearing advise the client of the order made.

Although unlikely in an application to strike out a statement of **9–14** case in a debt recovery action, if the costs were to be substantial then the court would be unlikely to deal with them summarily and they would need to move to detailed assessment. However it would be open to a successful applicant to ask for a payment on account of costs before costs are assessed on the basis of CPR 44.3 (8).

Practitioners need to be aware that the hearing of an application to strike out a statement of case would usually be in a public forum which means that members of the public and/or the media may attend.

Hearings before a district judge may take place in chambers or in open court and hearings before a Master will take place in chambers.

The rules do provide for hearings to be by means of telephone conference as provided under CPR PD 23.

9–15 An application to strike out is a full hearing and therefore one might expect the following persons to be in attendance:

- The solicitor responsible for the day-to-day case management of the case and who has authority to deal with issues arising from any order that is made.
- Counsel, if instructed in a very critical case or a debt recovery action of a large amount, although in debt recovery this may be seen as overkill.
- A junior solicitor or a trainee may be taken along to deal with administrative matters such as taking the notes of the hearing and ensuring that the bundles are readily available as well as carrying the books!
- The client, or a representative of the client, who has the authority again to deal with any issues arising if the court is minded to make further orders. If the client or representative cannot attend the hearing then it is always a good idea to have them available by telephone in case a solicitor needs to seek further instructions.

All hearings in the county court and High Court are recorded unless the judge orders otherwise (see CPR PD 39 para.6.1). However there can be delays in having the transcript prepared and even once it is prepared then this has to be approved by the judge.

The important thing to remember is that in having the application before the court it gives the court a further opportunity to review the conduct of a case as a whole and give necessary case management directions. Parties should be ready to assist the court in doing so and to answer any questions the court may ask for this purpose (see CPR PD 23 para.2.9).

9–16 As mentioned earlier the evidence to be provided to the court will be through the written evidence in witness statements, the application notice itself or affidavits.

The advocate or counsel of the applicant will open the matter and introduce the parties and their representatives to the court. He or she will then take the court through the documentary material such as the index of the bundle, the chronology and any skeleton argument. Reference will be made to the witness statements and authorities in support of the applicant's position.

The respondent's advocate of counsel will then reply.

The applicant's advocate or counsel will normally be allowed a right of response but clearly on the day it is very much a matter for the judge on how he wishes the proceedings to be dealt with.

Once the judge has heard everything the parties have to say, he or she will make the decision whether to grant the order to strike out or some other order that the judge thinks fit. Clearly the overriding objective will be very firmly in his or her mind as there is a clear duty on the court to deal with the matter justly and this is an application which can have devastating consequences for a defendant at an early stage in the proceedings. 9–17

The orders that may be made are set out below:

An Unless Order	The court has the power to make an Unless Order whereby, unless compliance is made by a specified date, the offending statement of case will be struck out and the defence or claim dismissed. In the event of non-compliance the court does not have to make an additional order for the strike out to be effective and indeed see the decision in *Marcan Shipping (London) Limited v Kefalas* [2007] EWCA Civ 463 where the Court of Appeal made that point very clearly. A party that wishes to obtain judgment against a party that has failed to comply can do so by filing a request for judgment, where the order includes the term "statement of case will be struck out for failure to comply" and, that order relates to the whole of the statement of case, i.e. the defendant's defence, and where the party that is wishing to obtain the judgment is a claimant seeking a specified amount of money. If the Unless Order does not go as far as striking out the whole claim then the successful applicant will need to make an application under Pt 23.
Consequential Orders	Consequential Orders may be made as a result of the application to strike out a statement of case and if the court has made the striking out order on its own initiative then it may order directions admitting a party to file an amended statement of case.
Summary assessment of costs	See above.

Just as a guide to any hearing before a High Court Master. Once the order is made then the general rule is that the court draws the order, but in the Queen's Bench Division and the Commercial Court the order will be drawn up by the parties. 9–18

At interim hearings in the Queen's Bench Division the Master himself will endorse the order in handwriting on the original application, will initial a draft order and, if needs be, will make any amendments. There is an art to listening carefully to what the Master is saying and making a contemporaneous note at the same time as the Master endorses the order just in case the handwritten order is abbreviated in any way.

Once back at the office the Practitioner must draw the order as per the Master's endorsement and take the prepared order for sealing and the Master's endorsement to Central Office where they will check the endorsement and the draft order and, if satisfied they coincide, will seal the order.

In complicated matters in any court then the procedure will be to submit the final form of order to the judge for approval and sealing with sufficient copies for each party to be sealed as well. In the Queen's Bench Division the order will be sealed by the Judgment and Orders Section in Room E17.

Copies of the order will be sealed by the court and in a County Court it will be served by the court, who will arrange for service on all the parties.

Application for Summary Judgment

9–19 Alongside the application to strike out under CPR 3.4 is the parallel application of applying for summary judgment.

The tactics behind the application are to achieve a decision from the court early on to avoid the time and expense of litigation and, in debt recovery terms, flush out any hint of further information and to put the other side on notice that one is serious about recovering the debt. The summary judgment application may also be the catalyst for achieving a settlement far earlier than the cost and time involved in preparing for a full-blown trial.

The downside of making the application is that if it is unsuccessful it may cause delay in the proceedings and lead to adverse costs orders being made against the applicant and any costs order that is made must usually be paid quickly within 14 days of the order being made so this needs to be factored into tactics. However, as said above, if the defendant is acting in person one should be asking what are the likely costs of the defendant's time in preparing and responding to such an application.

In addition a default judgment will not be available to a claimant against the defendant when the application for summary judgment has been made and has not yet been disposed of (see CPR 12.3(3)(a)(ii)).

9–20 A warning was sounded in the case of *Doncaster Pharmaceuticals Group Limited and Others v Bolton Pharmaceuticals Co 100 Limited*

[2006] EWCA Civ 661, in which Mummery L.J. warned "cocky claimants" about making their applications too simple to show that summary determination was suitable. This needs to be contrasted with the situation in which an application to strike out, if the application is made too complicated, the judge may feel it is not right for a strike out application. Applicants should also consider whether it would be quicker to go straight to trial particularly if a court has delays in listing a hearing for summary judgment.

As always the applicant should also be advised of the likely costs of a summary judgment application, including the preparation and attendance time. Even if the cost of the defendant's time is going to be manageable because the defendant is not legally represented, then an applicant who is legally represented can expect a large solicitor/own client bill, which may or may not be recoverable from the defendant. Again it is hoped that that sort of consideration will have been given before the claim was issued as to the make up and financial standing of the defendant in the proceedings.

Generally speaking summary judgment application allows the judge to look at claims or issues without the full cost of a trial. Once again the overriding objective to dispose of cases in order to save time and unnecessary legal costs is a continuing duty.

The ground for making the application is that the other party has no real prospect of succeeding in his defence and therefore, there is no compelling reason to have a trial.

The grounds for summary judgment are set out in CPR 24.2. **9–21**

The rules are on the face of it simple. The court may give summary judgment against a claimant or defendant on the whole claim, or a particular issue within that claim, if it considers that either the claimant has no real prospect of succeeding on the claim or issue, or that the defendant has no real prospect of successfully defending the claim or issue and, as a result, there is no other compelling reason why the case or issue should be disposed of at trial.

In a debt recovery action a claimant therefore makes the application on the basis the defendant has no real prospect of succeeding on the defence and there is no compelling reason why the defence should not be disposed of at a full trial. Conversely a defendant can use the basis for summary judgment to seek early judgment on a counter claim.

However, we will be looking at summary judgment in this book from the point of view of the claimant who wishes to seek early judgments on the basis there is no prospect of the defendant succeeding on the defence put forward.

As one might expect there is a series of case law surrounding the **9–22**
court's view of whether a defence has a real prospect of succeeding or not.

The leading case on the meaning of "real prospect of success" is

Terence Paul Swain v Mr T. Hillman [2001] 1 All E.R. 91 and in particular the judgment given by Lord Woolf.

It was held in that case under CPR 24.2 the court had a very "salutary power" to dispose summarily of claims or defences which had no real prospect of succeeding but the words "no real prospect of succeeding" did not need any further amplification and the word "real" required the court to see whether that was realistic, as opposed to a fanciful, prospect of success. The facts of the case involved a plank which had been left in a static position in a garden against a tree for three days. The plank fell on the claimant but no explanation could be given as to the reason for the cause of the fall and this claim was based on the assertion that the defendants were the site occupiers and that someone must have been negligent in leaving the plank balanced against the tree. In response, the defendants contended that this assertion was too weak and there was no real prospect of success.

Initially the trial judge decided that the claim was too weak and would inevitably fail. But at the appeal it was seen that there were issues, which unless the parties could reach agreement, would need to be investigated at trial and it could be argued that the plank should not have been in the position to have allowed it to fall. There was also the issue about whether site occupation had lead to the causation of the plank falling. These were held to be matters for trial and the application for summary judgment could therefore not succeed.

9–23 The point from this case, is that the respondent to an application for summary judgment does not need to show that he will probably succeed at trial (using the Swain case there could be a lot of discussion about who left the plank where it was and whose responsibility was it to ensure the site was safe) but that would be a matter for trial and therefore the respondent need only show that there is some prospect that at trial he has a defence and he may succeed. In getting to that point the court must not conduct a mini-trial in which effectively justice is shortcut.

Moreover, in the case of *Three Rivers DC v Bank of England* (3) *(Summary Judgment)* [2001] (UKHL) 16, HL, whether the action has a real prospect of success has to be determined having regard to the overriding objective of dealing with the case justly. Given that legal and factual issues raised were highly complex in that particular case it was inappropriate to attempt to dispose of the case on the basis of the documents alone. There was a risk of pre-judging the case if any attempt were made to evaluate the action's prospects of success by consideration at a stage when neither documents have been disclosed or evidence have been given.

In *Doncaster Pharmaceuticals Group Limited and others v Bolton Pharmaceutical Co 100 Limited* (2006) ([2006] EWCA Civ 661 as already mentioned, Mummery L.J. warned against "cocky claimants" presenting legal and factual issues to the court as simpler and easier than they really were and "rubbishy defences" designed to make matters look unsuitable for summary determination.

Clearly the judge was not impressed with the actions of the parties in this case and there lies a salutary point. Summary judgment must be played as a tactic with a straight bat. Trying to use it to circumvent the need for a full trial and being less than straightforward as to the causes to the facts involved will result in judges taking a dim view of what is presented to them.

In addition to the first limb of the test, i.e. that the defence has no **9–24** real prospect of success, the second limb should be remembered, in that there is "no other compelling reason for a trial". A respondent who has failed to established that he has a real prospect of success may still prevent an order for summary judgment being made against him if he can show there is a compelling reason for a trial. Examples of what might constitute a compelling reason include:

- a defendant who has not had an opportunity to establish a defence;
- an applicant who has acted harshly or unconscionably;
- a respondent who has been able to contact a material witness who may be able to help the defence; and
- a case where the issues are too complicated and which requires proper consideration at trial (as per the *Three Rivers DC* case above).

So where does all of this leave the Debt Recovery Practitioner? An **9–25** evaluation of what is put forward in a defence to the debt claim needs to be established and does it demonstrate that there is no real prospect of success? A bare denial that the debt is owing may clearly satisfy that part of the test but what if the defendant has been able to contact a material witness who can confirm that the goods supplied are not at the necessary standard? Care must be taken to take on board the comments made by judges in recent years involving summary judgment applications, and also to bear in mind that debt recovery itself often has straightforward contractual issues and not the kinds of complexities that many of the reported cases have dealt with.

Assuming that the grounds for making the application can be established and the two limb test satisfied, so far as the claimant is concerned the application should be made as soon as it becomes apparent that there is no real prospect of the defendant succeeding in order to prevent unnecessary costs being incurred. If the application is made late or is delayed for any reason this can affect its credibility, so the ideal time to make the application is either before filing the allocation questionnaire or when completing Section D of the allocation questionnaire to the effect that an application for summary judgment is intended.

If the case is not allocated and the application for summary judgment subsequently fails then the case will not have lost its place in the queue for trial. It is also important not to ask for directions to be deferred in the allocation questionnaire simply because of the application for summary judgment. The process of moving towards trial should continue and should not be varied simply because there is a summary judgment application on the horizon.

9–26 The application itself cannot be made until the defendant has filed an acknowledgment of service or defence or the court gives permission.

It should be noted that if the debt claim involves proceedings against the Crown a claimant cannot apply for summary judgment until after the period allowed for filing a defence has expired even if the Crown files an acknowledgment of service or defence before that date (see CPR 24.4.1A).

The application itself will be made on Form N244 which can be found on the court Service website at *http://www.hmcourts-service.gov.uk/courtfinder/forms/n244_e.pdf*. There is a guidance note to assist in the completion of this form.

The application notice itself must include a statement that the application is for summary judgment under Pt 24 of the rules along with other requirements set out in CPR PD 24: (the summary disposal of claims) para.2. This Practice Direction requires the applicant to identify concisely the points on which he intends to rely to demonstrate the respondent has no real prospect of succeeding to defend the claim and a statement that the applicant knows of no reason why the disposal of the issue should await a trial.

9–27 The relevant court guides should be checked for additional requirements in relation to hearings both under Commercial Court, Queen's Bench Division and Chancery Division.

As for other applications, written evidence must be verified by the accompanying statements of truth signed in the appropriate way as required by CPR Pt 22.

The applicant should attend court with a draft of the order sought. However, it is worth anticipating what other orders the court may be minded to make and ensuring that draft orders are prepared at least in outline to take along to the hearing.

As in the application to strike out a statement of case the application notice must be filed at court and the court fee must be paid and again details of the up-to-date fees for "on notice" applications can be found in the Civil Proceedings Fees Order 2008 as updated on the Court Service website.

9–28 The application notice together with the evidence in support and the draft order, such as it may be, should be served on every respondent to the application. Respondents should be given at least 14 days notice of the fixed date for the hearing along with notice of the issues that the court will be asked to decide at the hearing.

The same rules apply in relation to preparation of the application bundle as for an application to strike out (see above).

Again where the application is likely to take more than an hour then a skeleton argument will need to be prepared which, if counsel is involved, counsel will normally draft. Again, the same requirements as for an application to strike out a statement of case apply. Under CPR PD 24: (the summary disposal of claims) para.2(4), if an applicant wishes to submit witness evidence in response to any evidence put forward by the respondent he needs to file and serve copies on the respondent at least three days before the hearing but there is no requirement for this evidence to be identified in the application notice.

In relation to costs then a statement needs to be prepared if costs are to be assessed summarily on Form N260 as set out above for an application to strike out a statement of case. **9–29**

If the court fixes the date for the summary judgment hearing on its own initiative the parties will be given at least 14 days notice of the date of the hearing along with the issues to be considered by the court (see CPR 24.4(3)).

It is also worth bearing in mind that in a debt recovery action a defendant may come back on an application for summary judgment with a defence of "set-off" which is defined in CPR 16.6. The definition in the CPR as to "set-off" is where the defendant contends he is entitled to money from the claimant and he relies on this as a defence to the whole or part of his claim. This contention may be included in the defence and set-off against the claim whether or not it is part of a counterclaim.

A defendant may therefore seek to defeat the claimant's application for summary judgment on the basis that this is why the claim for the amount outstanding should proceed to a full trial. In the notes to CPR 16.6 (defence of set-off) if a court summarily disposes of the issues raised by the claimant's claim, the position of the defendant who has pleaded the set-off will need to be protected by an order delaying enforcement of the judgment until after the trial on the cross-claim.

It should be noted that if a claimant makes an application following the filing of an acknowledgment on of service for summary judgment then there is no requirement on the defendant to file a defence before the hearing of the application (see CPR 24.4(2)). However, there is nothing to prevent the defendant also filing a defence if he wishes to do so and probably from the point of view of getting all the issues out on the table it is better if a defence is prepared. **9–30**

Exactly the same issues in relation to the hearing of the application apply to a summary judgment application as they do to an application to strike out a statement of case.

The burden of proof firstly falls on the applicant to establish his case (see *ED&F Man Liquid Products Limited v Jitendra Patel* [2003] EWCA Civ 472 at para.7 to 9). The applicant has to prove the respondent has no real prospect of success in his defence or counterclaim and there is no compelling reason why the case should proceed to a full trial. If the applicant puts forward sufficient evidence to discharge the burden of proof then the evidential burden shifts to the respondent.

The respondent then is in the position of having to prove that the defence does have some real prospect of success and that there exists some other reason for a trial. The standard of proof required of the respondent in this scenario is not high. It will be enough for the respondent to rebut the applicant's statement of belief although the rebuttal must carry some conviction. Therefore, a respondent who could show that he may succeed, even if improbable that he will actually do so, will have discharged the burden of proof and the application so far as the claimant is concerned will be lost.

9–31 After the hearing the judge will then make his decision and then the order will be made. The orders that can be made following a summary judgment application include:

- judgment on the claim or issue;
- an order striking out the defence;
- dismissal of the application; and
- various conditional orders.

The court will also consider the question of who should bear the cost of the application.

The judge will dictate the terms of the order granted and where the parties are to draw up the order it is essential that a detailed note of the court's decision is taken by both counsel and solicitors; and indeed anybody else on behalf of the party who is in the court. It is surprising how often it becomes difficult to transcribe back that order in the office!

9–32 Should the application be dismissed the court will give case management directions as to the future conduct of the case (see CPR PD 24: (A summary disposal of claims) para.10).

This might include, if the respondent is a defendant, an order requiring a filing of a defence and directions as to the further management of the case.

If for any reason a party who was required to attend the summary judgment hearing remained absent and summary judgment was ordered against him he would be entitled to apply to have it set aside or varied by virtue of CPR PD 24 para.8.1 and on the hearing of any such application the court may make such order as it thinks fit.

An order for summary judgment may also be appealed, although the permission of the court will be required, and that appeal must be filed within 21 days of the date of the order.

Insofar as drawing up the order is concerned then the general **9–33** rule is that the court draws the order, although in the Queen's Bench Division and Commercial Court the order will be drawn by the parties, and in the Queen's Bench Division the Master will endorse the order in handwriting upon the original application or initial draft order having made the amendments, for the party then to produce the final order which will be sealed by the judgments and Order Section in Room E17 at Central Office.

When the court draws up the order sealed copies will be served on each party by the court which is the usual practice in the County Court. Where the parties draw the order then sufficient copies will need to be sealed by the court and returned to the applicant's solicitors for service.

How should accidental slips and omissions be dealt with in a debt recovery action?

It is part of life in a busy debt recovery department that there are **9–34** going to be mistakes and the person leading the team needs to have procedures in place for when these occur so they can be corrected quickly and with as little impact as possible on the action.

Fortuitously, r.40.12(1) is known as the "slip rule". Under this rule the court may at any time correct an accidental slip or omission in a judgment or order. Generally speaking it is used to correct typographical mistakes.

However, the slip rule can also be used to correct more substantial errors and omissions, although it cannot be used to correct errors of substance, or to detract from the original order made by the judge (see *R+V Versicherung AG v Risk Insurance and Reinsurance Solutions SA* [2007] EWHC 79).

In addition to the slip rule the court itself has an inherent power to vary its own orders or make the meaning and intention of the court clear (see CPR PD 40B para.4).

However, the slip rule cannot be used to amend an order, allow **9–35** time for consideration and then make a further order. The Court of Appeal in *Roadrunner Properties Ltd v Dean* [2004] EWCA Civ 376 made that perfectly clear. The court stated that the purpose of CPR 40.12 is only to enable the court to amend an order which has been perfected and as a result fails to implement the intention of the court by virtue of the order as drawn.

An application to use the slip rule may be made informally by letter or under CPR Pt 23. The application itself may be dealt with without notice if so requested by the applicant, or with the consent of the parties or without a hearing, if the court considers that appropriate.

If the application to amend the order is going to be opposed then it should be listed for hearing before the judge who made the judgment or order in question.

For practical purposes it should be remembered that the giving of any judgment will be in essence a two-stage process. At the end of the hearing a judge will give his decision or hand down a written judgment. That judgment will then be drawn and sealed by the court and in most cases there will be a period of time between the two events happening.

9–36 The date when the judgment is given, either through the judge giving it at the end of the hearing or the later written decision, becomes the date when the order takes effect (see CPR 40.7). This is important because the time to appeal the judgment begins to run from that date (see CPR 52.4). Of course it is open to the court to order that the time the order will run from can be different, but generally speaking that will be the situation.

Before the court close the order, even though it is made when it is given under CPR 40.7, there is a discretion for the judge to alter, or indeed reverse, its decision although this discretion will only be used in exceptional circumstances. In the case of *Venture Finance Plc v Mead* [2005] EWCA Civ 325 Arden L.J. explains a point in his judgment saying that from time to time a point would be made to the judge after his judgment has been given and that having considered that point he should consider the "materiality" of what has been said and if it undermines the judgment it may be necessary to change his decision. Arden L.J. felt this would not happen very often but it was worth reminding the parties of the judge's entitlement.

In the case of *Robinson v Bird* [2003] EWCA Civ 1820 the Court of Appeal emphasised that the court's jurisdiction to recall, vary or alter a judgment existed up to the time the order was perfected, whether the judgment had been given orally, handed down to the parties in draft, or formally handed down.

Debt Recovery Practitioners should not be surprised or fazed if any of these points happen and indeed should take advantage of the slip rule as and when required.

General Applications

9–37 Part 23 of the rules sets out the general rules about applications for court orders which Debt Recovery Practitioners need to be aware of and utilise from time to time when a case is found to be not straightforward when moving from claim to default judgment.

Varying A Default Judgment

As we saw in Chapter 7, many default judgments are obtained simply by the request being entered and involve no judicial scrutiny. Where a defendant considers that he has grounds to contend that a default judgment should be set aside then he should follow the procedures set out in CPR Pt 13. For Debt Recovery Practitioners they will need to know how to respond to such an application as it will be made frequently, particularly so in a busy department. **9–38**

If the default judgment was obtained by application as opposed to a simple request this means it will have been considered by a judge at Master/district judge level and therefore the defendant has two options either to apply to set aside the judgment under CPR Pt 13 or alternatively to appeal it. The application, if it is going to be made, is going to have to be made promptly by the defendant which is underlined in the contents of CPR 13.3(2).

The court will look at any delay that he has incurred in making the application and, if there has been a delay, that is going to have to be addressed in the supporting evidence as to why judgment should be set aside. The application itself will be made in accordance with CPR Pt 23 as it is an application, under CPR 13.4. This part of the rules expressly states that:

- where the claim is for a specified amount of money;
- judgment was obtained in a court which is not the defendant's home court;
- the claim has not been transferred to another home court; and
- the defendant is an individual,

then the court will transfer the application by the defendant under this rule to his home court to have the matter reviewed.

Generally speaking if the court has entered judgment wrongly it will be required to set it aside. Rule 13.2 sets out the categories in which this may be the case.

So a court must set aside a judgment which has been wrongly entered where: **9–39**

- the claimant obtained default judgment before the deadline to file the acknowledgement of service had expired;

- the claimant obtained default judgment before the deadline to file the defence had expired;
- the claimant obtained default judgment after the defendant had made a strike out application under CPR 3.4 or a summary judgment application under CPR Pt 24 and the relevant application had not been disposed of when default judgment was entered; and
- the whole of claim (including interests and costs) was satisfied before judgment was entered, or in relation to debt recovery claims, i.e. money claims, the claimant obtained default judgment after the defendant had filed or served an admission under CPR 14.4 or CPR 14.7 with a request for time to pay.

If any, of these situations apply then the court must set the judgment aside regardless of the defendant's lack of prospects of success (see *Credit Agricole Indosuez v Unicof Ltd* [2003] All E.R. (0)21).

9–40 In *Hart Investments v Fidler* [2006] EWHC 2857 it was held that for the default judgment to be valid it would have to be based on a correct certificate of service and a valid request for judgment. If the certificate of service was found to have had the wrong date and the request was premature then default judgment would be set aside.

In that case it was also noted that even if the judgment had been validly entered the court would have exercised its discretion under CPR 13.3 to set it aside because the claimant's solicitor's conduct was considered by the court to be aggressive and unreasonable—a warning for all Debt Recovery Practitioners anxious to recover a debt!

The issue of service can also lead to a court intervening and the court must be satisfied that the defendant was properly served (see Chapter 6 of this book) and the default judgment was obtained in accordance with CPR Pt 12. In the case of *Shiblaq v Sadikoglu (Application to Set Aside) (No.2)* [2004] EWHC 1890, the default judgment in that case was set aside under CPR 13.2 because there was no proof that the claim had been validly served.

This can be contrasted with the case of *Akram v Adam* [2004] EWCA Civ 1601 CA in which it was found that the defendant was unaware that proceedings had been served but the court held that if the claim was deemed to have been served in accordance with the CPR that would be sufficient service.

9–41 In those circumstances the defendant was not entitled to set the judgment aside under CPR 13.2, the court had to consider the application under CPR 13.3 if it could find the defendant had a real prospect of successfully defending the claim or there was some other good reason why the court should set aside or vary the judgment or the defendant should be allowed to defend the claim.

So this once again underlines the need for Debt Recovery Practitioners to be clear on the rules on service (see Chapter 6) and to ensure that they can prove service when the time comes. Practitioners need to ensure their systems, whether computerised or manual, diarise and allow time for acknowledgement of service and time to file defences to expire, as being eager to enter judgment will land them on the wrong end of an application to set aside.

As mentioned above if the default judgment was not wrongly entered under CPR 13.2 the court still has a discretion to set it aside pursuant to CPR 13.3 and the court may do that if it considers the defendant has a real prospect of successfully defending the claim or it appears to the court there is some other good reason why judgment should be set aside or varied.

The defendant should be advised of the likely cost of preparing the application and attending the application hearing, although in many instances in this day and age defendants are not legally represented and it will simply be the cost of their time in attending court together with their travel costs.

If the default judgment was entered wrongly a claimant, being **9–42** the respondent to the application to set aside or vary, will usually be ordered to pay the defendant's costs of bringing the application. This is another reason why Debt Recovery Practitioners must tread carefully to ensure that judgment is entered in the correct way. If default judgment is set aside pursuant to the court's discretion then the cost of the application will be at the discretion of the court but generally the claimant will bear the defendant's cost if he is successful in overturning the judgment.

If the application is unsuccessful then of course the defendant can expect to be on the wrong end of a costs order but again as we have said throughout this book the practical implications of that and the financial ones are, that even if a costs order is made against a defendant, will they have the means to actually pay it?

To prevent an application to set aside or vary the judgment getting out of hand if a claimant realises that judgment has been entered when it should not have been then the parties should seek to agree to set aside the default judgment by consent and a consent order should be made.

If, however, the claimant wishes to defend his position of judgment being entered then evidence is going to be needed to respond to the defendant's application. Consideration should be given to what conditional orders he contends the court should impose on the defendant if the application is successful and should specify how much the defendant should pay into court if the court is minded to make such an order.

If the claimant produces evidence then this needs to be filed and **9–43** served as soon as possible but in any event prior to the hearing.

If there is going to be a hearing then a bundle will probably need to be prepared and that has been dealt with elsewhere in this chapter. In this situation, however, there may be no co-operation between solicitors as to what goes into the bundle, or what should be in the bundle, and therefore the solicitors for both parties should check that all necessary documents have been included to deal with each party's position.

Once again a statement of costs should be prepared and signed by the party or his legal representative and filed not less than 24 hours before the date fixed for the hearing. The statement should follow closely Form N260 discussed elsewhere in this chapter.

9–44 A skeleton argument may be required if the hearing is likely to last more than one hour and certainly will be needed if counsel is likely to be the advocate on the day.

As in other applications there is always the opportunity for a consent order to be prepared and comments made elsewhere in this chapter apply to that type of order as much as they do to any other type of application.

As this is an interim application it will generally be heard by a Master in the High Court or a district judge in the county court, although applications can be referred to a judge depending on the complexities of the issues.

Once again the hearing will be, in theory, in public although more usually it will take place in chambers either before a Master or a district judge. Similar considerations apply about who should attend court.

9–45 At the hearing the counsel or the advocate for the applicant or indeed, in many cases, the applicant himself, will open the matter to the district judge but if the applicant is a litigant in person the district judge will generally take control of the proceedings to ensure that all the formalities are dealt with.

If the respondent is seeking a conditional order the applicant should provide the court with evidence of his means and whether or not he is able to make a payment into court.

If the order is made setting aside the default judgment under CPR 13.3(2) the court will not impose any conditions on the defendant and the defendant is likely to be awarded his costs to be paid by the claimant.

If the defendant is able to achieve an order setting aside the default judgment on the basis that he has a real prospect of successfully defending the claim, the court may make a conditional order, which may be on the basis that the defendant makes a payment into court. The court should consider any evidence put forward by the defendant as to how much he is able to pay into court.

9–46 As the hearing itself is likely to last less than a day the court will usually summarily assess the amount of costs.

If the default judgment was wrongly entered and is subsequently set aside under CPR 13.2 the claimant will probably be ordered to pay the defendant's costs of bringing the application. If however the default judgment is set aside pursuant to the court's discretion under CPR 13.3 then the cost of the application will be at the discretion of the court, and the general rule will be that the claimant will bear the defendant's cost if the defendant succeeds. Other possible costs orders include costs "thrown away" or "costs in the cause" or indeed no order for costs at all.

Whatever the final form of order the general rule is the court will draw up the order unless in the Queen's Bench Division or Commercial Court where the order is drawn up by the parties.

Finally, CPR 13.3(1) states that the court may vary a default judgment if the defendant has a real prospect of successfully defending the claim or it appears there is some other good reason why the judgment should be varied. For example a judgment may be varied so that it is judgment in part only or so that instalment arrangements are paid.

The procedure to apply to vary the default judgment is the same for setting judgment aside under CPR 13.4 and again an application notice must be served on Form N244 supported by a statement of truth and supporting evidence.

How is the Statement of Case Amended?

CPR Pt 17 deals with issues surrounding the amendment of a statement of case. **9–47**

It is important to note that once the statement of case has been served which includes the claim form, the particulars, the defence, counterclaim and reply then these can only be amended with the consent of all other parties or with the permission of the court.

The rules that impact on the amendments to the statement of case include Pt 1 in terms of the court and the parties meeting the overriding objective along with Pt 3 being the case management powers of the court, Pt 19 relating to the additional substitution of a party and Pt 36 offers.

When making an amendment to a statement of case the party should remember that the content of the original statement will have been verified by a statement of truth under CPR Pt 22 and any amendment inconsistent with the content of the original statement of case is therefore going to need an explanation. Such an amendment may also cause embarrassment in cross-examination and even expose the parties the risk of contempt of proceedings (see CPR 32.14). So this is not a step to be undertaken without careful consideration.

Can a statement of case be amended after Judgment?

9–48 Only in exceptional circumstances can the court allow an amendment to a statement of case after the Judgment has been given (see *Re Barrell Enterprise* [1972] 3 All E.R. 631).

This case was well before the CPR was ever contemplated but it was adopted in the case of *Stewart v Engel* [2000] 3 All E.R. 518 and it was held that the *Barrell* principles of the 1973 case remained relevant post CPR.

When can a statement of case be amended?

9–49 Debt recovery practitioners need to be aware that a statement of case can be amended anytime before it has been served on the other party.

Where the statement of case has been served, however, as mentioned earlier it can only be amended with the written consent of all the parties or the permission of the court.

Where the statement has been served the application to amend the statement of case by removing, adding or substituting a party is made in accordance with r.19.4.

The Practice Direction accompanying Pt 19 provides for the additional substitution of a defendant which is often the case in debt recovery proceedings when the claimant realises they may have sued the wrong person, such as a limited company, when in fact it was described as a partnership.

9–50 It is unlikely that the defendant is likely to want to be sued and therefore for practical purposes the application to substitute or add a new defendant is likely to be an on notice application. The application must be supported by evidence setting out the proposed new party's interest in or connection with the claim. The application itself should be filed in accordance with r.23.3 and be served in accordance with r.23.4.

The order giving permission to amend if made will unless the court decides otherwise, be drawn up and then it will need to be served by the court on all the parties, usually by the court itself.

Where the court makes an order adding or substituting a defendant it may direct:

- the claimant to file with the court within 14 days or any other period it orders an amended claim form and accompanying particulars for the court file;
- a copy of the order to be served on all parties to the proceedings; and

- the amended claim form, accompanying particulars and the response pack to be served on the new defendant and for the amended claim form and accompanying particulars to be served on any other Defendants.

It should then be noted that by virtue of the Practice Direction a new defendant will not become a party to the proceedings until the amended claim form has been served on him (see *Kettleman v Hansel Properties Ltd* [1987] A.C. 189 HL).

If the party is incorrectly named how easy is it for this to be amended?

Under CPR 17.4 if there is a genuine mistake in naming the party **9–51** to an action and for some reason there was no reasonable doubt as to the identity of that party when it was initially sued then the court will by applying the overriding objective, give permission to amend the statement of case so that the correct name is given and there is no need to rely on CPR 19.5 regarding special provisions in adding or substituting parties.

A good example of this is the case of *Gregson v Channel Four Television Corporation* [2000] All E.R.(D) 956 in which the Claimant mistakenly issued defamation proceedings against "Channel Four Television Co Ltd" which was found to be a dormant company, instead of against "Channel Four Television Corporation". However, Debt Recovery Practitioners, in making their pre-action checks and indeed from credit application forms, should be verifying the name of the party they are contracting with at the outset of the customer relationship and therefore it should be less likely in a debt recovery situation that name of the party is incorrectly sued.

Reference is also made to the case of *Morgan Est (Scotland) Ltd v Hanson Concrete Products Ltd* [2005] EWCA Civ 134 in which again the claimant has made a genuine mistake in the claim form as to the names of the parties. As the defendant had not been misled the court exercised its discretion to allow the claimant to join two other parties as first and third claimants respectively using the adding and substitution provisions of CPR Pt 19. The court in that case also permitted consequent amendments to the particulars of claim.

Chapter 10

The Enforcement Arena

Introductory Comments

The first nine chapters of this book have prepared a Debt Recovery Practitioner to achieve a judgment whether it be through a default hearing, or through one of the track processes culminating in a full hearing dependent on the value of the claim. The successful claimant will now have a piece of paper from the court, usually on Form N30, confirming judgment in their favour. If Practitioners have taken on the tenets of this book they will already have a strategy on how to enforce that judgment in the event the defendant decides not to pay. 10–01

For well prepared claimants who will now become the judgment creditors where they have the benefit of a judgment to enforce, the enforcement arena holds no fear. They should be able to move through the various methods of enforcement to achieve the ultimate outcome which is payment of their judgment debt.

For the less well prepared the enforcement arena can be a minefield of cost, delay and disappointment. It for this reason that we encourage reading of this book to take onboard the ideas and strategies set out in Chapters 1 and 3 of this book so that by the time they or their client reach this stage of the debt recovery process there is no need to incur unnecessary cost, suffer undue delay or be bitterly disappointed.

Enforcement is all about forcing the judgment debtor to pay. It is not going to be an exact science and it is not always going to be 100 per cent successful. What it should enable the judgment creditor to do is to understand if payment cannot be achieved why that is so, and close the file knowing that they navigated the system as well as they could but at the end of the day one cannot "get blood out of a stone".

With those thoughts in mind the enforcement arena itself is undergoing a significant change. 10–02

In 2007 the Tribunals Courts and Enforcement Act gained Royal Assent and is now on the statute books waiting for its enabling regulations by way of delegated legislation to be made.

References to the new Act will be made later on using the Enforcement Matrix. For the moment we must continue to enforce under the current Rules and highlight where the changes are likely to come and what may be the new regime for enforcement as a result of changes to be introduced.

What is the starting point for the enforcement arena within the rules?

10–03 The starting point within the rules for enforcement is CPR Pt 69 which deals with the appointment of a receiver and it has almost by historical accident ended up as Pt 69 when in fact it is not the section of the rules which sets out the structure for Civil Court enforcement. We will look at appointment of receivers later in this chapter.

The starting point then becomes CPR Pt 70. Ideally Pt 70 would have codified all the existing rules for enforcement into one new rule but unfortunately we still have to refer to High Court and county court business based on pre-CPR rules and which still exist in the CPR by virtue of Sch.1 and Sch.2. Schedule 1 deals with High court business and existing rules and Sch.2 deals with the county court part of the rules.

A Practitioner is therefope going to be need to be familiar with CPR Pt 70 as well as CPR Sch.1 RSC Orders 45, 46, 47 as well as CPR Sch.2 CCR Orders 25, 26 and 27.

What does CPR Part 70 cover?

10–04 CPR Pt 70 was added as part of a series of new rules published in March 2002 to start the codification of the existing rules on enforcement and to unify procedures between the county court and the High Court in relation to the enforcement of judgments. CPR Pt 70 was thought to be the corner stone for further rule changes starting with being CPR Pt 71 (orders to obtain information), CPR Pt 72 (third party debt orders), and CPR Pt 73 (Charging Orders).

CPR Pt 70 does set the scene for how the enforcement regime under the new rules will operate both now and in the future and again it is accompanied by the all important Practice Direction.

CPR 70.1 sets out a number of definitions in the relation to the enforcement of judgments and these definitions needs to be understood by Practitioners because once a debt passes the judgment milestone in proceedings the names of the parties change. Up until this point we have referred to the creditor as the claimant in proceedings and the debtor as defendant in proceedings. Once the judgment has been obtained then the claimant becomes the "judgment creditor" and the defendant becomes the judgment debtor". Of course it is always possible in a debt recovery action that in fact it will be the defendant who will win on a counterclaim or costs order and they then become the "judgment creditor" with the person against whom the order is made being the "judgment debtor". This is known as a "reverse action" and care needs to be taken when enforcing a reversed action because occasionally it is possible to send an HCEO to the door of the person who might be named the defendant in proceedings but who has the benefit of the judgment!

CPR 70.1(D) defines "judgment or order for the payments of money" to include a judgment or order for the payment of costs, however, to enforce a costs order the amount of costs payable must have been determined before enforcement begins.

What are the various methods of enforcing judgments and orders?

Under CPR 70 PD 1 the various methods of enforcing judgments and orders for the payment of money are set out. These includes: **10–05**

- a Writ of Fieri Facias or Warrant of Execution (see RSC Orders 45, 46, 47, and CCR Order 26 respectively;
- a third party debt order (see CPR Pt 72);
- a charging order (see CPR Pt 73);
- in the County Court an attachment of earnings order (see CCR Order 27); and
- the appointment of a receiver (see CPR Pt 69);

In relation to either a Writ of FiFa or a Warrant of Execution the process is "wholly administrative" and requires no judicial intervention or decision making. That said once the process is underway support and guidance from the court may well be necessary as execution against goods of a debtor often throws up a number of legal issues which need to be dealt with by judicial intervention including claims to goods by the parties and claims that the goods siezed are exempt from siezure.

Is simultaneous enforcement possible?

CPR 70.2(2) (b) expressly allows the simultaneous enforcement of judgments by different methods. By this we are describing the process where the judgment creditor can use one method of enforcement alongside another. Practitioners were often confused under the old rules as to whether or not they were allowed to use simultaneous **10–06** methods of enforcement but the new rules expressedly provide for this. The practical effect of this is that a Practitioner can seek to put a charge over a judgment debtor's property whilst at the same time instructing the County Court bailiff or High Court Enforcement Officer to levy execution on all available goods at that property. The only exception to simultaneous enforce ment is that an attachment of earnings order cannot be pursued in conjunction with any other method of enforcement.

What should the judgment creditor do if he is unsure as to the choice to make?

10–07 Hopefully by reading this book Practitioners will be much clearer about the choices open to them and build strategies to suit their debt recovery department! However, if a judgment creditor is stuck as to the method of enforcement to use, the Rules come to the aid of the Practitioner in the shape of CPR Pt 71 in which the judgment debtor can be cross-examined as to income and expenditure and other assets. More details about this procedure and how to use it strategically are set out in Chapter 11.

How can the enforcement of the judgment or order be affected?

10–08 The Practice Direction to CPR Pt 70 expressly confirms at para.1.3 that insolvency procedures and County Court administration orders can affect the enforcement of a court's judgment or order. Practitioners need to be aware of both of these types of issue because effectively if they come in to play then the enforcement of the judgment for the benefit of the creditor alone will be lost. This is one of the reasons why Practitioners need to move swiftly in making their enforcement choice and getting on with the procedure before insolvency intervenes or an administration order is made.

If a judgment is left on file for too long it is possible the judgment debtor will be advised to take shelter from creditors or to consolidate debts under an Administration Order and the benefit of achieving judgment will be lost to the judgment creditor.

How are proceedings transferred from one County Court to another?

10–09 CPR 70.3 provides for judgments to be transferred as allowed across the Civil Court system. A judgment creditor wishing to enforce a

High court judgment or order in the county court can apply to the High Court for an order transferring the proceedings to the county court in question. Under CCR Order 25 r.13 provisions regarding the transfer of county court proceedings to the High Court for enforcement are set out and follow the provisions of the High Court and County Court Jurisdiction Order 1991, art.8 (as amended).

Why would a judgment creditor wish to request a transfer from the county court to the High court?

The most common reason for transferring a judgment from the County Court to the High Court is to use the services of a High Court Enforcement Officer to seize goods belonging to a judgment debtor. This process called "execution against goods" is explained in Chapter 14. However there is a process to go through to arrange for the judgment to be transferred. As is said elsewhere in this book only judgments over £600 which are not regulated by the Consumer Credit Act 1974 (as amended) can be transferred to the High Court. If the decision is made to transfer the judgment then the starting point in the Rules is CPR Sch.2, CCR Order 25 r.13. **10–10**

To transfer the judgment, a judgment creditor will need to make a request to the court for a certificate of judgment (see CPR Sch.2, CCR Order 22 r.8). The certificate will enable him to take proceedings on the judgment in another court or to enforce the judgment or order in the High Court. The certificate actually comes in the form of a standard court form being Form N.293A. It is a form which needs to be completed on the front initially and then once the County Court has completed its part of the administration, and returns the form to the judgment creditor, it has to be completed on the reverse.

Where the certificate is required for the purpose of enforcing the judgment in the High Court the applicant being the judgment creditor, completes Form N.293A stating that it is intended to enforce the judgment or order by execution against goods. Provided this is approved the certificate itself will be signed by a court manager or other court officer on behalf of the court.

By virtue of s.42 of the county courts Acts 1984 (as amended by the Courts and Legal Services Act 1990), provision is made for specific judgments of the county court to be transferred to the High Court for enforcement. As a result when a judgment is transferred to the High Court it becomes a judgment as if it had been issued in the High Court to begin with, and will be treated as the judgment or order of the High Court for all purposes except in relation to the power to set aside the judgment, or correct or vary the judgment. These applications which often occur post judgment continue to be county court matters to be resolved in that court by application. In practice, however, a judgment debtor, if faced with High Court enforcement action may well apply to both the district judge in the County Court, and from time to time the Master, in the High Court to seek some reprieve against imminent enforcement action.

How can a non party enforce an order or judgment?

10–11 Under CPR 70.4 orders in favour of or against a non-party are "rare" but may arise where a costs order is given against a solicitor or a solicitor who perhaps undertakes to pay a non-party's costs. A non-party who has the benefit of such an order will not need permission to enforce that order against the party ordered to pay, and the same methods of enforcement are available to the non-party as are available for other enforceable judgments and orders.

How are awards of bodies other than the High Court and county courts enforced?

10–12 It is just worth noting that under CPR 70.5 provision is made for the enforcement of awards coming from tribunals. These forums may indeed award a sum of money to a successful applicant and as such this award creates a form of money judgment which needs to be enforced.

If a Practitioner is dealing with the enforcement of a money judgment arising from a tribunal award the salient point to remember is that the award itself has to be converted into an enforceable judgment before enforcement action can begin.

What is the effect of a successful application to set aside a judgment or order?

10–13 Under CPR 70.6 if a judgment or order is set aside then the enforcement of that judgment or order has to cease immediately unless the court makes an order to the contrary. There is also the issue of costs to consider. The issue of who is going to pay the costs will be dealt with at the application to set aside the judgment.

How is interest dealt with on judgment debts?

10–14 The accompanying Practice Direction to CPR Pt 70 deals with the issue of interest on judgment debts. The Practice Direction is not self-contained however due to the rather piecemeal approach surrounding interest in debt recovery proceedings and particularly that of interest on judgment debts.

If a judgment creditor is claiming interest on a judgment debt he must include in his application or request to issue enforcement proceedings details of the following:

- the amount of interest claimed and the sum on which it is claimed;
- the dates from and to which interest is accrued; and
- the rate of interest which has been applied, and where more than one rate of interest has been applied, the relevant days and dates used to compute the interest.

Interest on a High Court judgment runs from the date of judgment being the date when the judgment is pronounced, not the date when judgment is finally entered (see *Parsons v Mather & Platt Ltd* [1977] 2 All E.R. 715) and s.17 of the Judgments Act 1838.

The current prevailing rate for interest on judgment debts is 8 per cent per annum which has been in place since April 1, 1993 by virtue of the judgment Debts (Rate of Interest) Order 1993 (SI 1993/564).

The corresponding county court provision is s.74 of the County **10–15**
Courts Act 1984. Under this statutory provision the County Courts (Interest on judgment Debts) Order 1991 specifies when interest may be claimed on a county court judgment. County court judgments carry interest from the date of judgment only for sums over £5,000. For sums under this amount interest stops at judgment in a county court matter unless the contract allows for interest post judgment.

The rules on interest post judgment can therefore be summarised as follows:

- Interest on a county court judgment ceases at judgment unless there is a provision for interest under the contract or under statute for interest to run after judgment.
- Interest on county court judgments over £5,000 continues from the date of the judgment until the judgment is satisfied—Practitioners should, however, transfering judgments to the High Court for enforcement as for a judgment debt over £5,000.
- Interest on county court judgments between £600 and £5,000 is available from the date of when the certificate of judgment on Form N.293A is issued by the county court and again this could be a reason for a Practitioner making a decision to transfer to the High court.

- The statutory interest on a judgment or order for the payment of costs runs from the date of the judgment or order, which is a better position than the interest running from the date of the final costs certificate (see *Hunt v RM Douglas (Roofing) Ltd* [1988] 3 All E.R. 823, HL) and again may prove to a fiscal advantage to recoup as much as possible from the litigation process.

As can be seen the current situation regarding interest on judgments is messy and an opportunity to reform the position and to clarify the rules is well overdue.

What happens if a judgment debt is paid after the issue of enforcement proceedings?

10–16 In the Practice Direction to CPR Pt 70 at para.7, if a judgment debt is paid:

- after the enforcement proceedings have been issued;
- but before any Writ or Warrant has been executed; or
- before there has been any hearing on application to deal with the enforcement of the judgment such as the final hearing of a Charging Order application,

then the judgment creditor must notify the court in writing of the amount paid. If a judgment debt, or part of it, is paid after the judgment creditor has applied to the High Court for a Writ of Execution then the judgment creditor must immediately notify the relevant HCEO in writing of that fact as clearly the HCEO must not be taking further enforcement action if the full amount has been paid. However, it is worth pointing out at this stage, that the amount an HCEO will be looking for to clear the balance of the Writ if he has already levied, will be far higher than the amount of the judgment debt, any costs and interest on the judgment. An HCEO will be looking for payment of his fees which as a result of any Writ issued to him he will be entitled to charge if he as levied on any goods. The best way for Practitioners to approach this is to ask the HCEO to confirm the amount due throughout the progress of the enforcement of the Writ and ensure that if a proposal of payment is offered that the HCEO's position is always checked before accepting any sums for a lesser amount.

Clearly if payment in full is made then the enforcement of the judgment comes to a close, subject to the necessary paying away provisions being met. It is surprising how many cheques can bounce when intended for payment in full of the judgment debt.

What other areas of the rules should Practitioners be aware of?

As said at the outset of the this chapter not only does Pt 70 set the regime for the enforcement of judgments but Practitioners need to be able to navigate their way around CPR Sch.1 and CPR Sch.2 where the old Rules are still relevant when it comes to the enforcement of the court's judgment. 10–17

In essence, these rules can be summarised as follows:

CPR Sch.1, RSC Order 17	Interpleader proceedings in the High Court	Interpleader affects the execution of goods both when seized by a High Court Enforcement Officer and by a County Court bailiff but the County Court rules have their own provisions for interpleader (see below).
CPR Sch.1, RSC Order 45	General provisions	This deals with enforcement generally in the High Court.
CPR Sch.1, RSC Order 47	Writs of Fieri Facias (FiFa)	See Chapter 14.
CPR Sch.2, CCR Order 22	Judgments and orders	Deals with requesting a certificate of judgment.
CPR Sch.2, CCR Order 25	Enforcement of judgments and orders: general	Sets out county court procedures generally.
CPR Sch.2, CCR Order 27	Attachment of Earnings	See Chapter 15.
CPR Sch.2, CCR Order 33	Interpleader in the county court	See Chapter 14 generally.

How does a Stay of Execution impact on the enforcement of a judgment?

By CPR r.3.1(2) (f) the court has a general case management power to stay the whole or any part of any proceedings or judgment either generally or until a specified date or event. This rule itself is derived from the Supreme Court Act 1981 s.49(3). 10–18

A "Stay" imposes a halt on proceedings apart from taking any steps allowed by the CPR or the terms of the stay itself. Against the backdrop of legislation and rules, case law over the decade has embraced the overriding objective of the CPR with judges balancing the risks of granting an order "staying execution" against the risk of non-payment or repayment depending on the circumstances (see *Total*

M&E Services Ltd v ABB Building Technologies Ltd [2002] EWHC 248 (TCC)) and *Wimbledon Construction Company 2000 Ltd v Vago* [2005] EWHC 1086 (TCC)). In both cases the court was unimpressed by the arguments put forward and refused to grant orders staying execution.

A judgment debtor who is unable to pay a judgment debt or who has another reason for believing that a stay of execution should be granted may apply for a stay of execution under the CPR by virtue of RSC Order 47 r.1 in Sch.1 or CCR Order 25 r.8 under Sch.2.

Once the final judgment or order is made then execution can be issued immediately unless leave to issue execution is required or the court orders a stay.

10–19 Judgment creditors should be alive to the fact that a stay can come late in the day, particularly where a judgment debtor is desperate to prevent the removal of goods or to prevent an order for sale being executed in relation to the family home.

The court itself has wide powers to stay the execution of its order for the payment of money in both the High Court and County Courts.

When will a Stay of Execution be automatically granted?

10–20 It should be noted that on the issue of an interpleader application by an HCEO the execution of the Writ of FiFa will automatically be stayed until the third party claim has been dealt with by the court (see *Re Ford Ex p. Ford* [1886] 18 QBD 369).

An order for payment of a judgment debt by instalments is automatically stayed while the order allowing instalments is still in force. If the judgment debtor defaults in making the instalment payments an application for leave to issue execution will need to be made (see generally CPR Sch.1, RSC Order 47 r.1).

Does an appeal act as a Stay of Execution?

10–21 The answer simply is "no". An appeal does not operate as an order to stay the execution of the court's order and this does cause Practitioner's confusion from time to time.

If a stay is going to be needed the application should be made at the conclusion of the trial or hearing to the judge. The application should be made when the trial judge is asked to grant permission to appeal (see generally CPR 52.3(2)(a)).

If a stay is refused or is not applied for on that occasion in the lower court a separate application for a stay supported by evidence may be made or included in any application for permission to appeal to the Appeal Court.

The application is made after the filing of the Appeal Notice and will be in accordance with CPR Pt 23 (see also CPR PD 52, para.5.5 and 11.). **10–22**

Where the application to the Court of Appeal is urgent it is essential that a transcript of the judgment being appealed against is supplied and that the evidence in support of the application for a stay of execution is supported fully by the necessary evidence. The court's discretion to then grant an order staying execution is unfettered. The court will not order a stay unless satisfied there is full and frank disclosure of the evidence with a real risk to injustice being caused if the application is refused (see *Hammond Suddard Solicitors v Agrichem International Holdings Ltd* [2001] All E.R.(D) 258).

The common mistake by Practitioners is to presume that the issue of the application for an appeal acts as a stay of execution on any subsequent execution. A separate application for a stay must be made to ensure execution is prevented from escalating to, in the case of execution against goods, the seizure and removal of items pending appeal.

What is the effect of the registration of a civil court judgment against a person?

Finally, as a concluding comment to this chapter it is important to appreciate why taking judgment against a debtor is so important in debt recovery. As we have said at the outset a judgment in itself is not cash in the bank—it is only a milestone on the route to recovery. However for some debtors it is an important milestone which now means they are in a weaker position than at the outset of the claim. **10–23**

Once judgment is entered against a debtor he/she/it has one calendar month from the date judgment was entered against their name to show the court that payment has been made in full, or they risk having the judgment registered against them for six years regardless of any future payment. The position is improved slightly as the judgment will be marked as "satisfied". However, if the judgment is paid within the one month window then the judgment does not appear on any credit reference report and of course for some debtors it is vital they keep their credit rating clear of any adverse entries.

The website to visit with all the pertinent information about registration and a helpful Frequently Asked Questions page is the Registry Trust website at: *http://www.registry-trust.org.uk/FAQs*

Practitioners would also do well to think strategically about how they can use the milestone of judgment being entered to force a judgment debtor to pay, so as to avoid an adverse entry on appearing **10–24** credit the debtors score. This can be done by constructing a letter to be sent immediately when judgment is entered encouraging the debtor to pay or risk the consequences of registration for six years. The letter can explain the benefits of paying now rather than later, and point out the advantages of avoiding additional court fees. Too often Practitioners let this milestone pass without making use of the strategic advantages and savings on time and expense that a well timed letter or telephone call to the debtor can bring. There is still plenty of ignorance about the impact of a CCJ on a person's credit score and so Practitioners should not assume that the general public at large realise the implications. By pointing these out the judgment debtor may well be appreciative and consider him or herself to have been professionally well treated by the creditor's representative. Who knows the debtor may even want to do business again in the future!

What about assets outside the enforcement matrix?

What about assets outside the enforcement matrix?

10–25 As Debt Recovery Practitioners encounter more complex cases there will be a need to pursue assets which are outside the "norm" in terms of enforcement. The CPR caters for these instances through CPR Pt 69, which is a method of enforcement which evolved through the law of equity. As some readers may appreciate the law of equity over the centuries added a "gloss" to the common law to literally fill in the gaps where the common law had no remedy; and "equitable execution" was developed to cure defects in the common law arrangements for enforcement. As to the nature of the remedy in the 19th Century see *Levasseur v Mason & Barry* [1891] 2 Q.B. 73 and *Re Shepherd* [1889] 43 Ch D in which Bowen L.J. at p.137 described the position, "it is not execution but a substitute for execution".

CPR Pt 69 and its accompanying Practice Direction now covers the rules and procedure in both the High Court and county courts. The new rule provides a comprehensive procedural code to deal with the appointment by the court of receivers and managers which includes provisions relating to:

- the application for appointment;
- the evidence required in support of that appointment;
- security and remuneration of the receiver which is strictly controlled by the court;
- the receiver's accounts and discharge; and
- the termination of the receiver's appointment.

It should be borne in mind, that the power to appoint a receiver is discretionary and accordingly the court will do so whenever it appears to be just and convenient to do so in handling any application.

When should the appointment of a receiver be considered?

Part 69 is designed to cover both the appointment of receivers appointed for the purpose of preserving property during the course of litigation, as well as the appointment of receivers by way of equitable execution, a procedure which is said to be "comparatively rare" nowadays because of the availability of charging orders. **10–26**

What types of property may call for the appointment of a receiver by way of equitable execution?

The below sets out some examples of where the appointment of a receiver has been successfully appointed and instances where the application has not been successful: **10–27**

Examples of cases where property has been the subject of a successful application	Examples of cases where property has not been the subject of a successful application
The debtor's reversionary interest in the proceeds of sale of realty (*Tyrrell v Painton* [1895] 1 Q.B. 202).	Solicitor's costs untaxed.
The debtor's share of rent and profits of freehold and leasehold property held on a joint tenancy subject to mortgages (*Hills v Webber* (1901) 17 T.L.R. and see also *Hart v Emelkirk Ltd* [1893] 3 All E.R. 15—and see *Bank of Australasia v Whitehead* (1898) 24 V.L.R. 308 and *Cadogan v Lyric Theatre Ltd* [1894] 3 Ch 338 (rents and profits of theatre subject to a mortgage)).	Monies receivable from patents before license is granted.
Rents accruing but not accrued.	Salary of a public office not yet due and not assignable (*Cooper v Reilly* (1892) 2 Sim 560.
Pensions (except pensions of HM Forces personnel).	

Examples of cases where property has been the subject of a successful application	**Examples of cases where property has not been the subject of a successful application**
Income of a trust fund (*Oliver v Lowther* (1880) 42 LT 47).	
An interest in pure personality subject to a mortgage.	
Property subject to a lien (*Levasseur v Mason & Barry* [1891] 1 Q.B. 73).	
Debts where a third party debt order is inappropriate, e.g. *Moloney v Cruise* (1892) 30 LR Ir 99 (civil servant's pension) and see the more modern case of *Soinco S.A.C.I. and anor v Novokuznetsk Aluminium Plant and ors* [1988] Q.B. 406.	
Fund in the High Court, where the judgment is a county court judgment (see *London County Council v Monks* [1859] Ch 239).	
A reversionary interest under wills—*Fuggle v Bland* (1883) 11 QBD 711.	
Note: In the case of *Crowe v Price* [1889] 22 QBD 429, the sums in question were monies received on behalf of the debtor in commutation of part of his retired army pay, and monies received on behalf of the debtor for his retired pay. A receiver was appointed in respect of the first but not of the second!	

In practice the appointment of a receiver by way of equitable execution is designed to enable a judgment creditor to obtain payment of his debt when normal execution is not available because of the nature of the judgment debtor's interest in the property. In *Maclaine Watson and Co Ltd v International Tin Council* [1988] Ch 1 it was stated clearly by the court that such an order can only be made where:

- it is impossible to enforce using any of the other methods of enforcement; and
- the appointment of a receiver will be effective.

In the very recent decision of *Munib Masri v (1) Consolidated Contractors International Co Sal (2) Consolidated Contractors (Oil & Gas) Co Sal* [2008] EWHC 2492 (Comm) it was held that a judgment creditor was entitled to the continuation of freezing orders over certain assets of the judgment debtors, including receivables from a stake in foreign energy resources and construction projects, and to the appointment of a receiver by way of equitable execution in respect of the receivables.

Who can be a receiver?

The appointed receiver must be an individual and must not be someone who is in any way connected with the proceedings. **10–28**

How do you apply to have a receiver appointed?

Normally the application will be made during the course of the proceedings using Form N244 and the usual application process will be followed. It is, however, possible to apply for the appointment using a CPR Pt 8 claim form. **10–29**

In cases of urgency or where there are special circumstances, it is possible for the application to be made without notice.

Debt Recovery Practitioners are advised to read Atkin's Court Forms, Vol.33 for a more detailed explanation of the process for the appointment of receivers, together with examples of application notices and the various orders available to the court. Additionally both the Queen Bench and the Chancery Divisions have explanatory Guides relating to the procedure under CPR Pt 69.

Chapter 11

The Role of Information Hearings In Debt Claims—CPR 71

Introductory Comments

As has been detailed earlier in this book, the key to successful debt recovery is prevention rather than cure. If, however, despite the best organisation and credit policies a practitioner finds himself with a bad debt and is contemplating issuing proceedings, then again, as we have discussed earlier in the book, having consideration to the debtor's circumstances and possible assets, will greatly increase the possibility of successfully enforcing any judgment. **11–01**

Despite this there may still be times when a practitioner is unsure as to the exact financial circumstances of the debtor and wishes to make enquiries and obtain information before launching into a particular type of enforcement action.

Orders to Obtain Information are the method by which judgment creditors can obtain detailed information from their judgment debtor as to all aspects of their financial circumstances, with a view to then using this information to target the enforcement action and thereby increase the likelihood of successful enforcement.

The application requires the judgment debtor to complete a detailed questionnaire which the judgment debtor, whether the judgment debtor is an individual or a corporation, will have to answer, covering all aspects of the finances, such as, bank accounts, property ownership, employment and existing debts.

Unfortunately, this process has not been viewed as a method of enforcement as it does not actually result in the recovery of money itself. Judgment creditors have in the past, simply used this process as an administrative step once they have obtained judgment; usually because they have not thought about how they were going to enforce their judgment before they issued proceedings. **11–02**

However, used strategically Orders to Obtain Information, and getting the judgment debtor into court to provide that information, can be a very effective tool in the enforcement of a judgment.

Although this book does of course focus on the recovery of a debt, it is worth noting that this method of gaining information can also be used where a judgment debtor has failed to return goods, pursuant to this part of the Rules.

Enforcement Matrix

11–03 Using the Enforcement Matrix set out in Chapter 3, Debt Recovery Practitioners should be already identifying the type of information they hope to obtain from the judgment debtor before any enforcement application is made.

Where the judgment debtor is an individual, the Debt Recovery Practitioner should be looking to try and obtain information regarding the judgment debtor's employment, to enable an attachment of earnings order to be made; or possible property ownership which would allow a charging order to be obtained. If information is provided regarding bank or building society accounts, this could lead the way for a third party debt order against that account. The questionnaire also requests details regarding any assets owned by the judgment debtor, including vehicle information. Such information can then prove very useful in respect of pursuing execution against goods, either by way of a warrant of execution or a High Court Writ of Fifa.

11–04

Type of Debtor	Type of Premises	Possible types of assets	Type of Enforcement
Individual	Domestic address where the debtor may be viewed as a consumer of goods and services whether or not regulated under the CCA 1974 (as amended)—for sole trader see below.	Not sure what assets the debtor has.	Focussing on the income and expenditure and other assets of the debtor as per the record of examination questionnaire set out in Form EX140.
Sole Trader	Domestic—as above.	Not sure what assets the sole trader may have.	This time focussing on the accounts for the sole trader business including the sales ledger

Type of Debtor	Type of Premises	Possible types of assets	Type of Enforcement
			where the debtor may be owed money along with other financial information to draw conclusions on what assets may be available.
Sole Trader	Commercial	Not sure what assets the sole trader business has.	Again focussing on the accounts for the business—as above.
Partner	Domestic	Not sure what assets the partner has.	Again focussing on accounts for the business—as above.
Partner	Commercial	Not sure what assets the partner has.	Focussing on sales ledger and other assets and liabilities.
Company	Domestic	Not sure what assets the company owns.	Examining an officer of the company—with that officer completing form EX140A which focuses on the assets and liabilities of the debtor company.
Company	Commercial	Not sure what assets the company owns	Again a cross examination of the company's directors should take place and the company's directors should be required to bring the company's books to the hearing to verify whatever is stated by way of information.

How is the application commenced/started?

CPR 71.2 provides for the judgment creditor to be able to make an application to the court requiring the judgment debtor, or an officer of the judgment debtor company, to attend court to provide information regarding: 11–05

- the judgment debtor's means; or
- any other matter about which information is needed to be able to enforce the judgment or order.

The application is made without notice to the court where the judgment was obtained, unless the proceedings have already been transferred to another court.

Whilst the process is the same, the forms which need to be completed do vary depending upon whether or not the judgment debtor is an individual judgment debtor or a corporation. Form N316 is to be completed where the judgment debtor is an individual and Form 316A will be used where the judgment debtor is a company. There are also different forms which the respective judgment debtor's will complete to answer the questions and we will look at these later in this chapter.

Does the application need to contain any particular information?

11–06 The short answer is yes. The application must set out the information required in accordance with the Practice Direction which accompanies this rule. This includes the following:

- the name and address of the judgment debtor;
- details of the judgment which the judgment creditor is seeking to enforce;
- If the application relates to a money judgment, then the amount presently owed by the judgment debtor under that judgment;
- where the judgment debtor is a company then the name and address of the officer of that company whom the judgment creditor wishes to be ordered to attend court, together with details of that person's position in the company;
- if the judgment creditor requires the questioning to be conducted before a judge he must give his reason in the application form—if a request is not made then the application will be dealt with by a court officer without a hearing (the judgment creditor therefore needs to decide whether or not the additional gravitas added by conducting the hearing before a judge is needed to ensure the judgment debtor co-operates);
- if the judgment creditor wishes the judgment debtor, or any other person who is to be questioned, to be ordered to produce specific documents at court, then those must be identified in the application. Such documents may include: copies of utility bills to prove stated expenditure, copies of pay slips, copies of specific finance agreements, etc;
- on receiving the application the court officer may refer the matter to a judge and indeed will refer it to a judge for consideration if the judgment creditor requests the judgment debtor,

of officer of the judgment debtor company, to be questioned before a judge.

Providing that all of the above requirements are met then the court will issue an Order to Attend Court in the terms of CPR 71.6.

What happens once the order has been issued?

Once the court has issued the application and prepared the Order this will be sent to the judgment creditor who must then arrange for the Order to be personally served upon the judgment debtor in accordance with CPR 71.3. **11–07**

It is the responsibility of the judgment creditor to arrange for service of the Order. Normally service will be carried out by a process server and the judgment creditor should ensure that he obtains a detailed Statement of Service which can then be exhibited to the affidavit which the judgment creditor will need to file at court before the hearing. Unfortunately, although the requirement for personal service will inevitably result in the judgment creditor incurring additional expense, this cost is not recoverable from the judgment debtor.

Service of the Order must be effected not less than 14 days before the date fixed for the hearing/questioning. If a judgment creditor does not feel that he/she/it will be able to serve the Order by this time they will need to advise the court and seek an adjournment of the hearing. They must then obtain a fresh hearing date and get the Order amended accordingly. This notification must be made to the court not less than seven days before the hearing.

Once service has been carried out the judgment creditor must complete Form EX550 which is an affidavit of service and confirmation of whether travelling expenses have been offered/paid. The form requires the judgment creditor to provide details of the service of the Order upon the judgment debtor and to also indicate whether or not the judgment debtor has requested payment of travelling expenses to the hearing in accordance with CPR 71.4. If the judgment debtor intends to make such a request, they must do so within seven days of being served with the Order.

The judgment creditor must then ensure that the affidavit is filed at court at least two days before the hearing (CPR 71.5(2)(a)) or arrange for it to be produced at the hearing (CPR 71.5(2)(b)). It is always a good idea for a judgment creditor's representative to have a copy available at any hearing in case confirmation of service becomes an issue. **11–08**

It should also be noted that this is one of the few occasions where the document must be an affidavit which confirms service, rather than simply a statement that service has been effected. This is due to the serious ramifications for the judgment debtor if he/she/it fails to attend the hearing. Due to the potential for committal proceedings against the judgment debtor, the court requires the extra certainty and protection of an affidavit rather than merely a statement of service.

What if the judgment creditor is unable to personally serve the order?

11–09 Judgment debtors can be particularly elusive when it comes to trying to serve them with court documents. If the information being provided to the judgment creditor by the process server suggests that the judgment debtor is at the address where service is being attempted, but that the judgment debtor is deliberately evading service, then it is possible to make an application to the court for service by an alternative method; previously known as "substituted service".

Pursuant to CPR Pt 6 an application is made on Form N244 setting out the circumstances of the attempted service; ideally the judgment creditor should exhibit to the application a statement of attempted service from the process server. The Debt Recovery Practitioner should ensure that the paperwork from the process server is of a quality acceptable to the court.

Alternative service can be by any means appropriate to the particular judgment debtor to be served. Most commonly for individual judgment debtors it is by posting the Order through the letter box of the judgment debtor's property. It could, however, be by leaving it at a certain location where it is believed it will come to the judgment debtor's attention or by advertising it in the local press. Whatever means of alternative service intended to be used, this must be specified in the application.

11–10 Providing the court is satisfied that all attempts have been exhausted in trying to personally serve the judgment debtor an order for substituted service will be made specifying the exact method of service to be adopted. The judgment creditor must then ensure that service is effected using that exact method. Any deviation from that would result in the service being invalid.

Although alternative service is an option, it is important to note that if the Order is served using an alternative service method and the judgment debtor is not personally served, then it will not be possible to obtain a committal order against the judgment debtor should he or she fail to attend the court hearing. If committal is taken away as a sanction then the application loses its ferocity in ensuring compliance with the court's order to give the necessary information.

If it is, therefore, believed that there is a strong possibility that the judgment debtor will fail to attend when served with the order, yet the judgment creditor's strategy is to obtain a committal order, then the judgment creditor must persevere with the personal service route and not resort to service by an alternative method to ensure committal remains as a sanction.

How should the judgment debtor respond to an application under CPR Part 71?

As referred to above, if the judgment debtor intends to request travelling expenses in respect of the hearing they must do so within seven days of being served with the Order. If they judgment debtor makes such a request then the judgment creditor must ensure that such sums are paid as requested, in accordance with CPR 71.4(2). **11–11**

Most importantly, however, the judgment debtor must ensure that he/she/it attends the hearing specified in the Order to answer the questions to be put to them and to produce any documents which have been requested.

It is important for the judgment creditor to appreciate that there is no limit on the information which can be requested and the process should be used as a structure for detailed cross-examination of the judgment debtor regarding their income, expenditure and assets and finances.

The Order will contain a penal notice in the terms "You must obey this Order. If you do not, you may be sent to prison for contempt of court.". It is this wording which gives the Order To Obtain Information process its strength and consequently, where used properly, it can be a very effective tool in the enforcement arena where a judgment creditor wants to underline the seriousness of the need to comply with the Order for information to be given.

Where does the hearing take place?

Regardless of which court the judgment was obtained in, the actual hearing should take place in the county court within the district in which the judgment debtor resides or carries on business; unless the District Judge decides otherwise (see para.2.1 of CPR PD 71). **11–12**

So, although the application is submitted to the county court where the judgment was obtained, it is possible that the matter may be transferred to another county court for the purpose of the hearing.

What happens if the judgment debtor attends the hearing but refuses to answer questions?

11–13 In a nutshell the judgment debtor will be held to be in contempt of court in accordance with CPR 71.8.

Rather than being seen merely as an administrative procedure, the Order To Obtain Information route should be seen as a formidable weapon. The ultimate sanction of depriving the judgment debtor of its liberty for failing to comply with the Order should not be underestimated and judgment creditors should ensure that they utilise the application strategically and not simply "go through the motions".

If it is believed that the judgment debtor has assets overseas—will they be required to give information about these?

11–14 The judgment debtor is required to give information about *all* their assets. This includes assets outside of the jurisdiction (*Interpool Ltd v Galani* [1987] 2 All E.R. 981).

The judgment debtor is a company—can former officers of the company be questioned?

11–15 It has been held that "an officer" includes former officers of the company (*Societe Generale v JM Farin & Co* [1904] 1 K.B. 794).

How is the hearing conducted?

11–16 The most important point to note is that the judgment debtor, or officer of the judgment debtor company, will be required to answer questions on oath. The impact of this upon the judgment debtor should not be underestimated and this is something which should be spelt out to the judgment debtor before the application is even made. Indeed Debt Recovery Practitioners should underline this in the letters they send when notifying the judgment debtor of this course of action.

Who will carry out the cross examination?

11–17 In the case of *Republic of Costa Rica v Strousberg* [1880] 16 Ch D 8 it was stated that the hearing is to be conducted as "a cross of examination of the severest kind".

Today the questioning will be carried out by a court officer unless the judgment creditor has specifically requested that the hearing should be before a judge.

When considering making the application the judgment creditor should consider whether or not to request that the hearing be before a judge. This is far more intimidating for the judgment debtor than being asked questions by a court officer. As referred to above, this OTOI process should be a cross-examination of the severest kind rather than simply an administrative process and for this reason serious consideration should always be given to whether or not to request the hearing before a judge.

Alternatively, a "middle ground" may be for the judgment creditor or their representative to attend the hearing and ask the questions, where the questioning is to take place before the court officer. In this way the judgment creditor can maintain control of the process and ensure that the correct questions are asked of the judgment debtor and more importantly that appropriate and accurate answers are given. Unfortunately, costs are limited and a judgment creditor would only attend as a point of principle to get the information. This is no likelihood of the cost being recoverable.

If the hearing is to take place before a judge then the judgment **11–18** creditor must attend and ask the questions.

If the judgment debtor is an individual, then Form EX140 will be the standard form of questionnaire to be completed by the judgment debtor. If it is an officer of the judgment debtor company who is being questioned then Form EX141 will be used.

If the judgment creditor is asking the questions rather than the court officer they can of course use their own questions. However, due to the comprehensive nature of the court form questionnaires, the judgment creditor would be advised to use these at least as the basis of their questioning and ensure that answers are verified by documentary evidence.

What happens if the hearing is adjourned?

If the hearing is adjourned, for whatever reason, the court will give **11–19** directions regarding the service of the notice of the new hearing.

Common reasons for the hearing being adjourned are where the judgment debtor is required to produce additional documentation as part of the hearing process or because of some irregularity regarding service of the Order.

If the hearing is adjourned it is worth the judgment creditor trying to get the judgment debtor's agreement to accept service of notice of the new hearing by postal service. At least this way the further expense of arranging for personal service can be saved.

What happens if the judgment debtor fails to comply with the order to obtain information?

11–20 If the judgment debtor fails to attend court, or attends court and refuses to take the oath, then the court will refer to the matter to a High Court Judge or Circuit Judge.

The judge may then make a committal order against the judgment debtor for failing to obey the court's order. It is important to note here that the committal order is made for the judgment debtor's contempt of court in failing to comply with the court order and *not* because of the failure to pay the debt.

The judge cannot make a committal order unless the judgment creditor has complied with the following:

- CPR 71.4 in relation to travelling expenses; and
- CPR 71.5 in relation to filing the appropriate affidavit dealing with the issue of service of the Order.

11–21 As has been previously mentioned, the court is also unlikely to make a committal order where the Order has been served by means other than personal service.

Initially, the judge will order that the committal order be suspended provided that the judgment debtor attends court on a date and time specified in the further order and complies with the terms of the committal order and the original Order To Obtain Information.

Once again, the suspended committal order will have to be personally served upon the judgment debtor.

The suspended committal order will also state that if the judgment debtor fails to attend the hearing and comply with the suspended order then the judgment debtor will be bought before a judge to consider whether or not the committal order should be discharged.

11–22 If the judgment debtor does attend the hearing then the suspended committal order is discharged. If, however, the judgment debtor fails to attend the hearing a warrant for his/her arrest will be issued (see CPR PD71 para.8).

Rather than being taken straight to prison, the judgment debtor will be brought before the court pursuant to CPR 71.8(4)(b). The purpose of this is for the court to decide whether or not the committal order should be discharged. In practice this hearing is used to actually ask the judgment debtor the questions and to conduct the full hearing.

If the judgment debtor fails to answer any questions or to take the oath, then the judge will not discharge the committal order and will issue a warrant of committal immediately. The judgment debtor will then be taken to prison to serve a prison sentence. To do this the judgment must be satisfied "beyond reasonable doubt", as required under CPR PD71, para. 8 that the judgment debtor has failed to comply with both the original Order and the suspended committal Order and that both were properly served upon the judgment debtor.

Are there any human rights issues to be aware of?

It has been suggested by some commentators that the procedure for Order To Obtain Information is not compliant with the European Convention of Human Rights (ECHR). **11–23**

However, there is nothing within European jurisprudence to prevent civil courts from having the proper machinery in place for enforcing its orders.

The Order To Obtain Information procedure is clearly intended to be ECHR compliant. In practice actual committal to prison is extremely rare, and as explained above, is used only as an absolute last resort.

What will be the effect of The Tribunals, Courts and Enforcement Act 2007?

The existing system will continue, however, it is to be supplemented by the addition of Information Orders and Departmental Information Requests. **11–24**

Information Orders are to be used to acquire information from private individuals, with the Departmental Information Requests to be used to acquire information from Government departments.

The process will involve the courts making the application for either an Information Order or for a Departmental Information Request.

If information is obtained by the court through either process, then the court can use the information to provide the judgment creditor with information to assist in deciding upon the most appropriate enforcement action to pursue.

As with other aspects of the Act, the exact procedure for the applications are yet to be set down by Regulations to accompany the Act. Practitioners are therefore advised to watch developments closely in order to ensure that they are able to take advantage of the benefits the Act will bring as soon as possible.

Case Study

At pages 463 of the case study you will see examples of the forms completed by Tom to apply for an Order to Obtain Information and **11–25** the questionnaire which would be completed by Margot. The embarrassment factor for Margot having to attend court to answer questions regarding her financial affairs should not be underestimated and despite all the misgivings about the success or otherwise of this procedure it is the "embarrassment factor" which makes CPR 71 such a useful tool for Debt Recovery Practitioners.

Flow Charts

11–26 A flowchart outlining the process is set out in the Appendix.

Chapter 12

Third Party Debt Orders—CPR 72

Introductory Comments

Third Party Debt Orders (TPDO) are the replacement for the old "garnishee orders" and, although the name doesn't quite roll off the tongue in the same way, the purpose of the two is the same—to take a payment from any money owed to the judgment debtor by their own creditors, whether that is a bank, building society, trade debtors or their own judgment debtor. 12–01

If the judgment debtor is owed money by a third party, then the judgment creditor can obtain a TPDO. The judgment debtor's "debtor" is the third party and it is this person who is ordered to pay the judgment creditor the money they owe the judgment debtor rather than pay the judgment debtor directly.

Although it can be a tricky piece of enforcement to get right, due to requirements on service and obtaining initial information, which we will look at further in the chapter, it can nevertheless be an effective tool of enforcement as the interim order is obtained without notice to the judgment debtor. By the time the judgment debtor is made aware of the order, the judgment creditor has already, hopefully, obtained some protection for their debt by serving the TPDO on the Third Party.

The most common use of the order is against the judgment debtor's bank account. The account must be in credit as any overdraft would of course mean that the judgment debtor owed the bank money. In effect where the bank balance is in credit the bank is a "debtor" of the judgment debtor.

One of the main difficulties here can be the obtaining of the judgment debtor's bank account details. However, if the judgment creditor has a standard procedure in place regarding the copying of cheques used for payment of invoices during the course of business dealings, or a detailed credit checking system, then this information will be readily to hand. Of course in Chapter 1 and 2 we looked at credit application forms which should be the first port of call for bank account information. Alternatively, the judgment creditor may have utilised the Order To Obtain Information procedure detailed in the previous chapter and obtained the bank details that way.

Enforcement Matrix

12–02 Using the Enforcement Matrix set out in Chapter 3 Third Party Debtor Orders are an available option for all types of judgment debtors. Whether the judgment debtor is an individual, sole trader, partnership or limited company, the chances are that they will have a bank account.

Whilst Debt Recovery Practitioners and judgment creditors need to give consideration to the possibility that the bank or building society account may not be in credit the stealth approach afforded by the TPDO process, can be extremely effective in recovering judgment debts.

Practitioners, should of course be aware of the possibility that individual judgment debtors may well have joint accounts with their spouses, partners, etc. In the case study for example, it is possible that Margot will have a joint bank account with Jerry rather than an account in her sole name. In these circumstances a TPDO would not be possible and an alternative means of enforcement would need to be considered.

The table below sets out the options available to judgment creditors regarding this method of enforcement, regardless of the type of judgment debtor.

12–03

Type of Debtor	Type of Premises	Possible types of assets	Type of Enforcement
Individual	Domestic address where the debtor may be viewed as a consumer of goods and services whether or not regulated under the CCA 1974 (as amended)—for sole trader see below.	Bank account	Third Party Debt Order—CPR Pt 72.
Sole Trader	Domestic—as above.	Bank account	Third Party Debt Order—as above.
Sole Trader	Commercial	Bank account or debts owed to the business	Third Party Debt Order—as above.

Type of Debtor	Type of Premises	Possible types of assets	Type of Enforcement
Partner	Domestic	Bank account/debts owed to the business	Third Party Debt Order—as above.
Partner	Commercial	Bank account/debts owed to the business	Third Party Debt Order—as above.
Company	Domestic	Bank account/ debts owed to the company	Third Party Debt Order—as above.
Company	Commercial	Bank account/ debts owed to the company	Third Party Debt Order—as above.

How does a judgment creditor know if there is a debt due to the judgment debtor?

In order for the TPDO application to succeed, there must be the relationship of creditor and debtor between the judgment debtor and the third party. **12–04**

The test for this is if the judgment debtor could sue the third party for the outstanding amount then a TPDO is possible.

The debt must be "due" to the judgment debtor. Where the third party is the judgment debtor's bank, this situation is clear. However, it is possible to attach other types of debt provided that certain conditions are met.

For example, in the case of a building contract in a form published by the Royal Institute of British Architects (RIBA) where the builder is paid on the issue of the certificate from the architect, money in the hands of the building owner can be attached once the architect issues the necessary certificate, but only for the amount in the certificate (*Dunlop & Rankin Ltd v Hendall Steel Structure Pitchers (Garnishees)* [1957] 1 W.L.R. 1102). This is on the basis that the money is "due" once issued.

Where the money is not due there is nothing to attach (*Webb v Stenton* [1883] 11 QBD 518; *Re Greenwood* [1901] 1 Ch 887).

What types of "debt" can be attached?

Rent	Rent due can be attached (*Mitchell v Lee* [1867] L.R. 2 Q.B. 259). But although rent accrues from day to day under the Apportionment Act 1870, it is not attachable until it becomes payable by the tenant (*Barnett v*	**12–05**

	Eastman (1898) 67 L.J. Q.B. 517). Subject to the amount of the judgment debt and the rent payable the more usual way to attach rent is the appointment of a receiver under CPR Pt 69 but these applications are so rare that judicial statistics do not even recall the number of applications for the appointment of a receiver which are made in the courts.
Joint judgment against two or more persons	A judgment creditor with a judgment against two or more persons can attach a debt owing to any of his judgment debtors (see *Miller v Mynn* [1859] 23 L.J. Q.B. 324)
Debt of unascertained amount	The fact that the amount of a debt or accruing debt is not ascertainable will not prevent an interim TPDO being made (*Lucy v Wood* [1884] W N 58; *De Pass v Capital & Industries Corporation* [1891] 1 Q.B. 218. In *O'Driscoll v Manchester Insurance Company* [1915] 3 K.B. 499 money payable to a doctor by the Insurance Committee was held to be attachable after receipt by the committee of funds received by them to pay the doctor even though the precise sum due to the doctor had not been ascertained.
Debt already paid by cheque	Where the judgment debtor has been paid by a cheque which is stopped by the third party when served with an interim TPDO, there will be an attachable debt (*Coyne v Hale* [1878] 3 QBD 371). But the third party is not under any duty to stop a cheque already sent by him at the time of service of the interim TPDO and if he does not do so there will be no debt to be attached (*Elwell v Jackson* [1885] 1 T.L.R. 454).
Executors and personal representatives	Where a third party who was indebted to the judgment debtor dies an order can be served upon his executors or personal representatives but must be directed to them as Executors/Administrators and not personally (*Stevens v Phelips* [1875] L.R. 10 Ch 417).

What types of debt have been held to be "unattachable"?

12–06

Debt due to judgment debtor and another	In Hirschon v Evans [1938] 2 K.B. 801 it was held that it was not possible to obtain a garnishee order (now a TPDO) against a bank account in the joint names of the judgment debtor and his wife—although this authority was looked at in the government's review of enforcement in the White Paper "Effective Enforcement" it was suggested that the position will remain the same and it will not be possible to attach joint bank accounts.

A claim for unliquidated damages	*Johnson v Diamond* (1885) 11 Exch.73; *Jones v Thompson* (1858) EB & E 63.
A legacy in the hands of an executor	A legacy will not be attachable unless there has been an account stated which would constitute the legacy as a legal debt in the hands of a legal debtor (*McDowall v Hollister* (1855) 25 LTOS 185)
Money in court under a judgment	*Dolphin v Layton* (1879) 4 CPD 130, approved in *Spence v Coleman* [1901] 2 K.B. 199, CA (but see CPR 72.10).
A dividend distributable amongst creditors in the hands of an official receiver	*Prout v Gregory* (1889) 24 QBD 281.
A debt due to a judgment debtor and another who is not a party to the judgment	*Macdonald v Tacquah Gold Mines Co* (1884) 13 QBD 535.
Money which the judgment debtor and his wife have in a joint bank account, even though either has authority to draw on the account	*Hirschorn v Evans* [1938] 2 K.B. 801, [1938] 3 All E.R. 491, CA.
The future income of the tenant for life of a trust fund	*Webb v Stenton* (1883) 11 QBD 518, CA.
Salary accruing, but not actually due	*Hall v Pritchett* (1877) 3 QBD 215.
The pay of an officer	*Apthorpe v Apthorpe* (1886) 35 WR 728, CA and as to the pay or allowances due to a member of HM Forces see s.203 Army Act 1955.
The pension of an officer, though given solely in respect of past services	*Lucas v Harris* (1886) 18 QBD 127.
Fees due from a solicitor to counsel	*Wells v Wells* [1914] P 157, CA.
Money in the London banking account of a foreign state	Such monies cannot be the subject of a TPDO unless the judgment creditor can show that the money is solely intended to meet liabilities incurred in commercial transactions *Alcom Ltd v Republic of Colombia* [1984] A.C. 580, [1984] 2 All E.R. 6, HL.
Seamen's wages	By s.34 Merchant Shipping Act 1995, seamen's wages cannot be attached
Salary or compensation of customs officers	By s.7(1) Customs and Excise Management Act 1979 the salary or compensation of customs officers cannot be attached and see Vol.12(2), *Halsbury's Statutes*, 4th edn (1994, Reissue "Customs & Excise)

Does the third party have to be within the jurisdiction to be pursued?

12–07 In accordance with CPR 72.1 a judgment creditor is able to obtain a TPDO against a Third Party who is within the jurisdiction of the courts of England & Wales. There is no provision within the Rules for the court to make a TPDO against a party who is not within the jurisdiction.

However, the judgment creditor should note that even if the Third Party is only temporarily within the jurisdiction at the time that the interim TPDO is made this will be sufficient to take the application forward.

Alternatively, if the Third Party agrees to submit to the jurisdiction of the court for the purpose of the TPDO application then that agreement will be sufficient to enable an interim order to be made; even if the Third Party then leaves the jurisdiction before the final order is made (*SCF Finance Co. Ltd v Masri (No.3)* [1987] 1 All E.R. 194).

What is the definition of a bank or building society?

12–08 The definition is contained within CPR 72.1(2) which defines a "bank or building society" to include *"any person carrying on business in the course of which he lawfully accepts deposits in the United Kingdom"*. "Deposit" is defined within s.5 Banking Act 1987. Section 6 of the Banking Act 1987 describes a "deposit taking business" as one where:

- In the course of the business money received by way of deposit is lent to others; or
- Any other activity of the business is financed, wholly or to any material extent, out of the capital of all the interest on money received by way of deposit.

It should be noted that whilst the National Savings Bank is a "deposit taking institution" it remains under the control of the Crown and can therefore not be subject to a TPDO.

How is the application for a third party debt order started?

12–09 The application is made without notice to the court where the judgment was obtained, unless proceedings have been transferred to a different court in which case the application is made there.

The application is made on Form N349 and must contain all of the information as required by the Practice Direction to CPR 72.

As with the majority of court application forms, the application is verified by a statement of truth. It is important that Practitioners ensure that an appropriate procedure is in place to ensure that the statement of truth is signed in accordance with CPR 22 (see Chapter 5).

Applications for TPDOs are treated as "urgent business" by the court and will be placed before a District Judge or Master on the same day that they are received for consideration and the granting of the interim order.

The court will not grant speculative applications so Practitioners **12–10** must ensure that their applications are informative and supported by evidence. Unfortunately, by their very nature however, these types of applications may result in a certain amount of speculation being necessary.

One of the main difficulties is that information upon which an application for a TPDO is based can go out of date very quickly. By the time the judgment creditor has obtained details of the judgment debtor's bank account and submitted the application for a TPDO the balance in the account may have reduced and a TPDO will be ineffective.

One possible way around this problem is to take an application for a TPDO to the court at the same time as attending an Order To Obtain Information hearing. As soon as the judgment debtor provides details with regards to their bank account the seasoned Debt Recovery Practitioner should complete the TPDO application and submit this to the court before leaving the building.

Unfortunately the judgment creditor is not likely to learn that the information contained in the application may be out of date until after the interim order has been made and served.

Providing that the court is satisfied with the application and the information provided in the N349, the interim TPDO will be granted.

What happens once the interim TPDO has been made?

The interim TPDO will be made by the court without any notice **12–11** being given to the judgment debtor. The order will be made in the following terms:

- an order will be made fixing a hearing date to consider whether to make the interim order final; and
- directing that until that hearing the third party must not make any payment which reduces the amount he owes to

the judgment debtor to less than the amount specified in the interim order.

In addition the TPDO must specify the amount of money which the Third Party must retain. This will be a total of:

- the amount of money remaining due to the judgment creditor under the judgment or order; and
- an amount for the judgment creditor's fixed costs for the application for a TPDO as specified in the Practice Direction to CPR 72.

The interim TPDO only becomes binding upon the Third Party once it has been served.

The hearing for the making of the final order should not be less than 28 days after the making of the interim order.

How should the interim TPDO be served?

12–12 Of all the elements to consider regarding TPDOs the question of service is perhaps the most important. If this aspect is not dealt with properly the entire effect of the TPDO application will be lost. Service of TPDOs is perhaps the most strategic of all the enforcement processes and needs to be carefully thought through.

Copies of the TPDO, the application notice and any documents filed in support of the application must be served on:

- the third party, not less than 21 days before the date fixed for the hearing;
- on the judgment debtor not less than seven days after a copy has been served on the third party; and
- seven days before the date fixed for the hearing.

12–13 Once the judgment creditor has arranged for service of the interim TPDO it must:

- file a certificate of service not less than two days before the hearing; or
- produce the certificate of service at the final hearing

The usual rules regarding service as per CPR Pt 6 apply.

Worked Example of TPDO Timetable

Application for TPDO is made.	Interim TPDO is made by the court.	Final hearing date is set not less than 21 days before the final hearing date.	Third party is served not less than 21 days before the final hearing date.	Judgment debtor is then served not less than 7 days AFTER a copy of the interim TPDO has been served on the third party and 7 days before the final hearing date.	Final hearing takes place with all service require-ments having been met.

Parallel Chronology of Date

June 1	June 4	July 4	Service on third party to be com-pleted by June 14	Service on judgment to be com-pleted not earlier than June 21 and before June 23	Final hearing takes place on July 4

The above rules regarding service of the interim order are designed to ensure that any monies which are due to the judgment debtor by the third party are bound by the interim TPDO. By serving the third party first, the funds are frozen by the time the judgment debtor finds out about the order and finds cannot be dissipated so as to evade the judgment creditor's efforts to secure the fund.

How should a third party bank be served?

In order to effect service in accordance with the rules the following steps should be taken when serving a bank or building society: 12–14

- the bank/building society should be served at the principle office of the company or "any place of business of the company within the jurisdiction which has a real connection with the claim";

- following on from the old requirements under the garnishee proceedings, it is recommended that the interim order is served on the registered office of the bank together with the local branch where it is either known or suspected that the judgment debtor has an account.

What should the third party do once they have been served with the interim TPDO?

12–15 If the third party is a bank then its obligations are set out in CPR 72.6. Banks and building societies are subject to CPR 72.6(1), (2) and (3). All other third parties are subject to CPR 72.6(4).

If the third party fails to comply with CPR 72.6(4) the court will assume that the debt is not disputed and will make the final order. If the third party does dispute that they owe the judgment debtor the money they must notify the judgment creditor and the court in writing within seven days of being served with the interim TPDO.

In accordance with CPR 72.6 a bank or building society must carry out a search to identify all accounts held by the judgment debtor. Unless the court orders otherwise they are required to:

- retain money in accounts held solely for the judgment debtor (or if there are joint judgment debtors, accounts held jointly by them or solely by either of them); and
- search for and disclose information about such accounts.

12–16 Within seven days of being served with the interim TPDO the bank or building society must notify the court of the details of each account held by the judgment debtor including:

- the bank account number;
- whether the bank account is in credit and, if in credit:
  - whether the balance of the account is sufficient to cover the amount specified in the interim TPDO;
  - if the balance in the account is less than the amount specified in the interim TPDO then the amount in the account on the day the bank was served; and
  - where the bank or building society has served notice on the judgment debtor of its right to the money in the account, for example pursuant to a right of set off or some other reason—details of the bank's claim must be given.

What happens if the bank or building society does not have an account for the judgment debtor?

Once the bank or building society has made a search for accounts belonging to the judgment debtor it must confirm: **12–17**

- the judgment debtor does not hold an account with the bank; or
- the bank or building society is unable to comply with the order for any other reason, for example because it has more than one account holder whose details match the information contained in the Interim Order and cannot identify which account the order relates to.

The bank or building society must inform the court and the judgment creditor of this fact within seven days of being served with the Interim Order.

If the bank or building society is unable to comply with the TPDO for any reason and in the absence of any response from the bank or building society the court will use its discretion whether or not to make a Final Order based upon the facts before it including other evidence before the court.

It should be noted that in today's age of technology the search for accounts belonging to the judgment debtor should be a relatively easy process for the bank or building society. In addition, the Interim Order expressly provides for the bank or building society to deduct an amount from any money held for the judgment debtor for its expenses in complying with the Interim Order.

What happens if a third party makes an unauthorised payment?

The third party should not make any payment out of the funds they hold once they have been served with the Interim Order. If the third party does make a payment then they run the risk of having to pay the amount twice in the event that the Interim Order is made into a Final Order (*see Crantrave Ltd v Lloyds Bank Plc* [2000] 4 All E.R. 473). **12–18**

Whilst service of the Interim TPDO does not operate to transfer the property in the debt it is an equitable charge on the debt. The Third Party cannot pay the debt to anyone without incurring the risk of having to pay it over again (*Galbraith v Grimshaw* [1910] A.C. 508).

What happens if the judgment debtor has a joint account?

12–19 There has been considerable, consultation on the subject of whether or not it should be possible to obtain a TPDO against a joint bank account. So far the courts and government have been reluctant to allow TPDOs against joint accounts.

The original position stems from the case of *Beasley v Roney* (1891) 1 Q.B. 509. This was most recently confirmed in the case of *Hirschon v Evans* [1938] 3 All E.R. 491 by the Court of Appeal (as mentioned earlier in this chapter).

What is a hardship payment order within the TPDO procedure?

12–20 Hardship payments were introduced as part of the changes to the enforcement procedure in March 2002 (see Civil Procedure (Amendment No.4) Rules 2001 (SI 2001/2792)).

Service of the Interim Order on a bank or building society has the effect of freezing the account of the judgment debtor. Consequently, the third party bank cannot pay out on any of the judgment debtor's cheques or allow him to withdraw cash without the authority of the court.

As a result, the judgment debtor may be unable to pay day to day living expenses such as their mortgage or rent, or to buy food for himself or his family.

The provision for a hardship payment order aims to strike a balance between the rights of the judgment creditor and the needs of the judgment debtor. It enables the judgment debtor to apply to the court for specified payments to be made, notwithstanding that the account is frozen.

How does a judgment debtor make an application for a hardship payment?

12–21 The application can be made either to the High Court at the Royal Courts of Justice, or to any District Registry; however, the judgment debtor can only apply to one court for a Hardship Payment Order (HPO).

The application is made using Form N244 and must include detailed evidence explaining why the judgment debtor needs the payment and must be verified by a Statement of Truth.

If the Order is made it may permit the third party to make one or more payments from the account and will specify to whom the payments should be made.

The application for the HPO does not have to be made to the same court which has made the Interim TPDO and if it is made to a different court it will not be transferred. To ensure that both courts work in tandem the Practice Direction to CPR 72 makes the following stipulations:

- the application for the TPDO will not be transferred to the court hearing the HPO; but
- the court dealing with the TPDO will send copies of the application notice for the TPDO and the Interim TPDO to the court hearing the application for the HPO.

If the application for the HPO is a matter of exceptional urgency then the court can deal with the application without notice being served on the judgment creditor and allow representation on behalf of the judgment creditor to be made by appropriate methods of communication.

What orders can the court make at the final hearing of a TPDO?

Following on from the TPDO, and any hardship order application which might be applied for, the next stage is to apply for a final order. If either the judgment debtor or the third party objects to the court making a final TPDO then he/she/it must file and serve written evidence stating the grounds for his/her/their objection (see CPR 72.8(1)). 12–22

Or, if the judgment debtor or the third party believes that a person other than the judgment debtor has a claim to the money, then that person must also file and serve written evidence stating his knowledge of that matter (see CPR 72.8(2)). If the court is made aware that another person may have a claim to the money they will serve that person with a copy of the application for the TPDO and the Interim TPDO.

If the third party then gives notice under CPR 72.6 that he does not owe the money to the judgment debtor, or that the amount owed is less than the amount specified in the Interim TPDO and this is disputed by the judgment creditor, then it is for the judgment creditor to file and serve written evidence setting out the grounds on which he disputes the third party's position.

Any written evidence which is required to be filed and served must be served on the appropriate party as soon as possible and in any event not less than three days before the final hearing.

Most cases are straightforward once they reach the stage of the final hearing. The third party is not prejudiced by the making of a final order (see CPR 72.9) as they already owe the money to the 12–23 judgment debtor and they are simply being directed to pay out to the judgment creditor instead. The third party therefore receives discharge of his obligations to the judgment debtor.

At the hearing of the final TPDO the court may make any of the following orders:

- a final TPDO;
- an order discharging the Interim TPDO and dismissing the application;
- an order to decide any issues and disputes between the parties or between any of the parties and any other person who claims the money specified in the Interim Order; or
- an order directing a trial of any such issues with necessary directions being given although CPR 72.8(6) making it clear that the District Judge or Master can decide the issues raised by the parties but only exceptionally will it be necessary to give directions or order a trial pursuant to CPR 72.8(6)(d).

12–24 When considering whether or not to grant a final TPDO, the court must bear in mind the position of not only the judgment creditor but also the judgment debtor and third party. Previous cases where a final TPDO have not been granted include:

Where the court considers the making of a final order would be inequitable.	*Roberts Petroleum Ltd v Bernard Kenny Ltd* [1983] 1 All E.R. 564. *Pritchard v Westminster Bank Ltd* [1969] 1 W.L.R. 547.
If there are proceedings underway for the distribution of available assets to the judgment debtor amongst his creditors on a percentage basis.	*D. Wilson (Birmingham) Ltd v Metropolitan Property Developments Ltd* [1975] 2 All E.R. 814. *Rainbow v Moorgate Properties Ltd* [1975] 2 All E.R. 821.
If there is any doubt whether the estate of a deceased is insolvent then the money in the hands of a third party can be ordered to be paid into court pending any enquiry whether or not the estate is insolvent.	*George Lee & Sons (Builders) Ltd v Olink* [1972] 1 W.L.R. 214.
If money is due to the judgment debtor as a trustee for another.	*Roberts v Death* [1881] 8 QBD 319.
If the third party can prove that he would still be liable in a foreign court.	*Martin v Nadel* [1906] 2 K.B. 26.

What is the effect of a final TPDO?

The final TPDO is enforceable as an order to pay money as provided under CPR 72.9. 12–25

If the third party pays the money to the judgment creditor in compliance with the TPDO or the order is enforced against him then the third party is discharged from his debt to the judgment debtor.

Although it is unlikely that the third party, if they are a bank, will refuse to comply with the final TPDO and pay the money to the judgment creditor, a third party who owes money to the judgment debtor may not be quite so quick to comply with the TPDO and it may become necessary to enforce the order against them.

Can money in court be subject to a final TPDO?

Where money is paid into court either as security for costs in another claim or as part of a Pt 36 offer this is not "money standing to the credit of the judgment creditor" but instead is money to the credit of the claim in which payment was made and remains in court to await the court's direction or order in relation to those proceedings. 12–26

Consequently if there is money in court potentially standing to the credit of the judgment debtor, then the judgment creditor will need to make an application to the court for an order that the money in court, or at least a sufficient amount to satisfy the TPDO, be paid to him. The application must be served on the judgment debtor and the Accountant General of the Court Funds Office.

The money in court must not be paid out until the application has been dealt with.

Who pays the costs of the TPDO application?

Pursuant to CPR 72.11 if the judgment creditor is awarded costs on the application for an order under wither CPR 72.2 for an interim TPDO or a final TPDO under CPR 72.10, or money held in court, he must retain those costs out of the money recovered by him under the order. The costs should be deemed to be paid as a priority to the judgment debt unless the court orders to the contrary. 12–27

CPR 72.11 only deals with costs of the judgment creditor who has made a successful application for TPDO.

If the application is unsuccessful however, the judgment creditor may be ordered to pay costs; especially if the third party has been put to any expense.

If the third party is a bank or building society, in addition to any ordinary costs, they are entitled to deduct a sum for administrative expenses from the balance held when complying with a final TPDO. The amount they are entitled to deduct is specified under the Attachment of Debts (Expenses) Order 1996 (SI 1996/3098) and is currently £55.00.

What happens if there are insufficient funds in the judgment debtor's account?

12–28 The Interim TPDO will only succeed if there are actually funds in the judgment debtor's account *at the time of service* of the interim order, which are sufficient to satisfy the amount of the interim order.

Ways to improve the likelihood of funds being in the bank account include:

- obtaining further information from the judgment debtor under CPR 71;
- identifying dates of salary payments and other credits which may be paid to the judgment debtor on regular dates and ensuring that on the day the interim TPDO is served the funds have cleared and are available in the bank account;
- using information from Third Parties that they are about to make a payment to a judgment debtor—such as payment of a large invoice owed to the judgment debtor; and
- checking if assets have or are about to be sold by the judgment debtor, such as the judgment debtor's home, with funds being available in the judgment debtor's solicitor's bank account—the Interim TPDO will be served on the bank holding the client funds. If the money is wholly client's money it is subject to a trust and a Final TPDO cannot be made (*Plunkett v Barclays Bank* [1936] 2 K.B. 107).

What if further funds are received after the interim TPDO is made?

12–29 If funds are received into the account after service of the Interim TPDO then a further order will be needed to attach to those funds (*see Heppenstall v Jackson & Barclays Bank Ltd (Garnishees)* [1939] 2 All E.R. 10).

What is the effect of the judgment debtor's insolvency on a TPDO application?

Pursuant to s.346 Insolvency Act 1986 the judgment creditor cannot retain the benefit of the attachment of the debt against the judgment debtor's trustee in bankruptcy unless he has completed the attachment, i.e. by the receipt of the debt before the commencement of the bankruptcy. **12–30**

The definition of "receipt" was defined in the case of *George v Thompson's Trustee* [1949] Ch 322.

This position applies equally where the judgment debtor is a company subject to winding up proceedings and the relevant section of the Insolvency Act is s.183.

Case Study

At pages 495 of the case study, you will see an example of the forms which would be completed by Tom Good were he to contemplate pursuing a Third Party Debt Order against Margot for the recovery of his debt. **12–31**

Of course Tom would not be able to pursue a Third Party Debt Order against the joint bank account of Margot and Jerry, however were Margot to have a sole bank account such an application would be possible.

Flow Charts

A flow chart outlining the process for obtaining a Third Party Debt Order is included in the Appendix. **12–32**

Chapter 13

Charging Orders—CPR 73

Introductory Comments

In recent years applications for charging orders have seen something of a resurgence and have become an increasingly popular method of enforcement. Increased property prices and the existence of increased equity in properties has meant that the security offered by charging orders to a judgment creditor have increased. 13–01

Whilst CPR 73 provides the mechanism for judgment creditors to obtain security against a judgment debtor's interest in the real property, it also allows the judgment creditor to obtain security against the judgment debtor's share portfolio or partnership interest. It should however be said that these latter options are far less popular.

Enforcement Matrix

Using the Enforcement Matrix in Chapter 3 Debt Recovery Practitioners can begin to consider the options available to pursue this avenue of enforcement depending upon the type of judgment debtor. 13–02

As can be seen from the table below, the possibility of pursuing a charging order exists regardless of the type of judgment debtor—consideration simply needs to be given to the type of property which may be owned by the judgment debtor.

Type of Debtor	Type of Premises	Possible types of assets	Type of Enforcement
Individual	Domestic address where the debtor may be viewed as a consumer of goods and services swhether or not regulated under the CCA 1974 (as amended).	Equity in home	Charging Order—see CPR Pt 73.

Type of Debtor	Type of Premises	Possible types of assets	Type of Enforcement
Sole Trader	Domestic—as above.	Equity in home	Charging Order—as above.
Sole Trader	Commercial	Equity in property	Charging Order—as above.
Partner	Domestic/Commercial	Equity in home	Charging Order—as above.
Partner	Commercial	Equity in property	Charging Order—as above.
Company	Domestic/Commercial	Equity in director's home—if company owns the property.	Charging Order—as above—here a check needs to be done to see whether the property is owned by the company or whether it is owned by the director personally and again whether the director can be made personally liable for the company's debt.

What are the different types of charging order?

13–03 Broadly speaking there are three types of charging order; with charging orders against land being by far the most popular.

CPR Pt 73 is divided into three sections:

- Section I deals with charging orders over land;
- Section II deals with stock orders; and
- Section III deals with stop notices.

The guiding statute is the Charging Orders Act 1979. However, CPR 73.1 also refers to the Council Tax (Administration and Enforcement) Regulations 1992 (SI 1992/613). These regulations provide the mechanise whereby local authorities can enforce payment of council tax by charging order where the amount outstanding is over £1,000. Again over recent years more local authorities have used this Regulation to give them a further method of enforcement.

What is the effect of a charging order?

In essence a charging order made in accordance with CPR 73 is an "equitable mortgage under hand". Therefore, in respect of a charging order over land, the charging order provides the judgment creditor with security and protection similar to a mortgage over land. 13–04

It must be remembered that a charging order is an indirect method of enforcement as it does not immediately result in payment being made to the judgment creditor. To ensure payment is made, a judgment creditor will have to subsequently enforce the charging order by way of an application for an Order for Sale.

Which courts have jurisdiction?

The question of jurisdiction is set out in s.1(2) of the 1979 Act. Jurisdiction depends upon the value of the judgment debt according to the following principles: 13–05

- the county court has unlimited jurisdiction to make charging orders over land (see CPR 73.3(2))—and therefore the majority of charging orders are made in the county court.
- even in respect of one of its own judgments, the High Court only has jurisdiction to make a charging order over land where the original judgments is more than £5,000—this figure does not take into account any subsequent interest which may be charged or payments being made on account.

If the judgment creditor subsequently seeks to enforce the charging order by way of an Order for Sale however, it should be noted that where the Order for Sale involves a sum in excess of £30,000, the application for the Order must be made in the High Court, regardless of where the charging order was obtained. This means issuing the application for an Order For Sale in the High Court of one of its District Registries.

What consideration needs to be given by the court to other creditors?

When considering whether or not to grant a charging order, the court has to consider not only the needs of the judgment creditor but also of any other creditors of the judgment debtor, whether they already have protection registered against the judgment debtor's property or not. 13–06

It is therefore necessary for the judgment creditor to disclose details of any other creditors of the judgment debtor as part of the application process. Practically speaking a Debt Recovery Practitioner makes these enquiries by considering the Office Copy Entries obtained from the Land Registry and submitted with the Charging Order application. In addition any information known by the judgment creditor regarding the judgment debtor's circumstances, such as family living at the property, etc will be evaluated and disclosed as part of the application.

What happens if the judgment is in a foreign currency?

13–07 If a judgment creditor wishes to obtain a charging order in respect of a judgment which is expressed in a foreign currency then the court may order that the amount claimed be expressed in the sterling equivalent.

If the currency is converted, then the date for conversion will be as close as possible to the date of payment, having regard to the enforcement process (*see Miliangos v George Frank (Textiles) Ltd (No.1)* [1975] 3 All E.R. 801).

If the judgment debt has not been converted into sterling before the enforcement is completed, as determined by the above rule, then this doesn't mean the rules have been breached (*see Carnegie v Giessen* [2005] EWCA Civ 191, [2005] C.P. Rep 24).

How is the application for a charging order started?

13–08 The route to obtaining a Final Charging Order is a two stage process, with an Interim Charging Order being granted first and then the Final Charging Order being the second stage. The Interim Charging Order is obtained simply based upon the paper application submitted by the judgment creditor, with the Final Charging Order only being granted following a hearing where the judgment debtor has had the opportunity of making representations to the court.

The application is made by completing Form N379 setting out details of the judgment debt, the land to be charged, any other creditors, parties with interest in the land. In addition evidence must be submitted with the application showing the judgment debtor's interest in the land to be charged.

Usually this evidence is provided by way of Office Copy Entries obtained from HM Land Registry. Since the Land Registration Act 1988 came into force in December 1990 anyone can search against property which is registered at HM Land Registry.

The application will normally be made to the court where the judgment was obtained unless one of the following applies: 13–09

- the proceedings have been transferred to another county court; in this instance the application should be made to the new court;
- the application is to be made under 1992 Council Tax Regulations, in which case the application must be issued in the county court for the district in which the relevant dwelling is situated, pursuant to reg.50(3)(b);
- the application is for a charging order over an interest in a fund in court, in this instance the application must be made to the court where the claim relating to the fund is or was proceeding;
- the application is to enforce a judgment or order for the High Court and it is required by s.1(ii) Charging Orders Act 1979 to be made to a county court.

How is the application made against a jointly owned property?

Providing that the judgment debtor is the proprietor of the property to be charged, it doesn't matter whether or not the property is jointly owned with a party who is not the judgment debtor. So, for example, using the case study, Tom may seek a Charging Order against Margot's interest in her house even though the house is owned by Margot and Jerry. 13–10

Once the charging order is obtained it will be registered against the judgment debtor's beneficial interest in the property rather than their legal interest.

We will discuss the methods of registration of Charging Orders later in this chapter.

The judgment debtor owns more than one property—can a charging order be obtained against both properties?

The Practice Direction accompanying CPR 73 permits the judgment creditor to make a single application for multiple charging orders against multiple properties. 13–11

The Interim Charging Order which is then made will be in respect of all the properties and will subsequently be registered at the Land Registry against each of the respective Titles.

Again, it is usually possible to use the one application form to register the Order against more than one property (providing they are covered by the same District Land Registry), and thereby incur only one Land Registry fee. However, there does appear to be some variation in practice between District Land Registries and it is therefore worth checking the position with the Land Registry for the particular properties you are looking to register against before you send off the registration form.

What happens once the court receives the N379 application form?

13–12 The court will check the information completed on the form regarding the judgment debt details, and the evidence of the judgment debtor's interest in the land to be charged. Providing this information is correct the court will grant the Interim Charging Order without any further consideration.

It is possible for the court to refuse to grant the Interim Charging Order if it considers that the charging order process is taking a "sledgehammer to crack a nut" approach to the enforcement of the judgment debt.

The Interim Charging Order will contain a date for the hearing to take place for consideration to be given by the court as to whether or not a Final Charging Order should be granted.

What are the service requirements of the interim charging order?

13–13 It is the responsibility of the judgment creditor, or their legal representative, to arrange for the Interim Charging Order to be served on anyone with an interest in the property, whether that be the spouse of the judgment debtor, joint owner or existing chargees.

The spouse of the judgment debtor will need to be served with the Interim Charging Order as a consequence of one of the following provisions:

- as a "creditor" under CPR 73.5(1)(b) if there are pending proceedings;
- as a "trustee" under CPR 73.5(1)(c);
- as a person "in possession" under para.4.3(6) of the Practice Direction to CPR 73;

- as a person who has registered a class F land charge, or notice under s.31(10) of the Family Law Act 1996; and
- as a person specifically directed to be served by the court—in practice virtually all courts direct that the spouse should be served.

In addition to the spouse, anyone with an interest in the property and/or who is a creditor of the judgment debtor will also need to be served with the Interim Charging Order and therefore given the opportunity to make representations at the Final Order hearing.

Practically, service is usually effected by sending the Interim Charging Order, together with a copy of the application to the necessary parties by First Class post.

How is a charging order registered at the land registry?

It is important that the judgment creditor registers the Interim Charging Order at the Land Registry as soon as it is granted. It is only once it is registered that the judgment creditor receives the protection and security afforded by the Interim Order. **13–14**

It should be noted and remembered that it is not then necessary to register the Final Order once granted. The registration of the Interim Order is the vital step to take.

The way in which the Interim Order is registered the depends upon a number of factors, including whether or not the judgment debtor is the sole or joint proprietor of the property and whether or not the land is registered or unregistered.

The following table explains the different scenarios which may arise and the method of registration application to each scenario:

13–15

Judgment debtor Situation	Nature of Title To The Property	Interim Order Application	Resulting Registration	Withdrawal of Charge Application
Judgment debtor is sole owner	Registered Land	Form UN1	Notice	Form UN4
	Unregistered Land	Form CT1 and Form K4	Caution—will only last for five years. Practioners will need to diarise the matter for two months before	Judgment creditor can use WCT. Judgment debtor can use CCT. Also need to do Form K11.

Judgment debtor Situation	Nature of Title To The Property	Interim Order Application	Resulting Registration	Withdrawal of Charge Application
			the expiration of the five years. Use Form K7 to renew the charge.	
Judgment debtors who are jointly liable for the judgment debt	Registered Land	Form UN1	Notice	Form UN4
	Unregistered Land	Form CT1 and Form K4	Caution—will only last for five years. Practitioners will need to diarise the matter for two months before the expiration of the five years. Use Form K7 to renew the charge.	Judgment creditor can use WCT. Judgment debtor can use CCT. Also need to do Form K11.
Judgment debtor is the co-owner of property where the other co-owner(s) is/are not liable for the judgment debt, e.g. a spouse, co-habitee.	Registered Land	Form RX1 (restriction in Form K)	Restriction	Judgment creditor can use Form RX4 or Judgment debtor can use Form RX3.
	Unregistered Land	Form CT1 and Form K4	Caution—will only last for five years. Practitioners will need to diarise the matter for two months before the expiration of the five years. Use Form K7 to renew the charge.	Judgment creditor can use WCT. Judgment debtor can use CCT. Also need to do Form K11.

Judgment debtor Situation	Nature of Title To The Property	Interim Order Application	Resulting Registration	Withdrawal of Charge Application
Judgment debtor is a company.	Registered Land	Form UN1	Notice	Form UN4
	Unregistered Land	Form CT1 and Form K4	Caution—will only last for five years. Practitioners will need to diarise the matter for two months before the expiration of the five years. Use Form K7 to renew the charge.	Judgment creditor can use WCT. Judgment debtor can use CCT. Also need to do Form K11.

In theory, when registering a Charging Order by way of a Notice a Practitioner could also use Form AN1 and register an Agreed Notice. However, this process requires the agreement of the judgment debtor being the subject of the charge—which isn't likely to be forthcoming in the instance of a charging order. The Land Registry's recommendation therefore is that charging orders are registered as Unilateral Notices using Form UN1. 13–16

Where there are joint proprietors of the property and the charging order is against both proprietors, a judgment creditor would normally register the charge by way of a Unilateral Notice. However, if there is a Restriction already registered against one of the proprietors then the way to register the charging order is as a restriction against the beneficial interests of both proprietors.

What happens at the final hearing?

Any person objecting to the making of the Final Charging Order must file and serve on the applicant written evidence stating the grounds of his objections not less than seven days before the hearing. 13–17

At the hearing itself, the court may make any of the following orders:

- a Final Charging Order—this will verify the Interim Charging Order which has already been made, and will state that the Interim Charging Order will continue with or without modification;

- discharge the Interim Charging Order and dismiss the application;
- decide any issues of dispute between the parties and anyone objecting to the making of the Final Order; and
- direct a trial of any issues and, if necessary, give directions.

As with the Interim Charging Order, there is a requirement that the Final Charging Order is served upon all parties who were required to be served with the Interim Charging Order.

13–18 Judgment creditors, or Practitioners on their behalf, should ensure that they take with them to the hearing proof of service of the Interim Charging Order upon all necessary parties. This is usually by way of filing a Certificate of Service in Form N215, exhibiting a copy of the documents which have been served, namely the Interim Charging Order and application for the Order.

CPR 73.8(1) requires the judgment debtor to ensure that they serve evidence of any grounds they intend to raise to oppose the making of the Final Charging Order, rather than simply turning up at the hearing and raising their opposition at that late stage.

However, Practitioners should be aware that invariably, judgment debtors are not legally represented when it comes to Charging Order applications. Invariably therefore, judgment debtors do not serve evidence before the hearing in compliance with the Rules and simply turn up at the hearing.

Despite the Rules, the courts are more than willing to accommodate the judgment debtors and allow them to make representations at the hearing without having served any prior evidence. Practitioners and judgment creditors should be aware of this fact and prepare the cases accordingly with the expectation that they may be required to counter any arguments raised at the hearing by the judgment debtor.

How is a final charging order enforced?

13–19 A Charging Order itself does not actually achieve payment of the judgment debt; it provides the judgment creditor with a means of security for their judgment debt.

In order to actually achieve payment of the judgment debt, the judgment creditor must seek to further enforce the Final Charging Order by way of an application for an Order For Sale. CPR 73.10 expressly states that a person with the benefit of a charging order may enforce that order by way of an application for an order for sale to the court where the charging order was made; unless that court does not have the necessary jurisdiction.

In this respect it means the likelihood of the application having to be made in the High Court rather than the county court. Pursuant to s.23 county courts Act 1984 the county court has jurisdiction to hear applications in respect of judgment debts which do not exceed £30,000. Therefore if the charged judgment debt exceeds £30,000 the application for the Order for Sale must be made in the High Court. Regardless of the venue for the application, the application is made under Pt 8 of the CPR.

It is worth Practitioners being aware that an application for an Order for Sale is considered to be a new action taken by the judgment creditor and *not* an action on the judgment. Therefore it is not subject to the six year limitation period (see *Ezekiel v Orakpo* [1997] W.L.R. 340 CA).

What if the judgment debtor owns the property jointly with another—can the judgment creditor still obtain an order for sale?

Section 15 of the Trusts of Land and Appointment of Trustees Act 1996 will apply in this instance. This Section sets out the matters which the court will have to have consideration to when considering the application for the Order for Sale. These include: **13–20**

- the intentions of the person or persons (if any) who created the trust over the land which is charged;
- the purposes for which the property subject to the trust is held;
- the welfare of any minor who occupies or might reasonably be expected to occupy any land subject to the trust as a home; and
- the interests of any secured creditor of the beneficiary.

This in effect means that the court will consider the position of a joint owner, such as a spouse and the family of the judgment debtor, but this does not automatically mean that an Order for Sale cannot be granted.

Recent cases involving the application of s.15 include *Mortgage Corporation Ltd v Shaire* [2001] 4 All E.R. 364 and *Bank of Ireland Home Mortgages Ltd v Bell* [2001] 2 All E.R. (Comm) 920.

The judgment creditor is required to submit evidence in support of the application providing details regarding: **13–21**

- the value of the property;
- the value of any existing charges against the property; and

- details of anyone else who lives at the property with the judgment debtor.

When considering whether or not to make an Order For Sale the court will take into consideration the value of the judgment debt, the equity in the property and details of anyone else living at the property who would be affected by the Order For Sale being granted.

Practitioners should not be deterred from applying for an Order For Sale simply because the judgment debtor resides at the property with his/her family.

At the initial hearing of the application the court will either make the Order For Sale or they may adjourn the hearing to a fresh date. This latter option is likely where the judgment debtor provides evidence to the court to suggest that they may be in a position to pay the debt in full within a short time frame. Given the ultimate sanction of allowing the sale of the judgment debtor's property, the court is likely to allow the judgment debtor a degree of latitude in settling the debt before making the final Order.

What will be the effect of the Tribunals, Courts and Enforcement Act 2007?

13–22 Of all the enforcement options available to a judgment creditor, charging orders are likely to be the method most affected/amended by the Act.

The first area to be amended is in respect of judgments to be paid by instalments. Currently it is only possible to obtain a charging order in respect of a judgment payable by instalments where the instalments are in arrears. Section 93 of the new Act new ss.1(6), (7) and (8) of the Charging Orders Act 1979 have been created and will apply where the judgment debt is to be paid by instalments.

The effect is to allow a judgment creditor to obtain a charging order where the judgment debt is payable by instalments, even where the instalments are not in arrears.

Another area likely to be changed as a consequence of the new Act is the question of financial limits for applying for charging orders. Presently there are no financial limits regarding whether or not a charging order can be applied for, or whether or not an Order for Sale can be applied for. Obviously there is the question of the discretion of the court in whether or not to grant the charging order and whether the application for the order is a "sledgehammer to crack a nut" approach.

Under the new Act it is expected that there may be a minimum limit imposed in respect of the amount for which a charging order can be applied and the amount which needs to be outstanding before an Order for Sale can be applied for. At the time of writing, it is not known what these financial limits will be but it is hoped that they will not be unrealistically high, given the amounts for which charging orders are currently applied for.

Case Study

At pages 499 of the case study are examples of the forms to be completed by Tom in order to obtain a charging order against Margot's interest in her property. **13–23**

Due to the implications of a charging order and the possibility of Tom being able to subsequently apply for an order for sale, this is bound to be a step that Jerry will be most irritated by and one which could possibly result in payment being made so as to avoid the making of the Final Charging Order.

Flow Charts

A flow chart outlining the process to be followed to obtain a Charging Order is included in the Appendix to this book. **13–24**

Chapter 14

Using Writs and Warrants—CPR Schedules 1 and 2

Introductory Comments

Despite all the information contained within this book regarding the enforcement options available to a judgment creditor, the most commonly used method of enforcement is still execution against goods. **14–01**

Execution against goods can either be pursued through the county court or the High Court. Whichever route is pursued, the object of the process is the same, the seizure and sale of the judgment debtors' goods to satisfy the judgment debt.

In this chapter we will look at the similarities, and differences, between the process in the county court and High court.

Firstly, what does "execution against goods" mean?

The relatively recent case of *Society of Lloyds v Surman & Others* [2004] EWHC 2967 the explored the meaning of "execution". **14–02**

The dicta of Lord Denning from the, slightly less recent case of, *Re Oversees Aviation Engineering GB Ltd* [1962] 3 All E.R. 12 was referred to. At pages 39 to 40 of his judgment in that case, Lord Denning was quoted as saying:

> "[execution] . . . is of course . . . familiar to lawyers. 'Execution' means, quite simply, the process for enforcing or giving effect to the judgment of the court; and it is "completed" when the judgment creditor gets the money or other thing awarded to him by the judgment. That is the meaning".

In summary therefore "execution" means the process for enforcing or giving effect to the judgment of the court. Developing this further, then the phrase "execution against goods" means the process for enforcing or giving effect to the judgment of the court against the goods owned by the judgment debtor. The process is completed when the judgment creditor gets the money insofar as debt recovery is concerned.

Enforcement Matrix

14–03 When it comes to enforcing a judgment against a judgment debtor by way of execution against goods the key is for the judgment creditor or Debt Recovery Practitioner to consider what goods the judgment debtor would have which could be removed for sale at auction, as well as considering what goods they would expect a shop or office to have available for removal.

In the context of the case study, Tom would be able to instruct the bailiff or High Court Enforcement Officer to look to remove items that he can see in Margot's garden, the car parked on the drive, as well as the usual items Tom would have in his own home which could be removed by way of enforcement, i.e. computers, hi-fis, etc.

The table below shows the options available to judgment creditors for this method of enforcement against all types of judgment debtors.

14–04

Type of Debtor	Type of Premises	Possible types of assets	Type of Enforcement
Individual	Domestic address where the debtor may be viewed as a consumer of goods and service whether or not regulated under the CCA 1974 (as amended).	Goods—ranging from the family car to goods inside the premises such as state of the art television set, home entertainment system, antiques, jewellery, but consider carefully items which are exempt from seizure by virtue of s.99 Sch.7 of the Courts Act 2003.	Execution against goods using County Court bailiff and/or High Court Enforcement Officer (HCEO) Note: HCEO's cannot enforce judgment under £600 or judgment debts resulting from regulated agreements.
Sole Trader	Domestic—as above.	Goods—as above.	Execution—as above.
Sole Trader	Commercial	Goods—In this situation we are looking at the goods available	Execution against goods—here a County Court bailiff

Type of Debtor	Type of Premises	Possible types of assets	Type of Enforcement
		against the judgment debtor in his business property such as stock, plant and machinery, business equipment.	or a High Court Enforcement Officer is not prevented from forcing entry to a commercial property to levy execution and ultimately to remove goods for sale in the event of non-payment.
Partner	Domestic	Goods—as above	Execution against goods—as above
Partner	Commercial	Goods—as above	Execution against goods—as above
Company	Domestic	Goods	Execution against goods—the issue here to resolve is the goods the company's goods or do they belong to the director personally and can the director be made personally liable for the company's debt?
Company	Commercial	Goods—This will include stock, plant and machinery, business equipment within the company's premises.	Execution against goods—the issue to watch for here is that the correct company has been sued and judgment has been entered against the correct company

So what does "goods" mean in the context of execution?

Unfortunately, unlike the definition of "execution", there is no such specific definition regarding "goods". 14–05

Only the goods and chattels of the judgment debtor could be removed at common law. The Courts Act 2003, Sch.7, para.9 now provides a definition of the goods which may be seized in execution of either a warrant of execution or Writ of FiFa. These are:

- "any goods of the judgment debtor that are not exempt goods"; and
- "any money, banknotes, bills of exchange, promissory notes, bonds, specialities or securities for money belonging to the judgment debtor".

When a judgment creditor is considering what "goods" are and therefore potentially what they could instruct a bailiff or High Court Enforcement Officer to remove, they should consider what items they have in their own home as well as the mundane, such as the contents of a shop or office, to items such as trains, boats and aircraft.

What does "exempt goods" mean?

14–06 There are certain goods belonging to a debtor which cannot be removed by execution against goods. As with the definition of "goods", the definition of "exempt goods" is also contained within Courts Act 2003 Sch.7, para.9.

Exempt goods include:

- "such tools, books, vehicles and other items of equipment as are necessary to the judgment debtor for use personally by him in his employment, business or vocation"; and
- "such clothing, bedding, furniture, household equipment and provisions as are necessary for satisfying the basic domestic needs of the judgment debtor and his family".

It should be noted however that if the debtor is a limited company, it will not be able to claim that any goods seized are a "tool of the trade". This particular exemption is only available to individual debtors.

14–07 If a debtor tries to claim that an item seized is a tool of trade and is required by him for employment purposes, if it can be shown that the debtor could hire, or lease a replacement item, then it is unlikely that such a claim would succeed. This applies to sole traders and partners and is an important point to note when county court bailiffs or High Court Enforcement Officers are met with a tool of trade claim which could interfere with the execution.

The principle of the judgment debtor having to claim the statutory exemption is defined in the case of *Toseland Building Supplies Ltd v Bishop (t/a Bishop Groundworks),* October 28, 1993, CA, L.J. Steyn stated:

> "The general principle is that prima facie all the judgment debtor's goods are liable to seizure under a writ of fieri facias. If a judgment

debtor claims the benefit of a statutory exemption, the burden of showing that exemption applies, rests squarely on him."

What is the difference between a warrant of execution and writ of fieri facias?

Quite simply, the difference is that a Warrant of Execution is the method of enforcement in the county court and the Writ of FiFa (pronounced "By Bay") is the method in the High Court. **14–08**

Is there a limit regarding enforcement in the High Court?

Any High Court judgment and any county court judgment for over £600 (except where the judgment arises from a regulated agreement under the Consumer Credit Act 1974) may be enforced in the High Court. **14–09**

County court judgments of over £5,000 which are not regulated by the Consumer Credit Act 1974 (as amended) *must* be enforced in the High Court.

The Consumer Credit Act 2006 which came into force on March 30, 2006 makes provision to exempt:

- certain types of business agreement from the provisions of the 1974 Act—see s.4 of the Consumer Credit Act 2006;
- and also recognises that "high net worth" individuals cannot enjoy the protection afforded to debtors under the legislation—see s.3 of the Consumer Credit Act 2006,

which in turn makes those agreements (subject to all the various conditions which are attached) being on the face of it available for enforcement in the High Court (see Chapter 2).

What is the nature of a High Court writ of fieri facias (fifa)?

Much of the established case authority surrounding the use of execution, comes from the development of the Writ of FiFa over the centuries of the common law. **14–10**

There are however some procedural differences between Warrants of Execution and Writs of FiFa and these are set out in Sch.1 and Sch.2. Practitioners should therefore consult the Rules before assuming that the practice in either forum is the same as the other.

Basically, the High Court Writ provides for the seizure and sale of the judgment debtor's goods and chattels which are sufficient to satisfy the judgment debt, costs, interest and charges of the HCEO.

"Fieri Facias" comes from the latin meaning "that you cause to be done."

14–11 The forms of Writ of FiFa are set out in the Practice Direction (Forms) Table 2 at para.4PD 4. In the context of debt recovery the most common form of Writ is Form 53, an example of this form can be found at page 000 of the Appendix Case Study.

It is important that Practitioners appreciate that as the forms of Writ are prescribed they must be used wherever applicable with variations drafted into the writ as the case requires; for example in the case of a judgment expressed in a foreign currency this must include the sterling equivalent.

In addition a praecipe for the issue of the writ must first be indorsed and signed either by the judgment creditor, or by a solicitor on their behalf. Where necessary the requisite certificate under para.11(a) of the *Practice Direction (Judgment: Foreign Currency)* [1976] 1 W.L.R. 83; 1 A.E.R. 669 will then be entered on the Writ of FiFa by adapting the prescribed form to meet the circumstances of the case by substituting the requisite recital for the foreign element of the judgment.

The Writ follows the form of a royal direction to a named Authorised High Court Enforcement Officer or the enforcement officers for the district in which it is required to execute the Writ. The Writ then gives the HCEO the authority to carry out the Royal direction or command and, provided the HCEO acts lawfully, will protect the HCEO from future claims for trespass, etc.

When can a writ of fifa be issued?

14–12 A Writ of FiFa can be issued immediately after the court's judgment or order is made to enforce a judgment or order for either the payment or recovery of money and or costs by the successful party—subject to the points made below.

There is no need to seek the court's permission to issue the Writ, unless the court has attached any stipulations to the judgment or order when it was made. Neither is there any need to give prior notice to the judgment debtor that a Writ of FiFa has been issued (see *Land Credit Company of Ireland v Fermoy* (1870) L.R. 5 Ch 323 and other related cases).

For clarity, CPR 40.7(1) now expressly states that a judgment or order takes effect from the day when it is given or made, or any later date which the court may specify. This means that Practitioners don't need the drawn order from the court—an endorsement from a judge or Master will be sufficient.

A straightforward judgment without any other stipulations, can therefore be enforced immediately using a Writ of FiFa. However, there may be occasions when immediate enforcement cannot be initiated—for example:

- if the judgment contains directions allowing payment within a specified time, the writ of fifa cannot be issued within that specified time;
- if the judgment contains directions regarding service on the judgment debtor, then the writ of fifa cannot be issued until service of the writ has been effected and proof of service has been lodged with the court; and
- if the judgment or order is conditional, the writ can only be issued once the judgment debtor has defaulted in complying with any such conditions.

What happens if there are two more writs of fifa?

The general rule of practice is summed up in the maxim "One judgment, one execution,". **14–13**

In other words, a judgment creditor cannot issue a series of small executions on his judgment, making up the value of the judgment debt. For each judgment a judgment creditor can therefore only issue one execution (see *Forster v Baker* [1910] 2 K.B. 636 CA, per Vaughan Williams L.J. at 641; *Rothschild v Fisher* [1920] 2 K.B. 243 CA). It is for this reason assignees of part of a judgment debt cannot issue execution.

The position in the county court is dealt with in CPR Sch.2, CCR Order 26.

Can a writ of fifa be issued to recover a costs order?

Where the judgment or order is for the payment of money with costs to be assessed, then the usual practice is to issue separate Writs of FiFa; one for the judgment or order, and one for the costs after they have been assessed (see RSC Order 47, r.3). **14–14**

Is it possible to enforce an order for assessed costs after the original judgment?

14–15 Under RSC Order 47, r.3 a judgment creditor is entitled to enforce a judgment immediately without waiting for a detailed assessment of his costs under CPR Pt 47. Once costs have been assessed he can issue a second writ to enforce payment of the costs.

An order for payment of costs to be assessed is a judgment debt within the Judgments Act 1838 s.17 which means interest is payable from the amount of the costs from the date of which judgment was pronounced (see *Hunt v R. M. Douglas (Roofing) Ltd* [1990] 1 A.C. 398; [1988] 3 All E.R. 823, HL)

When is it wrong to issue a writ of fifa?

14–16 Judgment creditors need to be careful not to issue Writs in the following circumstances:

- after payment has been made (see *Clissold v Cratchley* [1910] 2 K.B. 244);
- or after a valid tender of payment (see *Cubitt v Gamble* (1919) 35 T.L.R. 223); and
- where the sum claimed in the writ is greater than the amount actually due at the time of issue.

If a Writ is issued in any of these circumstances the judgment creditor is liable in trespass to any action taken to enforce the Writ, although it should be noted that the liability rests with the judgment creditor and not necessarily the HCEO.

Ignorance that any payment has been made or tendered is no excuse.

If neither the judgment creditor, or any person authorised by them are within the jurisdiction of England and Wales to receive the money paid as a result of the Writ of FiFa being executed, then according to the case of *(Re A Debtor)* [1912] 1 K.B. 53 a stay of execution will be granted on payment into court.

When is permission necessary to issue a writ of fifa?

14–17 In accordance with Order 46 r.2, permission to issue a Writ of FiFa must be sought from the court in the following circumstances:

- where six years or more have elapsed since the date of the judgment or order;

- where any change has taken place, whether by death or otherwise, in the parties entitled or liable to execution under the judgment or order;
- where the judgment or order is against the assets of a deceased person coming into the hands of his executors or administrators after the date of the judgment or order, and it is sought to issue execution against such assets;
- where under the judgment or order any person is entitled to a remedy subject to the fulfilment of any condition which it is alleged has been fulfilled; and
- where any goods sought to be seized under a writ of execution are in the hands of a receiver appointed by the court or a sequestrator.

If the court grants permission, whether under this Rule or otherwise, for the issue of a Writ of Execution and the Writ is not issued within one year after the date of the order granting permission, the order will cease to have effect, without prejudice, however, to the making of a fresh order.

What happens if the judgment is over six years old—can it still be enforced?

To issue a Writ of FiFa on a judgment over six years old, an application needs to be made without notice, supported by the necessary evidence in the form of a witness statement either by the judgment creditor as the applicant, or the solicitor instructed by the judgment creditor. **14–18**

The evidence in support of the application should state:

- the date of the judgment;
- the amount of the original judgment debt;
- the amount remaining due;
- the causes of delay; and
- that the applicant is entitled to execution, i.e. that there has been no change of parties or devolution of interest (or, if there has been the precise nature of it).

In the case of *National Westminster Bank v Powney* [1990] 2 All E.R. 416 CA, the application to issue or to extend the time for execution under a judgment was held not to be an "action" within the meaning of s.38(1) of the Limitation Act 1980.

14–19 The effect of this decision meant that the application did not come within the provisions of s.24(1) of the Limitation Act 1980 which prohibits the bringing of an action on a judgment after the expiration of six years.

If an application is dismissed under this Rule it does not prevent the possibility of a second application but the second one, should not be granted unless it is founded on new evidence which has not previously been before the court (*W. T. Lamb & Sons v Rider* [1948] 2 K.B. 331).

The burden is on the judgment creditor to show the court that it is "demonstrably just" to grant permission to enforce after six years by say repeated attempts to enforce, or deviousness on the part of the judgment debtor or steps to locate the judgment debtor's assets (*Duer v Frazer* [2001] All E.R. 249).

If permission is needed, how is the application for permission to issue a writ of fifa made to the court?

14–20 Under CPR Sch.1, RSC Order 46 r.4, the application is made in accordance with CPR 23 but the application notice does not need to be served on the judgment debtor unless the court makes a specific direction to that effect.

The application for permission to issue the Writ must be supported by a witness statement or affidavit which identifies the judgment or order where permission is required.

For money judgments the evidence must include:

- details of the original amount due;
- the amount due at the date the evidence is filed; and
- the reasons for the application, i.e. the reason for the delay, details of change in the parties.

What paperwork is needed to issue a writ of fifa?

14–21 In accordance with RSC Order 46 r.6, which again is found in Sch.1 to the CPR, the Writ of FiFa needs to be prepared along with its accompanying form of praecipe and lodged in the court office out of which the writ is to be issued.

Both forms are taken to the court. A fee is payable on sealing the writ. The writ is checked by counter staff and then sealed. The

Praecipe is filed at the court, having been signed by or on behalf of the solicitor, or the judgment creditor, entitled to execute the writ.

To be valid the Writ needs to be sealed by the court.

Once the Writ and its accompanying praecipe and evidence of the judgment or order have been checked by the court counter staff, then the writ is sealed.

The court's seal includes the date on which it was issued along with details of the court out of which it was issued. This date is known as the "teste date". It is this date from which the 12 month time period of the life of the writ is calculated.

Where should the writ of fifa be issued?

The rules in which court to issue a Writ of FiFa are dictated by where the proceedings for the main action were commenced, so for example: 14–22

If the action was issued and heard in the District Registry	Then the writ of fifa will be issued in that District Registry
If the action was issued and heard in Admiralty or Commercial courts which are not in a District Registry	Then the writ of fifa will be issued in the Admiralty court or Commercial court in London
If proceedings have been dealt with in the Chancery Division, Chancery Chambers	Then proceedings will be issued in the Chancery Division
For all other cases not included as above	The writ of fifa will be issued in the Central Office of the Supreme Court in London

Can a county court judgment be enforced in the High Court?

Yes, provided that the judgment is for more than £600 and is not in respect of a Consumer Credit Act regulated agreement (see art.8 High Court and County Courts Jurisdiction Order 1991). 14–23

In order to be able to do this the judgment creditor will need to arrange for the county court judgment to be first be transferred to the High Court.

The county court judgment is transferred to the High Court for enforcement purposes by using Form N293A.

A directory of Authorised High Court Enforcement Officers can be found at *http://www.dca.gov.uk/directory/enforcement*. From this the judgment creditor can select the Authorised Officer to which they wish to direct their writ and thereby complete their details on the N293A.

Once a writ of fifa is issued what is its effect?

14–24 The issue of the Writ of FiFa "binds" the property in the goods of the judgment debtor from the time when the writ is received by the person who is under a duty to enforce it (see Courts Act 2003 Sch.7, para.8).

As it was said in the case of *Samuel v Duke* (1838) 3 M&W 622 it is as if ". . . from such delivery the goods become, as it were, impressed with a superimposed right of the [enforcement officer] to deal with the goods".

Once seized, the judgment debtor cannot deal with his goods except by sale to a bona fide purchaser for value and without notice of the delivery of the Writ. In these rare circumstances, the existence of the Writ of FiFa will not prejudice the title to goods acquired by:

- a person in good faith;
- who for valuable consideration, at the time when he acquired his title, had notice that the writ or any other writ, by virtue of which the goods of the judgment debtor might be seized or attached; and
- which had been delivered to and remained unexecuted in the hands of the enforcement officer

14–25 Occasionally a judgment debtor manages to sell the goods to a purchaser in good faith, at a market value, without telling the purchaser that a Writ of FiFa is in existence, either because the judgment debtor is not aware that a Writ has been issued, or because the judgment debtor conceals that information from the purchaser.

Although the debtor may pass a good title to a purchaser who buys these goods in good faith, for both valuable consideration and without notice of the writ or seizure, then under Courts Act 2003 Sch.7, para.8(2), the goods remain subject to the HCEO's rights.

Why is the timing of the writ so important?

14–26 On delivery of the Writ to the HCEO, the HCEO must endorse the Writ with the date and time of its receipt. The time which is endorsed is then used to establish the priority of the writ with competing judgment creditors, either in the High Court or county court, and so far as other proceedings are concerned, particularly where moves are afoot to make the judgment debtor insolvent.

The county court bailiff must also indorse on the back of the Warrant of Execution the hour/day/month/year when he received the application for the warrant, which again allows writs and warrants to be compared for issues of priority (County Courts Act 1984, s.99(3)).

There is a difference between the county court and High Court procedure in this regard.

The county court procedure differs from the High Court procedure as priority is calculated from the time the application for the warrant of execution is made, and not the time it is delivered to the county court bailiff for execution (see *Murgatroyd v Wright* [1907] 2 K.B. 333).

How does a judgment creditor know if there has been an effective seizure of the goods under the writ?

It is important to bear in mind that a seizure can take place: **14–27**

- regardless of whether a judgment debtor signs a Walking Possession Agreement—so if a judgment debtor refuses to sign a Walking Possession Agreement a valid seizure can still be achieved. HCEOs are encouraged to ensure that the document is signed as evidence that the judgment debtor, or some one representing the judgment debtor has accepted that a seizure was made—which can be useful for evidential purposes later on in the execution of the writ; and
- even though the enforcement officer leaves the premises in which the goods are situated with or without a signed Walking Possession Agreement.

What happens if the HCEO makes a wrongful seizure?

Where an HCEO is misled by an endorsement made by the judgment **14–28** creditor on the Writ of FiFa sent to him for enforcement, which then results in the HCEO seizing goods belonging to a person who has no connection to the judgment debt, it has been held that the judgment creditor is liable to an action of trespass (see *Morris v Salberg* (1889) 22 QBD 614).

This includes the judgment creditor taking care to ensure that the HCEO is directed to attend at an address where it is believed that the judgment debtor has goods. An HCEO will be exempt from penalties for an innocent mistake (see *Lee v Dangar* [1892] 2 Q.B. 337).

If there is nothing in the endorsement to mislead the enforcement officer, then an action for trespass cannot be maintained against the judgment creditor (see *Condy v Blaiberg* (1891) 7 T.L.R. 424).

Where neither the premises where the goods are seized, nor the goods seized, belong to the judgment debtor, the HCEO can apply to the court for an order to be protected against an action for trespass which may be taken against him by the owner of the address, or the true owner of the goods. This relief is available to the HCEO provided:

- no substantial grievance has been done to the person whose premises are wrongfully entered (see *Smith v Critchfield* (1885) 14 QBD 873); and
- the evidence shows that the HCEO has made all the necessary and proper inquiries as to the ownership of the goods (see *Salberg v Morris* (1888) 4 T.L.R. 47).

What happens if a sale of goods is made by an HCEO who has no notice of a third party claim?

14–29 Where an HCEO sells goods in the possession of the judgment debtor which turn out to belong to a third party, who has failed to inform the HCEO of this fact by making a valid claim under RSC Order 17, r.2, then the HCEO is protected from any liability by virtue of Sch.7 of s.99 to the Courts 2003 which replaced the Supreme Court Act 1981 s.138B(1).

However, to ensure that protection is secured, it is incumbent on the HCEO to make reasonable enquiries as to whether the goods seized, were or were not the property of the judgment debtor at the time of seizure.

In the case of *The Observer Ltd v Gordon* [1983] 2 All E.R. 945, Sheriff's Officers seized and sold a number of grand pianos which were in the piano repair shop of Reeva Gordon without making inquiries as to the ownership of each piano. Each person who had put a piano in for repair was made the subject of interpleader proceedings under what is now CPR Sch.1, RSC Order 17.

Can a HCEO force entry to a judgment debtor's premises?

14–30 A High Court Enforcement Officer is not entitled to break open the outer door of a dwelling house in order to levy execution which is the basis for the maxim "An Englishman's home is his castle" based on the decision in *Semayne's Case* (1604) 5 Co 91.

From this simple maxim the following points should be noted:

- An enforcement officer is not entitled to force his way in for the purpose of gaining entry (*Vaughan v McKenzie* [1968] 1 All E.R. 1154, DC).
- An enforcement officer may break open the outer door of the judgment debtor's workshop or other building not being his dwelling-house, nor connected with the dwelling-house (*Hodder v Williams* [1895] 2 Q.B. 663).
- An enforcement officer who has already entered the judgment debtor's dwelling house may lawfully break the lock to gain access to a house to seize the goods inside (*McLeod v Butterwick* [1998] 2 All E.R. 901)—although this decision remains open to criticism—particularly where vulnerable people are found to be inside the property.

What happens if an enforcement officer abandons possession of the goods which have been seized?

Where an HCEO, who has seized goods under a Writ of FiFa, fails in his duty to maintain "walking possession" of those goods, then a question may be raised as to whether he has "abandoned possession". **14–31**

Enforcement Officers are trained to ensure evidence of continued walking possession is secured by urging either:

- the judgment debtor; or
- a responsible person over the age of 18 who is at the premises at the time of the enforcement officer's visit,

to sign a Walking Possession Agreement on the initial attendance.

The form of the agreement is now regulated by reg.15 of The High Court Enforcement Officers Regulations 2004 and a form of agreement is set out in Sch.4 to those Regulations. **14–32**

If the judgment debtor refuses to sign a Walking Possession Agreement or a signed Walking Possession Agreement cannot be obtained then the HCEO is under a duty to remove the goods as soon as practicable or at the very least to inspect the goods at frequent intervals.

If this is not done the court may well hold that possession of the goods has been abandoned and the judgment debtor will be under no penalty if he disposes of them regardless of the initial seizure by the enforcement officer.

What happens if the goods seized are jointly owned by the judgment debtor and their spouse?

14–33 Where the HCEO seizes goods which appear to be co-owned, he is able to seize and sell those goods, and then seek interpleader relief from the court as to the division of the proceeds of sale (see *Farrar v Beswick* (1836) 1 M & W 682; *Mayhew v Herrick* (1849) 7 C.B. 229) and generally CPR Sch.1, RSC Order 17.

This is on the basis that where two or more people own chattels as co-owners whether as:

- "joint tenants" which means if one owner dies, the survivor automatically inherits the deceased's owner's share; or
- "tenants in common" which means if one owner dies, the other does not automatically take the entire estate of the deceased owner,

so that each co-owner is entitled to possession of those chattels or "goods" and can sell them without the consent of the other co-owner(s).

14–34 Accordingly, the HCEO acting under a Writ of FiFa on a judgment against one co-owner (named as the judgment debtor) is in no worse position than that of a "co-owner" and so can seize and sell the whole of the property.

If this happens the enforcement officer can then apply to the court under RSC Order 17, for interpleader relief, which in effect means he asks the court for a decision on how to divide the proceeds of sale based on the competing claims of the co-owners (*The James W. Elwell* [1921] P 351).

When two people have separate and different interests in a chattel(s), for example one person is an owner subject to another's charge or lien—i.e. goods stored in a warehouse—then the HCEO may seize the goods subject to that charge or lien. The charge or lien will then have to be discharged, before the goods are available for sale.

Can goods belonging to a company be seized?

14–35 Yes. There is no problem in an HCEO seizing goods belonging to a company as a legal person in its own right (see the Enforcement Matrix in Chapter 3 and 10).

In attending to seize goods of a company, the judgment creditor should direct the HCEO to the address where the company has goods.

This will usually be the trading address of the company, which is *not always* the same as the registered office.

What happens if the judgment debtor becomes insolvent whilst the writ of fifa is being executed?

The impact of insolvency on any enforcement method is to generally put the creditors on a pari passu footing and defeats a judgment creditor's sole right to enjoy the proceeds of the enforcement. **14–36**

In execution against goods the general rule is that an insolvency procedure may well defeat the position of a judgment creditor, unless the execution has been "completed" by the sale and holding of net proceeds for a 14 day statutory period after the receipt of monies. Consider here the quote of London Denning at the start of this chapter as to the definition of "Execution".

If money has been paid "to avoid sale" by a judgment debtor in some form of payment plan or instalment arrangement then each payment attracts its own 14 day window from the date of receipt by the High Court Enforcement Officer.

There are now a number of insolvency measures which can affect the execution of a Writ of FiFa, and therefore the table below seeks to provide an encapsulated guide on the impact of each on the execution of a Writ of FiFa (or indeed Warrant of Execution)

Corporate Insolvency Table

14–37

Type of Insolvency/ Charge	Reference	Impact on the Writ of Fifa
Compulsory Liquidation of Judgment debtor Company	See s.183 of the IA 1986 and s.129(2) IA 1986.	Under this section where execution has been issued against a company, and the company is subsequently wound up, the creditor cannot retain the benefit of the execution against the liquidator *unless* he has "completed" the execution *before* the commencement of the winding up (as to the definition of "commencement" see s.129(2) IA 1986 which in the case of compulsory liquidation means the date of commencement of the winding up is taken back to the date of the presentation of the petition on which the winding up order is subsequently made).

Type of Insolvency/ Charge	Reference	Impact on the Writ of Fifa
		The section does give the court a discretion to defeat the rights conferred on the liquidator, either wholly or partially, according to what is right and fair in the circumstances of the case (*Re Grosvenor Metal Co. Ltd* [1949] 2 All E.R. 948). "Completed" means there has been a sale of the goods (see *Re Standard Manufacturing Co* [1891] 1 Ch 627). However, if the company pays the HCEO a sum or sums to avoid the sale of its assets the money is not characterised as being paid in satisfaction of the writ of fifa but instead is viewed as "monies paid to avoid sale". In these instances the HCEO is bound to retain the money less the costs of execution for 14 days with time running from the time of payment (see *Re Walkden Sheet Metal Co Ltd* (1959) 3 All E.R. 333) but if no notice is served in the 14 days then the HCEO is at liberty to pay the money to the judgment creditor.
Appointment of Provisional Liquidator	Companies Act 1985, s.622.	Where any goods of a company are taken in execution, and before the sale or completion of the execution, notice is served on HCEO that a provisional liquidator has been appointed or a winding-up order made, etc. the HCEO on being required, must deliver up the goods or money seized to the liquidator, but the costs of the execution are a first charge on the goods or money so delivered, and the liquidator may sell the goods or a sufficient part of them to satisfy that charge. The "costs" referred to in this section only include costs incurred by the HCEO himself and do not include any costs of the judgment creditor (*Re Woods (Bristol) Ltd* (1931) 75 S.J. 458).
Voluntary Liquidation	See s.183 of the IA 1986 and s.129(1) IA 1986.	Similar considerations and timings apply to the voluntary liquidation of a judgment debtor company *except* where the company resolves to wind itself up the date of commencement begins on the date of the resolution.

Type of Insolvency/ Charge	Reference	Impact on the Writ of Fifa
Administration	Sch. B1, s.43(1) – (4) Insolvency Act 1986.	Introduced in September 2003 where a company is facing financial difficulties, it can be placed into "Administration" which is a procedure created under the Enterprise Act 2002 with streamlined objectives. The procedure places a company under the control of an insolvency Practitioner and the protection of the court with the objectives of rescuing the company as a going concern, or achieving a better result for creditors as a group and realising property in order to make a distribution to creditors. While a company is in administration creditors are prevented from taking any actions against it except with the permission of the court. A widely drafted moratorium expressly prevents execution being continued or commenced without the consent of the administrator or leave of the court.
Administrative Receiver	Insolvency Act 1986 Pt III	Administrative receivers are normally appointed by a bank or other lender when a company breaches the terms of its borrowing from a creditor. This type of receivership (there are others) is an enforcement remedy available to a creditor holding security which includes a floating charge over all (or substantially all) the assets of a company. An administrative receiver is appointed by the holder of the security but normally acts as agent of the company over whose assets he is appointed. His principal function is to recover the monies owed to the creditor *by whom he is appointed.* It is common for an administrative receiver to continue to operate the business, whilst trying to sell it as a going concern. However, an administrative receiver is simply a third party and does not enjoy any particular privilege as against the HCEO to surrender any goods which have been seized.
Company Voluntary Arrangement (CVA)	Insolvency Act 1986 Pt 1	As of January 1, 2003 CVAs were brought into line with IVAs and the courts are now given the power to order a moratorium of 28 days duration whilst the proposals for a CVA are formulated. The impact of

Type of Insolvency/ Charge	Reference	Impact on the Writ of Fifa
		such a moratorium is that "no other legal process may be commenced or continued, and no distress may be levied, against the company or its property except with the leave of the court and subject to such terms as the court may impose".
Debenture	Atkin's Court Forms Vol.9(1) Companies—General Vol.9(2) Companies—Insolvency	Where a charge under a debenture agreement crystallises by the valid appointment of a receiver before the completion of the execution, then the rights of the debenture holder will take priority over those of the judgment creditor (see *RE Standard Manufacturing Co* (1891) 1 Ch 627 CA; *Re Opera Limited* (1891) 3 Ch 260 CA; *Robinson v Burnell's Vienna Bakery Co Ltd* (1904) 2 K.B. 624; *Heaton and Dugard Ltd v Cutting Bros Ltd* (1925) 1 K.B. 655 DC). If the debenture holder decides to make a third party claim to the goods seized or intended to be seized then that claim will be treated as notice of a claim within the terms of RSC Order 17 r.2—which may occur, for example, if the validity of the receiver's appointment is disputed. The HCEO managing the execution of the writ will seek a copy of the debenture holder's agreement. This will then be submitted to the judgment creditor, for a decision on whether or not you admit or dispute the claim.

Personal Insolvency Table

14–38

Type of Insolvency	Reference	Impact on the Writ of Fifa
Bankruptcy	See s.346 of the IA 1986.	In order for a judgment creditor to retain the benefit of his execution against the trustee in bankruptcy of the judgment debtor, then as for liquidation, the judgment creditor must have *completed* the execution of his writ of fifa, by seizure *and* sale before the commencement of the bankruptcy order. To ensure the monies recovered under the writ of fifa are secure from any competing claim by the judgment debtor's trustee in bankruptcy then the following points should be noted.

Type of Insolvency	Reference	Impact on the Writ of Fifa
		a. the execution of the writ of fifa will be completed by the seizure and sale or receipt of the full amount of the levy (*Figg v Moore* [1894] 2 Q.B. 690).
		b. the execution of the writ of fifa will also be completed by a return of no goods (or as the form of return is commonly known a return of "nulla bona") as in *Re Fairley, Ex p. Low and Bonar Ltd* [1922] 2 Ch 791.
		c. the completion must have taken place before the commencement of the bankruptcy (*Burns v Brown* [1895] 1 Q.B. 324).
		d. the execution is not "completed" under Section 346 of the Insolvency Act 1986, unless payment has been made direct to the HCEO—and it is important to note that payment of monies directly to the judgment creditor or their solicitor, does not amount to completion (*Re Godding* [1914] 2 K.B. 70 *and Re Pollock* (1902) 87 L.T. 258).
		e. If a judgment debtor pays money to the HCEO in order to avoid a sale of goods taken in execution by the HCEO, then that money will be treated as "money in order to avoid sale" under s.346 of the Insolvency Act 1986, and not for "money received in part satisfaction of the execution" under the same section. The effect of this is that money paid to the HCEO in order to avoid a sale of the judgment debtor's goods becomes vested in the judgment creditor and can only be nullified if within 14 days of its receipt the HCEO receives notice of the debtor's bankruptcy (*Marley Tile Co Ltd v Burrows* [1978] 1 All E.R. 657 CA).
		f. A payment made by the judgment debtor to the enforcement officer even before a bankruptcy order is made against him, operates in satisfaction of a judgment creditor's debt only when the judgment creditor is in a position to maintain an action against the enforcement officer for money "had and received" (*Re A Debtor* (No.2 of 1977*), Ex p. the Debtor v Goacher* [1979] 1 All E.R. 870). In practical terms this means the payment must have been made to the enforcement officer, banked by the enforcement office, and then held for the statutory period of 14 days. The date for clearance of a cheque, or credit/debit card payment is computed from the date the enforcement officer's bank

Type of Insolvency	Reference	Impact on the Writ of Fifa
		account is actually credited with the funds which the enforcement officer could use to pay the judgment creditor, and not the date the payment (in the case in question it was a cheque) being received (*Parkside Leasing v Smith (Inspector of Taxes)* (1984) *The Times*, November 19, 1984).`
Individual Voluntary Arrangement (IVA)	S.252 Insolvency Act 1986	The making of an interim order prevents all execution being continued or commenced without leave of the court (IA 1986, s.252). However, the mere application for an interim order under that section is not a stay of execution, but the court may stay any action, execution or legal process pending the granting of the interim order. It should be noted that if a judgment creditor has not been served with the proposal or agreed to the proposal he is not bound by the terms of IVA. This becomes important if the HCEO has levied execution, in that following the little known case of *Peck v Craighead* [1955] 1 B.C.L.C. 337, seizure of goods by the Sheriff has been held to secure the goods for the benefit of the writ of fifa and the HCEO can continue with the execution of the writ by the sale and release of net proceeds of sale.
Administration Order	S.114 County Courts Act 1984	The effect of s.114 County Courts Act 1984 is that no creditor shall have any remedy against the property of the debtor in respect of those debts notified to the court before the AO was made or in respect of those debts which subsequently become scheduled to the order by addition to the list of debts. The object of the AO is to secure equal division of the debtor's property amongst all creditors and therefore leave is not given as to do so would in effect amount to setting aside the order (see *Re Frank* [1984] 1 Q.B. 9). An HCEO on learning that an AO has come into effect should confirm with the judgment creditor whether the debt is or is not a "scheduled debt" and therefore may or may not be bound by the order. Debts which have not been scheduled can be added at a later date which means any hint of an AO could thwart the successful execution of the writ of fifa.

14–39 Whilst all monies received from the judgment debtor must be applied to the Writ of FiFa in order of priority, payments made by third parties on behalf of the judgment debtor, may be allocated to specific writs (*Bower v Hett* [1895] 2 Q.B. 51).

A third party payment is not subject to the provisions of s.346 of the Insolvency Act 1986 as the payment does not deplete the assets of the judgment debtor and is therefore outside any issues involving the judgment debtor's bankruptcy.

What if the judgment debtor only has an equitable interest in chattels seized by the HCEO?

This is very rare. **14–40**

The general rule is that an HCEO cannot seize chattels in which the judgment debtor only has an equitable interest. However this rule does not extend to cases where the whole beneficial interest in the goods is vested in the judgment debtor, e.g. where furniture has been assigned to trustees upon trust to allow one of two judgment debtors to use it during the joint lives of himself and his wife (the other judgment debtor) and after the death of either upon trust for the survivor (see *Stevens v Hince* [1914] W.N. 148).

How long does a writ of fifa last for?

A Writ of FiFa is valid in the first instance for 12 months beginning **14–41**
with the date it was issued—RSC Order 46 r.8.

It is possible to apply to extend the Writ for a further 12 months.

If, during any 12 month period when the Writ of Fifa is valid, an interpleader application is issued in relation to a third party claim to goods seized by the enforcement officer, then the Writ is automatically extended for a 12 month period from the date of the final order in the interpleader proceedings. The purpose behind this rule is to allow the third party claim to be dealt with by the court, and then depending on the outcome of the interpleader proceedings for any further enforcement of the writ to be within the time frame of a valid writ instead of the writ expiring at some point during the interpleader proceedings.

Alternatively, it is possible to avoid making an application to renew the Writ of FiFa by allowing the 12 month period to expire and then simply complete a certificate confirming that nothing has been levied under the first writ which will allow a fresh writ to be issued. The risk in this approach is that another judgment will have been obtained against the judgment debtor, and that another judgment creditor issues a Writ of FiFa in between thereby gaining priority.

What is a "return" to a writ of fifa?

14–42 A "Return" by an HCEO is a form of report summarising the action taken by the HCEO in the execution of the Writ.

The "Return" must be sent by the HCEO to the judgment creditor or the judgment debtor, whoever requests it.

The rules are set out in RSC Order 46 r.9.

If an HCEO fails to then produce the necessary form of "Return" then the party making the request can apply to the court for an order compelling the enforcement officer to comply.

It should be noted that a party has no right to a "Return" whilst an interpleader is pending (*Angell v Baddeley* (1877) 3 ExD 49 CA).

Can the enforcement officer levy execution on a Sunday?

14–43 Generally speaking, the High Court Enforcement Officer cannot execute a Writ of FiFa on a Sunday, Good Friday or Christmas Day.

However, the claimant/judgment creditor/High Court Enforcement Officer can apply to the court for permission to execute a writ on these days by outlining why this permission is required.

An application for permission to continue the execution of a high profile writ of execution may well be permitted by the court to ensure enforcement action can continue on a Sunday or other day as necessary.

The judgment Debtor has offered to pay the amount due under the writ of fifa by instalments—is this allowed?

14–44 CPR Sch.1, RSC Order 47 does not contain an express provision to allow for payment by instalments. This contrasts with the position in the county court, where the county court rules do provide for an order to be stayed pending payment by instalments.

The mechanism to achieve payments by instalments in the High Court is for the judgment debtor to apply to the court for a stay under this order and seek a stay of execution on terms.

CPR Pt 40.11 provides both the High Court and county court with power to order payment by instalments at the time when judgment is given. Unless an order is therefore made allowing for payment by instalments a party must comply with a judgment or order for the payment of money to be made within 14 days of the date of the judgment or order.

What happens if it is decided to withdraw the HCEO?

Where the Writ of FiFa is withdrawn on instructions from the judgment creditor, then the HCEO cannot re-enter the premises without further instructions. 14–45

If a second judgment creditor subsequently issues a Writ against the same debtor the enforcement officer is justified in executing it without notice to the judgment creditor who has withdrawn him (see *Shaw v Kirby* (1888) 52 J.P. 182).

What are the courts powers to stay execution under a writ fieri facias?

Referring to the express rule on Writs of FiFa, under RSC Order 47 r.1, the High Court has the power to stay the execution of a Writ of FiFa either absolutely or for such period and subject to such conditions as the court thinks fit, provided that the applicant can satisfy the court that either: 14–46

- there are special circumstances which render it inexpedient to enforce the judgment or order; or
- that the applicant is unable from any cause to pay the money

The usual form of order granting a stay of execution under RSC Order 47, r.1 is as follows:

> "stay of execution (under O.47, r.1) so long as the defendant pays the judgment debt and costs by instalments at the rate of £—— per month on the —— day of each month, the first instalment to commence on the —— day of ——, 20—, provided that if he should make default in the payment of the said instalments or any part thereof on the due date, the stay be forthwith removed in respect of the whole outstanding balance at the time of such default and the judgment creditor do have permission forthwith to issue execution by writ of fifa on the said judgment and costs" (see *Chitty* and Jacob's Queen's Bench Forms, Form 1124).

Paragraph (2) of RSC Order 47 r.1 makes it clear that the judgment debtor is entitled to apply for a stay of execution by fifa, even if the judgment debtor has not acknowledged the service of the claim form or taken part in the proceedings.

The power to stay execution under this rule is separate and distinct from the power to stay execution pending an appeal under CPR 52 14–47 (see *Ellis v Scott (Practice Note)* [1964] 1 W.L.R. 976; [1964] 2 All E.R. 987).

The distinction between an order staying execution and a stay pending an appeal is important. The lodging of papers, or the issue of a notice to appeal a judgment will not be sufficient to prevent an HCEO from continuing with the execution of a writ of fifa.

If execution has been improperly issued it may be set aside even after execution has been levied. If the court sets aside a default judgment pursuant to CPR Pt 13 it will be necessary for the order to deal with payment of the costs of execution. These will have to be paid by the judgment debtor if the judgment was regular.

It is the duty of the judgment debtor to find the creditor if the latter is within the jurisdiction; but if neither the creditor nor anyone authorised to receive payment is within the jurisdiction a stay of execution may also be obtained (see *Re A Debtor* (1838 of 1911) [1912] 1 K.B. 53 at 62 CA).

The items seized are of specific value and interest—is it possible to sell the goods privately rather than by auction?

14–48 Under RSC Order 47 r.6 there is a handy little rule which enables an HCEO to apply for an order for sale "otherwise than by auction" on the basis he or she is under a duty to get the best price he can for the goods, and he or she is the person who may be likely to know whether and when this can be achieved by a private sale.

The overriding position that goods must be sold at public auction unless ordered to the contrary by the court, is set out in The Courts Act 2003 para.10, Sch.7 (which replaced the old provision under the Supreme Court Act 1981 s.138A(1)).

If it is thought that an application for permission to sell the debtor's goods by private contract will achieve more in terms of net proceeds than an application notice as prescribed by RSC Order 47 r.6 can be issued.

Usually this is done by the HCEO although under RSC Order 47 r.1, there is provision for the application to be made by either the judgment creditor or judgment debtor.

14–49 The application works best where the goods are unique, antique, or valuable.

Where the applicant for the order for private sale is not the HCEO, then on the demand of the applicant, the HCEO must send the applicant a list stating whether he has notice of the issue of another writ(s) of execution against the goods of the judgment debtor, and so far as is known to him, the name and address of every creditor who has issued a writ of execution.

If the HCEO is the applicant, then he or she must prepare such a list and have it available to show the court at the hearing of the application.

The application for permission to sell by private treaty needs to be served by the applicant at least four clear days before the date of the hearing on each person named in the list.

Each person who is served with the application may attend and be heard on the hearing of the application.

What happens if a third party claims ownership of the goods seized by the high court enforcement officer?

Where the HCEO has seized goods in execution of a Writ of FiFa and a person other than the judgment debtor makes a claim to ownership of the goods seized, the third party must give notice of its claim to the HCEO, including in its notice a statement of its address which will be his address for service. **14–50**

This is the start of the process of "interpleader" under CPR Sch.1, RSC Order 17.

When a third party claim is received the HCEO has to go through the process of giving notice of the claim to the judgment creditor on whose behalf the goods were seized in Form PF 23. This notice requires the judgment creditor to state whether he "admits or disputes" the claim.

If admitted the HCEO withdraws from possession of the goods which were the subject of the claim—and which may involve all or some of the goods seized or intended to be seized.

If disputed, the HCEO will apply to the court for interpleader relief.

The judgment creditor must respond to the notice of the third party's claim within seven days of receipt of the HCEO's notice and may use Form PF 24 to do so, although usually the response is in the form of a simple letter admitting or disputing the claim. **14–51**

Where the claim is admitted, the HCEO will withdraw from possession of the goods and may apply under RSC Order 17, r.2(4) for an order to restrain a claim being brought against him for having taken possession of the goods.

Where the claim is disputed, the HCEO may apply for interpleader relief. An application for interpleader relief if made in existing proceedings is made by an application in accordance with CPR 23, otherwise it is made by the issue of a Pt 8 claim form. Usually it is made within the existing proceedings.

The Master may deal with the third party claim summarily, or may direct an issue to be tried between the parties in dispute (see RSC Order 17, r.5) or make such other order as is appropriate.

14–52 There are some practical issues to consider if faced with a third party claim.

- What are the goods which have been claimed? Are they valuable, worth selling at auction to recover the full amount due under the Writ?
- Are other goods available to be seized if I win on the Interpleader?
- What will be the likely outcomes on costs—will I win costs against the third party (who becomes rather confusingly the "interpleader claimant")?
- What are the chances of enforcing any costs order against an interpleader claimant?
- What will be the costs of the HCEO and their legal team?
- What evidence do I have that the third party claim is worth disputing—i.e. do I have strong evidence that the goods really do belong to the judgment debtor and therefore the chances of winning the interpleader proceedings are strong?

Are there any particular obstacles I should be aware of regarding execution of a writ of fifa?

14–53

Rights of Landlords	As to the rights of a landlord to payment of arrears of rent by a judgment creditor, see Insolvency Act 1986, s.347(6). Sections 6 and 7 of Landlord and Tenant Act 1709 did not apply as against judgment creditors in favour of persons entitled to distrain (*Lewis v Davies* [1914] 2 K.B. 469 CA).
Interference With A Receiver	The court will not protect an HCEO who executes process after notice from a receiver that he is in possession (*Try v Try* (1851) 13 Beav 422; *Rock v Cook* (1848) 2 Ph. 691). An HCEO who seizes goods in the possession of a receiver is guilty of a contempt of court (*Lane v Sterne* (1862) 3 Giff 629) and may be subject to an action for committal.
Reserve and Auxiliary Forces (Protection of Civil Interests) Act 1951	Armed forces personnel are treated differently in relation to enforcement action and a petitioner should be aware of the potential difficulties before proceeding with enforcement against a member of the armed forces.

Crown's Position	Save as provided by s.25(1)–(3) of the Crown Proceedings Act 1947, no execution or attachment or process in the nature of execution or attachment can be issued to enforcing payment from the Crown of money or costs, and no person can be made individually liable under any order for payment by the Crown, or any government department, or any officer of the Crown as such, for any such money or costs
The Position of a Foreign Sovereign	A sovereign state does not by initiating proceedings in this country render its property within the jurisdiction liable to execution. To enforce an order for payment of costs (*Duff Dev Co v Kelantan* [1923] 1 Ch 385)—see also State Immunity Act 1978 s.20

What value of debt can be enforced in the county court using a warrant of execution?

Where the judgment amount to be enforced is £5,000 or more, it can only be enforced in the High Court and should not be accepted by county court staff in the issuing of the Warrant. **14–54**

The sums that can be enforced in the county court using warrants of execution, are judgment debts below £5,000 and judgments regulated under the Consumer Credit Act 1974 (as amended).

For judgments between £600 and £5,000 which are not regulated by the Consumer Credit Act there is currently a choice for court users on which agency they choose for enforcement, be it the county court bailiffs or the HCEOs, either of choice, or by using the HCEO cab rank system.

The following table offers a quick guide to the value of debts and their location of enforcement: **14–55**

Judgment debt amount to be enforced (including costs and interest where applicable)	County Court	High Court
Below £600	Yes	No
Consumer Credit Act debt	Yes	No
Consumer Credit Act debt which is exempt	Yes	Yes
Between £600–£5,000	Yes	Yes
Above £5,000	No	Yes

Is permission needed to issue in the county court?

14–56 CCR Order 26 r.5(1) outlines the the circumstances where permission must be sought. The most common situation is where six years have elapsed since the judgment or order (see *Duer v Fraser* [2001] 1 All E.R. 249).

Application for leave is made on Form N244, supported by a witness statement or affidavit and is initially made without notice.

What is the procedure for issuing a warrant of execution

14–57 In accordance with CCR Order 26 r.1 the request is made on Form N323.

The fee in the County Court for issuing the warrant is currently £35 if the debt does not exceed £125; or above £125, the fee is £55. You can obtain up to date details of the fees from the Court Service website at *http://www.hmcourts-service.gov.uk/infoabout/fees/county.htm*.

If the judgment to be enforced is a High Court judgment or order you must also file:

- an office copy of the judgment or order on Form N326 or N327;
- a certificate verifying the amount due;
- if a writ of execution has been issued, a copy of the relevant HCEO's return; and
- a copy of the order for transfer.

How will the court note the priority of the warrant?

14–58 Brief details of the differences in this regard between the county court process and the High Court process have been given above.

In accordance with s.85(3) County Courts Act 1984, the court staff must enter into their records the precise time of the making of the application to issue the warrant and/or, under s.103(1) County Courts Act 1984, of the time they send the warrant of execution to another county court.

The court officer will issue the warrant, give it a number, give notice to the judgment debtor and forward the warrant to the bailiff.

How long does a county court warrant last for?

A warrant of execution is valid for 12 months initially from the date of its issue, and can be renewed for a period of 12 months at any one time from either: **14–59**

- the day after its expiry if it is renewed pursuant to an application made before that day; or
- from the day it expires or such later day (if any) as the court shall allow if not made until after expiry.

How is the application to renew the warrant made?

The application is be made on Form N445 and submitted to the court with the appropriate fee; currently debts below £125 attract a fee of £35 and those above £125 have a fee of £55. **14–60**

As with the majority of the court forms referred to throughout these notes, you can obtain a copy of the form, and complete it on-line, at the Court Service website at *http://www.hmcourts-service.gov.uk/HMCSCourtFinder/FormFinder.do*.

Agreement has been reached regarding payment of the debt—how does this affect the warrant?

If the judgment creditor reaches agreement with the judgment debtor regarding payment, the court can be asked to suspend execution of the warrant. **14–61**

If the debtor then defaults on the arrangement to pay, the judgment creditor can ask the court to re-issue the warrant as advised above.

Stays of execution are more common in the county court with the power of the court to suspend or stay a warrant of execution exercisable by a district judge and in accordance with the rules by a court officer (see CCR Order 25 r.8).

If the judgment debtor makes the application it should be on form N245, with any reply by the judgment creditor being on Form N246A. If the judgment or order is suspended the order is in Form N41.

What if a third party claims the goods seized by the bailiff?

The situation in this case is the same as with a High Court Writ—interpleader proceedings will be needed to resolve who owns the goods. **14–62**

If the judgment creditor disputes the third party claim then, in accordance with CPR Sch.2, CCR Order 33, the court has the same procedural rules to deal with the claim by the use of interpleader proceedings.

If the bailiff seizes goods, how will he deal with the sale?

14–63 This procedure is dealt with under CCR Order 26, r.12.

The court will send the judgment debtor an inventory of the goods removed and, not less than four days before the auction sale, will provide the judgment debtor with details of the date/time and location of the sale.

The sale itself is governed by s.97 County Courts Act 1984.

Following the sale the court must provide the judgment debtor with a detailed account, in writing, of the sale and of the application of the proceeds of sale.

There is also provision for the goods to be sold by means other than by auction (see CCR Order 26, r.15).

The judgment creditor must make an application to the court for permission to sell in this manner.

What will be the effect of the Tribunals, Courts and Enforcement Act

14–64 Execution against goods is perhaps the area to be most amended by Pt 3 of the new Act.

One of the biggest changes is actually in relation to the name of the Writs and Warrants. Rather than being Warrants of Execution and Writs of FiFa, they are both renamed Warrants and Writs of Control.

There is to be a requirement for notices to be served on the judgment debtors before either the county court bailiffs or the HCEOs are able to attend to execute the Warrant or Writ.

There is to be a minimum period of time for which goods seized are to be held before they can be sold at auction; although this minimum period has yet to be specified.

There will no longer be bailiffs and High Court Enforcement Officers, but "Enforcement Agents".

As with other areas of the Act, the majority of the detail has yet to be agreed and specified, but it is certain to be a period of massive change and Practitioners should be aware of the changes in terminology and practice to ensure that they are ready to comply with the new requirements once introduced.

Case Study

Tom knows, that Margot has a number of large oil paintings hanging in her property as well as driving a very nice car, and having several "large" pieces of ornamental garden furniture; all of which could be removed under a Warrant of Execution or Writ of FiFa and sold in satisfaction of his judgment Debt. **14–65**

Examples of the forms Tom would complete to pursue either of these routes are shown in the Case Study example at pages 459, 460–462. Practitioners should particularly note the amount of information which Tom has provided to both the bailiff and Enforcement Officer in his instructions to increase the likelihood of a successful execution.

Too often judgment creditors make the mistake of thinking that bailiffs and Enforcement Officers are clairvoyant and will somehow miraculously know of the judgment debtor's assets. Simply providing details of the times of the day when the judgment debtor is believed to be at home, or the make and model of the vehicle they are believed to drive, will significantly increase the prospects of a successful enforcement.

Flow Charts

A flowchart outlining the process for enforcement by way of execution against goods in both the county court and High Court is included in the Appendix to this book. **14–66**

What does it cost to use a High Court Enforcement Officer?

A High Court Enforcement Officer is entitled to costs and charges pursuant to the High Court Enforcement Officers Regulations 2004. These regulations updated the old Sheriff's scale of fees which dated back to 1920. **14–67**

Many Practioners may not be familiar with these regulations which set out a scale of fees that High Court Enforcement Officers are entitled to charge upon the issue of a Writ. These fees can be best described and separated into two categories.

Nominal fixed and percentage fees

These fees are chargeable on any Writ that is enforced and are based upon either a very nominal fixed fee such as £2.00 for investigating a **14–68** third party claim to goods and percentage fees based on the value of the goods seized or monies recovered.

Discretionary fees

14–69 These are charges made pursuant to Fee Item 12 in the Regulations and are charged by most High Court Enforcement Officers in respect of additional and administrative costs incurred to meet the cost of the High Court enforcement service.

The fees charged under this provision often relate to the time of the High Court Officer spent in attending and managing the execution and the financial costs attributable to the overall cost of managing a Writ.

It is important to remember that a High Court Enforcement Officer will always attempt to recover his charges of execution from the Judgment Debtor. There are, however, some circumstances where this may prove difficult and as a result a Judgment Creditor may be faced with a liability to the High Court Enforcement Officer.

When will a High Court Enforcement Officer look to a Judgment Creditor for payment of his fees?

14–70 As has already been outlined, a High Court Enforcement Officer will always attempt to recover his full fees from the Judgment Debtor, however, where the execution of the Writ proves fruitless and ultimately unsuccessful the Judgment Creditor will need to pay an abortive charge, usually the fee charged will be a nominal fee in the region of £60 plus VAT.

If an arrangement is made with the Judgment Debtor to settle the outstanding amount by way of an instalment arrangement the High Court Enforcement Officer is, according to the rules and common law, entitled to his fees based upon a successful recovery. Most High Court Officer's will take a commercial view in relation to the fees charged in these circumstances and are likely to base their fees on the work undertaken to achieve the payment arrangement and take a percentage of the sums that have been recovered.

As a cautionary note, it should be remembered that it is set out at common law that ultimate liability for the High Court Enforcement Officer's charges does rest with the Judgment Creditor, a fact set out in the High Court Enforcement Officer's Regulations and as such it is very important that practitioners do bear in mind the High Court Enforcement Officer's charges before and during and negotiations with the Judgment Debtor to settle the matter. The best way of avoiding any liability in these circumstances is to contact the High

Court Enforcement Officer before agreeing any proposal with the Judgment Debtor or by referring the Judgment Debtor to the High Court Enforcement Officer who can deal with the Judgment Debtor's offer or proposal to settle.

What happens if I disagree with the High Court Enforcement Officers charges?

If a Judgment Creditor or a Judgment Debtor disputes any charge being made by the High Court Enforcement Officer then their remedy is set out in Pt 4 of the High Court Enforcement Officers Regulations. This allows for detailed assessment of the High Court Enforcement Officer's charges by a Costs Judge pursuant to CPR Pt 47. **14–71**

Most HCEO's will be prepared for their fees to be assessed by a Costs Judge and many will prefer to make the application themselves for a detailed assessment of the charges in question to ensure any charge which is made can be justified to the Court.

What does it cost to use a county court bailiff?

In contrast the cost of using a county court bailiff less complex but one has to ask if it is as effective. The Judgment Creditor will pay a fee on the issue of the Warrant of Execution for either a full recovery or part recovery (which is a lower fee). Any cost incurred by the bailiff in executing the Warrant will be passed on o the Judgment Debtor, such as the cost of attending to remove goods. **14–72**

However, compared to the High Court Enforcement Officers, county court bailiffs often lack the resources and or infrastructure to carry out the removal and sale of goods compared to their High Court colleagues. The effect of this is that whilst county court bailiffs have far greater numbers of warrants the actual cash recovered from the process can appear considerably less.

Chapter 15

Attachment Of Earnings—CPR Schedule 2, CCR Order 27

Introductory Comments

15–01 Attachment of Earnings Orders (AEOs) are only obtainable within the County Court for the purposes of debt recovery proceedings. Where the judgment debtor is in paid employment, it is possible to obtain an order effectively ordering the judgment debtor's employer to deduct payments from the judgment debtor's salary for the payment and benefit of the judgment creditor.

Attachment of Earnings Orders are one of the most popular methods of enforcement action. This is primarily because where the judgment debtor is in paid employment an Attachment of Earnings Order is a straightforward remedy.

Practitioners should, however, be aware that, unlike other methods of enforcement, where an AEO is granted, the judgment creditor cannot pursue other methods of enforcement whilst the AEO is in force. So they cannot issue a warrant or writ, or seek a charge over the judgment debtor's property.

Enforcement Matrix

15–02 Debt Recovery Practitioners will usually consider an AEO against an individual judgment debtor who is employed, but rarely do Practitioners consider the possibility of obtaining an AEO against a judgment debtor who is a director of a company. This is on the basis that they consider them to be self employed and therefore view an AEO as not being obtainable.

However, what Practitioners should be considering is the fact that as a company director, the judgment debtor is likely to be receiving an income from the company by way of PAYE salary as a director.

As the table below shows, it is not just individual judgment debtors who can therefore be subject to Attachment of Earnings Orders.

15–03

Type of Debtor	Type of Premises	Possible types of assets	Type of Enforcement
Individual	Domestic address where the debtor may be viewed as a consumer of goods and service whether or not regulated under the CCA 1974 (as amended)—for sole trader see below.	Employment	Attachment of Earnings—CPR Sch.2, CCR Order 27
Company	Not applicable	Director's salary	Attachment of Earnings—as above—if the company director can be found to be made personally liable for the company's debt then the salary can be attached.

How does an AEO actually work in practice?

15–04 An AEO works by telling the judgment debtor's employer how much to deduct from the judgment debtor's salary for the benefit of the judgment creditor.

The employer is told:

- the total debt owed by the judgment debtor;
- the amount of the weekly or monthly deductions to be made; and
- the amount below which the court considers that a judgment debtor's earnings should not be reduced.

It is then the responsibility of the employer to ensure that the deductions are made in accordance with the court order. The payments are sent to CAPS (Centralised Attachment of Earnings Payment System) and are than passed on to the judgment creditor.

How does the court decide the amount of the deductions?

There are two "rates" fixed by the order under s.6(5) of the 1971 Act. These are: 15–05

- **Normal Deduction Rate**—this is the rate at which the court thinks it is reasonable for the judgment debtor's earnings to be applied.
- **Protected Earnings Rate**—this is the rate below which the court will not allow the judgment debtor's earnings to fall. The method of calculation is based upon the state benefits to which the judgment debtor would be entitled. In *Billington v Billington* [1974] Fam 24, it was stated that the best guide in most cases was to apply the calculation or normal requirements under the Supplementary Benefits Act.

Can all of the judgment debtor's earnings be attached?

No. There are certain earnings which cannot be attached. These include: 15–06

- State "old age" pension;
- Disability pensions;
- Benefit payments;
- Tax credits;
- Armed forces pay;
- Merchant seaman's wages; and
- Self-employed earnings.

How is an application for an AEO started?

Firstly, it should be mentioned that an application for an AEO is to be made to the court for the district in which the judgment debtor lives—CPR Sch.2, CCR Order 27 r.3. This may mean the case being transferred to the judgment debtor's local court if proceedings have been commenced through the County Court Bulk Centre. 15–07

However, having ascertained where the application should be

made, the first stage of the process is not in fact to submit the application for the AEO. Instead it should be to make a search of the AEO Index.

County Courts are required to keep a record of all AEOs made against judgment debtors residing within their district. Using Form N336 a judgment creditor can submit a request to the County Court that they search the index and advise as to whether or not there are any existing AEOs against the judgment debtor.

In the event that the search reveals that other AEOs are in existence, the judgment creditor can either decide not to proceed with their application, or alternatively request a Consolidated Attachment of Earnings Order, pursuant to CPR Sch.2, CCR Order 27 r.19.

Consideration should however be given to the fact that if a Consolidated AEO is made this will not increase the level of deductions made from the judgment debtor's earnings. Instead, the deductions which are already being made will continue and will simply be "shared" amongst all of the judgment creditors who are party to the Consolidated AEO.

Once the search of the index has been completed, and on the basis that the judgment creditor decides to proceed with the application for an AEO, the full application is then made to the court on Form N337.

15–08 Once in receipt of the N337 the court will complete and issue Form N55. However, CPR r.5.2(1) does permit the judgment creditor to complete the Form N55 and thereby negate the need for the N337; in practice this rarely happens.

The court will serve notice of the application on the judgment debtor and provide the judgment debtor with Form N56. If the judgment debtor does not pay the debt in full at this stage, then he/she must complete and return the Form N56 within eight days of being served with the notice.

If the judgment debtor fails to return the Form N56 then the court will serve the judgment debtor with a Form N61 (an Order for Production of Statement of Means). Again this should be completed and returned to the court within eight days of service upon the judgment debtor.

If the judgment debtor still fails to comply with the court order, the court will serve Form N63 upon the judgment debtor (Failure to Comply With Statement of Means). This requires the judgment debtor to attend court and provide a good reason as to why they should not be sent to prison for 14 days or fined up to £250. Failure of the judgment debtor to attend at this stage will result in the court issuing an order for their arrest.

All these steps are taken by the court without any need for the judgment debtor to proactively request that these steps are taken.

What are the employer's duties with an AEO?

Once the AEO is served on the employer the employer has seven days before being bound to comply with the order. The employer has a further ten days in which to advise the court if the judgment debtor is no longer employed. Failure to notify the court is an offence under s.7(2) of the 1971 Act. **15–09**

It is then the responsibility of the employer to ensure that deductions are taken from the judgment debtor's earnings in accordance with the order. The employer is entitled to deduct £1 for the administrative costs of dealing with the AEO, providing that a deduction is in fact made. Simply checking whether or not a deduction can be taken does not entitle the employer to make the deduction for administrative costs.

The employer must then send the deductions made to CAPS at regular intervals.

What happens if the judgment debtor becomes self-employed?

As an AEO cannot operate against self-employed earnings and any AEO in force will be discharged and a judgment creditor will have to pursue an alternative means of enforcement action to recover the outstanding balance of the judgment debt. **15–10**

What happens if the judgment debtor leaves their employment?

The AEO remains in force but is ineffective until such time as it is redirected to the new employer. **15–11**

Whilst the judgment debtor is under an obligation to advise any new employer of the existence of the AEO against them so that it can be "reactivated" (s.15 of the 1971 Act) in practice this rarely happens. This leaves the judgment creditor in the position of having to try and track down the new employers details so that information can then be passed to the court and the AEO can be redirected.

Once the new employers details are know, the AEO can be redirected and deductions can recommence as before.

Can the judgment creditor vary the AEO?

It is open to both parties to apply to the court within 14 days of service of the AEO to apply to the court for the order to be reconsidered. **15–12**

The application is made using Form N244 and is usually made on the basis that the judgment creditor believes that increased deductions should be made.

Can the court vary the AEO?

15–13 Yes. The court can vary or discharge the AEO at any time of its own motion. It must however first give notice to the judgment creditor and the judgment debtor and allow both parties the opportunity to be heard (see CPR Sch.2, CCR 27.13).

How does the court actually manage the payments?

15–14 The two prescribed forms of AEO are Form N60 or N64 (Suspended). Both forms identify the judgment debtor by name and, where appropriate, the employer reference. It directs the employer to make the deductions and pay the amounts to CAPS.

CAPS then processes the payments and pays out to the judgment creditor.

What costs are permitted under an AEO?

15–15 The answer is two-fold:

- A solicitor who has prepared a witness statement or affidavit or request for a judgment creditor under r.7(8) is treated as having attended the hearing. The cost may be fixed and allowed without detailed assessment under CPR 47; and
- An employer making deductions pursuant to an AEO is entitled to deduct £1 for their administrative costs pursuant to Attachment of Earnings (Employers Deductions) Order 1991 (SI 1991/356).

How is a consolidated AEO obtained?

15–16 Section 17 of the 1971 Act allows a consolidated AEO to be obtained from the court. It is possible for either the judgment creditor or judgment debtor to apply to the court for a consolidated order. It is also possible for the court to make a consolidated order of its own motion.

If the judgment debtor makes the application the court will notify all parties of the application and any party objecting to the making of the consolidated order must notify the court in writing within 14 days of their grounds for objection. Any objections will then be referred to the District Judge for consideration and appropriate directions.

If the judgment creditor makes the application he/she/they must do so on Form N66A with a covering letter to the court, detailing the amount outstanding at that time.

What about deductions from armed forces personnel?

It is not possible to obtain an AEO against armed forces personnel. However, it is possible to arrange for compulsory deductions to be made from the judgment debtor's salary under the following legislation: **15–17**

- s.151A Army Act 1955;
- s.151A Air Force Act 1955; and
- s.128E Naval Discipline Act 1957.

Whilst the judgment creditor should firstly approach the judgment debtor for payment, either in full or to agree instalments if the judgment debtor fails to respond or co-operate, then the judgment creditor should write to the appropriate pay authority with details of the judgment order, providing full details of the judgment debtor and requesting that compulsory deductions be made.

What will be the effect of the Courts, Tribunals and Enforcement Act?

The two main areas of change under the new Act are the introduction of a fixed deduction scheme and a system for "following" judgment debtors to new employment. **15–18**

Section 91 of the new Act introduces a fixed rate deduction scheme rather than deductions being made in accordance with Pt 1 of Sch.3 of the 1971 Act as they are at present. The level and frequency of the fixed deductions are yet to be set down in regulations and are therefore at present unknown.

One of the biggest problems with the current AEO system is the fact that it can be incredibly difficult for the judgment creditor to track the judgment debtor down if they change employment whilst the AEO is in place.

The new Act aims to alleviate this problem by making it easier for the judgment creditor to redirect an AEO when the judgment debtor changes employment (ss.15A–15D). It is intended that HMRC will provide the necessary information to the court, using tax and NI details, to enable the AEO to be redirected.

15–19 Unfortunately, as with a lot of the "detail" of the new Act, the necessary regulations governing the use and supply of the judgment debtor's information, have yet to be drafted. Until such time as those regulations have been drafted and approved no requests can be made of the HMRC for information to assist in the redirection of the AEO.

Once the Regulation is in force however, the new ss.15A–15D will apply to all AEOs whether they were granted before or after the commencement of the new Act.

Case Study

15–20 At pages 497 and 498 of the case study is an example of the form of application which would be completed by Tom were he to pursue an Attachment of Earnings Order against Margot, together with examples of the forms issued by the court.

Although such an application is only likely to result in small value payments being received by Tom, in this particular case, the embarrassment to Margot of her employers finding out about the debt, could well result in an offer of payment being forthcoming and therefore a Suspended Attachment of Earnings Order being made.

Flow Charts

15–21 A flow chart in the Appendix outlines the process to be followed in order for a judgment creditor to successfully obtain an Attachment of Earnings Order against their judgment debtor.

Chapter 16

Enforcing Judgments with a Foreign Element—CPR Part 74

Introductory Comments

Debt Recovery Practitioners are becoming increasingly aware of the need to be able to move judgments out of the jurisdiction of England and Wales to collect debt. Today court users have to be more and more confident about being able to enforce judgments within the UK, Europe and across the world as handling instructions from foreign clients who wish to enforce judgments within England and Wales. 16–01

Fortunately the Civil Procedure Rules has streamlined the enforcement of foreign judgments with such foreign elements. CPR Pt 74 is a comprehensive code to handle enforcement of judgments with a series of countries within Europe and beyond. This chapter will look at how Pt 74 is structured and offer solutions on countries which are outside the Rule.

To start with Practitioners need to be clear in their own minds how judgments are treated within the Rules and essentially this boils down to two clear concepts:

- "Incoming judgments" for judgments coming into England and Wales for enforcement; and
- "Outgoing judgments" for judgments entered in the civil courts in England and Wales and which needed to be sent outside of the jurisdiction for enforcement.

How is CPR Part 74 structured?

The Rule is structured into five separate sections with two accompanying practice directions. The sections divide the business of foreign judgment enforcement as follows: 16–02

Section I—Enforcement in England and Wales of judgments of foreign courts.	This section of the CPR Pt 74 contains provisions for the registration in the High court of the Enforcement of judgments from the courts of members states of the European Union, the European Free Trade Areas ("EFTA"), certain Commonwealth countries in certain states with which the United Kingdom has reciprocal treaties and conventions for the enforcement of "incoming judgments".
Section II—Enforcement in foreign countries of judgments of the High court and County courts	This section of CPR Pt 74 deals with the procedure of transferring "outgoing judgments" from the courts of England and Wales to courts in foreign jurisdictions under the provision of various Acts dealing with reciprocal enforcement which date back to 1920, 1933 and 1982. The application to transfer judgments out of the jurisdiction is usually made without notice to the court where the judgment was given. The application is in effect a request for a certified copy of the English or Welsh judgment to be made available as the basis for the transfer. In the case of judgments with registration in member states of the EU the certificate needed is annexed to the Judgment Regulation which is set out in the Appendix to CPR PD 74. The important point to note here is that the evidence in support of the application needs to fully comply with CPR 74.13. There is some debate as to whether a judgment obtained in a county court in England and Wales which is then transferred to the High Court for enforcement can be enforced through a court abroad. This comes from the fact that the judgment may not meet the criteria of the 1920 and/or 1933 reciprocal treaty Acts to be a judgment "given" or "obtained" in a "Superior Court". If there is doubt about whether a county court judgment will be recognised in another jurisdiction (Jersey is an example where a county court judgment will not be recognised), then a suggested alternative course is to issue the proceedings within the High Court where possible so that the resulting judgment is a judgment of the Superior Court. If this is not possible because the current rules of CPR prevent this, for example, where the claim is under £15,000, then the claim should be started in the county court and before any further step is taken an application should be made to transfer the claim to the High Court (see CPR 30.3) to ensure any resulting judgment is a High Court judgment and thus will be recognised as a judgment of a "superior court".

Section III—Enforcement of the United Kingdom judgments in other parts of the United Kingdom.	This section provides for the registration of "incoming judgments" from courts in other parts of the United Kingdom by a certificate for the enforcement of "money provisions" and for the obtaining of certificates for "outgoing money judgments" to other part of the United Kingdom being Scotland and Northern Ireland.
Section IV—Enforcement in England and Wales of European community judgments	The European Communities (Enforcement of Community judgments) Order 1972 (SI 1972/1590) was made as part of the United Kingdom's accession to the Treaty of Rome. It provides for the enforcement of certain judgments of the European Community/Union and its institutions, provided that the Secretary of State has appended an order for enforcement of the judgment. It is important to note that the 1972 order and this part of CPR Pt 74 do not apply to the judgments of the domestic courts of Member States of the EU as these come under s.I of the CPR Pt 74 as set out above. The 1972 Order and this section apply to the judgments and orders against persons made by communities institutions, such as the Council of the Commission, often in the nature of a penalty for breach of regulatory requirements (e.g. in respect of anti-competitive activities) under the European Court. It also includes Euratom inspection orders (see para.9 of CPR PD 74).
Section V—European Enforcement orders	This section of CPR Pt 74 provides the cross border mechanism to transfer judgments from England and Wales to the rest of Europe through the recent innovation of a European Enforcement Order. It also provides for the recognition and enforcement in England and Wales of the judgments of other contracting states that have been certified as European Enforcement Orders (EEOs) under the necessary Regulations. EEOs have been available since October 21, 2005 for all judgments dated after January 20, 2005.

What is the supporting legislative framework to CPR Part 74?

One of the success stories of the English Common Law has been its portability across the world and today its legacy is the foundation of many of the legal systems which make up the Commonwealth. This means much of how judgment enforcement works across the world is based on the English system so it is not usual to find Writs of Fieri Facias in precedent books in Singapore, and the USA. **16–03**

If a debt recovery practitioner wants to enforce a judgment in another part of the world, whether it be another part of the UK, Europe or somewhere further afield, the easiest way to start the process is to look at the country where the assets are believed to be and work out which treaty applies to that country. Once the treaty process is identified then the rules applicable to that treaty can be used. This will mean the outgoing judgment can be moved out of the jurisdiction of England and Wales to the jurisdiction where enforcement is to take place.

In the Appendix to this book the reader will find a "Look Up Table" of all the countries in the world where reciprocal treaties are in place. If the country is not showing in the table it means we have to go about carrying the enforcement in a slightly different way. However we have anticipated that as well in the Scenarios set out below.

Under CPR Pt 74.1(5), the reciprocal treaties which have developed over the last century are set out and will be found in the "Look Up Table" set out in the Appendix to this book. There are as follows:

- The Administration of Justice Act 1920—referred to as "1920 Act";
- The Foreign Judgments (Reciprocal Enforcement) Act 1933—referred to as the "1933 Act";
- The Civil Jurisdiction and Judgments Act 1982—referred to as the "1982 Act";
- The Judgments Regulation under Council Regulation (EC) No. 44/2001—published as part of an initiative to streamline the recognition and enforcement of judgments across Europe; and
- Council Regulation (EC) No.805/2004 which created the European Enforcement Order for uncontested claims—referred to as the "EEO Regulation"—which came into being in January 2005—a copy of the EEO Regulation is annexed to Practice Direction 74B and can be found at: *http://europa.eu.int/eurlex/pri/en/oj/dat/2004/1–143/1–14320040430en00150039.pdf*

Which section applies to the enforcement of a judgment with a foreign element?

16–04 Building on the need to make this area of enforcement easier for practitioners CPR Pt 74 can be split into a number of different scenarios which when confronted with a problem to resolve should make it easier for practitioners to navigate where they are in the Rules. These eight scenarios are set out below:

8 Key Scenarios For Enforcement With a Foreign Element	Which Section of CPR P 74 applies
Scenario 1 —judgments to be enforced as "**incoming judgments**" into England and Wales from another part of the United Kingdom, i.e. Scotland or Northern Ireland	Section III
Scenario 2 —judgments to be enforced as "**incoming judgments**" into England and Wales from another part of the European Union	Section V
Scenario 3—judgments to be enforced as "**incoming judgments**" into England and Wales from another country with which England and Wales has a reciprocal treaty (see the Look Up Table in the Appendix to this book)	Section I
Scenario 4—judgments to be enforced as "**incoming judgments**" into England and Wales from another country with which England and Wales has **NO** reciprocal treaty, i.e. USA/China/Russia	See the notes below
Scenario 5—judgments to be enforced as "**outgoing judgments**" in England and Wales to another part of the United Kingdom, i.e. Scotland or Northern Ireland	Section III
Scenario 6—judgments to be enforced as "**outgoing judgments**" in England and Wales to another country within the European Union	Section V
Scenario 7—judgments to be enforced as "**outgoing judgments**" in England and Wales from another country with which England and Wales has a reciprocal treaty such as Canada and Australia	Section II
Scenario 8—judgments to be enforced as "**outgoing judgments**" in England and Wales to another country where there is no reciprocal treaty such as the USA/China/Russia	See the notes below.

Of course the enforcement of judgments with a foreign element is a complex area and reference should be made to both the White Book service and the leading civil procedural text for updates, precedents and current case law should further guidance or information be necessary.

Having identified the eight Key Scenarios we can now look at each of these in turn.

Scenario 1—what is the outlined process for handling an incoming judgment into England and Wales from another part of the United Kingdom?

16–05 Practitioners should look to s.III of CPR Pt 74 under r.74.14. This is entitled "Enforcement of United Kingdom judgments in other part of the United Kingdom".

As has been said elsewhere in this book the jurisdiction of the United Kingdom is defined in CPR 2.3 to include England and Wales and any part of the territorial waters of the United Kingdom adjoining England and Wales.

"Other parts" of the United Kingdom for practical purposes means Scotland and Northern Ireland but does not include the Isle of Man, or the Channel Islands. Practitioners are also referred to the note at CPR 74.0.5 of the White Book Service 2007 as to the position in relation to both of these jurisdictions.

In enforcing an incoming judgment from another part of the United Kingdom the debt recovery practitioner is looking to enforce a "money provision" judgment as opposed to a "non-money provision". A "money provision" judgment is one in which the court has ordered the payment of one or more sums of money under a judgment. The process is governed by s.18, Sch.6 to the 1982 Act (see above).

16–06 CPR 74.15 deals with the registration of the incoming money provision judgment from either Scotland or Northern Ireland. The process is relatively straightforward. A money judgment coming from Scotland or Northern Ireland will first of all be registered in the High Court under para.5 of Sch.6 of the 1982 Act by way of a certificate issued by either the court in Scotland or Northern Ireland. This must be registered in the Central Office of the High Court within six months of issue.

The certificate will be filed together with a copy certified by written evidence to confirm it is a true copy. The effect of registering the judgment in the High Court means the incoming judgment becomes a High Court judgment within England and Wales and the enforcement of the incoming judgment is therefore subject to the rules on enforcement of High Court judgments currently dealt with under CPR Sch.1, RSC Orders 45, 46, 47. For example once registered it is possible for a Scottish decree to be enforced using the services of a High Court Enforcement Officer by issuing a Writ of Fi Fa based on the Scottish decree.

A judgment debtor may apply to stay the enforcement of a money judgment under para.9 of Sch.6 of the 1982 Act and an application may be made to stay the enforcement with a certificate issued under CPR 74.15. If such an application is made then the registering court being the High Court in England and Wales has to be satisfied that the applicant is entitled to and intends to apply to the judgment court being the court in Scotland or Northern Ireland which made the judgment, to set aside or grant a stay on the enforcement of the judgment. If the High Court is satisfied that such an application is going to be made then it may make an order staying the enforcement proceedings on such terms as it thinks fit and for such period as may be reasonably sufficient to enable the application in the judgment court to be disposed of.

Scenario 2—is the judgment to be enforced an incoming judgment in England and Wales from another part of the European Union?

If the judgment to be enforced is coming from another country within **16–07** the European Union then the procedure to enforce the judgment in England and Wales as an incoming judgment comes under the recently introduced European Enforcement Order Regime or "EEO" as it will be termed throughout the rest of this chapter.

Countries in the European Union which come within this section of the Rules are set out in the Appendix under the "Look Up Table". Once again practitioners are encouraged to look at the country where they wish to enforce rather than the necessary legislation.

Under CPR 34.31 a person seeking to enforce an EEO in England and Wales must lodge at the court in which enforcement proceedings are to be brought, the documents required by art.20 of the EEO regulation. The documents in art.20 include:

- a sealed order of the judgment;
- the sealed EEO certificate; and
- a translation of the EEO certificate into the language of the country of enforcement which must be then certified by a "person qualified to do so in one of the member states".

In addition where a person applies to enforce an EEO expressed in **16–08** a foreign currency in either the High Court or the county court then the application must contain a certificate of the sterling equivalent of the judgment sum at the close of business on the date nearest to the date preceding the date of issue of the application for the EEO.

The evidential requirements of an application for an EEO are set out in CPR 74.4 at paras 1(b) and 2(e) and include a translation of the judgment into English certified by a Notary Public or other qualified person or accompanied by written evidence confirming the translation is accurate along with an up-to-date interest calculation.

European Enforcement Orders also have their own Practice Direction in CPR PD 74(B) supplementing the rules in Section V of CPR P 74. Under para.1 of the Practice Direction it is confirmed that the rules relating to the certification and Enforcement of EEOs are governed by the Council Regulation (EC) No.805/2004. The EEO regulation is annexed to the Practice Direction and using an online reference for the Rules can be accessed through a hyperlink.

Provision is made in the Practice Direction that if the claim does not meet the requirements of the EEO Regulation for any reason or if a judgment creditor does not wish to enforce the judgment using the EEO regulation it can be enforced using another method of enforcement.

16–09 Paragraph 5 of the Practice Direction confirms that when the EEO is lodged at a court in England and Wales where enforcement proceedings are to be commenced then the enforcement proceedings will be assigned a case number. An official copy from the court of the member state of origin will satisfy the requirement of art.20 above, for a "sealed copy of the judgment". Rules on monetary limits for enforcement also need to be borne in mind when bringing an EEO into the courts of England and Wales for enforcement. These are:

- Section I of the Charging Orders Act 1979 provides that only the High Court has jurisdiction to make a charging order where the amount of the original judgment exceeds the county court limit, currently set at £30,000.
- Article 8 of the High Court and County Courts Jurisdiction Order 1991 ("HCCCJO 1991") provides that judgment in excess of £5,000 must only be enforced by an execution against goods in the High Court.
- The HCCCJO 1991 also stipulates a judgment in excess £600 may be enforced in the High Court and judgment for less than £600 must only be enforced in the county court.

The judgment debtor can seek an application for enforcement to be prevented under CPR Pt 23 to the court in which the EEO is being sought to be enforced.

At the time of preparing this book there is very little information or statistical analysis about the use of EEOs and how successful or otherwise they are. There is also a little or no information about how often judgment debtors apply to try and either stay the enforcement of an EEO or in some way impede its process through the courts in this jurisdiction. No doubt in time, more statistical analysis will emerge on the use of EEOs and their effectiveness.

Scenario 3—is the judgment to be enforced an incoming judgment into England and Wales from another country with which there is a reciprocal treaty?

As mentioned earlier the English Common Law was exported all over the world and forms the basis of many of the legal systems in Commonwealth countries. For most of these countries there is a reciprocal treaty system and reference is again made to the Look Up Table in the Appendix to this book. **16–10**

Evidence in support of an application for an incoming judgment to be recognised by the courts of England and Wales has to be filed in accordance with the requirements of the 1920, 1933 and 1982 Acts. CPR 74.4 sets out the evidential requirements for such applications.

The process of registration is made through the High court and may be made without notice being given to the judgment debtor. The application to register a judgment either under the 1920 or the 1933 Act will be made to the Master supported by a witness statement or affidavit. The application should be lodged in room E17 at the Royal Courts of Justice, Central Office.

The application will be checked in the Action Department by foreign process specialists before being submitted to a Master for him or her to consider the application. The Master may direct that, instead of dealing with the application without notice, it is served on any other party.

The witness statement in support of the application needs to expressly state whether it is made "In the matter of the Administration of Justice Act 1920, Part II" or "In the matter of the Foreign Judgments (Reciprocal Enforcement) Act 1933". **16–11**

In either case the title of the witness statement or affidavit should also identify the judgment by reference to the court in which it was obtained and its date. The rate of exchange of the foreign judgment also has to be dealt with. Following the decision in *Miliangos v George Frank (Textiles) Ltd* [1976] A.C. 433 the witness statement or affidavit in support of the application for registration should not convert the amount of the foreign judgment debtor into UK currency at the prevailing exchange date at the date of judgment. Instead the foreign judgment must be registered in the foreign currency in which it is expressed or the sterling equivalent at the time of payment. There is no power entitling the claimant to convert the currency of the foreign judgment to the rate of exchange prevailing at any earlier or other date except the date of payment. This requirement applies to judgments under both the 1920 and 1933 Acts.

When it comes to actually enforcing the registered incoming foreign judgment then it will be necessary to convert it into the **16–12** foreign currency at the date of enforcement in accordance with the method employed and set out in the Queen's Bench Guide at para.11.2.4. This stipulates that a party who wishes to enforce a judgment or order expressed in a foreign currency by the issue of a Writ of FiFa must endorse the praecipe with the following certificate:

> "I/We certify that the current rate in London for the purchase of [*state the unit of foreign currency in which the judgment is expressed*] at the close of business on [*state the nearest preceding date of the date of issue of the Writ of Fiera Facias*] was [*amount*] to the nearest £ and at this rate the sum of [*state the amount of judgment debt in foreign currency*] amounts to £ [*amount*]"

The schedule to the Writ of FiFa should also be amended to show the amount of the judgment or order in the foreign currency and include the new paragraph which includes the amount of the sterling equivalent taken from the certificate appearing on the praecipe with the remaining paragraphs of the Writ of FiFa being renumbered as necessary.

16–13 Applications under the 1920 and 1933 Acts do provide for the enforcement of any order for costs given or made in any country to which the Acts apply.

If a judgment is found to have a technical defect, for example, the omission of certain words prescribed by the foreign law then this will not render the judgment a nullity that will make it voidable, and so long as it stands it will be capable of enforcement by execution and therefore capable of being registered in this country (see *SA Consortium General Textiles v Sun & Sand Agencies Ltd* [1978] 2 All E.R. 339 CA).

Under CPR 74.5 there is provision for an application for security of costs being made in accordance with the specific rule on this subject being CPR Pt 25 except in relation to a French judgment which is outside of this particular rule.

16–14 Under this scenario it is also possible for an application to be made to set aside the registration as provided under CPR 74.7. There is also the right to appeal the registration under CPR 74.8.

Once registered the foreign judgment may become the basis of a bankruptcy petition (see *Re A Judgment Debtor* (No.2176 of 1938) [1939] 1 All E.R. 1).

Enforcement can begin once the registration order is complete (see CPR 74.9) although there is a period allowed under the Rules to allow for any appeal which is provided under CPR 74.9(1) and the judgment creditor must file the necessary evidence of service on the judgment debtor of the registration order.

Scenario 4—is the judgment to be enforced an incoming judgment in England and Wales from another country with which England and Wales has no reciprocal treaty?

There are certain countries in the world where there is no reciprocal treaty to enable enforcement to move from England and Wales to that country or indeed to come from another country into England and Wales. Many of our trading partners including USA, Japan and Russia have no such reciprocal treaty in place. 16–15

A Claimant from a foreign jurisdiction who does not have the benefit of a reciprocal treaty to rely on will need to issue a claim under CPR Pt 7 using the judgment of the foreign court as the basis for the claim. It will be entirely within the discretion of the court within England and Wales as to whether the judgment of the foreign court will be recognised. Under CPR Pt 24 an application may be made almost immediately for summary judgment on the basis the defendant has no real prospect of successfully defending the claim because judgment has already been entered in the foreign country. The application for summary judgment can be made at any time after the defendant has stated an intention to defend the claim. In effect Pt 74 allows the usual process of setting out the nature of the claim in a Statement of Case to be expedited and the court is asked to make a final judgment on the basis of evidence which relies on the foreign judgment as the justification for judgment being entered in favour of the claimant.

If judgment is given then the practicalities of enforcement involve the location of the judgment debtor's assets and ensuring the correct procedure is chosen in the foreign court to be able to enforce the judgment.

Scenario 5—is the judgment to enforce an outgoing judgment within England and Wales to another part of the United Kingdom?

This is going to be the most likely form of foreign judgment enforcement that Debt Recovery Practitioners will experience and it is certainly something that they will need to add to their repertoire as their practice grows. Judgments moving from England and Wales to either Scotland or Northern Ireland are becoming more frequent. 16–16

The process is relatively simple. The judgment creditor in England and Wales applies to the court where judgment was entered for a certified copy of the judgment. This certificate forms the basis of seeking registration outside of England and Wales.

CPR 74.17 provides the mechanism for this application in both the High Court and county courts in relation to money provision judgments.

An application for the certificate of judgment is made under para.2 of Sch.6 of the 1982 Act to enable the money provision judgment of the High Court or county court to be enforced in either Scotland or Northern Ireland. The judgment creditor may apply for a certificate on Form 111 which is filed at the court where judgment was entered along with written evidence setting out:

- the name and address of the judgment creditor and if known the name and address of the judgment debtor;
- the sums payable and unsatisfied under the money provisions of the judgment;
- where interest is recoverable on the judgment, either the amount of interest which is accrued after the date of the application or the rate of interest from the date interest is recoverable to the date on which it ceases to accrue;
- confirmation that the judgment is not stayed;
- the date on which time for appealing a judgment has expired or will expire;
- whether an appeal notice has in fact been filed;
- the status of any application for permission to appeal; and
- whether an appeal is actually pending.

16–17 A form of witness statement in support of the application can be found in any of the leading civil procedure texts.

If the court issues the certificate of judgment then the Debt Recovery Practitioner must then arrange to register the judgment in the foreign country. As stated above, enforcement in Scotland and Northern Ireland is becoming more frequent. Set out below is the process to be followed in order to register and then enforce a judgment in these two countries.

Scotland

16–18 Before any enforcement proceedings can begin the original certificate of judgment (Form 111) must be registered in the Books of Council and Sessions at Erskine House, Queen Street, Edinburgh, EH2 4NF, contact telephone number 0131 659 6111. The fee for registering the judgment, at the time of writing this book, is £10, payable to the "Registers of Scotland".

The Debt Recovery Practitioner must consider which of the enforcement options available in Scotland is the most appropriate, given the circumstances of the judgment debtor. Again, the Enforcement Matrix referred to throughout this book can be just as easily applied to the enforcement of a judgment abroad as within England & Wales. To enforce in Scotland contact should be made with a Scottish Sheriffs Officer in whom a practitioner feels confident. Details of Sheriffs Officers can be found at *www.scottishlaw.org.uk/lawfirms/shoff.htm.* Alternatively contact a Scottish solicitor using The Law Society of Scotland website at *http://www.lawscot.org.uk.*

Northern Ireland

The original certificate of judgment (Form 111) must be photocopied and certified on the reverse that it is a true copy. Both must be forwarded to the Front of House Office, Royal Courts of Justice, Chichester Street, Belfast, BT1 3JF, (contact telephone number 028 9072 4619) to be registered. This service is free of charge. **16–19**

Once this process is completed, a request is made to the Enforcement of Judgments Office, at 6th Floor, Bedford House, 16–22 Bedford Street, Belfast, BT2 7FD to enforce the judgment. The initial fee when sending an instruction is, at the time of writing this book, £20, payable to the "Enforcement of Judgments Office".

The Enforcement Office serves a Notice of Intention to enforce the judgment on the judgment debtor, by post, giving the judgment debtor 10 days to pay the judgment debt.

In the event that the judgment debtor does not pay the judgment debt and enforcement action becomes necessary, the Debt Recovery Practitioner can obtain full details of the enforcement methods available, and the fees payable, directly from the Enforcement of Judgments Office on telephone number 028 9024 5081 or by using the Northern Ireland Enforcement of Judgment Office website at: *http://www.courtsni.gov.uk/en-GB/services/enforcement+of+judgments+office.*

Scenario 6—is the judgment to be enforced on an outgoing judgment in England and Wales to another country within the EU?

The momentum to streamline cross border enforcement within the European Union has recently culminated in the creation of the EEO and is available for any judgment dated after January 20th, 2005. **16–20**

The EEO allows a judgment creditor who has an uncontested

judgment from an English or Welsh court to obtain a certificate from the court where the judgment was entered and effectively transport that judgment to another EU country where the judgment debtor has assets. It also allows for an uncontested judgment for an EU country to be enforced in the High Court or county court in England and Wales as an incoming judgment.

The application is made for an outgoing judgment to be transferred on Form N219 or Form 219A. Her Majesty's Courts Service also provides an advice sheet in the form of EX375.

The application is made on the form and must comply with art.6 of the European Council Regulation 805/2004. The form will contain the names and address of the parties, the amount of a claim, interest sought, the rate of interest, the period for which interest is claimed and the basis of reason for the claim.

16–21 The application will be made to a Master/district judge in either the Chancery or Queen's Bench Division of the High Court where the judgment was entered in the High Court or one of the High Court's District Registries. In the case of a county court judgment the application will be made to the district judge.

When an application is granted the court will send the EEO certificate and a sealed copy of the judgment to the person making the application. If the court refuses the application it will have to give reasons and may give further directions.

Article 17 of the Regulation requires that information must also be supplied to the judgment debtor advising how the claim can be contested.

Once the application is prepared it needs to be served in accordance with the requirements set out in arts 13, 14 and 15 of the Regulation. Service can be by personal or postal service.

The EEO is only available where the claim is "uncontested". Article 3 of the regulation defines what constitutes an "uncontested claim" which basically "equates" to the English or Welsh form of default judgment.

16–22 ***If a claim appears to be contested then the EEO procedure will not be available.*** However, if a claim is settled by consent then the EEO procedure will be available.

The application itself is a very much "on paper" application. Once the EEO is made it needs to be sent to the member state for enforcement. The paperwork includes the need for a sealed copy of the judgment, the sealed EEO certificate and any necessary translation. The biggest hurdle in relation to this form of enforcement is actually finding the enforcement professionals within the country concerned who will carry out the work. A very useful website is: *http://europa.eu.int/comm/justice-home/ejn/index-en.htm* Where information about enforcement procedures and enforcement officers is given for all EU countries. It is one thing to have navigated the court system in England and Wales to get an EEO but it is quite another to actually then be able to enforce it in the country where the judgment debtor has assets.

It is important to remember the cost of enforcement outside of England and Wales is often not on a fixed fee basis as one would expect in the county court bailiff system, for example, and enforcement professionals are more expensive with often irrecoverable cost being payable by the judgment creditor. 16–23

Practitioners should seriously consider what other options they have to be able to enforce the judgment where the judgment debtor is abroad including telephone collections either pre-action or post judgment. If necessary this can be outsourced to a specialist service provider who will often work on a no-win no-fee basis.

Scenario 7—is the judgment to be enforced an outgoing judgment from England and Wales to another country with which England and Wales has a reciprocal treaty?

Under s.II of CPR Pt 74 the enforcement of English and Welsh judgments in foreign countries where there is a reciprocal enforcement treaty is started by the application for a certified copy of the judgment. This certified copy is then sent to the country where there is a reciprocal treaty for enforcement to begin. The same issues in terms of understanding how enforcement actually works in a foreign country is important. Execution against goods is often available as a method of enforcement, as are "garnishee procedures", and attaching from salary. Practitioners may be surprised as to how similar the procedures can be although they still need to be understood in terms of timescale and cost. 16–24

Which acts apply to which countries?

The "Look Up Table" in the Appendix is the easiest way to identify which legislation applies. It should be remembered that this list is subject to change and therefore reference should always be made to the most up to date version of the White Book Service and the accompanying commentary. 16–25

How is the application started?

The application for a certified copy of the English or Welsh judgment is made without notice supported by written evidence which must include: 16–26

- copies of the claim form in the proceedings in which the judgment was given;
- evidence of service of the claim form on the defendant;
- the statements of case made in the claim; and
- where relevant, a document showing whether the applicant was an assisted person or an LSC funded client.

The written evidence must also deal with:

16–27
- the grounds on which the judgment was obtained;
- whether the defendant has objected to the jurisdiction and the grounds of his objection;
- confirmation that the judgment has been has been served in accordance with CPR P 6 and CPR 40.4 (regarding the service of order where it has been drawn by a party);
- confirmation that the judgment is not subject to a stay of execution;
- the date on which time for appealing the judgment expired or will expire; and
- or whether an appeal notice has been filed and the status of any application for permission to appeal, and whether an appeal is pending.

NOTE: The statement about "the time for appealing has expired" does not of course apply to a judgment entered in default of any acknowledgment of service or defence under CPR Pt 12. Where judgment has been entered in default the application must show that no application has been made to set aside the judgment. The form of certificate issued by the court will then state that the defendant may apply to set the judgment aside although he has not yet done so (Practice Direction, July 17, 1962 seems to be the authority for this practice followed by the Judgment and Orders Section of the Central Office of the Royal Courts of Justice). For default judgments intended to be enforced in European Member States the approach should be to follow the procedure set out in Scenario 6 above and to apply for an EEO.

- whether the judgment provides for the payment of a sum of money, and if so, the outstanding and unsatisfied amount;
- the interest position—stating whether interest is recoverable on the judgment, and if so, either the amount of interest which has accrued up to the date of the application, or the rate of

interest, the date from which it is recoverable, and the date on which it ceases to accrue.

Are there any pitfalls in using scenario 7?

There are a couple of pitfalls that the judgment creditor needs to be aware of in seeking to enforce a judgment under s.II of CPR Pt 74. Firstly, under s.10 of the 1933 Act a certificate of judgment cannot be issued where the sum payable is "… in respect of taxes or other charges of a like nature or in respect of a fine or other penalty". Secondly, there is some debate as to whether a judgment obtained in a county court and transferred to the High Court for enforcement can be enforced through a court abroad, as it has been queried as to whether such a judgment meets the criteria of the 1920 and/or 1933 Acts that it should be a judgment "given" or "obtained" in a "superior court". The question is "will the foreign court recognise the county court judgment as a judgment given or obtained in a superior court?" As the 1920 and 1933 Acts are based on reciprocity it cannot be assumed that countries with which these reciprocal arrangements exist will enforce judgments other than those of the "High Court" or "Superior Court" as defined in the Acts. If reciprocity cannot be shown then the solution is to base a claim based on the solution for Scenario 8 (and also see notes at the beginning of this chapter). 16–28

What is the procedure for applying for a certificate where judgment has been entered at a district registry?

Applications for certified copies of judgments entered in District Registries should be sent to the District Registry where the judgment was obtained and the district judge can then exercise his/her powers as a Master under this Rule (and see CPR 2.4 relating to the interchangeability of powers of district judges and Masters). 16–29

This brings the procedure under the 1933 Act into line with the procedure under the Brussels Convention and Judgments Regulation regime.

Scenario 8—is the judgment to be enforced on an outgoing judgment from England and Wales to another country where there is no reciprocal treaty in place?

As can be seen from Scenario 4 there are major trading partners with whom England and Wales does not enjoy the benefit of reciprocal 16–30 treaty including the US, China and Russia. So how does a judgment creditor who obtains a judgment in this country enforces against the assets of a judgment debtor living in say America?

The options are to start proceedings in the English or Welsh courts and obtain summary judgment and then issue proceedings in the foreign jurisdiction using the English or Welsh judgment as a basis for the claim. Alternatively, it would be possible but risky to issue proceedings in the foreign jurisdiction and seek judgment based on that jurisdiction rules of the foreign court. This might be in the face of it easier however there is always a risk on costs, and twists and turns in the procedures which may result in what looked like on the face of it a straightforward claim turning out to be anything but.

In this scenario again a creditor is well advised to look at what alternative collections strategy he/she/it might employ. Collection companies do work across the world using the telephone and indeed personal visit to seek payment from judgment debtors on no-win no-fee basis. In many ways such an approach is going to be more satisfactory particularly if payment is achieved rather than going to the legal system in the country concerned and trying to navigate this as with all of the different nuances that that entails.

Concluding comments

16–31 The enforcement of judgments with a foreign element is a specialised area and practitioners need to be aware that often court staff will not be familiar with this area of practice and procedure. Close attention should be paid to the rules and where necessary reference should be made to the White Book Service which is the leading text on this area of procedure.

Reference should also be made to one of the leading precedent books such as Atkin's Court Forms to ensure that the application, the evidence in support by way of witness statement or affidavit and any order which is to be drawn are all technically correct to ensure that there are no delays in the transfer of the matter nor out of the jurisdiction.

Practitioners should be encouraged to have confidence not to worry so much about the procedure but to focus on the assets of the debtor, what is it that the creditor is trying to enforce against?

Universally it will be the debtor's goods, the debtor's equity, the debtor's salary, or the debtor's bank account. The practitioner should try and take a simple approach focusing on assets and not getting too bogged down in the procedural nuances which if working outside of the jurisdiction a lead agent should look after who is familiar with the area of law in that jurisdiction.

Finally, all the points made at the outset of this book in relation to keeping focus on knowing the debtor, knowing the contract and knowing the remedy are extremely important when working outside the jurisdiction because there is no point chasing a debtor who has either no assets or who cannot be pinpointed and who could therefore escape liability simply on a technicality. Preparation, investigation and attention to detail will enable practitioners to navigate this area of the rules using all the basic skills set out in the previous chapters of this book.

Chapter 17

Insolvency Procedures—Their Place In Debt Collection

Introductory Comments

Insolvency is not a debt recovery process as such, and indeed is frowned upon by the courts if used in this way. It is, however, worth discussing the question of insolvency as a method of recovering a debt as part of this book as so many Debt Recovery Practitioners will use the insolvency measures in the day to day work. **17–01**

The official use of an insolvency procedure is as a last resort to recover a debt from a debtor where there are no other means of recovery possible. However, strategic use of insolvency procedures can have the result of recovering payment from a debtor, whether a judgment debtor or pre-legal, where other attempts have failed.

For the purpose of discussing insolvency within this chapter, we will look at:

- Corporate insolvency by way of winding up proceedings.
- Individual insolvency by way of bankruptcy.
- Insolvency against partnerships.

Insolvency is also a much larger topic than this book is designed to cover. There are specialist Practitioner books available on the topic of insolvency and these should be consulted for more detailed discussion of this area. Reference should also be made to the resources available on the Insolvency Service website at *http://www.insolvency.gov.uk*.

Whether considering corporate or individual insolvency the creditor needs to ensure the following issues have firstly been dealt with: **17–02**

- re-check the identity and status of the debtor;

- assess whether the use of insolvency proceedings is available and will result in payment;
- assess whether the debtor has any other creditors who will benefit from any insolvency action; and
- asssess the cost of the entire process.

Corporate Insolvency

17–03 Insolvency against companies can either be pre or post judgment.

Whilst winding up proceedings may be viewed as a method of enforcement of a court judgment, it is possible to pursue insolvency immediately for a debt without the need for a court judgment and indeed some Practitioners find this to be a very effective form of debt management.

Either way the process is almost identical, the main issue is the question of time taken to achieve the winding up.

Enforcing a judgment or serving a statutory demand—is there an option?

17–04 Rather than issuing court proceedings and then pursuing insolvency as a method of "enforcement" of the judgment, a creditor may decide to immediately proceed to insolvency.

In this instance the creditor has the option of either serving a statutory demand upon the debtor company, or simply proceeding directly to the filing of the winding up petition. For the purpose of this chapter, and in order to ensure that the full process can be covered, we will assume that the creditor is pursuing the route to insolvency via a statutory demand.

Practitioners can regularly use the service of a statutory demand as a means to recover a debt rather than issuing court proceedings. In effect the issue and service of a statutory demand is a parallel process to the issue of a claim. It can be particularly useful where the debtor business cannot afford to be involved in insolvency proceedings, for example, a business which is perhaps about to float on the stock exchange. Quite often the ramifications of failing to pay a debt upon service of a statutory demand are enough to ensure that the debtor does pay and that full insolvency proceedings do not become necessary.

The statutory demand must be completed with precision and there must be adherence to the Insolvency Rules. The form and content of the statutory demand can be found in rr.4.5 and 4.6 of the Insolvency Rules 1986. Failure to ensure the accurate completion of the form will result in any subsequent petitions potentially being invalid and challengable.

When pursuing this procedure the following points should be noted: 17–05

- the debt should be for a minimum of £750;
- the demand should be in the prescribed form as stated above;
- it must be served by the creditor on the debtor company at the company's registered office address—usually service is effected by utilising the services of a Process Server to personally deliver the statutory demand to the registered office address; and
- it must be dated and authorised by the creditor or person authorised by the creditor, most commonly their solicitor or legal representative. Whoever signs the demand will have state the capacity in which they are signing and their relationship to the creditor.

Reference should also be made to Atkin's Court Forms Vol. 7 in relation to the preparation and drafting of a Statutory Demand.

What are the grounds for the pesentation of a winding up petition?

Moving on of a Petitioner who wishes to move to wind up a debtor company, the debtor company again has to be in a position where it is unable to pay its debts. A company is deemed to fall into this category pursuant to s.123 of the Insolvency Act 1986 as follows: 17–06

- if a creditor has served a statutory demand upon the company and the company has failed to pay the debt (s.123(1)(a) IA 1986);
- within England and Wales, execution or other process on a judgment has been returned unsatisfied (s.123(1)(b) IA 1986); and
- it is proved to the courts' satisfaction that the company is unable to pay its debts as they fall due (s.123(1)(e) IA 1986).

In which court should the winding up petition be presented?

17–07 The High Court has the jurisdiction to hear any winding up petition. In London this business will be carried out by the Companies Court, Chancery Division. Outside London there are eight District Registries which have Chancery jurisdiction and are able to deal with winding-up proceedings. These are:

- Birmingham
- Bristol
- Cardiff
- Leeds
- Liverpool
- Manchester
- Newcastle Upon Tyne
- Preston

For companies whose:

- issued and paid up share capital does not exceed £120,000; and
- the registered office is in the county court district of the court designated as having winding up jurisdiction (see IA 1986, ss.117 and 118),

the county court has concurrent jurisdiction.

17–08 It should be noted that not every county court has jurisdiction, but those which have bankruptcy jurisdiction also have winding up jurisdiction. County courts in London do not have jurisdiction to deal with either bankruptcy or winding up petitions.

The Court of Appeal only has jurisdiction to hear appeals relating to winding up petitions and is not a court of first instance for these actions (*see Re Dunraven Adare Coal & Iron Co* (1875) 33 L.T. 371).

What is the procedure for obtaining a winding up petition?

17–09 As with all aspects of the insolvency procedure, the paperwork to apply for a winding up petition has to be extremely precise. Any errors or discrepancies can completely invalidate the process.

Rule 4.7 of the Insolvency Rules 1986 sets out the requirements for the presentation and filing of a winding up petition.

The format of the petition is set out in Form 4.2 of the Insolvency Rules 1986. The need for absolute precision extends to the recital of the debtor company's name. Failure to be accurate in this regard can be fatal to the process (*see Re Vidiofusion Ltd* [1974] 1 W.L.R. 1548).

The information which is required in the petition includes:

- the amount of the debt;
- the consideration for the debt;
- details of the debtor company's registered office;
- the date of incorporation of the debtor company;
- the authorised and issued share capital of the debtor company
- whether the EC Regulations on insolvency apply; and
- the principal objects of the debtor company

Again reference should be made to Vol. 7 of Atkin's Court Forms as to the form and content of a petition.

Should any checks be made before the winding up petition is presented?

A check should be made to ensure that there are no existing winding up petitions against the debtor company. If the petitioning creditor fails to do this and it transpires that there is another petition against the debtor company then the petitioning creditor may not be able to recover their petition costs—*Re Dramstar Ltd, The Times,* October 29, 1980. **17–10**

The court will carry out the check at the time that the petition is submitted. However, by this stage a certain amount of work will already have been conducted in the preparation of the petition and cost incurred. Practitioners would therefore be advised to conduct their own checks prior to the preparation of the petition by checking the London Gazette or using the telephone enquiry service at Companies Court on 0906 754 0043.

Do the limitation rules apply to the presentation of petitions in relation to judgment debts?

Recent case law has decided that the six year limitation period under s.24(1) Limitation Act 1980 does not apply regarding winding up **17–11** proceedings (*see Ridgeway Motors (Isleworth) Ltd v Altis Ltd* [2005] 2 All E.R. 304).

Once the petition is prepared how is it issued?

17–12 Pursuant to r.4.7 Insolvency Rules 1986 the following steps must be taken:

- three copies of the petition should be taken to the court for sealing and issue;
- a copy of the petition, together with a verifying affidavit or witness statement—in the High Court attendance should be made at the Companies Court;
- a hefty deposit in respect of the Official Receiver's fee is payable, together with a court fee. Details of the current fees can be found at *http://www.hmcourts-service.gov.uk/court-finder/forms/ex50.pdf*. The cheque should be made payable to HMCS. In the event that the petition is withdrawn, or if the winding up order is made and funds are subsequently recovered, the Official Receiver's fee will be repaid. If, however, the petition is dismissed there will be no repayment of fees; and
- when issuing a petition in the High Court, a fee of £5 is payable in respect of the search to ensure there are no existing petitions (this is payable even if you have conducted your own search beforehand).

The court will then list the matter for a hearing and seal the petition and the copies for service.

17–13 Practitioners should note that the court will expect the petition to proceed swiftly through the court and will not normally allow adjournments to happen whilst the petition hangs over the debtor company.

Is there any evidence which needs to be filed in support of the petition?

17–14 Yes. The petitioning creditor must file either an affidavit, in Form 4.3, or a witness statement verifying the information contained within the winding up petition, with a copy of the winding up petition exhibited to the affidavit or witness statement.

The deponent to the affidavit or witness statement can be either the petitioning creditor, the petitioning creditor's solicitor, or a person authorised to sign on behalf of the petitioning creditor.

How is the winding up petition served?

Pursuant to IR 1986 r.4.8 the petition must be served personally on the following: 17–15

- a director of the debtor company; or
- a duly authorised person of the debtor company; or
- by leaving a copy of the petition at the registered office of the debtor company.

It is advisable to utilise the services of a very reputable process server to effect service and for a witness statement of service (in Form 4.4) to be prepared, exhibiting a copy of the petition. This should then be filed at court. Failure to prove service can also be fatal to this procedure.

If service is made following an application for substituted service, then Form 4.5 should be used for the witness statement of service.

In addition to the above parties to be served with the petition, the following should also be served within two days of requesting a copy of the petition, pursuant to IR 1986 r.4.13: 17–16

- any director of the debtor company;
- contributory; and
- any creditor.

The party requesting the petition will however be responsible for the payment of an appropriate fee for the provision of a copy of the petition.

The petition has to be advertised—what are the requirements for this?

The petition must be advertised in the London Gazette, pursuant to IR 1986 r.4.11. 17–17

The timing of the advert is crucial and needs to be:

- at least seven days after service of the petition—with the purpose of allowing the debtor company the time to object; and
- at least seven days before the hearing.

Failings in the timing of the advertisement can result in the court dismissing the petition (*see Re Signland Lt* [1982] 2 All E.R. 609), or at best a criticism of the failure to comply with the correct procedure (*Re Shusella Ltd* [1983] B.C.L.C. 505).

The purpose of the advertisement of the petition is to provide notice to the world of the existence of the petition.

What if the petitioning creditor wants to withdraw the petition?

17–18 This may arise if the debt is paid before the final order is made. The mechanism for withdrawing the petition is provided for in r.4.5 IR 1986.

This allows for the petition to be withdrawn upon an ex parte application being made, if at least five days before the hearing the petitioning creditor can satisfy the court that the petition has not been advertised and that no notices have been received by him, and that the debtor company consents to the petition being withdrawn (of course this last requirement is hardly likely to be a problem).

How does the creditor show compliance?

17–19 At least five days before the hearing of the petition, the petitioning creditor must file a Certificate of Compliance pursuant to r.4.14(2) IR 1986.

The Certificate must show:

- the date of the presentation of the petition;
- the date fixed for the hearing of the petition;
- the date of service of the petition; and
- that the advertising rules have been complied with—a copy of the advert should be filed with the Certificate.

Should the petitioning creditor fail to file the Certificate it can lead to the petition being dismissed by the court.

What about other creditors of the debtor company?

17–20 Other creditors are required to give notice to the Petitioning Creditor indicating whether or not they support or oppose the petition.

The Petitioning Creditor is required to prepare a list (Form 4.10) for the court indicating which creditors have given notice and whether that notice is in support or opposition of the petition.

Pursuant to r.4.19 IR 1986 it is also possible for a creditor to be substituted for the Petitioning Creditor. This situation can arise where the Petitioning Creditor is paid the debt due to them but another creditor is still owed their money and wishes to pursue the insolvency action.

There is no need for re-advertisement of the petition in the event of substitution, pursuant to *Re Commercial and Industrial Insulations Ltd* (1986) 2 B.C.C. 98,901.

What are the possible outcomes at the hearing of the winding up petition?

The ultimate decision of whether or not to make a winding up order is at the discretion of the court (IA 1986, s.125(1)). **17–21**

At the hearing, the court may:

- dismiss the petition;
- adjourn the hearing conditionally or unconditionally;
- make a compulsory winding up order; and
- make any other order it sees fit.

The Petitioning Creditor must file with the court the list detailing the creditors who have filed notice indicating their intention to appear at the hearing of the petition, either to support or oppose the petition. If there are no creditors, then the Petitioning Creditor must still file Form 4.10 indicating "none".

What is the position on costs on the petition?

If the Winding Up Order is made then costs will usually be ordered to be paid out of the debtor company's assets. **17–22**

The costs will be a first charge on the assets of the company and are payable ahead of the claims of all other secured creditors. However, a creditor will have to wait for the return on this investment.

In the event that the petition is dismissed, then the Petitioning Creditor will be liable to meet costs. If, however, the court considers that the debtor company was in any way responsible for the petition being presented in the first place due to its behaviour, then the court may not award costs to be paid by the Petitioning Creditor after all.

If the petition is dismissed as a result of the debtor company paying the debt at the "eleventh hour" then it is quite common for the court to order that the debtor company pay the Petitioning Creditor's costs.

If a Winding Up Order is made following a debtor company wrongfully opposing the petition, then it is possible that the court may order that the directors or shareholders pay the costs (*Re A Company* (No.004055 of 1991), *Ex p. Doe Sport Ltd* [1991] 1 W.L.R. 1003).

What happens after the winding up order is made?

17–23 If a Winding Up Order is made then the date of the compulsory liquidation procedure will be the date when the petition was presented to the court.

When the Winding Up Order is granted it should:

- be officially notified in the London Gazette; and
- recorded at the Companies Registry.

It is the court's responsibility to notify the Official Receiver of its Order. The Official Receiver will then notify the company of his appointment and deal with the necessary requirements concerning the notification of the Winding Up Order pursuant to IA 1986 s.130(1).

Who appoints the official receiver?

17–24 Whilst it is possible for a private insolvency Practitioner to be appointed by the company's creditors, ordinarily the Official Receiver is appointed by the court.

Three sealed copies of the Winding Up Order will be sent by the court to the Official Receiver who will then serve a copy on the Registrar of Companies and on the company itself.

It is also the Official Receiver's responsibility to advertise the Winding Up Order in the London Gazette, as well as one other local newspaper (IA 1986, s.130 and IR 1986, rr.4.20 and 4.21).

What is the effect of a winding up order on the debtor company?

17–25 The main effects can be summarised into four points as follows:

- no actions or proceedings against the debtor company or its property can be commenced or continue except with the leave of the court—IA 1986, s.130(2);
- the winding up will be deemed to commence at the time of the presentation of the winding up petition—IA 1986, s.129;
- execution against goods is effectively stayed and the duties of the High Court Enforcement Officer are set out in the IA 1986, s.184; and
- unless the court orders otherwise, any disposition of the company's property between presentation of the petition and the order are void—IA 1986, s.127.

Partnership Insolvency

So what happens if the debtor is a partnership and not a limited company? Can insolvency action be pursued against the partnership? The answer is yes—and a lot of the procedure is very similar to that pursued against a limited company. 17–26

This area of insolvency is governed by the Insolvent Partnerships Order 1994 (SI 1994/2421) ("the IPO").

What is the definition of a partnership?

As we have seen in Chapters 1 and 3 a partnership is a relationship which exists between two or more persons carrying on a business together with a view to making a profit. 17–27

A partner in this relationship can be either an individual or a company (known as a corporate member) and they are individually liable (usually without limit) for the debts of the partnership.

As a creditor therefore it is possible to pursue one or more of the partners individually, as well as the partnership itself, for recovery of the debt.

What options are available to pursue insolvency against a partnership?

As with corporate insolvency, the point to remember is that insolvency is not intended to be a debt recovery process as such. The idea of pursuing insolvency as a last resort in the debt recovery process should still apply. 17–28

It is possible to be able to pursue the partnership, but not the individual partners individually, as they will be pursued under the bankruptcy procedure in their personal capacity (see below).

This can mean that the individual partners can continue to trade in other businesses thereby generating profits which may be used for the settlement of the debt.

If this is the case, the form of the petition closely follows that for company winding up.

Alternatively, the individual partners can be pursued. In this situation, the only ground upon which the partnership can be wound up is if the partnership is unable to pay its debts.

What is the definition of "unable to pay its debts"?

17–29 In respect of a partnership, the circumstances under which it will be considered to be unable to pay its debts are set out in s.222(1) IA 1986, as modified by the IPO 1994.

In respect of individual partners, they will be considered to be unable to pay their debts if the partnership owes a debt in excess of £750 and a statutory demand has been served on both the partnership and the individual partner and payment has not been forthcoming. The form of statutory demands are the same as those for corporate and individual insolvency and again reference should be made to Vol. 7 of Atkin's Court Forms on Insolvency.

How is a partnership wound up?

17–30 As explained above, the partnership and the individual partners can be held liable for a debt.

This means that a practitioner can wind up a partnership and proceed for bankruptcy against the individual partners in respect of the same debt.

An insolvent partnership can be dealt with under the provision of the IPO 1994 as follows:

The partnership can be wound up	This involves presenting a winding up petition which will need to be prepared/ served and presented against the insolvent partnership. The form of petition is in the same form as a petition to wind up an unregistered company and can be used with the necessary modifications (see Form 4.2 in Sch.4 IR 1986)

The partnership can be wound up and the individual partners can be made bankrupt	The ground for presenting a petition in these circumstances is that the partnership is unable to pay its debts. Evidence of that fact will be the failure to pay a debt in excess of £750 following service of a statutory demand served both on the partnership and the individual partners.
One or more of the individual partners can be made bankrupt without making all the partners bankrupt and without winding up the partnership and the individual partners can be made bankrupt	Individual partners can be made bankrupt and a Practitioner has the choice of whether to also wind up the partnership.

Which courts have jurisdiction for winding up partnerships?

As with a petition to wind up a company, a petition to wind up an insolvent partnership can be presented in either the High Court or County Court, providing that the court has insolvency jurisdiction. The same principles apply regarding which courts have insolvency jurisdiction as for corporate insolvency. 17–31

It is a requirement that the partnership must have carried on business in England and Wales within a period of three years ending with the day on which the petition is presented to the court.

What are the necessary grounds for an IPO petition?

The various grounds on which an insolvent partnership may be wound up are set out in s.221(7) IA 1986 as amended by, Sch.3(3) Pt I IPO 1994. 17–32

The main ground to consider for debt recovery purposes and the one which is going to be of most relevance, to debt recovery Practitioners is the one regarding the partnerships inability to pay its debts.

When will a partnership be considered unable to pay its debts?

This will be in the same way as an unregistered company as follows: 17–33

- a statutory demand has been served upon the partnership in the proper form and no payment has been forthcoming;

- any action or proceeding has been instituted against a member of the partnership for a debt or demand, or a sum has been claimed as due from either the partnership or the partner and written notice has been served on the partnership of the commencement of proceedings and payment has not been made (see s.222 IA 1986 as modified by Sch.3(5), Pt 1 IPO 1994);
- execution or other process issued following a judgment against the partnership has been returned unsatisfied;
- it is proven to the court's satisfaction that the partnership is unable to pay its debts as they fall due; and
- the court is satisfied that the value of the partnership liabilities outweighs the assets.

What happens at the hearing of the petition?

17–34 If the creditor is applying to wind up the partnership and make the partners bankrupt, the hearing of the winding up petition will be heard before the bankruptcy petitions.

Schedule 9 IPO 1994 requires that the creditor complete Form 9 to advise the court as to the progress of any other petitions.

The petition may only be withdrawn at the hearing if notice has been given to the court at least three days prior to the hearing of the creditor's intention to do so.

As with corporate and individual insolvency, the court has the power to substitute another creditor in respect of both the partnership and partners' insolvency.

The petition in respect of the individual partners will follow the same procedure as individual insolvency.

What happens after the partnership is wound up?

17–35 Once the winding up petition has been made against the partnership, its affairs are dealt with in the same way as a company which has been wound up (see above).

Individual Insolvency

17–36 Whilst once again it should be reiterated that insolvency is not intended to be used as a debt recovery process, there are of course going to be times when there are no other options available to the creditor other than insolvency, whether this is genuinely as a last resort, or as a method of achieving payment from the debtor by threatening to pursue the full insolvency process.

What conditions must be satisfied to be able to pursue bankruptcy?

The conditions are set out in s.265 of the IA 1986. The debtor must: **17–37**

- be domiciled in England and Wales;
- be personally present within the jurisdiction of England and Wales on the day the bankruptcy petition is presented to the court; or
- at any time within three years following the day on which the petition is presented to the court have been ordinarily resident, or have had a place of residence in England and Wales; or have carried on business in England and Wales.

What grounds need to be met for the creditor to present a bankruptcy petition?

The creditor must be owed a debt, or debts, by the debtor in accordance with IA 1986 s.267(1). Subject to this initial requirement the following conditions need to be present (IA 1986 s.267(2)): **17–38**

- the amount of the debt or the aggregate is equal to or exceeds the bankruptcy level (at present £750);
- the debt is for a liquidated sum payable either immediately or at some certain future time, and is unsecured;
- the debt is one which the debtor appears either to be unable to pay, or to have no reasonable prospect of being able to pay; and
- there is no outstanding application to set aside a statutory demand which has been served under IA 1986 s.268 in respect of the debt (this condition will be outside the scope of the circumstances where the petition is based on a return that execution was unsatisfied in whole or in part).

What is the definition of "unable to pay"?

This will be either: **17–39**

- a failure to comply with a "statutory demand" in the prescribed form; or
- the result of an execution for a judgment or order of the court in favour of the petitioning creditor which has been returned unsatisfied in whole or in part (IA 1986 s.268 (1)(a) and (b)).

Full details of the statutory demands which can be used can be obtained from the Insolvency Service website at *http://www.insolvency.gov.uk*.

17–40 There are three different versions of statutory demands depending upon the stage at which the debt is at:

- Form 6.1—Statutory Demand under s.268(1)(a) of the Insolvency Act 1986. Debt for Liquidated Sum Payable Immediately.
- Form 6.2—Statutory Demand under s.268(1)(a) of the Insolvency Act 1986. Debt for Liquidated Sum Payable Immediately Following a Judgment or Order of the Court.
- Form 6.3—Statutory Demand under s.268(2) of the Insolvency Act 1986. Debt Payable at Future Date.

Evidence of an unsatisfied execution is provided by the HCEO's return obtained under the provisions of RSC Order 46 r.9 but see *Re a Debtor* [1996] 2 All E.R. 211, in which the court indicated that where the sheriff had been unable to execute the Writ of Fifa, a return of *nulla bona,* meaning "no goods", would not be sufficient evidence of the debtor's inability to pay. In that case the sheriff had not levied execution and not been inside the debtor's house. The court found there was insufficient evidence to substantiate a finding of "inability to pay".

What is the procedure following service of the statutory demand?

17–41 As with service of a statutory demand upon a limited company, the statutory demand in respect of individual insolvency again sets out details of the debt due to the creditor.

The creditor must arrange for the statutory demand to be served upon the debtor and this is most usually arranged by employing the services of a process server. The process server will usually arrange to personally serve the debtor with the statutory demand and then exhibit a copy to a statement of service.

Once served with the statutory demand, the debtor has 18 days in which to apply to have the statutory demand set aside. Failure to make such an application and failure to pay the debt within 21 days of service of the demand upon him shall mean that the debtor is then at risk of the creditor presenting a bankruptcy petition.

Can the debtor seek to set aside the statutory demand?

In order to be successful with an application to set aside the statutory demand the debtor must be able to show that there is a genuine dispute regarding the non payment of the outstanding debt. In these circumstances the court will normally agree to set aside the statutory demand on the basis that the proper arena for the creditor to pursue recovery of the debt is through the court by way of a money claim, which the debtor can then properly defend. Debt Recovery Practitioners should not be surprised if a debtor makes this application. It is common and the Practitioner should anticipate it and have another strategy. 17–42

Which court has jurisdiction for bankruptcy petitions?

The High Court (IR 1986 r.6.9(1)) has jurisdiction if: 17–43

- the debtor has resided or carried on business within the London insolvency district for the greater part of the six months immediately preceding presentation of the petition, or for a longer period in those six months than in any other insolvency district;
- the debtor is not resident in England and Wales; and
- the petitioner is unable to trace the residence of the debtor or his place of business.

The London insolvency district is made up of the City of London together with the districts of the county courts for:

- Barnet
- Bow
- Brentford
- Central London
- Clerkenwell

- Edmonton
- Lambeth
- Shoreditch
- Wandsworth
- West London
- Willesden

17–44 The county court has jurisdiction in all other cases:

- if the debtor has not carried on business or resided within the London insolvency district as set out above, then the petition should be presented in the insolvency court for the insolvency district in which the debtor has resided or carried on business for the longest period of time during those six months;
- if the debtor has carried on business in one insolvency district and resided in another, the petition should be presented in the insolvency court for the district in which he has carried on business; and
- if the debtor has carried on business in more than one insolvency district then the petition must be presented to the court for the district in which he has had his principal place of business for the longest period within those six months

It should be noted that not all county courts have insolvency jurisdiction. It may therefore not necessarily be the debtor's local county court to which a Practitioner would submit a bankruptcy petition. If in doubt regarding whether or not a particular court has insolvency jurisdiction, a check can be made by looking at the Court Service website at *http://www.hmcourts-service.gov.uk/cms/index.htm.*

If proceedings are issued in the wrong court, it is possible to arrange for the proceedings to be transferred to the correct court. However, it should be noted that any costs associated with the transfer are not likely to be recoverable by the creditor.

What is the format of the bankruptcy petition?

17–45 The petition has to be in the prescribed form and the usual form will be Form 6.7 or Form 6.9 where execution is returned unsatisfied.

As with the documentation for corporate insolvency, accuracy and up-to-date information is paramount.

Shortcomings in paperwork will result in adjourned or dismissed petitions which inevitably cause problems in explanations to clients.

What are the required contents of the bankruptcy petition?

The petition must, so far as it is within the creditor's knowledge, state the following matters relating to the debtor (IR 1986 r.7): 17–46

- the debtor's name, place of residence and occupation (if any);
- the name or names in which the debtor carries on business, if other than the debtor's true name, and whether, in the case of any business of a specified nature, the debtor carries it on alone or with others;
- the nature of the debtor's business and its address;
- any name, other than the debtor's true name, in which the debtor has carried on business at, or after the time the debt was incurred, and whether the debtor has done so alone or with others; and
- any address or addresses at which the debtor has resided or carried on business at or after that date, and the nature of that business.

It must also state the following details relating to the debt itself (IR 1986 r.6.8): 17–47

- the amount of the debt, the consideration for it and the fact that it is owed to the petitioner;
- the date the debt was incurred or became due;
- details of any interest charge not previously notified to the debtor, and the grounds on which it is claimed to form part of the debt;
- and that the debt is for a liquidated sum payable immediately and that the debtor appears to be unable to pay it or that the debt is for a liquidated sum payable at some future certain time (the date must be specified) and that the debtor appears to have no reasonable prospect of being able to pay it;
- that the debt is unsecured—but this is subject to the exception set out in IA 1986 s.269; and

- whether the EC Regulation on Insolvency applies (see Canal Regulation (EC) No.1346/2000).

What is the procedure for presenting and filing the bankruptcy petition?

17–48 Again, as with the procedure for pursuing insolvency against a company, the procedure is very similar for individual insolvency. The petition must be verified by a witness statement (IR 1986 r.6.10) and delivered to the court.

Two extra copies will be required, one of which is for service on the debtor and the other will be exhibited to the witness statement of service of the petition. The court will fix the date and time for hearing the petition when it is filed.

In addition, the creditor must also file at the same time as the petition and witness statement the statement of service in respect of service of the statutory demand.

How is the petition verified?

17–49 The petition must be verified by a witness statement or an affidavit, completed by the creditor or their legal representative, verifying that the statements in it are true to the best of your knowledge, information and belief. The witness statement or affidavit must exhibit a sealed copy of the petition (IR 1986 r.6.12)

Where the deponent to the witness statement or affidavit verifying the petition is not the creditor, the capacity of the deponent must be stated, together with the deponent's authority in which the witness statement or affidavit is made and the deponent's means of knowledge of the matters deposed to.

Although reference is made to verification by witness statement or affidavit, in practice the usual method is by witness statement. The reason for this is that there is no fee involved in preparing a witness statement, whereas there is the oath fee for swearing an affidavit.

A witness statement is acceptable to the court hence the reason for its use. The format for a witness statement in support of a bankruptcy petition is the same as the format for any other witness statement.

What are the costs on issuing a bankruptcy petition?

17–50 A Practitioner will need to pay an Official Receiver's deposit as well as a court fee when issuing a petition.

At the present time the Official Receiver's deposit is £400 and the court fee is £190. The cheque should be made payable to HMCS.

A search fee of £5 is payable when issuing a petition in the High Court for the court to check whether there are any existing petitions.

Of course the Official Receiver deposit and the court fee can change. Up-to-date details will be published by the court and you should always check the Court Service website at *http://www.hmcourts-service.gov.uk/infoabout/fees/county.htm* and with the court where it is intended to issue the petition.

The deposit will be repaid if funds are available, or the petition is **17–51** withdrawn because the debt is paid, but it will not be repayable if the petition is struck out. Even if the petition is withdrawn, whilst the deposit will be repayable, the court fee will not.

It is very important to check the Insolvency Service website at *http://www.insolvency.gov.uk/eiir/* to see whether or not the debtor has already been declared bankrupt, or has entered into an Individual Voluntary Arrangement.

NOTE: Do not include any unnecessary "space" marks when typing in the debtor's details into the search facility as this could result in "false" results being returned.

What happens once the bankruptcy petition is filed?

The court will issue the petition and list the petition for hearing. **17–52**

Once the petition has been filed and issued by the court, the court automatically sends a notice to the Chief Land Registrar of the petition together with a request that it is registered in the register of pending actions at HM Land Registry (IR 1986 r.6.13).

How is service of the petition effected?

As with service of a winding up petition, in order to ensure compli- **17–53** ance with the rules, it is best for the creditor to instruct a process server to arrange for service of the petition.

They must serve a sealed copy to the debtor (IR 1986 r.6.14) and then prepare a witness statement or affidavit of service exhibiting a sealed copy of the petition.

The witness statement or affidavit of service must then be filed at court immediately after service has been effected.

Service of the petition must be by personal service, again utilising the services of a process server. If the debtor deliberately attempts to evade service then it is possible to make an application to the court under CPR 23, using Form N244 for an order for substituted service (see Chapter 6).

17–54 The creditor must specify in their application the method of substituted service required, i.e. advertisement or leaving at the debtor's property.

If the court is satisfied that the debtor is avoiding service then they will usually grant the order. Service will then need to be effected in the manner ordered and a witness statement or affidavit of service prepared confirming the details of service, including the method used.

If a debtor dies before service of the bankruptcy petition the court may order service on the debtor's personal representatives or such other persons as it thinks fit (IR 1986 r.6.16).

How might the debtor oppose the bankruptcy order?

17–55 Firstly, it should be noted that the court has discretion to make the bankruptcy order whether or not the application is opposed by the debtor (IA 1986 s.271).

If a debtor intends to oppose a bankruptcy petition, then IR 1986 r.6.21 provides that not later than seven days before the day fixed for the hearing of the petition the debtor must:

- file in court a notice specifying the grounds of objection to a bankruptcy order being made;
- send a copy of the notice to you or to his solicitor.

The form to be used by the debtor is Form 6.19.

What happens at the hearing of the bankruptcy petition?

17–56 At least 14 days must elapse between the presentation of the bankruptcy petition and the date of the hearing to ensure the Official Receiver's fees are paid.

If the creditor is presenting the petition as an "enforcement" method following a judgment or court order, the court may stay or dismiss the petition on the ground that an appeal is pending from the judgment or order, or that there has been a stay of execution on the judgment (IR 1986 r.6.25).

If the court makes an order adjourning the hearing of the bankruptcy petition the petitioning creditor must, subject to any order made by the court to the contrary, send the debtor a notice of the adjournment and stating the new time, date and venue for the hearing. In *Re Williams (a bankrupt)*, *The Times,* July 16, 1997, the court held that where a bankruptcy petition had been presented and the debtor had indicated that he could repay his debt by instalments, yet there was no reasonable prospect that repayment could be made within a reasonable time, it was not open to the court to grant repeated adjournments of the bankruptcy proceedings.

If an order is made dismissing the bankruptcy petition or the court allows the petition to be dismissed with leave, then an order must also be made allowing the registration of the petition to be vacated from the register of pending actions.

The court will send a sealed copy of any such order to the debtor.

Is there anything else needed before the hearing?

Yes. **17–57**

The creditor must prepare a list of creditors (if any) who have given notice under IR 1986 Rule 6.23 of their intention to either support or oppose the petition. This must be filed at court before the hearing.

What will happen at the hearing of the petition?

At least 14 days must have elapsed between the presentation of the **17–58** bankruptcy petition and the hearing, in order to ensure that the Official Receiver's fees are paid.

The court may:

- dismiss the petition;
- adjourn the hearing conditionally or unconditionally;
- make a bankruptcy order; or
- make any other order it thinks fit.

If the court makes a bankruptcy order, then, pursuant to IA 1986 s.278 the commencement date of the bankruptcy is the date on which the order is made, as opposed to the date of the petition (as with corporate insolvency).

Case Study

At pages 510–519 of the case study examples can be seen of the forms **17–59** which may be completed by Tom if he were to decide to pursue individual insolvency against Margot for the recovery of his debt.

Flow Charts

17–60 The process for pursuing insolvency against either against an individual or a corporation is outlined in the flow chart in the Appendix to this book.

Appendix A

Flow Charts

Description of Flow Charts	Chapter
Overview of Debt Recovery Process Through The Court	Chapter 1
Interest On A Claim	Chapter 5
Claimant Accepts Defendant's Part 36 Offer within Relevant Period	Chapter 7
Part 36—Offer Defendant Accepts Claimant's Part 36 Offer within Relevant Period	Chapter 7
Part 36 Offer—Claimant Equals or Beats Own Part 36 Offer at Trial	Chapter 7
Part 36 Offer—Claimant Fails to Beat Defendants Part 36 Offer at Trial	Chapter 7
Part 36 Offer—Claimant Fails to Establish Liability at Trial—Doesn't Beat Defendant's Part 36 Offer at Trial	Chapter 7
Part 36 Offer—Claimant Beats Defendant's Part 36 Offer but Doesn't Equal or Beat own Part 36 Offer	Chapter 7
Application To Apply For An Order To Obtain Information—CPR 71	Chapter 11
Application For A Third Party Debt Order—CPR 72	Chapter 12
Application For A Charging Order Against Land—CPR 73	Chapter 13
Process For Execution Again Goods By Way of Warrant of Execution (CCR Order 26) Or Writ of Fieri Facias (RSC Order 47)	Chapter 14
Application For An Attachment Of Earnings Order—CCR Order 27	Chapter 15
Process to Pursue Insolvency Against a Limited Company	Chapter 17
Process To Pursue Insolvency Against An Individual	Chapter 17

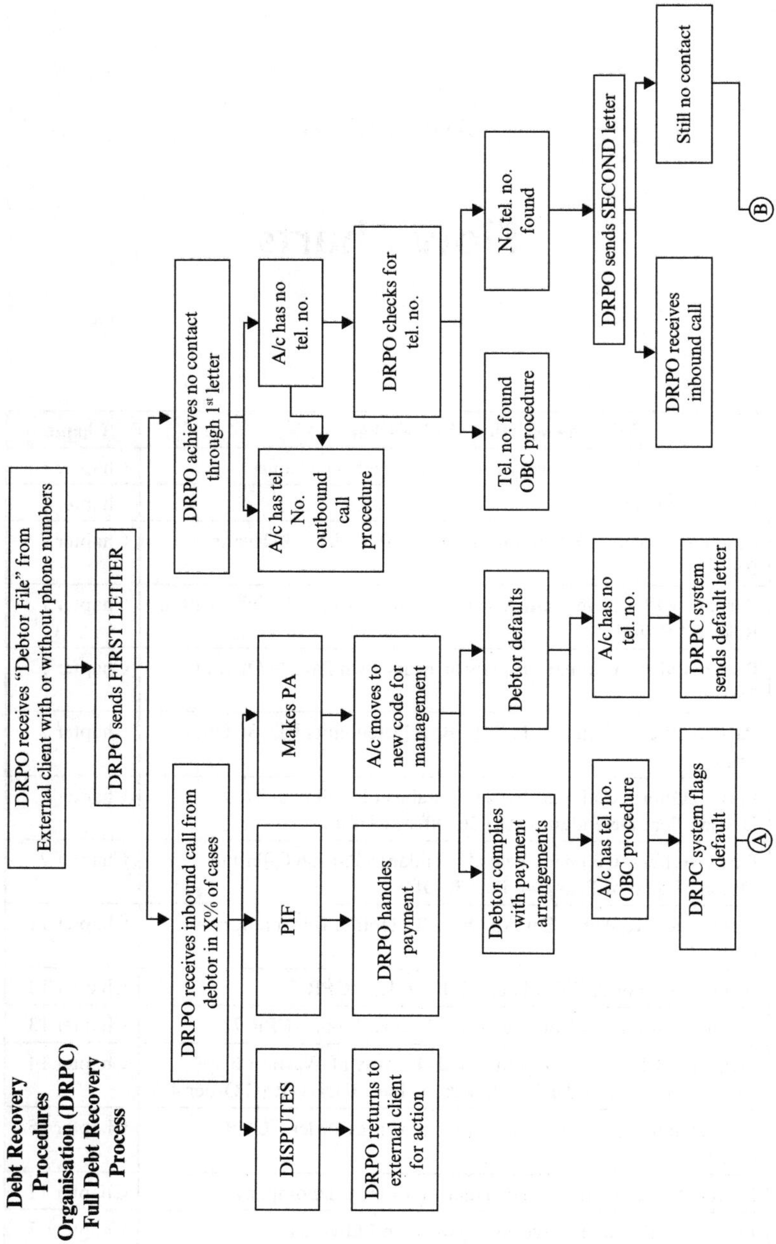
Debt Recovery Procedures Organisation (DRPC) Full Debt Recovery Process
DRPO receives "Debtor File" from External client with or without phone numbers
DRPO sends FIRST LETTER
DRPO receives inbound call from debtor in X% of cases
DRPO achieves no contact through 1st letter
DISPUTES
PIF
Makes PA
DRPO returns to external client for action
DRPO handles payment
A/c moves to new code for management
Debtor complies with payment arrangements
Debtor defaults
A/c has tel. no. OBC procedure
A/c has no tel. no.
DRPC system flags default
DRPC system sends default letter
A
A/c has tel. No. outbound call procedure
A/c has no tel. no.
DRPO checks for tel. no.
Tel. no. found OBC procedure
No tel. no. found
DRPO sends SECOND letter
DRPO receives inbound call
Still no contact
B

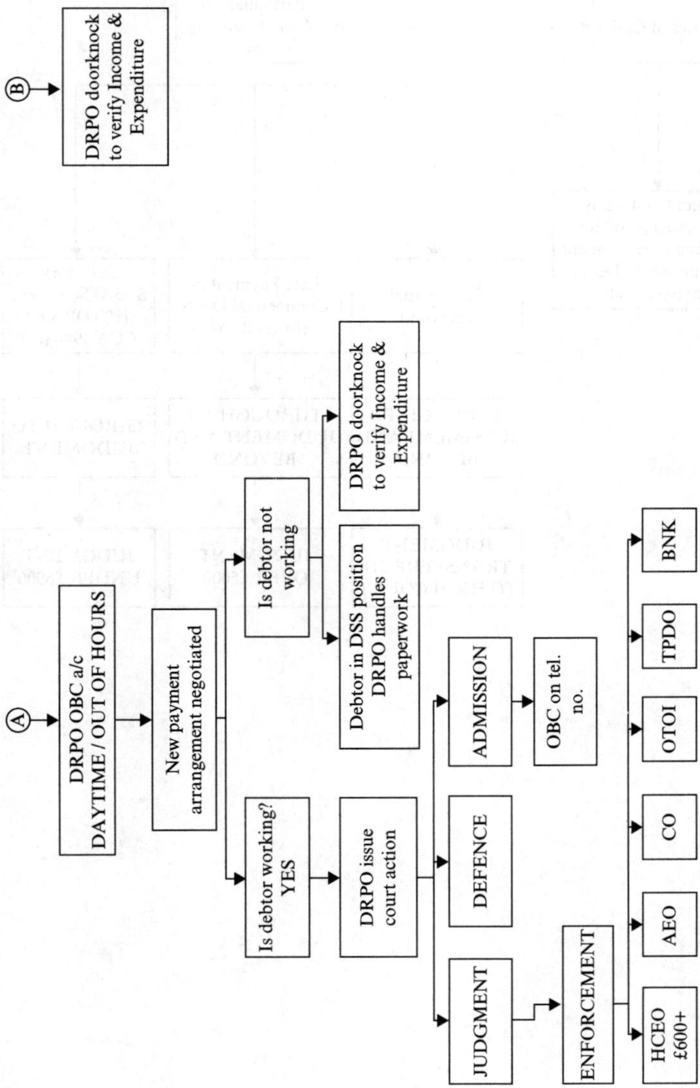
B
DRPO doorknock to verify Income & Expenditure
A
DRPO OBC a/c DAYTIME / OUT OF HOURS
New payment arrangement negotiated
Is debtor working? YES
Is debtor not working
DRPO issue court action
Debtor in DSS position DRPO handles paperwork
DRPO doorknock to verify Income & Expenditure
JUDGMENT
DEFENCE
ADMISSION
OBC on tel. no.
ENFORCEMENT
HCEO £600+
AEO
CO
OTOI
TPDO
BNK

Interest on A Claim

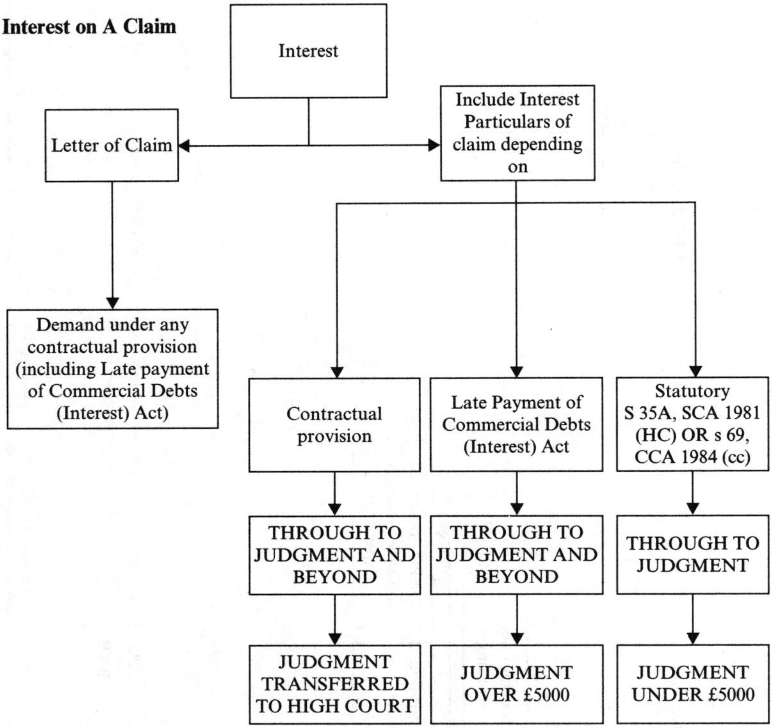

Part 36 Offer – Claimant Accepts Defendant's – Part 36 Offer Within Relevant Period

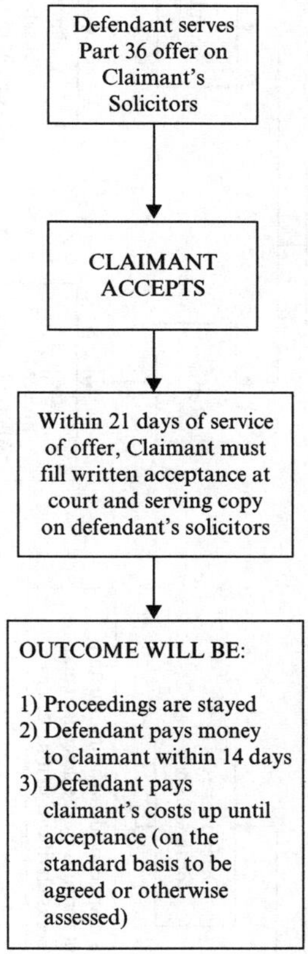

Defendant Responds With An Admission – Process To Be Followed

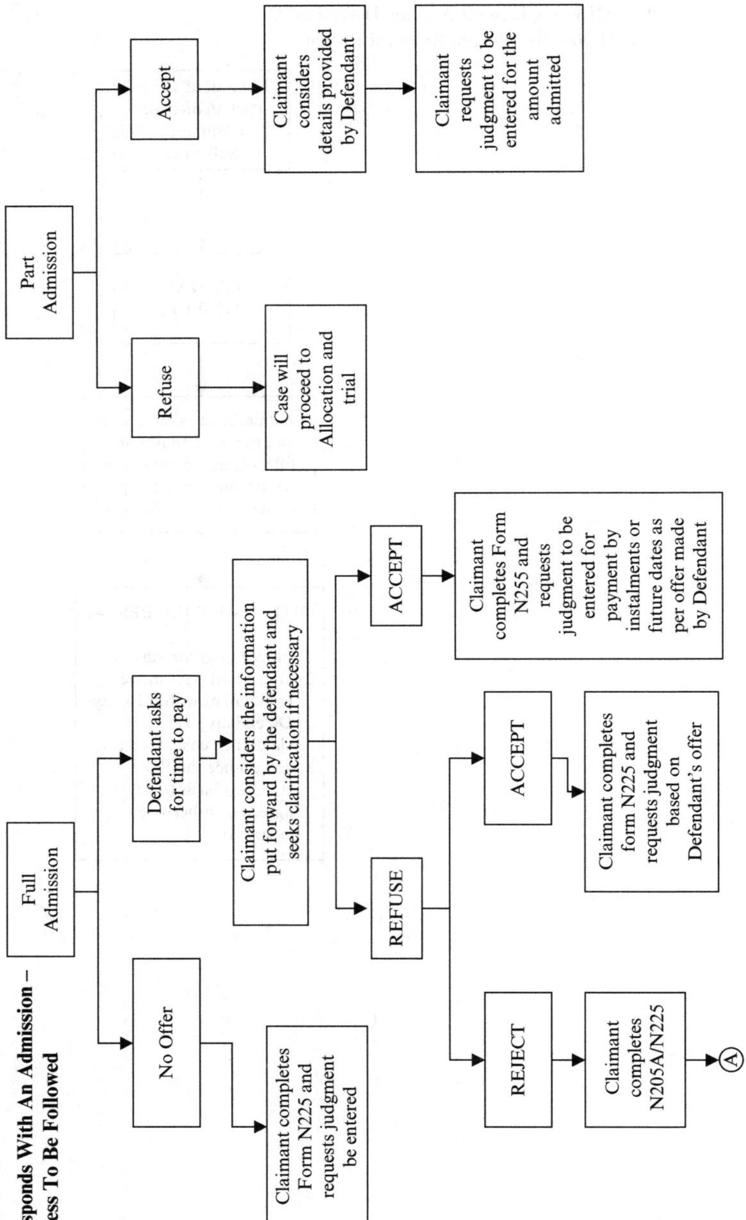

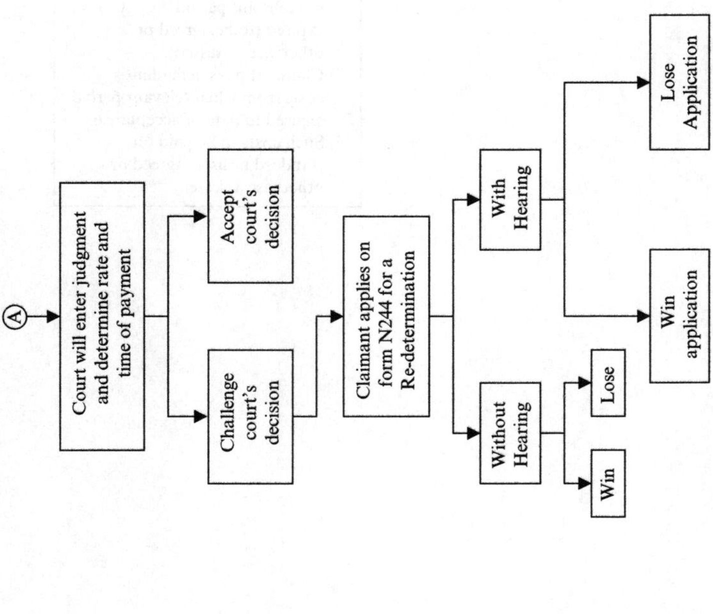
A
Court will enter judgment and determine rate and time of payment
Accept court's decision
Challenge court's decision
Claimant applies on form N244 for a Re-determination
With Hearing
Without Hearing
Lose Application
Win application
Lose
Win

Part 36 Offer – Claimant Accepts Defendant's Part 36 Offer after the Relevant Period has Expired

Defendant serves Part 36 offer on claimant's Solicitors.

↓

CLAIMANT'S ACCEPTS

↓

After 21 days of service of offer, claimant accepts by filing written acceptance at court and serving copy on defendant's solicitors.

↓

OUTCOME:

1) Proceedings will be stayed.
2) Defendant pays money to claimant within 14 days.
3) Defendant pays claimant's costs up until the relevant period expired (to be agreed or otherwise assessed).
4) Claimant pays defendant's costs from when relevant peroid expired to date of acceptance.
5) Such costs to be paid on standard basis as agreed or otherwise assessed.

Part 36 Offer – Claimant Equals or Beats Own Part 36 Offer at Trial

Claimant makes Part 36 offer

↓

Defendant does not accept

↓

Case proceeds to trail

↓

Claimant wins and is awarded the same as or more than the amount of his offer

↓

Claimant will receive:

A) The damages awarded by the court:

B) Interest at the court's discretion on the damages awarded provided claimed in the particulars of claim, normally from when the loss was sustained to and including the day before the last date when the Defendant could have accepted Claimants Part 36 Offer, ie the day before the relevant period expired (day 20)

C) Under r 36.14 (3) 'enhanced' interest on the damages awarded at a maximum rate of 10% pa over base rate from and including the last date when Defendant could have accepted Claimants Part 36 offer, ie the day the relevant period expired (day 21) until judgment:

D) Costs on the standard basis potentially from when first incurred by Claimant up to and including the day before the last date for acceptance of Claimants Part 36 offer, ie the day before the relevant period expired (day 20)

E) Under r 36.14 (3) costs on the indemnity basis from and including the last date for acceptance of Claimants Part 36 offer, ie the day the relevant period expired (day 21) up to judgment:

F) Under r 36.14 (3) interest on those indemnity basis costs at a maximum rate of 10% pa over base rate from when each item was incurred. Note the norm is 4% pa over base rate(Rowlands v Bryn Alyn Community (Holdings) Ltd {2003}).

Part 36 Offer – Claimant Fails to Beat Defendant's Part 36 Offer at Trial

Claimant wins but is awarded at trial the same as or less than Defendants Part 36 offer.

↓

OUTCOME:
Claimant will receive:

1) The amount awarded by the court:
2) Interest at the court's discretion on the amount claimed in the particluars of claim:
3) Costs on the standard basis potentially from when first incurred by Claimant up to and including the last date for acceptance of Defendants Part 36 offer, ie expiry of the relevant period (day 21)
   Claimant will pay Defendant

Under r 36.14(2) Defendants costs on the standard basis from and including the day after the last date for acceptance of Defendants part 36 offer, ie the day after the relevant period expired (day 22) up to judgment, plus interest on the costs incurred during this time.

Part 36 Offer – Claimant Fails to Establish Liability at Trial – Doesn't Beat Defendant's Part 36 Offer at Trial

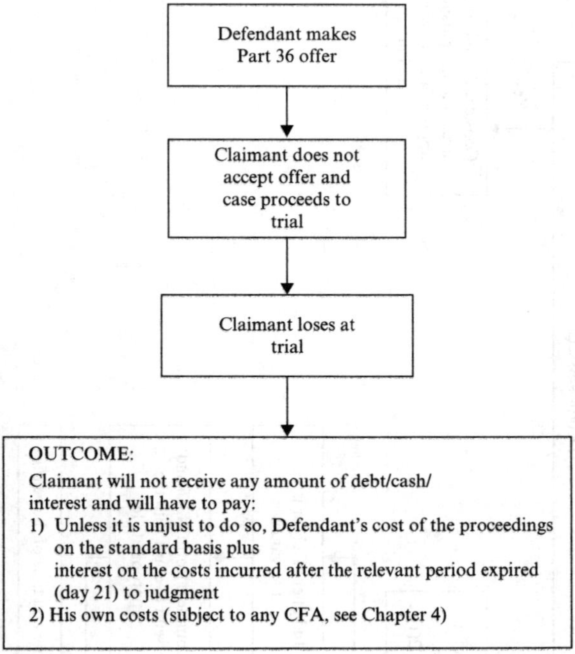

Part 36 Offer – Claimant Beats Defendant's Part 36 Offer but Doesn't Equal or Beat own Part 36 Offer

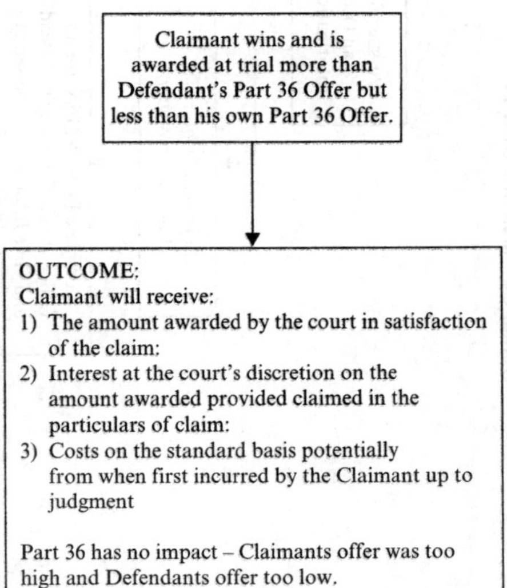

Application To Apply For An Order To Obtain Information – CPR 71

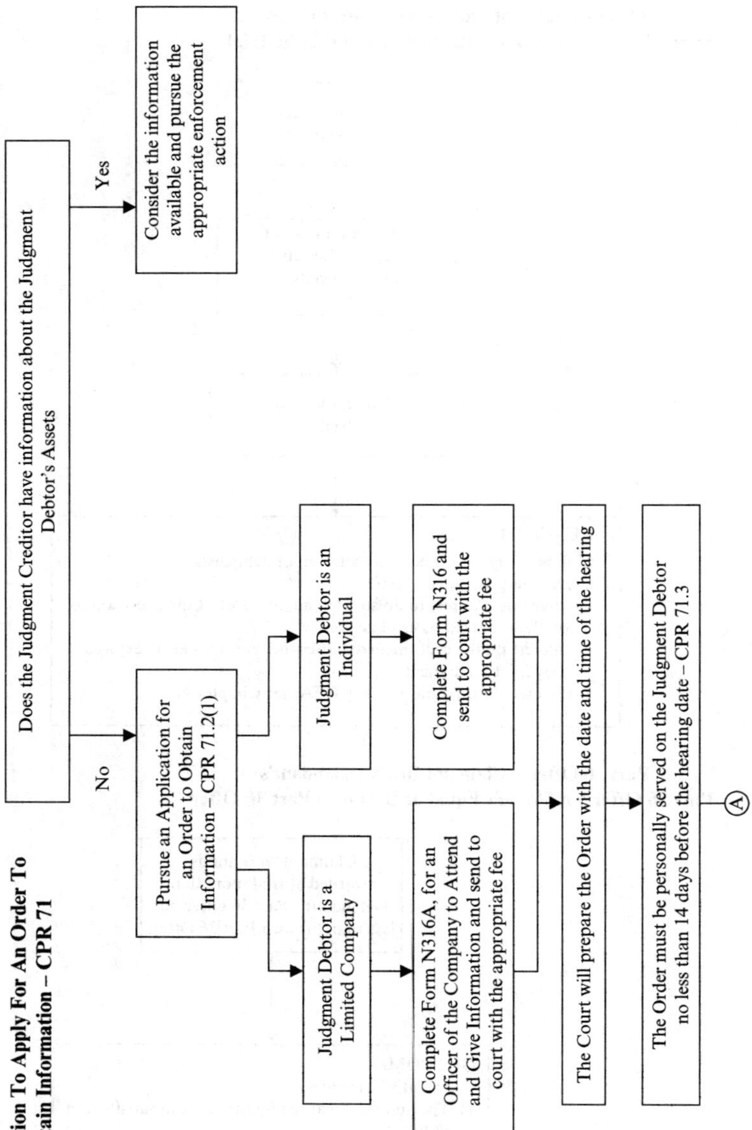

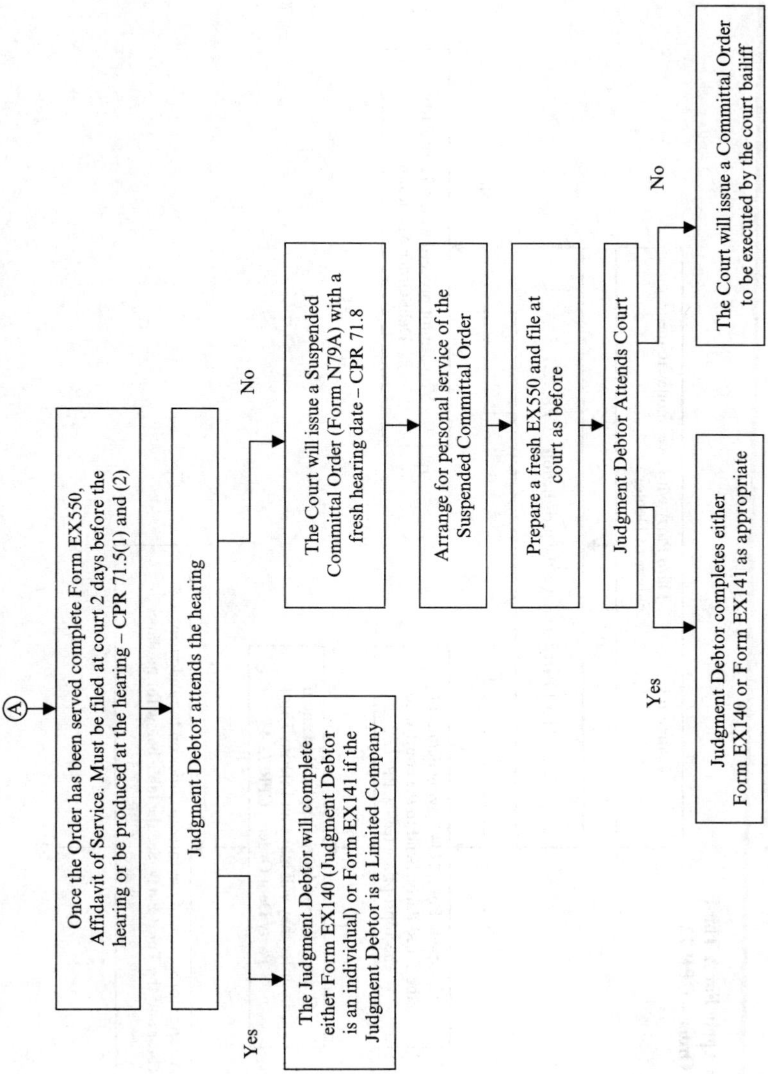
A
Once the Order has been served complete Form EX550, Affidavit of Service. Must be filed at court 2 days before the hearing or be produced at the hearing – CPR 71.5(1) and (2)
Judgment Debtor attends the hearing
Yes
The Judgment Debtor will complete either Form EX140 (Judgment Debtor is an individual) or Form EX141 if the Judgment Debtor is a Limited Company
No
The Court will issue a Suspended Committal Order (Form N79A) with a fresh hearing date – CPR 71.8
Arrange for personal service of the Suspended Committal Order
Prepare a fresh EX550 and file at court as before
Judgment Debtor Attends Court
Yes
Judgment Debtor completes either Form EX140 or Form EX141 as appropriate
No
The Court will issue a Committal Order to be executed by the court bailiff

Application To Apply For A Third Party Debt Order – CPR 72

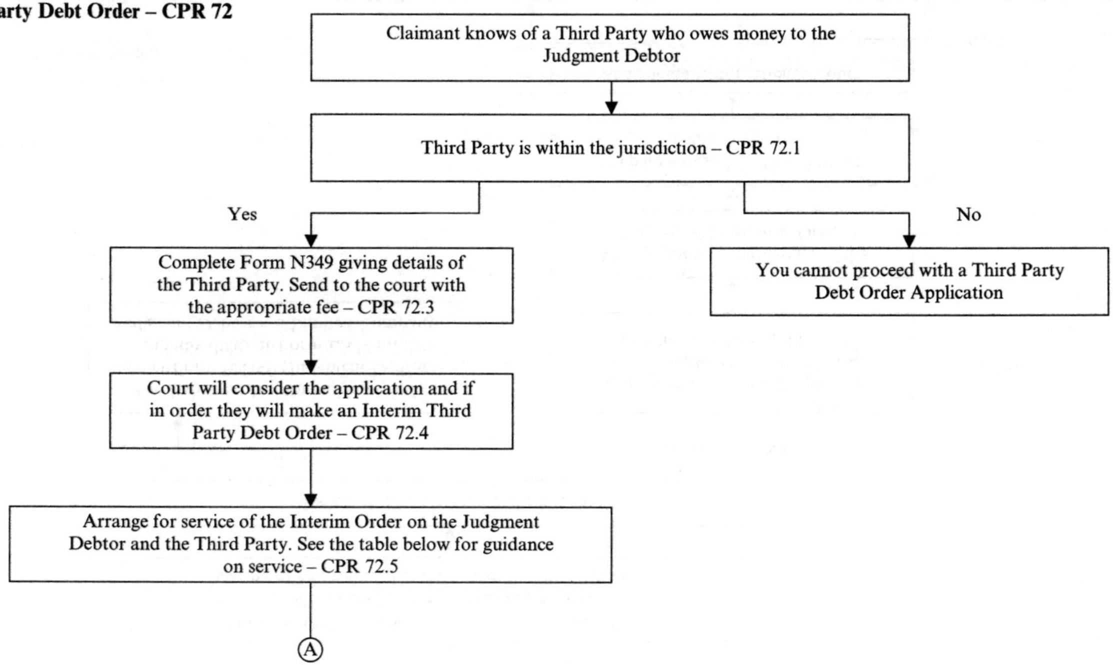

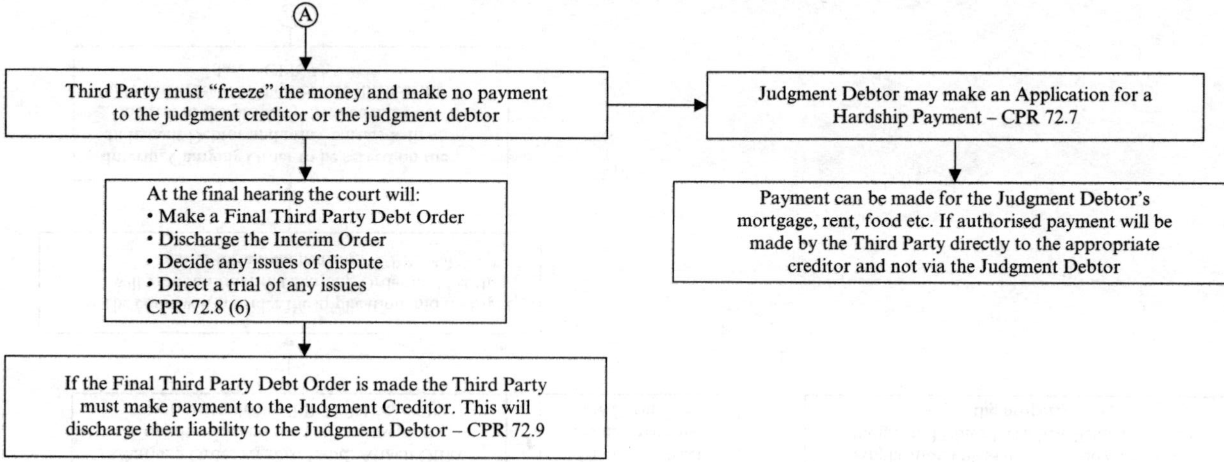

Third Party Debt Order Table For Service – CPR 72.5

Application for TPDO is made	Interim TPDO is made by the court	Final hearing is set not less than 28 days ahead	Third Party is served not less than 21 days before the final hearing date	Judgment Debtor is served not less than 7 days after a copy of the Interim TPDO has been served on the Third Party and 7 days before the final hearing	Final hearing takes place with all service requirements having been met
1st June	**4th June**	**4th July**	**Service on Third Party to be completed by 14th June**	**Service on Judgment Debtor to be completed not earlier than 21st June and before 28th June**	**Final hearing takes place on 4th July**

Application To Apply For A Charging Order Against Land – CPR 73

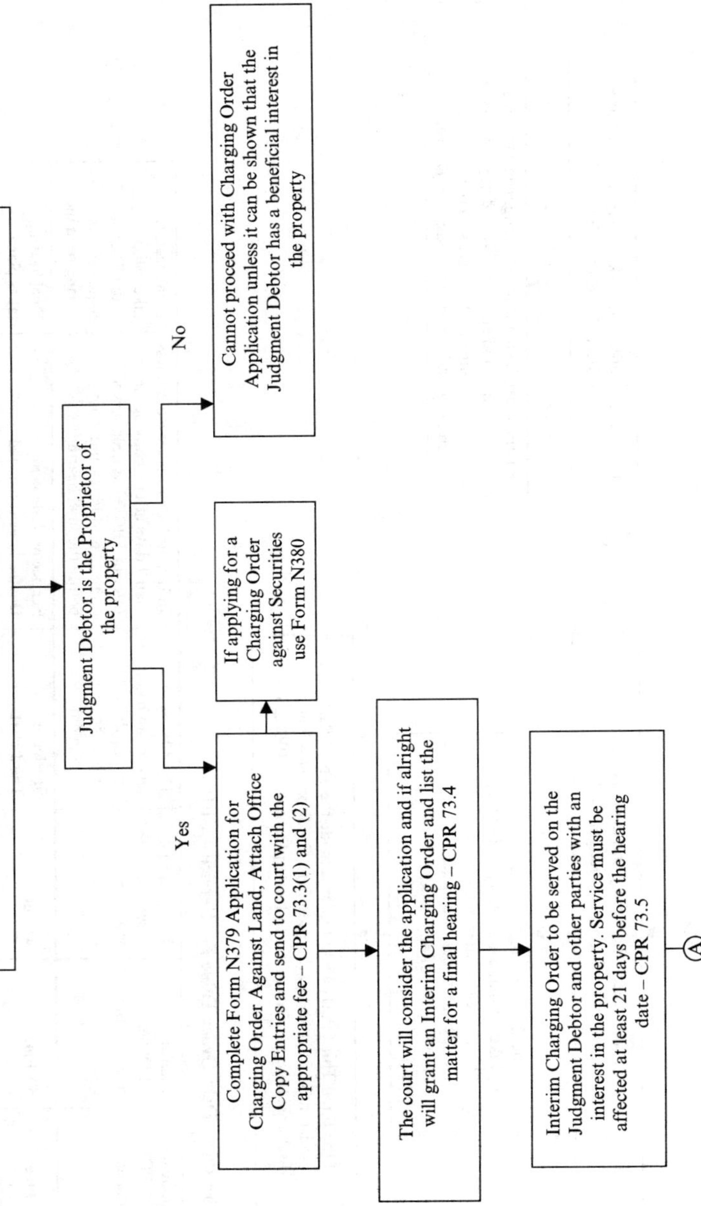

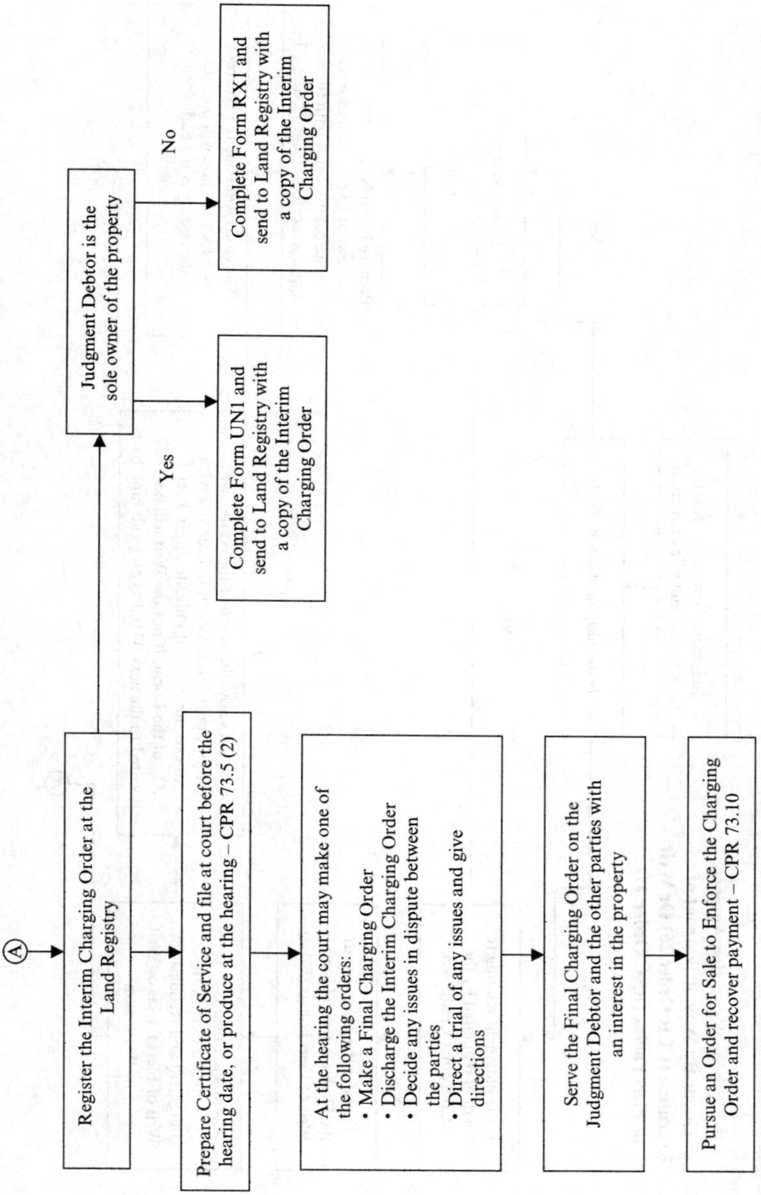
A
Register the Interim Charging Order at the Land Registry
Judgment Debtor is the sole owner of the property
Yes
Complete Form UN1 and send to Land Registry with a copy of the Interim Charging Order
No
Complete Form RX1 and send to Land Registry with a copy of the Interim Charging Order
Prepare Certificate of Service and file at court before the hearing date, or produce at the hearing – CPR 73.5 (2)
At the hearing the court may make one of the following orders:
• Make a Final Charging Order
• Discharge the Interim Charging Order
• Decide any issues in dispute between the parties
• Direct a trial of any issues and give directions
Serve the Final Charging Order on the Judgment Debtor and the other parties with an interest in the property
Pursue an Order for Sale to Enforce the Charging Order and recover payment – CPR 73.10

Process For Execution Against Goods By Way of Warrant of Execution (CCR Order 26) Or Writ of Fieri Facias (RSC Order 47)

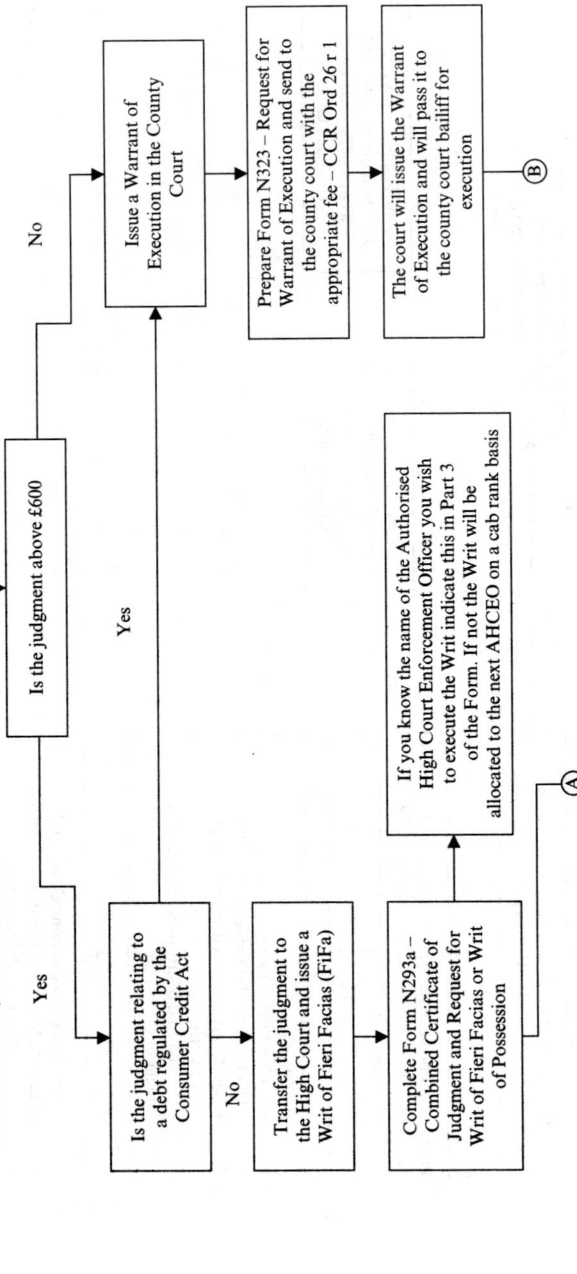

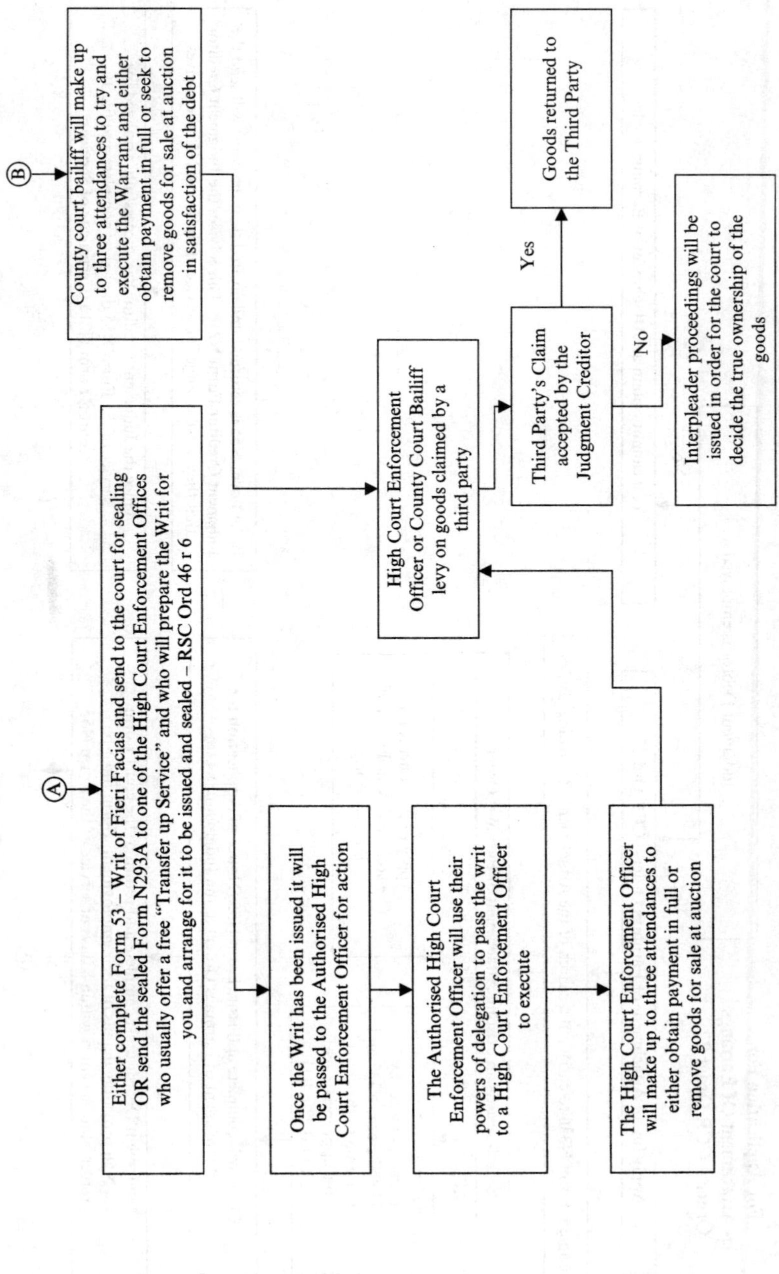
A
Either complete Form 53 – Writ of Fieri Facias and send to the court for sealing OR send the sealed Form N293A to one of the High Court Enforcement Offices who usually offer a free "Transfer up Service" and who will prepare the Writ for you and arrange for it to be issued and sealed – RSC Ord 46 r 6
Once the Writ has been issued it will be passed to the Authorised High Court Enforcement Officer for action
The Authorised High Court Enforcement Officer will use their powers of delegation to pass the writ to a High Court Enforcement Officer to execute
The High Court Enforcement Officer will make up to three attendances to either obtain payment in full or remove goods for sale at auction
B
County court bailiff will make up to three attendances to try and execute the Warrant and either obtain payment in full or seek to remove goods for sale at auction in satisfaction of the debt
High Court Enforcement Officer or County Court Bailiff levy on goods claimed by a third party
Third Party's Claim accepted by the Judgment Creditor
Yes
Goods returned to the Third Party
No
Interpleader proceedings will be issued in order for the court to decide the true ownership of the goods

For Application For An Attachment Of Earnings Order – CCR Order 27

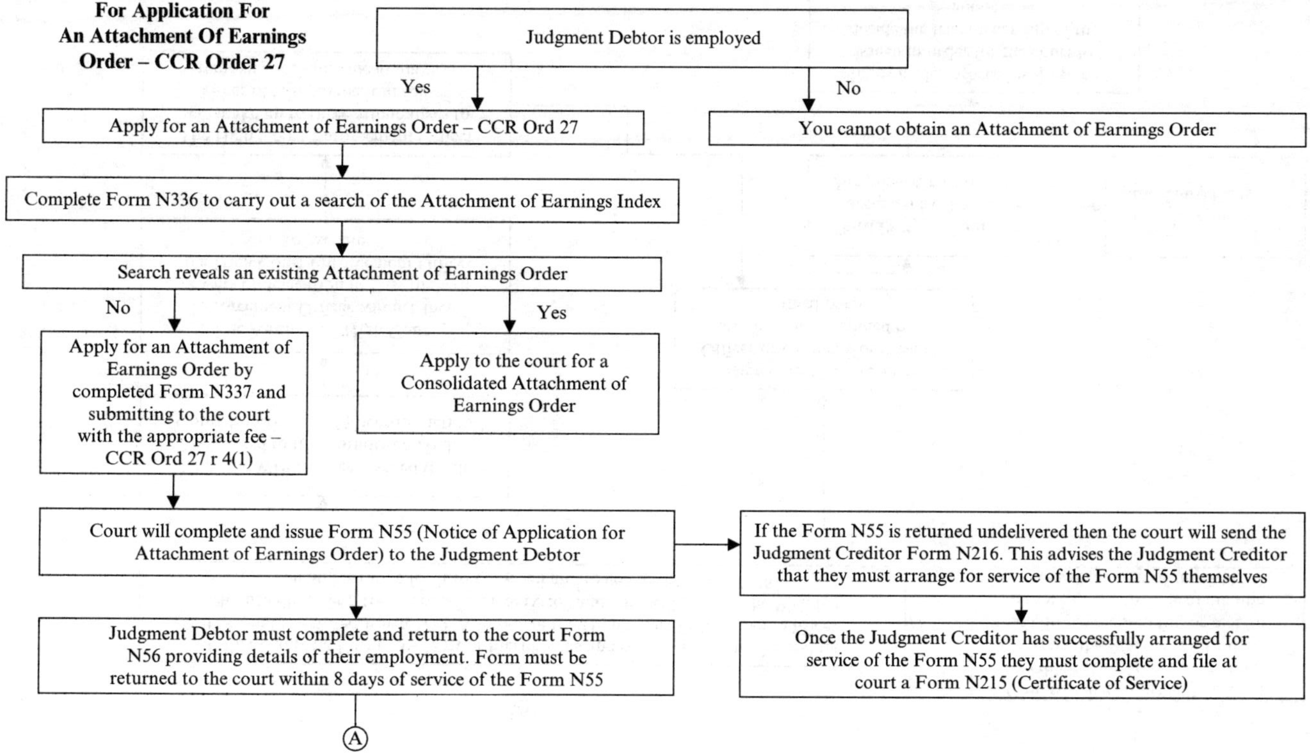

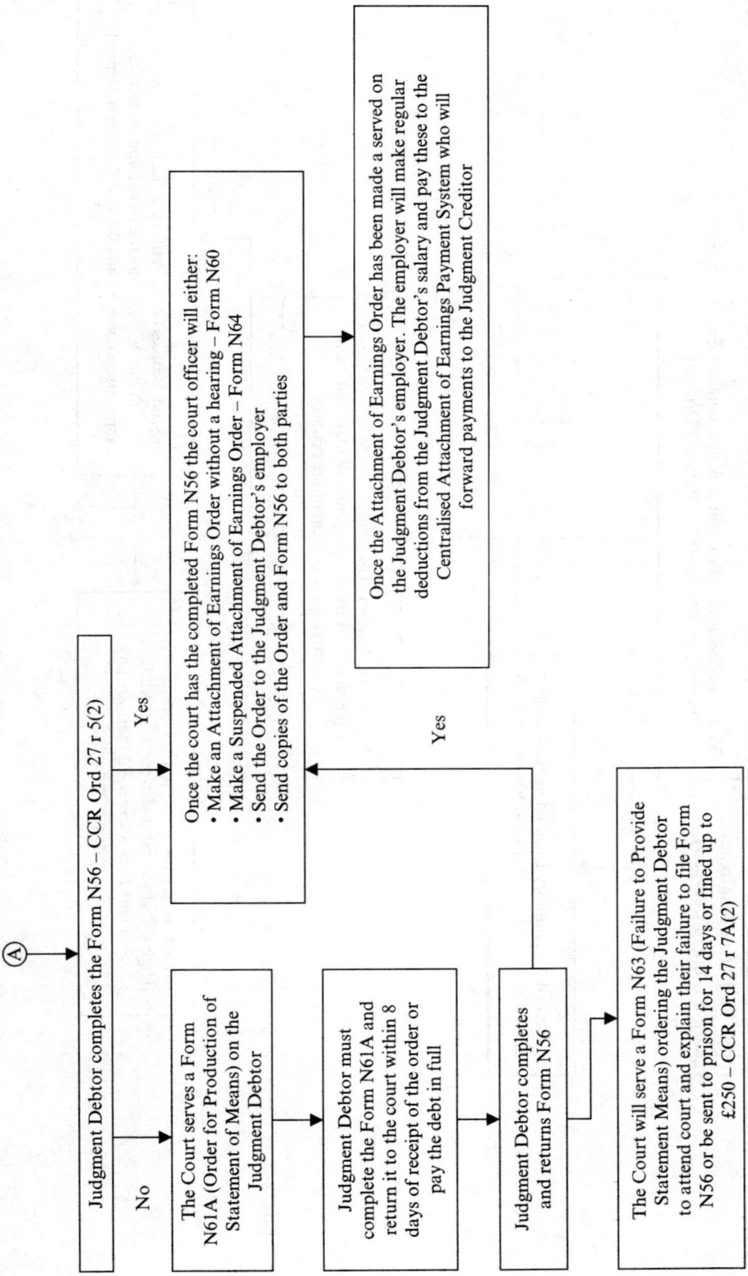
A
Judgment Debtor completes the Form N56 – CCR Ord 27 r 5(2)
Yes
Once the court has the completed Form N56 the court officer will either:
• Make an Attachment of Earnings Order without a hearing – Form N60
• Make a Suspended Attachment of Earnings Order – Form N64
• Send the Order to the Judgment Debtor's employer
• Send copies of the Order and Form N56 to both parties
Once the Attachment of Earnings Order has been made a served on the Judgment Debtor's employer. The employer will make regular deductions from the Judgment Debtor's salary and pay these to the Centralised Attachment of Earnings Payment System who will forward payments to the Judgment Creditor
No
The Court serves a Form N61A (Order for Production of Statement of Means) on the Judgment Debtor
Judgment Debtor must complete the Form N61A and return it to the court within 8 days of receipt of the order or pay the debt in full
Judgment Debtor completes and returns Form N56
Yes
The Court will serve a Form N63 (Failure to Provide Statement Means) ordering the Judgment Debtor to attend court and explain their failure to file Form N56 or be sent to prison for 14 days or fined up to £250 – CCR Ord 27 r 7A(2)

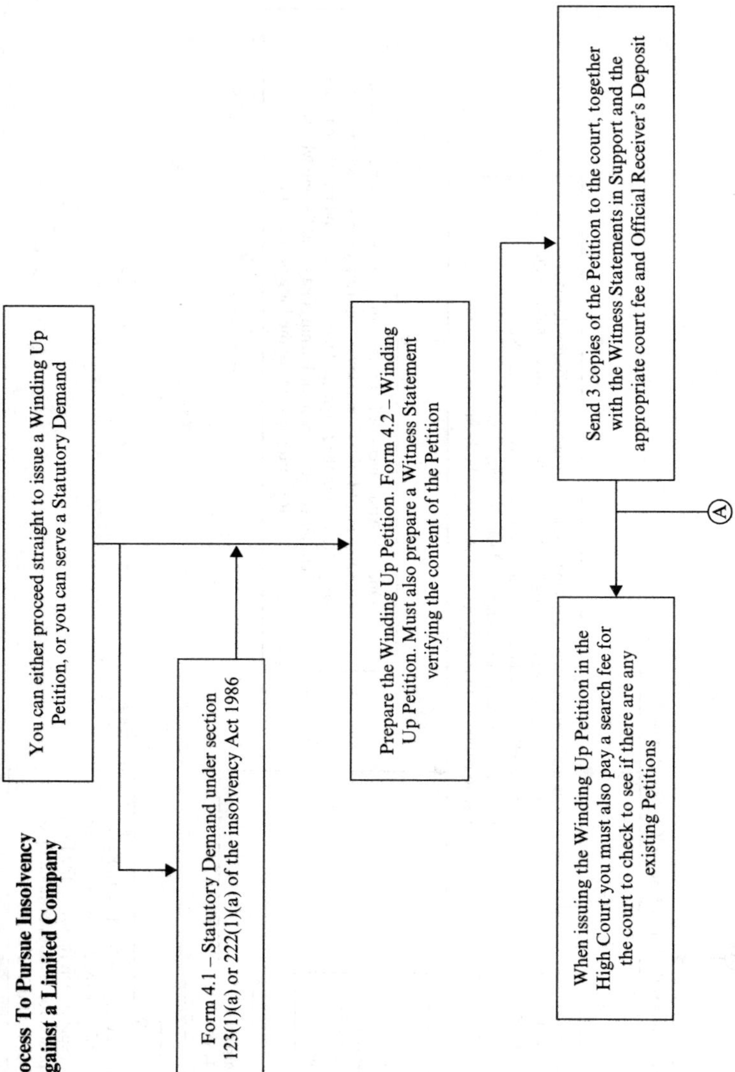
Process To Pursue Insolvency Against a Limited Company
You can either proceed straight to issue a Winding Up Petition, or you can serve a Statutory Demand
Form 4.1 – Statutory Demand under section 123(1)(a) or 222(1)(a) of the insolvency Act 1986
Prepare the Winding Up Petition. Form 4.2 – Winding Up Petition. Must also prepare a Witness Statement verifying the content of the Petition
Send 3 copies of the Petition to the court, together with the Witness Statements in Support and the appropriate court fee and Official Receiver's Deposit
When issuing the Winding Up Petition in the High Court you must also pay a search fee for the court to check to see if there are any existing Petitions
A

(A)

↓

Once the Petition is issued and the hearing date listed, the court will return the Petition to you for service upo the Company.
It must be served personally on:

- A director of the company
- A duly authorised person of the debtor company
- Leaving it at the debtor company's registered office

↓

You must also arrange for the Winding Up Petition to be advertised in the London Gazette. The advert must be placed:

- At least 7 days after the service of the petition; and
- At least 7 days before the hearing of the petition

↓

At least 5 days before the hearing of the petition you must file a Certificate of Compliance at court showing:

- The date of the presentation of the petition; the date fixed for the hearing; the date of service of the petition; and
- The advertising rules have been complied with (a copy of the advert should be filed with the Certificate)

↓

At the hearing of the petition the court will make one of the following orders:

- Dismiss the petition
- Adjourn the hearing conditionally or unconditionally
- Make a compulsory winding up order
- Make any other order it thinks fit

Process To Pursue Insolvency Against An Individual

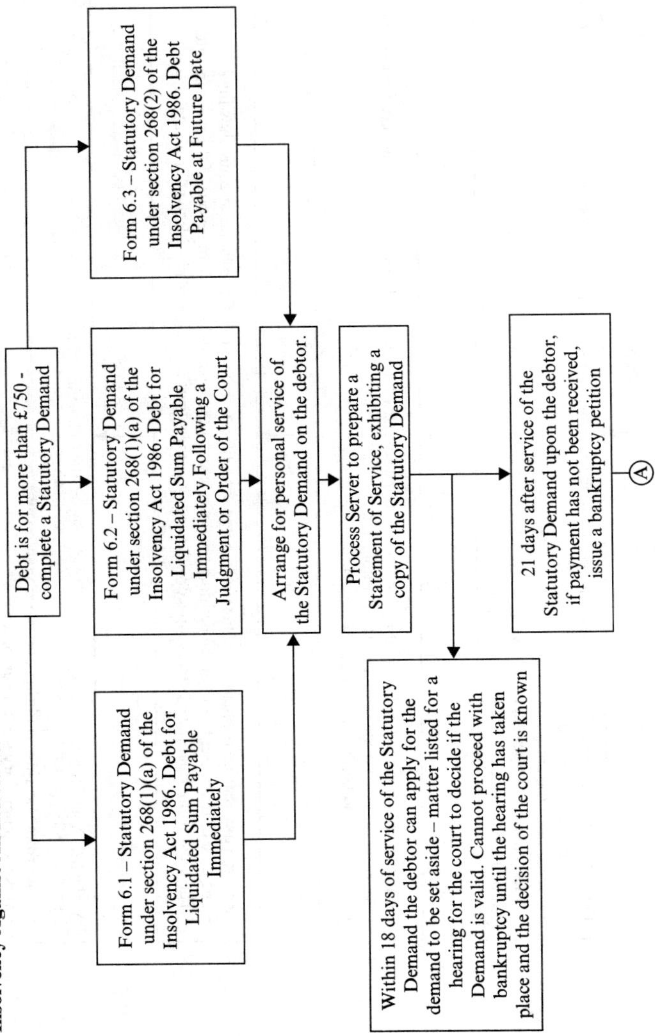

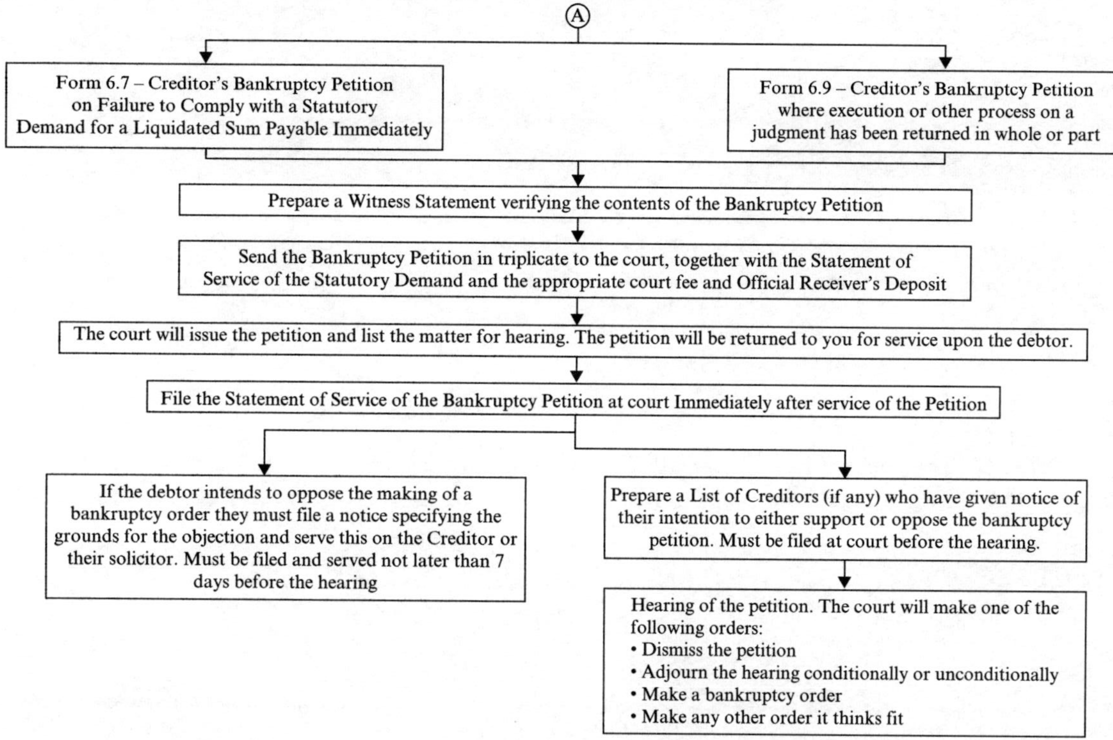
A
Form 6.7 – Creditor's Bankruptcy Petition on Failure to Comply with a Statutory Demand for a Liquidated Sum Payable Immediately
Form 6.9 – Creditor's Bankruptcy Petition where execution or other process on a judgment has been returned in whole or part
Prepare a Witness Statement verifying the contents of the Bankruptcy Petition
Send the Bankruptcy Petition in triplicate to the court, together with the Statement of Service of the Statutory Demand and the appropriate court fee and Official Receiver's Deposit
The court will issue the petition and list the matter for hearing. The petition will be returned to you for service upon the debtor.
File the Statement of Service of the Bankruptcy Petition at court Immediately after service of the Petition
If the debtor intends to oppose the making of a bankruptcy order they must file a notice specifying the grounds for the objection and serve this on the Creditor or their solicitor. Must be filed and served not later than 7 days before the hearing
Prepare a List of Creditors (if any) who have given notice of their intention to either support or oppose the bankruptcy petition. Must be filed at court before the hearing.
Hearing of the petition. The court will make one of the following orders:
• Dismiss the petition
• Adjourn the hearing conditionally or unconditionally
• Make a bankruptcy order
• Make any other order it thinks fit

Appendix B

Case Study Documents for a Commercial Debt Claim

Index

Description of Documents	Page Number
Application Notice (Form N244)—Notes for Guidance	479
Trial Bundle Index	480
Record of Examination	481
Affidavit (order to attend for questioning and suspended committal order)	493
Application for Third Party Debt Order	495
Request for Attachment of Earnings Order	498
Application for Charging Order on Land or Property	499
Certificate of Service	501
Application to Enter a Restriction—RX1	503
Claim Form (CPR Part 8)	506
Witness Statement in Support of Claim for Order for Sale	508
Statutory Demand under section 268(1)(a) of the Insolvency Act 1986, Debt for Liquidated Sum Payable Immediately—Form 6.1	510
Statutory Demand under section 268(1)(a) of the Insolvency Act 1986, Debt for Liquidated Sum Payable Immediately—Form 6.2	514
Creditor's Bankruptcy Petition on Failure to Comply with a Statutory Demand for Liquidated Sum Payable Immediately—Form 6.7	518

Case Study Introduction

Tom Good lives in a detached house in suburbia. Several years ago he decided to start to grow his own vegetables in his back garden. He made such a success of it that he had an abundance of vegetables and started to share these with his neighbours.

As time went by and he started to grow more and more vegetables and decided to set up a business supplying seasonal vegetables to local business and his neighbours.

Tom then expanded his business and started to keep livestock, including chickens and pigs. Ever the entrepreneur he decided to make the most of the "by product" of keeping animals and also started to supply manure to his neighbours for their gardens.

One of Tom's customers included his neighbour Margot Ledbetter. Not only did Margot regularly receive Tom's vegetable boxes, but she also had manure from Tom's animals to place on her flower beds. Margot was a keen participant in the local flower shows and prided herself on the roses she grew, convinced that the use of the manure would help her win first prize in the flower show.

Despite being friends and neighbours, Tom always made sure that he provided an invoice to Margot in respect of both the supply of the vegetables and the manure. Ordinarily Margot paid the invoices on time, however after the recent supply of some vegetables and manure, Margot has failed to pay the invoice.

Tom has repeatedly requested payment yet nothing has been forthcoming. Margot is now alledging that the vegetables were supplied as a gift and that she does not have to pay for the manure as the wrong manure has been provided and has resulted in her prize roses dying.

The following forms have been completed as if by either Tom as the Claimant, or Margot as the Defendant, as appropriate in the course of Tom pursuing a claim against Margot for the non payment of his invoice, and Margot counterclaiming against Tom for the damage to her roses.

Credit Account Application Form

Tom Good T/a Good Food & Manure
1 Cuckoo Lane
Braintree
Essex
CM6 3RT

Please complete ALL the details on this form and return it to us as soon as possible. This form MUST be completed in full and signed before credit can be issued.

I/We request you to open a credit account in the name of:

Business Name:	Tel:
Address:	Mobile:
	Fax:
	E-mail:
Post Code:	

Trading Name (if different):	Trading Fax (if different):
Trading Address (if different):	
Post Code:	

Legal Type (please tick)	**Credit**
Sole Trader (please set out full name)	Maximum Monthly Credit Requested: If in excess of £5000 we will require 2 references, one of which must be your bank
Partnership (please set out in full the names of all proprietors)	
Limited Partnership	
Limited Company/PLC – Registration No.	
Other – please state	

Important

Payment to be made within 30 days from the date of invoice for any goods supplied. Goods will remain the property of Tom Good until payment for them has been received in full. Claims regarding damage, short delivery, non-delivery, or quality of work cannot be entertained unless confirmed in writing by recorded delivery within seven days of the dispatch date. Please see overleaf for full terms and conditions.

I/we the undersigned wish to apply for credit facilities with Tom Good and agree to abide by the terms and conditions overleaf.

Signed:	Please print name:
Position:	Date:

Thank you. A copy of this form will be sent to you as confirmation that the credit facilities have been established.

Tom Good t/a Good Food & Manure

Terms and Conditions of Contract

Name of Business/Individual: MARGOT LEDBETTER

- Tom Good t/a Good Food and Manure's contracts are based on standard service periods (quarterly or monthly) during which period we undertake to provide specified goods and services in return for specified payments
- Our commitment to you is to provide the specified services at the required time to a high standard. We aim to provide you with a high quality and adaptable service
- Your commitment to us is to make the specified payments at the required time and to notify us within 7 days if our service falls below the standard you expect so that we can rectify the issue
- Payment is due on all standard service contracts 14 days in advance of the relevant service period, unless payment is by standing order, in which case payment will be due on the first day of the relevant service period
- Where credit arrangements are agreed, payment will be 30 days from the date of our invoice
- Notice of cancellation of a service contract is required in writing, one complete service period in advance of cancellation by either party
- In the event that payment is not received by the required date, provision of the service may be suspended without notice. Liability for any charges due under the service contract will continue until notice of cancellation has been received and the required notice period has expired
- An account may not be cancelled while overdue payments are outstanding
- In the event that Tom Good t/a Good Food & Manure needs to take measures to recover any overdue debts, the customer is liable to reimburse Tom Good t/a Good Food & Manure for the cost
- We reserve the right to withdraw credit facilities at any time

Signed:

We/I have read your terms and conditions and agree to abide by them

Signed:
Tom Good t/a Good Food & Manure

Dated:

Good Food & Manure

Invoice No. A789

Date: 30th June 2007

Description	**Amount**
4 Medium seasonal vegetable boxes	£100.00
10 Sacks of manure	£400.00
2 Small seasonal vegetable boxes (provided to Mrs K Ledbetter as gifts as per your order)	£ 30.00
SUB TOTAL	**£530.00**
VAT	**£ 92.75**
TOTAL	**£622.75**

Tom Good
T/a Good Food & Manure
1 Cuckoo Lane
Braintree
Essex
CM6 3RT

STATEMENT

To: Margot Ledbetter
3 Cuckoo Lane
Braintree
Essex
CM6 3RT

Account No: 445566

Statement No: 1

Statement Date: 17th July 2007

Details for Period: 01.06.07 – 30.06.07

Date	**Invoice No.**	**Details**	**Amount**	**VAT**
30th June 2007	A789	4 Medium vegetable boxes 10 sacks of manure 2 small vegetable boxes	£530.00	£92.75

For Payment:

Sub total: £530.00
VAT: £ 92.75
TOTAL AMOUNT DUE: £622.75

Please detach this slip and forward with your remittance to:

Tom Good T/A Good Food & Manure 1 Cuckoo Lane, Braintree Essex CM6 3RT	In any correspondence please quote: Account No: 445566 Statement No: 1

Cheques should be crossed and made payable to:

Tom Good t/a Good Food & Manure

T/A Good Food & Manure
1 Cuckoo Lane
Braintree
Essex
CM6 3RT

Tel: 01543 456332

Date: 24th July 2007

Ref: TG/445566

To: Margot Ledbetter
3 Cuckoo Lane
Braintree
Essex
CM6 3RT

Dear Madam,

Invoice No. A789
Invoice Date: 30th June 2007
Amount Due: £622.75

Our records indicate that the above account remains outstanding. We would be grateful for an early remittance.

If you have paid the amount within the past seven days please telephone us to ensure we have received it.

We will pursue legal action in the absence of settlement of the outstanding invoice.

Yours faithfully,

T Good
T/A Good Food & Manure

L A LAW, Solicitors, Boston House, New Street, Nottingham, NN4 8SD
Tel. 01357 556442 Fax. 01357 84621

Mrs M Ledbetter
3 Cuckoo Lane
Braintree
Essex
CM6 3RT

Our Ref: JB/Good

Date: 22nd December 2007

Dear Madam

Balance owed by you to Mr Tom Good t/a Good Food & Manure: £622.75
URGENT: NOTICE OF INTENDED LEGAL ACTION

We are instructed by Mr Tom Good t/a Good Food & Manure to recover the above sum in relation to an outstanding debt you owe to our client in respect of an unpaid invoice for goods supplied.

If payment is not received by **4pm 29th December 2007** then we are instructed to prepare the matter for litigation by issuing a county court claim. If this step is taken we will add solicitors costs, interest at 8% per annum and court fees to the amount of the debt. These additional sums will increase you account by at least a further £150.00.

Once a county court claim is issued, then in the absence of payment we will ask the court to record a county court judgment against you. This step may adversely affect your credit rating for up to 6 years. We also have standing instructions from Mr Good to enforce payment of all county court judgments in the absence of payment.

To avoid the consequences of a county court judgment being registered against you, or enforcement proceedings being taken at a future date you should arrange for the immediate payment of your account in full to ourselves at the above address.

To assist you payment can be made in the following ways:

Cheque – please quote the reference given above on the back of any cheque which should be made payable to "LA Law Solicitors"
Credit or Debit Card – please complete the details below and return to us by **4pm 29th December 2007.** Alternatively, you can telephone us with your credit/debit card details

Your prompt attention to this matter is now required. No further notice of our client's intention will be given.

Yours faithfully

L A Law Solicitors

Remittance Slip Amount to be paid £ **Payment by Cheque/Postal Order/Credit/Debit Card***

CREDIT/DEBIT CARD DETAILS (*Delete as applicable)

Cardholders Name :

Card Type : Mastercard/Visa/Switch/Delta*

Card Number :

Valid From : Expiry Date: Issue No: (if applicable)

Signature :

Your contact telephone number:

Claim Form

Click here to clear your data after printing

In the NORTHAMPTON COUNTY COURT

	for court use only
Claim No.	
Issue date	

SEAL

Claimant

TOM GOOD T/A GOOD FOOD & MANURE
1 CUCKOO LANE
BRAINTREE
ESSEX
CM6 3RT

Defendant(s)

MARGOT LEDBETTER
3 CUCKOO LANE
BRAINTREE
ESSEX
CM6 3RT

Brief details of claim

1. £622.75 that being the amount owed by the Defendant to the Claimant for the goods supplied.
2. Interest on the sum pursuant to Section 69 County Courts Act 1984.

Value

NOT EXCEEDING £5,000

Defendant's name and address

MARGOT LEDBETTER
3 CUCKOO LANE
BRAINTREE
ESSEX
CM6 3RT

	£
Amount claimed	646.64
Court fee	65.00
Solicitor's costs	70.00
Total amount	781.64

The court office at

is open between 10 am and 4 pm Monday to Friday. When corresponding with the court, please address forms or letters to the Court Manager and quote the claim number.

N1 Claim form (CPR Part 7) (01.02)

Printed on behalf of The Court Service

Claim No.

Does, or will, your claim include any issues under the Human Rights Act 1998? ☐ Yes ☑ No

Particulars of Claim (attached)(to follow)

1. At all material times the claimant was a supplier of manure/fertiliser and seasonal vegetable boxes of seasonal vegetables and fruit.

2. On or around May 1, 2007 the Defendant ordered from the claimant 4 medium seasonal boxes of vegetables, 10 sacks of manure and 2 small seasonal vegetable boxes ("the order"). The claimant supplied the order on May 3, 2007.

3. On June 16, 2007 the claimant rendered an invoice number A789 for the order in the sum of £622.75. Payment was due 30 days after invoice.

4. The defendant has failed to pay all or any part of the price of the order and therefore owes the claimant £622.75.

5. Further, the claimant claims interest on the above sum at the rate of 8% per annum pursuant to section 69 County Courts Act 1984.

AND the claimant claims:

a. The sum of £622.75.

b. Interest on the sum of £622.75 amounting to £23.89 from July 16, 2007 to January 7, 2008 and continuing at a daily rate of £0.14.

Dated this 7th Day of January 2008

Statement of Truth
*(I believe)(The Claimant believes) that the facts stated in these particulars of claim are true.
* I am duly authorised by the claimant to sign this statement

Full name JOSEPH BLOGGS

Name of claimant's solicitor's firm LA LAW SOLICITORS

signed ______________ position or office held SOLICITOR

*(Claimant)(Litigation friend)(Claimant's solicitor) (if signing on behalf of firm or company)

**delete as appropriate*

LA Law Solicitors
Boston House
New Street
Nottingham
NN4 8SD

Claimant's or claimant's solicitor's address to which documents or payments should be sent if different from overleaf including (if appropriate) details of DX, fax or e-mail

Click here to reset form | Click here to print form

Response pack

You should read the 'notes for defendant' attached to the claim form which will tell you when and where to send the forms

Included in this pack are:

- either **Admission Form N9A** (if the claim is for a specified amount)
  or **Admission Form N9C** (if the claim is for an unspecified amount or is not a claim for money)
- either **Defence and Counterclaim Form N9B** (if the claim is for a specified amount)
  or **Defence and Counterclaim Form N9D** (if the claim is for an unspecified amount or is not a claim for money)
- **Acknowledgment of service** (see below)

	Complete
If you admit the claim or the amount claimed and/or you want time to pay	the admission form
If you admit part of the claim	the admission form and the defence form
If you dispute the whole claim or wish to make a claim (a counterclaim) against the claimant	the defence form
If you need 28 days (rather than 14) from the date of service to prepare your defence, or wish to contest the court's jurisdiction	the acknowledgment of service
If you do nothing, judgment may be entered against you	

Acknowledgment of service

Name of court	NORTHAMPTON COUNTY COURT
Claim No.	8NN123456
Claimant (including ref.)	TOM GOOD T/A GOOD FOOD & MANURE
Defendant	MARGOT LEDBETTER

Defendant's full name if different from the name given on the claim form

Address to which documents about this claim should be sent (including reference if appropriate)

MRS MARGOT LEDBETTER
3 CUCKOO LANE
BRAINTREE
ESSEX

Postcode CM3 3RT

If applicable	
Telephone no.	
Fax no.	
DX no.	
Your ref.	

E-mail

Tick the appropriate box

1. I intend to defend all of this claim ☑
2. I intend to defend part of this claim ☐
3. I intend to contest jurisdiction ☐

(My) (Defendant's) date of birth is 16/07/1956

If you file an acknowledgment of service but do not file a defence within 28 days of the date of service of the claim form, or particulars of claim if served separately, judgment may be entered against you.

If you do not file an application to dispute the jurisdiction of the court within 14 days of the date of filing this acknowledgment of service, it will be assumed that you accept the court's jurisdiction and judgment may be entered against you.

If served outside the jurisdiction see CPR rule 6.35 and 6.37(5).

Signed

(Defendant) (Defendant's solicitor) (Litigation friend)

Position or office held (if signing on behalf of firm or company)

Date / /

The court office at

is open between 10 am and 4 pm Monday to Friday. When corresponding with the court, please address forms or letters to the Court Manager and quote the claim number.

N9 Response pack (10.08)

Click here to reset form | Click here to print form

Defence and Counterclaim (specified amount)

Name of court	NORTHAMPTON COUNTY COURT
Claim No.	8NN123456
Claimant (including ref.)	TOM GOOD T/A GOOD FOOD & MANURE
Defendant	MARGOT LEDBETTER

- Fill in this form if you wish to dispute all or part of the claim and/or make a claim against the claimant (counterclaim).
- You have a limited number of days to complete and return this form to the court.
- Before completing this form, please read the notes for guidance attached to the claim form.
- Please ensure that all boxes at the top right of this form are completed. You can obtain the correct names and number from the claim form. The court cannot trace your case without this information.

How to fill in this form

- Complete sections 1 and 2. Tick the correct boxes and give the other details asked for.
- Set out your defence in section 3. If necessary continue on a separate piece of paper making sure that the claim number is clearly shown on it. In your defence you must state which allegations in the particulars of claim you deny and your reasons for doing so. **If you fail to deny an allegation it may be taken that you admit it.**
- If you dispute only some of the allegations you must
  - specify which you admit and which you deny; and
  - give your own version of events if different from the claimant's.

- If you wish to make a claim against the claimant (a counterclaim) complete section 4.
- Complete and sign section 5 before sending this form to the court. Keep a copy of the claim form and this form.

Need help with your legal problems?
Community legal advice is a free confidential service, funded by legal aid. They can help you find the information and advice you need by putting you in touch with relevant agencies, helplines or local advice services. And if you are eligible for legal aid, the service can offer specialist legal advice over the telephone in cases involving: debt; housing; employment; benefits; and education.
Call **0845 345 4 345** or **www.communitylegaladvice.org.uk**

1. How much of the claim do you dispute?

☑ I dispute the full amount claimed as shown on the claim form.

or

☐ I admit the amount of £

If you dispute only part of the claim you must **either**:
- pay the amount admitted to the person named at the address for payment on the claim form (see How to Pay in the notes on the back of, or attached to, the claim form). Then send this defence to the court

or
- complete the admission form **and** this defence form and send them to the court.

☐ I paid the amount admitted on __/__/____

or

☐ I enclose the completed form of admission *(go to section 2)*

2. Do you dispute this claim because you have already paid it? *Tick whichever applies*

☐ **No** *(go to section 3)*

☐ **Yes** I paid £ to the claimant

on __/__/____
(before the claim form was issued)

Give details of where and how you paid it in the box below *(then go to section 5)*

3. Defence (If you need to continue on a separate sheet put the claim number in the top right hand corner.)

1. The defendant denies that the claimant is a supplier of manure and fertilisers or of vegetable boxes. The claimant has an allotment and small holding in his back garden. He grows a variety of vegetables and has a small number of animals, including chickens and pigs. At no time has the claimant indicated that this was anything more than a pastime or hobby and has certainly never mentioned that it was a
2. It is agreed that the claimant provided the defendant with sacks of manure. This followed a request by the defendant to the claimant for manure for her garden if the claimant was willing to provide the same and had surplus. It is denied that the request was in the form of an order or that there was any business or contractual relationship between the claimant and the defendant. It is agreed that the defendant received vegetables from the claimant but she viewed these as gifts
3. The defendant had requested that the claimant provide her with chicken manure if possible for her rose bushes which

(continue over the page)

Claim No.	8NN123456

Defence (continued)

she was trying to grow for the local flower show.
4. The claimant agreed to provide the defendant with any surplus manure for use on her roses.
5. The claimant duly provided the sacks of manure which the defendant placed on her roses. It was not until the defendant had used the manure that she became aware that the claimant had in fact provided her with pig manure and not chicken manure as requested. This resulted in all of the defendant's rose bushes dying.
6. The defendant admits that the claimant provided an invoice for the sacks of manure and vegetable boxes.
7. The invoice remains unpaid as the defendant denies there was any contractual relationship between the claimant and the defendant and, or in the alternative, the claimant did not provide the manure requested.
8. The defendant therefore denies that she is indebted to the claimant in the said sum or at all.

4. If you wish to make a claim against the claimant (a counterclaim)

- To start your counterclaim, you will have to pay a fee. Court staff can tell you how much you have to pay.
- You may not be able to make a counterclaim where the claimant is the Crown (e.g. a Government Department). Ask at your local county court office for further information.

If your claim is for a specific sum of money, how much are you claiming? £150.00

I enclose the counterclaim fee of £30.00

My claim is for *(please specify nature of claim)*

The cost of replacement rose bushes

What are your reasons for making the counterclaim?
If you need to continue on a separate sheet put the claim number in the top right hand corner.

1. As a result of the claimant providing the defendant with the wrong manure, rather than improving the defendant's rose bushes, they all died and the defendant has consequently been put to the cost of purchasing replacement rose bushes.
2. In addition the defendant has suffered inconvenience and stress in not being able to enter the local flower show as intended and having to destroy the rose bushes and buy new ones.

5. Signed - To be signed by you or by your solicitor or litigation friend.

*(I believe) (The defendant believes) that the facts stated in this form are true.
*I am duly authorised by the defendant to sign this statement.

**delete as appropriate*

Position or office held
(If signing on behalf of firm or company)

Date __/__/____

Defendant's date of birth, if an individual __/__/____

Give an address to which notices about this case can be sent to you

Postcode C M 6 3 R T

If applicable	
Telephone no.	
Fax no.	
DX no.	

E-mail	

Click here to print form

Check here to clear your data after printing

Admission (specified amount)

- You have a limited number of days to complete and return this form
- Before completing this form, please read the notes for guidance attached to the claim form

Name of court	NORTHAMPTON COUNTY COURT
Claim No.	8NN123456
Claimant (including ref.)	TOM GOOD T/A GOOD FOOD & MANURE
Defendant	MARGOT LEDBETTER

When to fill in this form

Only fill in this form if:

- you are admitting all of the claim **and** you are asking for time to pay; or
- you are admitting part of the claim. (You should also complete form N9B)

How to fill in this form

- Tick the correct boxes and give as much information as you can. **Then sign and date the form.** If necessary provide details on a separate sheet, add the claim number and attach it to this form.
- Make your offer of payment in box 11 on the back of this form. **If you make no offer the claimant will decide how much and when you should pay.**
- If you are not an individual, you should ensure that you provide sufficient details about the assets and liabilities of your firm, company or corporation to support any offer of payment made in box 11.
- You can get help to complete this form at **any** county court office or Citizens Advice Bureau.

Where to send this form

- **If you admit the claim in full**
  Send the completed form to the address shown on the claim form as one to which documents should be sent.
- **If you admit only part of the claim**
  Send the form to **the court** at the address given on the claim form, together with the defence form (N9B).

How much of the claim do you admit?

☐ I admit the full amount claimed as shown on the claim form **or**

☐ I admit the amount of £

1 Personal details

Surname: LEDBETTER

Forename: MARGOT

☐ Mr ☑ Mrs ☐ Miss ☐ Ms

☑ Married ☐ Single ☐ Other *(specify)*

Date of birth: 1 6 0 7 1 9 5 6

Address: 3 CUCKOO LANE
BRAINTREE
ESSEX

Postcode: CM6 3RT

Tel. no.

2 Dependants *(people you look after financially)*

Number of children in each age group

under 11 ☐ 11-15 ☐ 16-17 ☐ 18 & over ☐

Other dependants *(give details)*

3 Employment

☐ **I am employed as a**

My employer is

Jobs other than main job *(give details)*

☐ **I am self employed as a**

Annual turnover is.......................... £

☐ **I am not in arrears with my national insurance contributions, income tax and VAT**

☐ **I am in arrears and I owe**.......... £

Give details of:
(a) contracts and other work in hand
(b) any sums due for work done

☑ **I have been unemployed for** 23 years months

☐ **I am a pensioner**

4 Bank account and savings

☑ **I have a bank account**

☐ The account is in credit by....... £ 2,300.00

☐ The account is overdrawn by.... £

☐ **I have a savings or building society account**

The amount in the account is.......... £ 15,000.00

5 Residence

I live in ☐ my own house ☐ lodgings ☑ my jointly owned house ☐ council accommodation ☐ rented accommodation

6 Income

My usual take home pay *(including overtime, commission, bonuses etc)*	£ per
Income support	£ per
Child benefit(s)	£ per
Other state benefit(s)	£ per
My pension(s)	£ per
Others living in my home give me	£ per
Other income *(give details below)*	
	£ per
	£ per
	£ per
Total income	**£** 0.00 **per**

7 Expenses

(Do not include any payments made by other members of the household out of their own income)

I have regular expenses as follows:

Mortgage *(including second mortgage)*	£ per
Rent	£ per
Council tax	£ per
Gas	£ per
Electricity	£ per
Water charges	£ per
TV rental and licence	£ per
HP repayments	£ per
Mail order	£ per
Housekeeping, food, school meals	£ per
Travelling expenses	£ per
Children's clothing	£ per
Maintenance payments	£ per
Others *(not court orders or credit debts listed in boxes 9 and 10)*	
	£ per
	£ per
	£ per
Total expenses	**£** 0.00 **per**

8 Priority debts

(This section is for arrears only. Do not include regular expenses listed in box 7.)

Rent arrears	£ per
Mortgage arrears	£ per
Council tax/Community Charge arrears	£ per
Water charges arrears	£ per
Fuel debts: Gas	£ per
Electricity	£ per
Other	£ per
Maintenance arrears	£ per
Others *(give details below)*	
	£ per
	£ per
Total priority debts	**£ per**

9 Court orders

Court	Claim No.	£ per
Total court order instalments		**£ per**

Of the payments above, I am behind with payments to *(please list)*

10 Credit debts

Loans and credit card debts *(please list)*

	£ per
	£ per
	£ per

Of the payments above, I am behind with payments to *(please list)*

11 Offer of payment

☑ I can pay the amount admitted on 01.02.08

or

☐ I can pay by monthly instalments of £

If you cannot pay immediately, please give brief reasons below

12 Declaration

I declare that the details I have given above are true to the best of my knowledge

Signed

Position or office held (if signing on behalf of firm or company)

Date 12.01.08

IN THE NORTHAMPTON COUNTY COURT **CLAIM NO. 8NN123456**

B E T W E E N:

TOM GOOD
T/A GOOD FOOD & MANURE

Claimant

and

MARGOT LEDBETTER

Defendant

DEFENCE TO COUNTERCLAIM

---

1. It is denied that the Claimant provided the Defendant with the wrong manure as alleged in Paragraph 1 of the Counterclaim. Further, it is denied that the manure provided caused the Defendant's rosebushes to die, and the Defendant is put to strict proof of the same. Except that it is denied that it was necessary to purchase replacement rosebushes, the Claimant is unable to admit or deny the rest of Paragraph 1 and puts the Defendant to strict proof of the same.

2. The Claimant neither admits nor denies that the Defendant has suffered inconvenience and stress as alleged in Paragraph 2 of the Counterclaim or at all. The Defendant is put to strict proof of the same.

STATEMENT OF TRUTH

(I believe)(The Claimant believes) that the facts stated in this Defence are true.
I am duly authorised by the Claimant to sign this statement.

Full Name: ....

Name of Claimant's solicitors firm: ....

Signed: ....

Position:...

Date: ....

LA Law Solicitors
Boston House
New Street
Nottingham
NN4 8SD

Filed on behalf of the Claimant
Mr Tom Good
1st
Exhibit:
Signed:
Filed:

IN THE NORTHAMPTON COUNTY COURT **CLAIM NO. 8NN123456**

B E T W E E N:

TOM GOOD
T/a GOOD FOOD & MANURE

Claimant

and

MARGOT LEDBETTER

Defendant

WITNESS STATEMENT OF TOM GOOD

I, TOM GOOD of 1 Cuckoo Lane, Braintree, Essex, CM6 3RT, Market Gardener, **WILL SAY AS FOLLOWS:**

1. I am a market gardener trading as Good Food & Manure from my address at 1 Cuckoo Lane, Braintree, Essex, CM6 3RT. I am the Claimant to this claim and make this statement in support of my claim against the Defendant.

2. I have for a number of years been interested in gardening and have always had a small plot in my garden where I have grown vegetables for my own use.

3. When I moved to my property at 1 Cuckoo Lane, Braintree, Essex in 2000 the garden there was much larger than I had previously had and therefore it opened up the possibility of me being able to start to grow my own vegetables and subsequently keeping livestock.

4. Shortly after moving to the property I began to cultivate the garden and began to set it out into various vegetable beds and areas for livestock. I planted a number of vegetables, including: potatoes, cabbages, carrots, peas, cucumbers, lettuces etc. I also purchased a number of chickens, two pigs and a goat.

Filed on behalf of the Claimant
Mr Tom Good
1st
Exhibit:
Signed:
Filed:

5. My aim in doing this was to become more self-sufficient and to also be in a position to sell any surplus vegetables to earn a small income.

6. The business became very popular and successful in the local area very quickly. I was fortunate to have an abundance of vegetables and was therefore in a position to start offering a box scheme to my neighbours. They would place an order each week for the size of box that they wanted and I would then select whatever surplus, in season, vegetables were available and would make up the appropriate boxes. The price of the boxes would vary depending upon the size and I would then invoice the customer accordingly.

7. After several months of supplying vegetables, I decided that I could also start to supply the surplus manure being generated by the pigs and chickens as fertiliser for their gardens.

8. As soon as I started to advertise to my customers that I was also able to provide fertiliser I started to receive orders for this as well as the vegetable boxes. I would again invoice the customers for the fertiliser with the cost being determined by the size of the sack or bag that the customer ordered.

9. Initially, the Defendant was a little upset by the way that I had decided to use my garden and particularly didn't like the idea of livestock being kept in the garden. However, once the Defendant began to see the quantity and quality of the produce being grown she began to place regular orders for the vegetable boxes. As with all my other customers, I would invoice the Defendant for the box provided. Prior to the invoice which forms the basis of this claim, the Defendant always paid the invoices submitted on time.

10. I knew that the Defendant was keen on gardening and was particularly proud of the rose bushes in her garden. I had also seen her exhibiting some of the roses on one occasion at the local flower show.

11. When I began to sell manure as fertiliser to my other customers I mentioned this to the Defendant as I thought she would be interested in using the manure for her rose bushes.

Filed on behalf of the Claimant
Mr Tom Good
1st
Exhibit:
Signed:
Filed:

12. The Defendant immediately placed an order for a bag of manure and I subsequently saw her in the garden digging the manure into the ground around her rose bushes. The Defendant subsequently placed regular orders for sacks of manure and particularly paid attention to her rose bushes.

13. At no time did the Defendant ever express a preference for the type of manure she wanted, nor did she ever raise a complaint regarding the manure which was being provided or any problems with it.

14. In readiness for the local flower show, the Defendant placed an order for some manure which was duly supplied and invoiced for in the usual way.

15. Normally, as stated above, the Defendant was very prompt in paying the invoices I submitted to her for both the vegetables and the manure. However, on this occasion the invoice was not paid on time. As we are neighbours, I initially mentioned the outstanding invoice to the Defendant when we saw each other in the garden. The Defendant apologised for the oversight and confirmed that she would arrange for payment of the invoice as soon as possible.

16. When payment was still not forthcoming I decided to instruct a solicitor to arrange for a formal letter to be sent to the Defendant requesting payment of the invoice. Unfortunately this still did not produce payment from the Defendant and consequently proceedings were issued for recovery of the outstanding sum.

17. I was amazed when the Defendant's defence and counterclaim were received as the Defendant had never raised and concerns or issues of complaint with me up to that point.

18. I strenuously deny that, if any damage has indeed occurred, that it was in anyway as a result of the manure supplied by me. The Defendant has been supplied with the same manure over several months and has never raised any complaints, or to my knowledge, ever experienced any problems.

19. I would also advise that I have supplied manure to several other customers at the same time as the Defendant and that no one else has raised any complaints with regards to

Filed on behalf of the Claimant
Mr Tom Good
1st
Exhibit:
Signed:
Filed:

the quality of the manure provided or indicated any problems.

STATEMENT OF TRUTH

I believe that the facts of this witness statements are true.

FULL NAME: THOMAS GOOD

SIGNED: ....

DATED: 7th April 2008

L A Law Solicitors
Boston House
New Street
Nottingham
NN4 8SD
Solicitors for the Claimant

Click here to reset form | Click here to print form

Request for judgment and reply to admission (specified amount)

- Tick box A or B. If you tick box B you must complete the details in that part and in part D. Make sure that all the case details are given. Remember to sign and date the form. Your signature certifies that the information you have given is correct.
- If the defendant has given an address on the form of admission to which correspondence should be sent, which is different from the address shown on the claim form, you must tell the court.
- Return the completed form to the court.

In the	NORTHAMPTON COUNTY COURT
Claim No.	8NN123456
Claimant (including ref)	TOM GOOD T/A GOOD FOOD & MANURE
Defendant (including ref)	MARGOT LEDBETTER

A ☑ **The defendant has not filed an admission or defence to my claim**

Complete all the judgment details at D. Decide how and when you want the defendant to pay. You can ask for the judgment to be paid by instalments or in one payment.

B ☐ **The defendant admits that all the money is owed**

Tick only one box below and complete all the judgment details at D.

☐ **I accept the defendant's proposal for payment**

Say how the defendant intends to pay. The court will send the defendant an order to pay. You will also be sent a copy.

☐ **The defendant has not made any proposal for payment**

Say how you want the defendant to pay. You can ask for the judgment to be paid by instalments or in one payment. The court will send the defendant an order to pay. You will also be sent a copy.

☐ **I do NOT accept the defendant's proposal for payment**

Say how you want the defendant to pay. Give your reasons for objecting to the defendant's offer of payment in the space opposite. (Continue on the back of this form if necessary.) Send this form to the court with **defendant's admission N9A**. The court will fix a rate of payment and send the defendant an order to pay. You will also be sent a copy.

C

☐ Defendant's date of birth is not stated in the form of reply but is known to the claimant as

D D M M Y Y Y Y

☐ Defendant's date of birth is not stated in the form of reply and is not known to the claimant.

D Judgment details

I would like the judgment to be paid

☑ (immediately)

☐ (by instalments of £ ______ per month)

☐ (in full by ______)

Amount of claim as admitted (including interest at date of issue)	646.64
Interest since date of claim (if any)	2.24
Period from 07.01.08 to 23.01.08	
Rate 8 %	
Court fees shown on claim	65.00
Solicitor's costs (if any) on issuing claim	70.00
Sub Total	783.88
Solicitor's costs (if any) on entering judgment	22.00
Sub Total	805.88
Deduct amount (if any) paid since issue	
Amount payable by defendant	

I certify that the information given is correct

Signed ______ (Claimant)(Claimant's solicitor)(Litigation friend)

Position or office held ______ (if signing on behalf of firm or company)

Date ______

The court office at

is open between 10 am and 4 pm Monday to Friday. When corresponding with the court, please address forms and letters to the Court Manager and quote the Claim number

Click here to clear your data after printing

Request for Warrant of Execution

to be completed and signed by the claimant or his solicitor and sent to the court with the appropriate fee

1 Claimant's name and address
MR TOM GOOD T/A GOOD FOOD & MANURE
1 CUCKOO LANE
BRAINTREE
ESSEX
CM6 3RT

In the NORTHAMPTON **County Court**

Claim Number 8NN123456

2 Name and address for service and payment (if different from above)
LA LAW SOLICITORS
BOSTON HOUSE
NEW STREET
NOTTINGHAM
NN4 8SD
Ref/Tel No. JB/GOOD 01234 567890

for court use only
Warrant no.
Issue date:
Warrant applied for at o'clock
Foreign court code/name:

3 Defendant's name and address
MARGOT LEDBETTER
3 CUCKOO LANE
BRAINTREE
ESSEX
CM6 3RT

4 Warrant details

(A) Balance due at date of this request	805.88
(B) Amount for which warrant to issue	805.88
Issue fee	55.00
Solicitor's costs	2.25
Land Registry fee	
TOTAL	863.03
If the amount of the warrant at (B) is less than the balance at (A), the sum due after the warrant is paid will be	

I certify that the whole or part of any instalments due under the judgment or order have not been paid and the balance now due is as shown

Signed

Claimant (Claimant's solicitor)

Dated 01.02.08

IMPORTANT
You must inform the court immediately of any payments you receive after you have sent this request to the court

You should provide a contact number so that the bailiff can speak to you if he/she needs to:

Daytime phone number: 01234 567890 Evening phone number (if possible):

Contact name (where appropriate): JOE BLOGGS

Defendant's phone number (if known):

If you have any other information which may help the bailiff or if you have reason to believe that the bailiff may encounter any difficulties you should write it below.

The defendant is known to drive a black BMW with 06 licence plates. In addition there a number of marble garden statues in the defendant's garden which are believed to be of some value.

N323 -w3- Request for warrant of execution (4.99) *Produced on behalf of The Court Service*

Click here to clear text after printing

Combined certificate of judgment and request for writ of fieri facias or writ of possession

In the NORTHAMPTON County Court	
Claim No.	8NN123456
Creditor's/ Claimant's Ref.	JB/GOOD
Debtor's/ Defendant's Ref.	
Date	

Creditor/Claimant
TOM GOOD T/A GOOD FOOD & MANURE

Debtor/Defendant
MARGOT LEDBETTER

I certify that the details I have given are correct and that to my knowledge there is no application or other procedure pending.

I request an order for enforcement in the High Court by

☐ Writ of Fieri Facias

☐ Writ of Possession

I intend to enforce the judgment or order by execution against goods, and/or against trespassers in the High Court and require this Certificate for this purpose.

....

signed - (Creditor/Creditor's solicitor)
(Claimant/Claimant's solicitor)

....date

Part 1

Date of judgment or order 28.01.08

Total amount of judgment *including any costs* 805.88

or

Details of order for possession *including any costs*

Total amount of interest accrued at the rate of _____ per day to date *(if any)*

Part 2 ***(for court use only)***

I certify that this is a true extract of the court record in this case.

Seal

Order for enforcement in the High Court by

☐ Writ of Fieri Facias

☐ Writ of Possession

made on (date)..

....An Officer of the Court

Please Note:

This judgment or order has been sent to the High Court for enforcement by (Writ of Fieri Facias) (Writ of Possession against trespassers) only.

The county court claim has not been transferred to the High Court. Applications for other methods of enforcement or ancillary applications must be made to the county court in which the judgment or order was made, unless the case has since been transferred to a different court, in which case it must be made to that court.

The court office at

is open between 10 am and 4 pm Monday to Friday. When corresponding with the court, please address forms or letters to the Court Manager and quote the claim number.

THE ACTION DEPARTMENT of the High Court is open between 10am and 4.30pm. All correspondence should be sent to the Court Manager, Action Department, Royal Courts of Justice, Strand, London WC2A 2LL

N293A Combined certificate of judgment and request for writ of fieri facias or writ of possession (04.04)

/ continued overleaf

Part 3

In the High Court of Justice

Queen's Bench Division

(Sent from the Northampton County Court by Certificate dated the day of)

High Court Enforcement Number

County Court Claim Number

Address of (Debtor)
(property of which possession is to be given)

3 CUCKOO LANE
BRAINTREE
ESSEX
CM6 3RT

Seal a Writ of (Fieri Facias)(Possession) directed to the:

To: " CLAIRE SANDBROOK, an enforcement officer authorised to enforce writs of execution from the High Court'.

Or,

'The enforcement officers authorised to enforce writs of execution from the High Court who are assigned to the district of [1] ____________ in England and Wales'.

Note: If you have chosen this option you must send this writ to the National Information Centre for Enforcement for allocation.

against MARGOT LEDBETTER

for: ***(Complete A, B, C as approriate)***

A. the sum of:

(a) debt	£805.88
(b) costs and interest	£101.75
(c) Subsequent costs *(if any)*	£

B. and interest thereon at 8 ....% per annum from the date of transfer and costs of execution

C. possession of

and £ for costs.

Signed

Address for service
LA LAW SOLICITORS, BOSTON HOUSE, NEW STREET, NOTTINGHAM, NN4 8SD

Date

Guidance Notes

Enforcement in the High Court of county court judgments or orders.

The practice for the enforcement in the High Court of those county court judgments or orders to which Article 8(A) and (B) of the High Court and County Court Jurisdiction Order 1991 applies shall be as follows:

1. The applicant shall present to the judgment counter clerk a certificate of judgment of the county court sealed with the seal of that court, setting out details of the judgment or order to be enforced, together with a copy of the same. There is no fee payable on registration.

2. The judgment counter clerk will check that the certificate has been signed by an officer of the issuing court (a rubber stamp is not sufficient), dated and that the certificate complies with CCR 0.22, r8 (1A) (Sched. 2 to the CPR), and in particular with the requirement that on its face it states that it is granted for the purpose of enforcing the judgment or order by execution against goods or for possession against trespassers in the High Court.

3. Provided that paragraphs 1 and 2 have been complied with, the counter clerk will:-
   (a) Allocate a reference number, and year and endorse that on the top right hand corner of the certificate and copy.
   (b) Date and seal the certificate and copy. Return the original to the applicant who should send the writ to the appropriate enforcement officer or the National Information Centre for Enforcement for allocation and retain a copy for the court records.

4. The Certificate shall be treated for enforcement purposes as a High Court judgment or order and interest at the appropriate rate shall run from the date of the certificate. Such interest as claimed on the judgment in the county court should be incorporated in the judgment as above.

5. The title of all subsequent documents shall be as follows:-

IN THE HIGH COURT OF JUSTICE — High Court No.
QUEEN'S BENCH DIVISION — County Court Claim No
(Sent from the County Court by Certificate dated the day of)

A.B.
Claimant

C.D.
Defendant

6. When the appropriate fee is paid and a writ of *fieri facias* or possession is issued, the Certificate of Judgment retained by the applicant shall be date sealed by the counter clerk on the bottom left hand corner.

7. **Any application for a stay of execution should be made by application notice in the High Court returnable before a Queen's Bench Master. All other applications for enforcement or ancillary relief must be made to the county court in which the judgment or order was made, unless the case has since been transferred to a different court, in which case that court.**

R L Turner, Senior Master
Queen's Bench Division

[1] This should reflect the Districts as set out in the High Court Enforcement Officers Regulation 2004

No. 53 - Writ of fieri facias

In the High Court of Justice
[ ] Division
[ ] District Registry
High Court Claim No.
[County Court Claim No.]

[Sent from the [ ] County Court by Certificate dated]

Claimant

Defendant

ELIZABETH THE SECOND, by the Grace of God, of the United Kingdom of Great Britain and Northern Ireland and of Our other realms and territories Queen, Head of the Commonwealth, Defender of the Faith.

TO: *"........, an enforcement officer authorised to enforce writs of execution issued from the High Court."*
Or,
"The enforcement officers authorised to enforce writs of execution issued from the High Court who are assigned to the district of[1] .... in England & Wales.

[**Note** If you have chosen this option you must send this writ to the National Information Centre for Enforcement for allocation.]

IN THIS CLAIM a Judgment or Order was made as set out in the Schedule.

YOU ARE NOW COMMANDED to seize in execution the goods, chattels and other property of the defendant authorised by law and raise therefrom the sums detailed in the Schedule, [together with fees and charges to which you are entitled]. And immediately after execution to pay the [claimant][defendant](*name*) the said sums and interest.

YOU ARE ALSO COMMANDED to indorse on this writ immediately after execution a statement of the manner in which you have executed it and send a copy of the statement to the [claimant][defendant]

THIS WRIT WAS ISSUED by the Central Office ~~[the District Registry]~~ of the High Court on (*date*) on the application of LA LAW SOLICITORS OF BOSTON HOUSE, NEW STREET, NOTTINGHAM, NN4 8SD ~~of (*address*) [agent for (*name*) of (*address*)]~~ solicitor for [the claimant] ~~[or the claimant (*name*) in person] who resides at (*address*)~~.

WITNESS (name) Lord High Chancellor of Great Britain, the (date)

The address[es] for enforcement are (give address[es] including county and postcode).
3 CUCKOO LANE
BRAINTREE
ESSEX
CM6 3RT

SCHEDULE

1. Date of Judgment or Order: 28th JANUARY 2008	
2. Amount of Judgment or Order (including interest awarded by Judgment or Order)	£805.88
3. Fixed costs on Judgment or Order	£
4. Assessed costs (if any) [by costs certificate dated (date)]	£
5. (If sent from county court by certificate) Interest[2] post-Judgment or Order on county court judgment or order over £5,000) until date of certificate	£
6. **LESS** credits or payments received since Judgment or Order	£
Sub Total	**£805.88**
7. Costs of execution	£101.75
Total	**£907.63**

Together with: -
A. Judgment interest[3] at [8]% from;_________20__
date of Judgment on sub-total above, or
(if sent from county court by certificate) date of county court certificate on paragraphs 1,2 and 3 above until payment,
B. Fees and Charges to which you are entitled (where appropriate).

1 This should reflect the Districts as set out in the High Court Enforcement Officers Regulation 2004
2 Interest under s.74 of the County Courts Act 1984
3 S.17 Judgments Act 1838

Application for order that debtor attend court for questioning

Click here to reset form

In the NORTHAMPTON COUNTY COURT	Claim No. 8NN123456
	Appn. No.
TOM GOOD T/A GOOD FOOD & MANURE	Claimant
MARGOT LEDBETTER	Defendant

The [claimant] [defendant] ('the judgment creditor') applies for an order that the [defendant] [claimant] ('the judgment debtor') attend court to provide information about the judgment debtor's means and any other information needed to enforce the judgment or order given on 28TH JANUARY 20 08 [by the in claim no.].

1. Judgment debtor

The judgment debtor is MARGOT LEDBETTER
whose address is 3 CUCKOO LANE, BRAINTREE, ESSEX
Postcode CM6 3RT

2. Judgment debt or order

[The judgment or order required the judgment debtor to pay £ 805.88 (including any costs and interest). The amount now owing is £805.88 [which includes further interest payable on the judgment debt]].

[The judgment or order required the judgment debtor to]

Note:

Questioning and documents

Questioning will be by a court officer unless a judge agrees there are compelling reasons for questioning to take place before a judge. Normally the court officer will ask the questions set out in Form EX140 and the judgment debtor will be told to produce all relevant documents including:

- pay slips
- bank statements
- building society books
- share certificates
- rent book
- mortgage statement
- hire purchase and similar agreements
- court orders
- any other outstanding bills
- electricity, gas, water and council tax bills for the past year.

and in the case of a business

- bills owed to it
- 2 years' accounts
- current management accounts.

Complete sections 3,4 and 5 only if applicable.
The statement of truth overleaf must be completed.

3. [Attached is a list of questions which the judgment creditor wishes the court officer to ask the judgment debtor in addition to those in Form EX140.]

4. [Attached is a list of documents which the judgment creditor wishes the judgment debtor to be ordered to produce in addition to those listed in the note above.]

5. [The judgment creditor requests that the judgment debtor be questioned by the judgment creditor before a judge. The reason for this request is

]

Statement of Truth

*(I believe)(The judgment creditor believes) that the facts stated in this application form are true.
* I am duly authorised by the judgment creditor to sign this statement.

signed ____________________ date ____________________

(Judgment creditor)(Litigation friend(where judgment creditor is a child or a patient)*)(Judgment creditor's solicitor)
**delete as appropriate*

Full name JOE BLOGGS

Name of judgment creditor's solicitor's firm LA LAW SOLICITORS

position or office held SOLICITOR
(if signing on behalf of firm or company)

Judgment creditor's or judgment creditor's solicitor's address to which documents should be sent.

LA LAW SOLICITORS
BOSTON HOUSE
NEW STREET
NOTTINGHAM

Postcode NN4 8SD

Tel. no. 01357 556442

if applicable	
Ref. no.	JB/GOOD
fax no.	01357 84621
DX no.	65432 NOTTINGHAM
e-mail	

List of documents: standard disclosure

Notes

- The rules relating to standard disclosure are contained in Part 31 of the Civil Procedure Rules.
- Documents to be included under standard disclosure are contained in Rule 31.6
- A document has or will have been in your control if you have or have had possession, or a right of possession, of it **or** a right to inspect or take copies of it.

In the	NORTHAMPTON
Claim No.	8NN123456
Claimant (including ref)	TOM GOOD T/A GOOD FOOD & MANURE
Defendant (including ref)	MARGOT LEDBETTER
Date	

Click here to clear all fields

Click here to print form

Disclosure Statement

I, the above named

☑ Claimant ☐ Defendant

☐ Party (if party making disclosure is a company, firm or other organisation identify here who the person making the disclosure statement is and why he is the appropriate person to make it)

state that I have carried out a reasonable and proportionate search to locate all the documents which I am required to disclose under the order made by the court on (date of order) JANUARY 10, 2008

☑ I did not search for documents:-

☑ pre-dating JANUARY 1, 2007

☑ located elsewhere than

WITHIN MY OWN FILING SYSTEM

☐ in categories other than

☐ for electronic documents

☑ I carried out a search for electronic documents contained on or created by the following:
(list what was searched and extent of search)

CREDIT CONTROL SYSTEM

☑ I did not search for the following:-

☑ documents created before JANUARY 1, 2007

documents contained on or created by the ☑ Claimant ☐ Defendant

☐ PCs	☑ portable data storage media
☐ databases	☑ servers
☑ back-up tapes	☑ off-site storage
☑ mobile phones	☑ laptops
☑ notebooks	☑ handheld devices
☑ PDA devices	

documents contained on or created by the ☑ Claimant ☐ Defendant

☑ mail files	☑ document files
☑ calendar files	☑ web-based applications
☐ spreadsheet files	☑ graphic and presentation files

documents other than by reference to the following keyword(s)/concepts
(delete if your search was not confined to specific keywords or concepts)

I certify that I understand the duty of disclosure and to the best of my knowledge I have carried out that duty. I further certify that the list of documents set out in or attached to this form, is a complete list of all documents which are or have been in my control and which I am obliged under the order to disclose.

I understand that I must inform the court and the other parties immediately if any further document required to be disclosed by Rule 31.6 comes into my control at any time before the conclusion of the case.

☐ I have not permitted inspection of documents within the category or class of documents (as set out below) required to be disclosed under Rule 31(6)(b)or (c) on the grounds that to do so would be disproportionate to the issues in the case.

Signed ______________ **Date** ______________

(Claimant)(Defendant)('s litigation friend)

List and number here, in a convenient order, the documents (or bundles of documents if of the same nature, e.g. invoices) in your control, which you do not object to being inspected. Give a short description of each document or bundle so that it can be identified, and say if it is kept elsewhere i.e. with a bank or solicitor

I have control of the documents numbered and listed here. I do not object to you inspecting them/producing copies.

1. Copy invoice dated June 16, 2007.
2. Copy letter from claimant's solicitors to the defendant dated July 28, 2007.

List and number here, as above, the documents in your control which you object to being inspected. (Rule 31.19)

I have control of the documents numbered and listed here, but I object to you inspecting them:

1. Correspondence between claimant and the claimant's solicitor.

Say what your objections are

I object to you inspecting these documents because:

They are by their very nature privileged.

List and number here, the documents you once had in your control, but which you no longer have. For each document listed, say when it was last in your control and where it is now.

I have had the documents numbered and listed below, but they are no longer in my control.

1. The originals of those documents listed above.

Click here to reset form | Click here to print form

Allocation questionnaire

To be completed by, or on behalf of,

TOM GOOD T/A GOOD FOOD & MANURE

who is [1st][2nd][3rd][ ][Claimant][Defendant] [Part 20 claimant] in this claim

Name of court	NORTHAMPTON COUNTY COURT
Claim No.	8NN123456
Last date for filing with court office	

Please read the notes on page six before completing the questionnaire.

You should note the date by which it must be returned and the name of the court it should be returned to since this may be different from the court where the proceedings were issued.

If you have settled this claim (or if you settle it on a future date) and do not need to have it heard or tried, you must let the court know immediately.

Have you sent a copy of this completed form to the other party(ies)? ☑ Yes ☐ No

A Settlement

Under the Civil Procedure Rules parties should make every effort to settle their case before the hearing. This could be by discussion or negotiation (such as a roundtable meeting or settlement conference) or by a more formal process such as mediation. The court will want to know what steps have been taken. Settling the case early can save costs, including court hearing fees.

For legal representatives only

I confirm that I have explained to my client the need to try to settle; the options available; and the possibility of costs sanctions if they refuse to try to settle. ☑

For all

Your answers to these questions may be considered by the court when it deals with the questions of costs: see Civil Procedure Rules Part 44.3 (4).

1. Given that the rules require you to try to settle the claim before the hearing, do you want to attempt to settle at this stage? ☐ Yes ☑ No
2. If Yes, do you want a one month stay? ☐ Yes ☐ No
3. Would you like the court to arrange a mediation appointment? ☐ Yes ☑ No
   (A fee will be payable to the mediation provider appointed by the National Mediation Helpline.)
4. If you answered 'No' to question 1, please state below the reasons why you consider it inappropriate to try to settle the claim at this stage.

Reasons:

Full details regarding the debt have already been provided to the defendant and attempts have been made to settlement this matter before proceedings were issued. The defendant has failed to respond to any previous attempts to settle and it is felt that any stay granted now would not result in a settlement due to the defendant's lack of response.

B Location of trial

Is there any reason why your claim needs to be heard at a particular court? ☐ Yes ☑ No

If Yes, say which court and why?

C Pre-action protocols

You are expected to comply with the relevant pre-action protocol.

Have you done so? ☐ Yes ☑ No

If No, explain why?

No pre-action protocol exists for this claim. However, full details of the claim have been provided to the defendant and the opportunity to settle this case have already been given to the defendant before proceedings were issued.

D Case management information

What amount of the claim is in dispute? £781.64

Applications

Have you made any application(s) in this claim? ☐ Yes ☑ No

If Yes, what for? (e.g. summary judgment, add another party) For hearing on

Witnesses

So far as you know at this stage, what witnesses of fact do you intend to call at the trial or final hearing including, if appropriate, yourself?

Witness name	Witness to which facts
TOM GOOD	CONTRACT AND SUPPLY OF GOODS
MARGERY MOUNTSHAFT	BUSINESS ENTITY

Experts

Do you wish to use expert evidence at the trial or final hearing? ☐ Yes ☑ No

Have you already copied any experts' report(s) to the other party(ies)? ☐ None yet obtained ☐ Yes ☐ No

Do you consider the case suitable for a single joint expert in any field? ☐ Yes ☐ No

Please list any single joint experts you propose to use and any other experts you wish to rely on. Identify single joint experts with the initials 'SJ' after their name(s).

Expert's name	Field of expertise (eg. orthopaedic surgeon, surveyor, engineer)

Do you want your expert(s) to give evidence orally at the trial or final hearing? ☐ Yes ☐ No

If Yes, give the reasons why you think oral evidence is necessary:

Track

Which track do you consider is most suitable for your claim? Tick one box

☑ small claims track
☐ fast track
☐ multi-track

If you have indicated a track which would not be the normal track for the claim, please give brief reasons for your choice

E Trial or final hearing

How long do you estimate the trial or final hearing will take?

days	4 hours	minutes

Are there any days when you, an expert or an essential witness will not be able to attend court for the trial or final hearing? ☐ Yes ☑ No

If Yes, please give details

Name	Dates not available

F Proposed directions *(Parties should agree directions wherever possible)*

Have you attached a list of the directions you think appropriate for the management of the claim? ☐ Yes ☑ No

If Yes, have they been agreed with the other party(ies)? ☐ Yes ☐ No

G Costs

*Do **not** complete this section if you have suggested your case is suitable for the small claims track **or** you have suggested one of the other tracks and you do not have a solicitor acting for you.*

What is your estimate of your costs incurred to date? £

What do you estimate your overall costs are likely to be? £

In substantial cases these questions should be answered in compliance with CPR Part 43

H Fee

Have you attached the fee for filing this allocation questionnaire? ☐ Yes ☑ No

An allocation fee is payable if your claim or counterclaim exceeds £1,500.

Additional fees will be payable at further stages of the court process.

I Other information

Have you attached documents to this questionnaire? ☐ Yes ☑ No

Have you sent these documents to the other party(ies)? ☐ Yes ☑ No

If Yes, when did they receive them?

Do you intend to make any applications in the immediate future? ☐ Yes ☑ No

If Yes, what for?

In the space below, set out any other information you consider will help the judge to manage the claim.

Signed

[Counsel] [Solicitor] [for the][1st][2nd][3rd][ ]
[Claimant] [Defendant] [Part 20 claimant]

Date

Please enter your name, reference number and full postal address including (if appropriate) details of telephone, DX, fax or e-mail

Postcode NN4 8SD

If applicable	
Telephone no.	01357 556442
Fax no.	01357 84621
DX no.	65432 NOTTINGHAM
Your ref.	JB/GOOD

E-mail

Click here to reset form | Click here to print form

Notes for completing an allocation questionnaire

- If the claim is not settled, a judge must allocate it to an appropriate case management track. To help the judge choose the most just and cost-effective track, you must now complete the attached questionnaire.
- If you fail to return the allocation questionnaire by the date given, the judge may make an order which leads to your claim or defence being struck out, or hold an allocation hearing. If there is an allocation hearing the judge may order any party who has not filed their questionnaire to pay, immediately, the costs of that hearing.
- Use a separate sheet if you need more space for your answers marking clearly which section the information refers to. You should write the claim number on it, and on any other documents you send with your allocation questionnaire. Please ensure they are firmly attached to it.
- The letters below refer to the sections of the questionnaire and tell you what information is needed.

A Settlement

Under the Civil Procedure Rules parties should make every effort to settle their case before the hearing. This could be by discussion or negotiation (such as a roundtable meeting or settlement conference) or by a more formal process such as mediation. The court will want to know what steps have been taken. If you think that it would be worthwhile you and the other party trying to negotiate a settlement at this stage you should tick the 'Yes' box. The court may order a stay, whether or not all the other parties to the claim agree. Even if you are requesting a stay, you should still complete the rest of the questionnaire.

More information about settlement options is available in the Legal Services Commission leaflet 'Alternatives to Court' free from any county court or the LSC leaflet line on 0845 3000 343. If you would like to find out more about mediation, and the fees charged, contact the National Mediation Helpline on 0845 60 30 809 or go to www.nationalmediationhelpline.com. Although you may appoint a mediator of your choice, if you would like the court to arrange a mediation for you please tick 'Yes'. By ticking this box you are consenting to your contact details being passed via the Helpline to an accredited external mediation provider.

B Location of trial

High Court cases are usually heard at the Royal Courts of Justice or certain Civil Trial Centres. Fast or multi-track trials may be dealt with at a Civil Trial Centre or at the court where the claim is proceeding.

C Pre-action protocols

Before any claim is started, the court expects you to have complied with the relevant pre-action protocol, and to have exchanged information and documents relevant to the claim to assist in settling it. To find out which protocol is relevant to your claim see: http://www.justice.gov.uk/civil/procrules_fin/menus/protocol.htm

D Case management information

Applications

It is important for the court to know if you have already made any applications in the claim, what they are for and when they will be heard. The outcome of the applications may affect the case management directions the court gives.

Witnesses

Remember to include yourself as a witness of fact, if you will be giving evidence.

Experts

Oral or written expert evidence will only be allowed at the trial or final hearing with the court's permission. The judge will decide what permission it seems appropriate to give when the claim is allocated to track. Permission in small claims track cases will only be given exceptionally.

Track

The basic guide by which claims are normally allocated to a track is the amount in dispute, although other factors such as the complexity of the case will also be considered. Leaflet EX305 - The Fast Track and the Multi-track, explains this in greater detail.

E Trial or final hearing

You should enter only those dates when you, your expert(s) or essential witness(es) will not be able to attend court because of holiday or other commitments.

F Proposed directions

Attach the list of directions, if any, you believe will be appropriate to be given for the management of the claim. Agreed directions on fast and multi-track cases should be based on the forms of standard directions set out in the practice direction to CPR Part 28 and form PF52.

G Costs

Only complete this section if you are a solicitor and have suggested the claim is suitable for allocation to the fast or multi-track.

H Fee

For more information about court fees please go our website www.hmcourts-service.gov.uk or pick up a fees leaflet EX50 from any county court. If you cannot afford the fee, you may be eligible for remission of the fee. More details can be found in the leaflet EX160A, which can be downloaded from our website or you can pick up a copy from any county court.

I Other Information

Answer the questions in this section. Decide if there is any other information you consider will help the judge to manage the claim. Give details in the space provided referring to any documents you have attached to support what you are saying.

Listing questionnaire (Pre-trial checklist)

Click here to clear all fields

To be completed by, or on behalf of,

TOM GOOD T/A GOOD FOOD & MANURE

who is [1st][2nd][3rd][ ][Claimant][Defendant] [Part 20 claimant][Part 20 defendant] in this claim

In the	NORTHAMPTON COUNTY COURT
Claim No.	8NN123456
Last date for filing with court office	MARCH 18, 2008
Date(s) fixed for trial or trial period	

This form must be **completed** and **returned** to the court no later than the date given above. If not, your statement of case may be struck out or some other sanction imposed.

If the claim has settled, or settles before the trial date, you must let the court know immediately.

Legal representatives only: You must **attach** estimates of costs incurred to date, and of your likely overall costs. In substantial cases, these should be provided in compliance with CPR Part 43.

For multi-track claims only, you must also **attach** a proposed timetable for the trial itself.

A Confirmation of compliance with directions

1. I confirm that I have complied with those directions already given which require action by me. ☑ Yes ☐ No

If you are unable to give confirmation, state which directions you have still to comply with and the date by which this will be done.

Directions	Date

2. I believe that additional directions are necessary before the trial takes place. ☐ Yes ☑ No

If Yes, you should attach an application and a draft order.

Include in your application all directions needed to enable the claim ***to be tried on the date, or within the trial period, already fixed.*** *These should include any issues relating to experts and their evidence, and any orders needed in respect of directions still requiring action by any other party.*

3. Have you agreed the additional directions you are seeking with the other party(ies)? ☐ Yes ☑ No

B Witnesses

1. How many witnesses (including yourself) will be giving evidence on your behalf at the trial? *(Do not include experts - see Section C)* 2

Continued over

Witnesses continued

2. If the trial date is not yet fixed, are there any days within the trial period you or your witnesses would wish to avoid if possible? *(Do not include experts - see Section C)*

Please give details

Name of witness	Dates to be avoided, if possible	Reason

Please specify any special facilities or arrangements needed at court for the party or any witness (e.g. witness with a disability).

3. Will you be providing an interpreter for any of your witnesses? ☐ Yes ☑ No

C Experts

You are reminded that you may not use an expert's report or have your expert give oral evidence unless the court has given permission. If you do not have permission, you must make an application (see section A2 above)

1. Please give the information requested for your expert(s)

Name	Field of expertise	Joint expert?	Is report agreed?	Has permission been given for oral evidence?
		☐Yes ☐No	☐Yes ☐No	☐Yes ☐No
		☐Yes ☐No	☐Yes ☐No	☐Yes ☐No
		☐Yes ☐No	☐Yes ☐No	☐Yes ☐No

2. Has there been discussion between experts? ☐ Yes ☐ No

3. Have the experts signed a joint statement? ☐ Yes ☐ No

4. If your expert is giving oral evidence and the trial date is not yet fixed, is there any day within the trial period which the expert would wish to avoid, if possible? ☐ Yes ☐ No

If Yes, please give details

Name	Dates to be avoided, if possible	Reason

D Legal representation

1. Who will be presenting your case at the trial? ☐ You ☑ Solicitor ☐ Counsel

2. If the trial date is not yet fixed, is there any day within the trial period that the person presenting your case would wish to avoid, if possible? ☐ Yes ☑ No

If Yes, please give details

Name	Dates to be avoided, if possible	Reason

E The trial

1. Has the estimate of the time needed for trial changed? ☐ Yes ☑ No

If Yes, say how long you estimate the whole trial will take, including both parties' cross-examination and closing arguments ☐ days ☐ hours ☐ minutes

2. If different from original estimate have you agreed with the other party(ies) that this is now the **total** time needed? ☐ Yes ☐ No

3. Is the timetable for trial you have attached agreed with the other party(ies)? ☐ Yes ☐ No

Fast track cases only

The court will normally give you 3 weeks notice of the date fixed for a fast track trial unless, in exceptional circumstances, the court directs that shorter notice will be given.

Would you be prepared to accept shorter notice of the date fixed for trial? ☐ Yes ☐ No

F Document and fee checklist

Tick as appropriate

I attach to this questionnaire -

☐ An application and fee for additional directions
☐ A proposed timetable for trial
☐ A draft order
☐ An estimate of costs
☐ Listing fee

Signed

[Counsel][Solicitor][for the][1st][2nd][3rd][ ]
[Claimant][Defendant]
[Part 20 claimant][Part 20 defendant]

Date

Please enter your [firm's] name, reference number and full postal address including (if appropriate) details of DX, fax or e-mail

LA LAW SOLICITORS, BOSTON HOUSE, NEW STREET, NOTTINGHAM

Postcode NN4 8SD

Tel. no.	01357 556442	DX no.	65432 NOTTINGHAM	E-mail	
Fax no.	01357 84621	Ref. no.	JB/GOOD		

3 of 3

Click here to reset form | Click here to print form

Application notice

For help in completing this form please read the notes for guidance form N244Notes.

Name of court NORTHAMPTON COUNTY COURT	
Claim no.	8NN123456
Warrant no. (if applicable)	
Claimant's name (including ref.)	TOM GOOD T/A GOOD FOOD & MANURE JB/GOOD
Defendant's name (including ref.)	MARGOT LEDBETTER
Date	

1. What is your name or, if you are a solicitor, the name of your firm?

2. Are you a ☐ Claimant ☐ Defendant ☑ Solicitor
   ☐ Other *(please specify)*

   If you are a solicitor whom do you represent? CLAIMANT

3. What order are you asking the court to make and why?

   ORDER FOR SUMMARY JUDGMENT AS THE DEFENDANT'S DEFENCE HAS NO REAL PROSPECTS OF SUCCESS

4. Have you attached a draft of the order you are applying for? ☐ Yes ☑ No

5. How do you want to have this application dealt with? ☑ at a hearing ☐ without a hearing ☐ at a telephone hearing

6. How long do you think the hearing will last? [ ] Hours [30] Minutes

   Is this time estimate agreed by all parties? ☐ Yes ☑ No

7. Give details of any fixed trial date or period: NONE

8. What level of Judge does your hearing need? DISTRICT JUDGE

9. Who should be served with this application? DEFENDANT

10. What information will you be relying on, in support of your application?

☐ the attached witness statement

☐ the statement of case

☑ the evidence set out in the box below

If necessary, please continue on a separate sheet.

1. The defendant has stated in their claim that they were not aware that the goods had been supplied in a business capacity and have stated that they considered the goods were a gift.

2. The claimant is able to demonstrate that the defendant has been provided with goods previously in a business capacity and previously paid the invoices rendered in respect of those goods.

3. The claimant is able to produce witness statements from other customers to confirm and verify the claimant's business identity.

4. The defendant has no real prospect of successful defending the claim based upon the evidence against her.

Statement of Truth

(I believe) (The applicant believes) that the facts stated in this section (and any continuation sheets) are true.

Signed ______________________ Dated ______________________

Applicant('s Solicitor)('s litigation friend)

Full name JOE BLOGGS

Name of applicant's solicitor's firm LA LAW SOLICITORS

Position or office held SOLICITOR
(if signing on behalf of firm or company)

11. Signature and address details

Signed ______________________ Dated ______________________

Applicant('s Solicitor)('s litigation friend)

Position or office held SOLICITOR
(if signing on behalf of firm or company)

Applicant's address to which documents about this application should be sent

LA LAW SOLICITORS
BOSTON HOUSE
NEW STREET
NOTTINGHAM

Postcode N N 4 8 S D

If applicable	
Phone no.	01357 556442
Fax no.	01357 846442
DX no.	65432 NOTTINGHAM
Ref no.	JB/GOOD

E-mail address	

Click here to print form

Application Notice (Form N244) – Notes for Guidance

Court Staff cannot give legal advice. If you need information or advice on a legal problem you can contact Community Legal Service Direct on 0845 345 4 345 or www.clsdirect.org.uk, or a Citizens Advice Bureau. Details of your local offices and contact numbers are available via their website www.citizensadvice.org.uk

Paying the court fee
A court fee is payable depending on the type of application you are making. For example:

- To apply for judgment to be set aside
- To apply to vary a judgment or suspend enforcement
- To apply for a summons or order for a witness to attend
- To apply by consent, or without service of the application notice, for a judgment or order.

No fee is payable for an application by consent for an adjournment of a hearing if it is received by the court at least 14 days before the date of the hearing.

What if I cannot afford the fee?
If you show that a payment of a court fee would involve undue hardship to you, you may be eligible for a fee concession.

For further information, or to apply for a fee concession, ask court staff for a copy of the combined booklet and form EX160A - Court fees - Do I have to pay them? This is also available from any county court office, or a copy of the leaflet can be downloaded from our website www.hmcourts-service.gov.uk

Completing the form

Question 3
Set out what order you are applying for and why; e.g. to adjourn the hearing because..., to set aside a judgment against me because... etc.

Question 5
Most applications will require a hearing and you will be expected to attend. The court will allocate a hearing date and time for the application. Please indicate in a covering letter any dates that you are unavailable within the next six weeks.

The court will only deal with the application 'without a hearing' in the following circumstances.

- Where all the parties agree to the terms of the order being asked for;
- Where all the parties agree that the court should deal with the application without a hearing, or
- Where the court does not consider that a hearing would be appropriate.

Telephone hearings are only available in applications where at least one of the parties involved in the case is legally represented. Not all applications will be suitable for a telephone hearing and the court may refuse your request.

Question 6
If you do not know how long the hearing will take do not guess but leave these boxes blank.

Question 7
If your case has already been allocated a hearing date or trial period please insert details of those dates in the box.

Question 8
If your case is being heard in the High Court or a District Registry please indicate whether it is to be dealt with by a Master, District Judge or Judge.

Question 9
Please indicate in the box provided who you want the court to send a copy of the application to.

Question 10
In this section please set out the information you want the court to take account of in support of the application you are making.
If you wish to rely on:

- **a witness statement,** tick the first box and attach the statement to the application notice. A witness statement form is available on request from the court office.
- **a statement of case,** tick the second box if you intend to rely on your particulars of claim or defence in support of your application.
- **written evidence** on this form, tick the third box and enter details in the space provided. You must also complete the statement of truth. Proceedings for contempt of court may be brought against a person who signs a statement of truth without an honest belief in its truth.

Question 11
The application must be signed and include your current address and contact details. If you agree that the court and the other parties may communicate with you by Document Exchange, telephone, facsimile or email, complete the details

Before returning your form to the court

Have you:

- signed the form on page 2,
- enclosed the correct fee or an application for fee concession,
- made sufficient copies of your application and supporting documentation. You will need to submit one copy for each party to be served and one copy for the court.

IN THE NORTHAMPTON COUNTY COURT **CASE NO. 8NN123456**

B E T W E E N:

TOM GOOD
T/A GOOD FOOD & MANURE

Claimant

and

MARGOT LEDBETTER

Defendant

TRIAL BUNDLE INDEX

Description of Documents	Page No.
Pleadings	
Claim Form	1-2
Defence and Counterclaim	3-4
Defence to Counterclaim	5
Claimants Allocation Questionnaire	6-11
Statements	
Witness Statement of Tom Good	12-15
Documents	
Invoice No. A789 dated 30th June 2007	16

Record of examination
(Individual)

Click here to reset form

In the	
Claim No.	
Appn. No.	

Judgment Creditor:

Judgment Debtor:

1 Personal Information

Full Name

Your age?

Present address

National insurance no.

Are you ☐ married? ☐ single? ☐ separated? ☐ divorced? ☐ living with partner?

Phone numbers:

home

work

mobile

other

Do you intend moving to another address? ☐ Yes ☐ No

If Yes, what will your new address be and when are you moving?

Date

Do you have any dependant children? ☐ Yes ☐ No

If Yes, what are their names and ages?

Name	Age

Do you have other dependants living with you, *eg. elderly relatives?* ☐ Yes ☐ No

If Yes, what are their names and ages and to what extent are they dependant?

2 Employment Status

Are you ☐ employed? Go to section 3 below ☐ self employed? Go to section 4 page 3 ☐ unemployed? Go to section 5 page 5 ☐ retired? Go to section 6 page 5

3 Employment Details

What is your occupation?

Where is your place of work if different?

What is the name and address of your employer and your employee number?

employee number

What is your gross pay *ie. before tax, national insurance deductions?* £ per

What is your average take home pay including overtime and commission? £ per

Do you receive Working Tax Credit? ☐ Yes ☐ No

If Yes, how much? £ per

How often are you paid? ☐ weekly ☐ monthly ☐ other

On which day are you paid?

Is your pay paid ☐ in cash ☐ by cheque ☐ direct to bank or building society account?

If direct to bank or building society account what is the name and address of the branch and account number?

account number

Do you have any jobs other than your main job? ☐ Yes ☐ No

If Yes, ask for all the above details in relation to all other jobs and set out information below.

[Go to Section 7 page 5]

4 Self Employed

How long have you been self employed? ☐

What work do you do? ☐

What is the name of your business? ☐

Do you have business premises? eg. shop, yard, lockup ☐ Yes ☐ No

If Yes, what is their address? ☐

What is your annual turnover? £

What amount of profit did the business make over the last year? £

How much do you draw from the business? £ per

What were your total drawings in last 12 months? £

Are you a ☐ sole trader? ☐ partner? If a partner,

(a) How many partners are there? ☐

(b) What is your share of the partnership ? %

How many employees do you have? ☐

Do you complete Inland Revenue self assessment? ☐ Yes ☐ No

Do you have accounts? ☐ Yes ☐ No

Do you employ an accountant? ☐ Yes ☐ No

If Yes, what is the accountant's name and address? ☐

If you don't have an accountant are accounts audited by a third party? ☐ Yes ☐ No

If Yes,give name and address and say when audit takes place?

Date of audit

Will you allow the creditor to approach your accountant or auditor or Inland Revenue to verify the information you have given in this section? ☐ Yes ☐ No

Are you working on any contracts at the moment? ☐ Yes ☐ No

If Yes, give details below

Name and address of customer	Nature of work	Contract price £	Amount outstanding £	Date payment expected

Is any money still due to you for work already done? ☐ Yes ☐ No If Yes, give details below

Name and address of customer	Nature of work	Contract price £	Amount outstanding £	Date payment expected

If money (see above) is overdue what steps are you taking to recover it?

Do you have contracts for work in the future? ☐ Yes ☐ No If Yes, give details below

Name and address of customer	Nature of work	Expected price £

Go to Section 7 page 5

5 Unemployed

How long have you been unemployed? [ ]

What is your trade / training /profession? [ ]

What steps are you taking to obtain employment? [ ]

Do you have any outstanding job interviews? ☐ Yes ☐ No   If Yes, when? [ ]

What state benefits do you receive? *(Housing benefit, if any should be included section 8b on page 7)*

Type of benefit	Amount	Frequency of payment	DSS/BA ref.

Go to Section 7 below

6 Retired

When did you retire? [ ]

By whom are your pension(s) paid, how much is paid and when? *(include both state and private pensions)*

Pension from	Amount	Frequency of payment

Go to Section 7 below

7 Other Income

Is there anyone else in your household who is employed? *(Do not include tenants/lodgers. See section 8 on page 6)* ☐ Yes ☐ No

If Yes, how much do they contribute to the running of the home? £ per

What other state benefits do you receive? *(Housing benefit, if any should be included section 8b on page 7)*

Type of benefit	Amount	Frequency of payment	DSS/BA ref.

Go to Section 8 page 6

8 Residence

Is your home
- ☐ your own property? Go to 8a below
- ☐ lodgings? Go to 8b page 7
- ☐ rented from a council or housing association? Go to 8b page 7
- ☐ rented unfurnished from a private landlord? Go to 8b page 7
- ☐ rented furnished from a private landlord? Go to 8b page 7
- ☐ other ______ (*e.g. mobile home*) Go to 8b page 7

8a Your own property

Are you the sole owner? ☐ Yes ☐ No — If No, name joint owner(s) [ ]

Do you own the ☐ freehold? ☐ leasehold? — When did you buy the property? [ ]

Is your home a ☐ house? ☐ bungalow? ☐ flat?

Is it ☐ detached? ☐ semi-detached? ☐ terraced?

How many of the following rooms does it have? ☐ living rooms? ☐ kitchens? ☐ bedrooms? ☐ bath/shower rooms?

How much Council Tax do you pay per year? £

What was the purchase price of property? £ — What is its value now? £

Is your home mortgaged? ☐ Yes ☐ No — If Yes, what is the name and address of your mortgage lender? [ ]

How much are your mortgage payments per month? £ — What type of mortgage do you have? *eg. repayment, endowment etc.* [ ]

How long is the mortgage for? years — When did you take out the mortgage? [ ]

How much is currently owed under the mortgage? £ — Is some or all of the interest paid by the Benefits Agency? ☐ Yes ☐ No

If Yes, how much is paid each month? £

Do you let any part of your home? ☐ Yes ☐ No

If Yes, give names of the tenants/lodgers and details of rent received

Do you have any loans secured on your home? (e.g. further mortgage) ☐ Yes ☐ No

If Yes, give the same details as for the first mortgage

[Go to Section 9 page 8]

8b Rented property

Do you rent ☐ on your own? ☐ jointly?

What is the name and address of your landlord?

How long have you lived at the property? _____months _____years

Do you share parts of your home with someone unconnected with you? ☐ Yes ☐ No

Do you pay any additional service charges in connection with the premises? ☐ Yes ☐ No

If Yes, give details £ per

How much rent do <u>you</u> pay? £ per none ☐

How much Council Tax do <u>you</u> pay a year? £ none ☐

Do you sub-let any part of your home? ☐ Yes ☐ No

If Yes, give names of tenants/lodgers and details of rent received.

Do you receive housing benefit? ☐ Yes ☐ No

If Yes, give details £ per paid to

[Go to Section 9 page 8]

9 Savings, Investments and other Assets

Do you own any property other than your home? ☐ Yes ☐ No

If Yes, give the address and value and details of any mortgages and lettings

Do you have any bank, building society or other accounts? ☐ Yes ☐ No

If Yes, give details below

Name & Address of Bank Building Society	Account No.	Type of Account	Balance	Sole or joint A/c	Name(s) of joint account holder(s)

Do you have any shares, investments (eg. ISAs, Tessas etc.), insurance/assurance policies or premium bonds? ☐ Yes ☐ No

If Yes, give details below

Are you making contributions to a pension scheme? ☐ Yes ☐ No

If Yes, give details

Do you have any of the following items and how long have you had them?

	Age (years)	Is it owned by you, on hire purchase credit sale or rented?	If not owned by you, give; Name of Creditor	Amount still owed	Payments
☐ Microwave					
☐ Hi-fi / surround sound					
☐ Television (No._____)					
☐ Video					
☐ Camcorder					
☐ Computer					
☐ Dishwasher					
☐ Camera					
☐ Dining Room suite					
☐ Caravan					
☐ Mobile telephone					
☐ Musical instruments..					
☐ Other items....					

Do you own a motor vehicle? ☐ Yes ☐ No

If Yes, give age, make, model value and registration number. State whether it is owned by you, or subject to a hire purchase/ rental agreement.

Do you have any assets not previously mentioned? ☐ Yes ☐ No

If Yes, give details

Assets	Value

Does anyone owe you money, which is not a business debt or for work you have done? ☐ Yes ☐ No

If Yes, who owes you money and how much do they owe?

	Value

10 Other Debts or regular payments and court orders

Expenses
Do not include payments made by other members of your household out of their own income or priority debts listed opposite

Mortgage	£	per
Rent	£	per
Council tax	£	per
Gas	£	per
Electricity	£	per
Water charges	£	per
Housekeeping, food, school meals	£	per
Travelling expenses	£	per
Children's clothing	£	per
Maintenance/child support payments	£	per
Student loan repayments	£	per
Mail order payments	£	per
HP repayments	£	per
Digital/satellite TV subscriptions	£	per
Telephone	£	per
Mobile phone	£	per
Other expenses	£	per
(*not court orders, priority debts or credit debts listed left*)	£	per
	£	per
Total Expenses	**£**	**per**

Priority Debts
This section is for arrears only. DO NOT include regular expenses listed left

			Total arrears outstanding
Rent arrears	£	per	£
Mortgage arrears	£	per	£
Council tax/Community charge arrears	£	per	£
Water charge arrears	£	per	£
Fuel arrears: Gas	£	per	£
Electricity	£	per	£
Other	£	per	£
Maintenance arrears	£	per	£
Income tax	£	per	£
VAT	£	per	£
National Insurance	£	per	£
Others (*give details below*)	£	per	£
	£	per	£
	£	per	£
	£	per	£
Total Priority Debts	**£**	**per**	**£**

Have any court orders been made against you? ☐ Yes ☐ No If Yes, give details below

Name of court and case number	Date of Judgment or order	Amount of Judgment or order	Instalments payable per month	Name of creditor	Total still owed	Are payments up to date? (yes/no)	If no, how much in arrears?
	TOTALS						

Do you owe money on credit cards or any other loans (not mortage or business)? ☐ Yes ☐ No If Yes, give details below

Name of Creditor	Total amount owing	Instalments payable per month	Are payments up to date? (yes/no)	If no, how much in arrears?
TOTALS				

Have any bankruptcy proceedings been issued against you? ☐ Yes ☐ No

If Yes, what is the court name and case no.

Is the petition ☐ still pending? ☐ order made but discharged? ☐ order has been made but not discharged? ☐ other outcome? *(give details below)*

Has an Individual Voluntary Arrangement been made? ☐ Yes ☐ No

If Yes, give the date

If No, is there a current proposal for one? ☐ Yes ☐ No

Give details of Trustee/ Insolvency Practitioner/ Administrator, supervisor

10

11 Offer of Payment

Can you make an offer of payment? ☐ Yes ☐ No

If No, please explain why

What is your offer of payment?

Pay in full by ______ day of ______

Instalments of £ ______ per ______ to start on ______

Method of payment ☐ postal order ☐ cheque ☐ direct debit ☐ standing order ☐ payment book ☐ cash

I certify that this is a correct record of the answers I gave to the questions in this document.

Signed ______ Judgment Debtor
Print name ______
Date ______

The judgment debtor refused to sign this record of evidence.

Signed ______ Court Officer
Print name ______
Date ______

The following costs of the examination have been allowed and added to the judgment debt £ ______

12 Documents produced

The judgment debtor produced the following documents:

Affidavit
(order to attend for questioning and suspended committal order)

Sworn by JOE BLOGGS	
on FEBRUARY 17, 2008	
This is the 1st [ ] affidavit filed on behalf of the judgment creditor by this deponent on 20	
Claim No.	8NN123456
Appn. No.	
In the NORTHAMPTON County Court	

TOM GOOD T/A GOOD FOOD & MANURE -V- MARGOT LEDBETTER

Give full name, address and occupation (or description)

I, JOE BLOGGS, SOLICITOR

of L.A. LAW SOLICITORS, BOSTON HOUSE, NEW STREET, NOTTINGHAM, NN4 8SD

state on oath [on affirmation] that:

Part A Service

A1 I served the [order to attend court for questioning] [suspended committal order] upon MARGOT LEDBETTER , [the officer of] the judgment debtor named in the order, on FEBRUARY 10 20 08 , by delivering a copy to [him] [her] personally at
3 CUCKOO LANE, BRAINTREE, ESSEX, CM6 3RT

A2 (a) [I already knew the person served]

Delete or complete as appropriate to show how the person served was identified as the person named in the order

(b) [The person served admitted [his] [her] identity to me]

(c) [ ]

A3 A copy of the order marked 'A' is exhibited to this affidavit.

Part B Continuing Debt

B1 (a) I am the judgment creditor and the following statement[s] [is] [are] true to my own knowledge.

Complete either (a) or (b) as appropriate (b) I am the

of the judgment creditor and the following statement[s] [is] [are] true to the best of my knowledge and belief having enquired of the judgment creditor's staff and consulted its records

B2 The balance due under the judgment is £805.88

Part C Travel expenses

C1 (a) The person ordered to attend court has not requested payment of [his] [her] travelling expenses.

Complete either (a) or (b) as appropriate (b) On 20 , the person ordered to attend court requested payment of travelling expenses and, in accordance with that request, the sum of £ was paid to that person on 20 [in cash] [by cheque] [by postal order] sent by first class post.

Sworn [affirmed] at____________________

____

on____________________20___ } ____________________

before me____________________

an officer of the court appointed by the judge to take affidavits

Application for third party debt order

Click here to reset form

In the
NORTHAMPTON COUNTY COURT

Claim No.
8NN123456

Appn. No.

TOM GOOD T/A GOOD FOOD & MANURE
Claimant

MARGOT LEDBETTER
Defendant

LOADSAMONEY BUILDING SOCIETY
Third Party

The [claimant] [defendant] ('the judgment creditor') applies for an order that the third party pay to the judgment creditor the debt which the third party owes to the [defendant] [claimant] ('the judgment debtor') (or so much of it as is necessary to discharge the amount owing under the judgment or order given on JANUARY 28 20 08 [by the in claim no.] and the costs of this application).

1. **Judgment debtor**
The judgment debtor is MARGOT LEDBETTER
whose address is
3 CUCKOO LANE, BRAINTREE, ESSEX
Postcode CM6 3RT

2. **Judgment debt**
The judgment or order required the judgment debtor to pay £ 805.88 (including any costs and interest). The amount now due is £ 805.88 [which includes further interest].

☐ £ of the instalments due under the judgment or order has fallen due and remains unpaid.

☑ The judgment or order did not provide for payment by instalments.

3. **Third party**
The third party is within England and Wales and owes money to (or holds money to the credit of) the judgment debtor.

The third party is a bank or building society.
Its name is LOADSAMONEY BUILDING SOCIETY
Its head office address in England and Wales is:
8 POUND PLAZA, COLCHESTER, ESSEX, CO2 4BT

The branch at which the account is held is
☐ not known

☑ the whose address is 4 HIGH STREET, BRAINTREE, ESSEX, CM4 8GY

The account number is
☐ not known
☑ 456321

The sort code is
☐ not known
☑ 60-43-88

[The third party is not a bank or building society.

☐ the third party is

whose address in England and Wales is

4. **Other persons' interests**

The persons (in addition to the judgment debtor) who have a claim to the money owed by the third party are

☑ None

☐ The following: *(names and address(es))*

Information known about each person's claim:

5. **Sources and grounds of information**

The judgment creditor knowns or believes that the information in section 3 and 4 is correct because:

The judgment creditor kept a copy of a cheque used by the judgment debtor to pay a previous invoice.

6. **Other applications**

In respect of the judgment debt,

☑ the judgment creditor has made no other applications for third party debt orders.

☐ the judgment creditor has already made the following application(s) for third party debt order:

Details of application(s)

Third party's name

Address

Postcode

Statement of Truth

*I believe (the judgment creditor believes) that the facts stated in this application form are true.

*I am duly authorised by the judgment creditor to sign this statement

signed ______________________ date ______________

*(Judgment creditor)(Litigation friend *(where judgment creditor is a child or a patient)*)(Judgment creditor's solicitor)

**delete as appropriate*

Full name JOE BLOGGS

Name of judgment creditor's solicitor's firm LA LAW SOLICITORS

position or office held SOLICITOR *(if signing on behalf of a firm or company)*

Judgment creditor's or judgment creditor's solicitor's address to which documents should be sent.

L.A. LAW SOLICITORS
BOSTON HOUSE
NEW STREET
NOTTINGHAM
NN4 8SD

Postcode

if applicable

Ref. no.	JB/GOOD
fax no.	01357 84621
DX no.	65432 NOTTINGHAM
e-mail	
Tel. no.	01357 556442

Click here to clear your data after printing

IN THE NORTHAMPTON **COUNTY COURT**

BETWEEN TOM GOOD T/A GOOD FOOD & MANURE . . . . . . CLAIMANT

AND MARGOT LEDBETTER . . . . . . DEFENDANT

To the Court Manager of the NORTHAMPTON County Court

Please search your attachment of earnings order index and notify me whether any, and if so what, information is recorded in the name of
MARGOT LEDBETTER

whose address is
3 CUCKOO LANE, BRAINTREE, ESSEX, CM6 3RT

against whom I have obtained a judgment in the NORTHAMPTON COUNTY Court, under claim number 8NN123456

DATE

Signed
Claimant('s Solicitor)

Solicitor's Address LA LAW SOLICITORS, BOSTON HOUSE, NEW STREET, NOTTINGHAM, NN4 8SD

Solicitor's Ref:- JB/GOOD

To the Claimant('s Solicitor)
A search of the attachment of earnings order index has been made against the above named defendant and I certify that:-

(1) delete where inapplicable

(1) There are no subsisting entries.

(1) An attachment of earnings order in respect of a judgment debt is in force in the County Court. The normal deduction rate is £ per week/month (1) and the balance outstanding is £

(1) A priority attachment of earnings order in respect of a fine/maintenance order (1) is in force in the Court.

DATE

Court Manager

Click here to clear your text after printing

Request for Attachment of Earnings Order

to be completed and signed by the claimant or his solicitor and sent to the court with the appropriate fee

In the NORTHAMPTON **County Court**

Claim Number

1 Claimant's name and address

TOM GOOD T/A GOOD FOOD & MANURE
1 CUCKOO LANE
BRAINTREE
ESSEX
CM6 3RT

2 Name and address for service and payment (if different from above) **Ref/Tel No.**

L.A. LAW SOLICITORS
BOSTON HOUSE
NEW STREET
NOTTINGHAM
NN4 8SD
JB/GOOD 01234 567890

For court use only

A/E application no

Issue date:

Hearing date:

on

at o'clock

at (address)

3 Defendant's name and address

MARGOT LEDBETTER
3 CUCKOO LANE
BRAINTREE
ESSEX
CM6 3RT

4 Judgment details

Court where judgment/order made if not court of issue: NORTAMPTON

5 Outstanding debt

Balance due at date of request* (excluding issue fee but including unsatisfied warrant costs)	805.88
Issue fee	65.00
AMOUNT NOW DUE	870.88

* you may also be entitled to interest to the date of request where judgment is for £5,000 or more, or is in respect of a debt which attracts contractual or statutory interest for late payment

I apply for an attachment of earnings order

I certify that the whole or part of any instalments due under the judgment or order have not been paid and the balance now due is as shown

Signed

Claimant(Claimants solicitor)

Date

6 Employment Details *(please give as much information as you can – it will help the court to make an order more quickly)*

Employer's name and address:

Greenfingers Nursery
High Street
Braintree
Essex

Defendant's place of work *(if different from employer's address)*: As above

The defendant is employed as: Florist Assistant

Works No / Pay Ref:

7 Other details

(Give any other details about the defendant's circumstances which may be relevant to the application)

Defendant works part time - 4 days per week

IMPORTANT
You must inform the court immediately of any payments you receive after you have sent this request to the court

N337 - w3 Request for attachment of earnings order (4.99)

Printed on behalf of The Court Service

Application for charging order on land or property

Click here to reset form

In the
NORTHAMPTON COUNTY COURT

Claim No.
8NN123456

Appn. No.

TOM GOOD T/A GOOD FOOD & MANURE

Claimant

MARGOT LEDBETTER

Defendant

The [claimant] [defendant] ('the judgment creditor') applies for an order imposing a charge on the interest of the [defendant] [claimant] ('the judgment debtor') in the land or property mentioned below to secure payment of the amount owing under the judgment or order given on JANUARY 28 20 08 [by the in claim no.].

1. Judgment debtor
The judgment debtor is
whose address is
3 CUCKOO LANE, BRAINTREE, ESSEX

Postcode CM6 3RT

2. Judgment debt
The judgment or order required the judgment debtor to pay £ 805.88 (including any costs and interest). The amount now owing is £ 805.88 [which includes further interest payable on the judgment debt].

☐ £ of the instalments due under the judgment or order has fallen due and remains unpaid.

☑ The judgment or order did not provide for payment by instalments.

3. The land or property
The address of the land or property upon which it is sought to impose a to charge is
3 CUCKOO LANE, BRAINTREE, ESSEX, CM7 8YG

[the title to which is registered at H. M. Land Registry under Title No. CM987654
An Office Copy of the Land Register entries for this title is attached.]

4. Judgment debtor's interest in the land or property
The judgment debtor is:

☐ the sole owner ☑ a joint owner ☐ a beneficiary under a trust

☑ This is shown by the Office Copy Land Register entries attached.

☐ The judgment creditor believes this to be so because

5. Other creditors

☐ The judgment creditor does not know of any other creditors of the judgment debtor.

☑ The judgment creditor knows of the following other creditors of the judgment debtor:
(names and addresses and, if known, nature of debt and amount)

6. Other persons to be served

☐ No other person has an interest in the property (including any co-owners, trustees and persons with rights of occupation).

☑ The following persons have or may have an interest in the property:
(name and address and, if known, nature of interest)

MONEY BANK, 1 THE HIGH STREET, STIRLING TOWN, ST2 8SS - REGISTERED CHARGE

JERRY LEDBETTER, 3 CUCKOO LANE, BRAINTREE, ESSEX, CM6 3RT - SPOUSE AND JOINT OWNER

7. Further information

The judgment creditor asks the court to take account of the following:

8. Sources of information *(Complete only where the judgment creditor is a firm or a company or other corporation)*

[The information in this application is given [by me] [by of who is the of the judgment creditor] after making proper enquiry of all persons within the judgment creditor's organisation who might have knowledge of the facts.]

Statement of Truth

*I believe (the judgment creditor believes) that the facts stated in this application form are true.
*I am duly authorised by the judgment creditor to sign this statement

signed ______________________ date 03.02.08

*(Judgment creditor)(Litigation friend *(where judgment creditor is a child or a patient)*)(Judgment creditor's solicitor)

**delete as appropriate*

Full name JOE BLOGGS

Name of judgment creditor's solicitor's firm LA LAW

position or office held SOLICITOR *(if signing on behalf of a firm or company)*

Judgment creditor's or judgment creditor's solicitor's address to which documents should be sent.

LA LAW SOLICITORS
BOSTON HOUSE
NEW STREET
NOTTINGHAM

Postcode

if applicable

Ref. no.	JB/GOOD
fax no.	01357 84621
DX no.	65432 NOTTINGHAM
e-mail	
Tel. no.	01357 556442

Click here to reset form | Click here to print form

Certificate of service

Name of court	Claim No.
NORTHAMPTON COUNTY CT	8NN123456
Name of Claimant	
TOM GOOD T/A GOOD FOOD & MANURE	
Name of Defendant	
MARGOT LEDBETTER	

On what day did you serve? 2 6 / 0 2 / 2 0 0 8

What documents did you serve?
Please attach copies of the documents you have not already filed with the court.
Application for charging order and interim charging order

On whom did you serve?
(If appropriate include their position e.g. partner, director).
1. MARGOT LEDBETTER 2. JERRY LEDBETTER 3. MONEY BANK

How did you serve the documents? - *please tick the appropriate box*

- [x] by first class post or other service which provides for delivery on the next business day
- [ ] by Document Exchange
- [ ] by delivering to or leaving at a permitted place *(see notes overleaf)*
- [ ] by fax machine (..........time sent, where document is other than a claim form) *(you may want to enclose a copy of the transmission sheet)*
- [ ] by personally handing it to or leaving it with (..............time left, where document is other than a claim form) *(please specify)*
- [ ] by other electronic means (................time sent, where document is other than a claim form) *(please specify)*
- [ ] by other means permitted by the court *(please specify)*

Give the address where service effected, include fax or DX number, e-mail address or other electronic identification
1&2 - 3 Cuckoo Lane, Braintree, Essex, CM6 3RT
3 - 1 The High Street, Stirling Town, ST2 8SS

Being the
- [ ] claimant's
- [x] defendant's
- [ ] solicitor's
- [ ] litigation friend
- [ ] usual residence
- [ ] last known residence
- [ ] place of business
- [ ] principal place of business
- [ ] last known place of business
- [ ] principal office of the partnership
- [ ] principal office of the corporation
- [ ] principal office of the company
- [x] other *(please specify)* Address given in Office Copy Entries

The date of service is *(see overleaf for guidance)* __/__/____

I believe that the facts stated in this certificate are true.

Full name JOE BLOGGS

Signed

(Claimant) (Defendant) ('s solicitor) ('s friend)

Position or office held SOLICITOR

(If signing on behalf of firm or company)

Date __/__/____

N215 Certificate of service (10.08)

Notes for guidance

Please note that these notes are only a guide and are not exhaustive. If you are in doubt you should refer to Part 6 of the rules

Where to serve	
Nature of party to be served	**Permitted place of service**
Individual	Usual or last known residence
Individual being sued in the name of a business	Usual or last known residence; **or** principle place of business or last known place of business
Individual being sued in the business name of a partnership	Usual or last known residence; **or** place of business or last known place of business of the partnership
Limited liability partnership	Principal office of the partnership; **or** any place of business of the partnership within the jurisdiction which has a real connection with the claim
Corporation (incorporated in England and Wales) other than a company	Principal office of the corporation; **or** any place within the jurisdiction where the corporation carries on its activities and which has a real connection with the claim
Company registered in England and Wales	Principal office of the company or corporation; **or** any place of business of the company within the jurisdiction which has a real connection with the claim
Any other company or corporation	Any place within the jurisdiction where the corporation carries on its activities; **or** any place of business of the company within the jurisdiction

Personal Service - A document is served personally on an individual by leaving it with that individual. A document is served personally on a company or other corporation by leaving it with a person holding a senior position within the company or corporation. In the case of a partnership, you must leave it with either a partner or a person who at the time of service has the control or management of the partnership business as its principal place of business.

Service on a solicitor - Where a solicitor is authorised to accept service, see CPR rule 6.7.

Deemed Service - Rule 6.26. A document which is served in accordance with these rules or any relevant practice direction shall be deemed to be served on the day shown in the following table.

Method of service	**Deemed day of service**
First class post or other service which provides for delivery on the next business day.	The second day after it was posted, left with, delivered to or collected by the relevant service provider provided that day is a business day; or if not, the next business day after that day
Document exchange	The second day after it was left with, delivered to or collected by the relevant service provider provided that day is a business day; or if not, the next business day after that day
Delivering the document to or leaving it at a permitted address	If it is delivered to or left at the permitted address on a business day before 4.30pm, on that day; or in any other case, on the next business day after that day
Fax	If the transmission of the fax is completed on a business day before 4.30pm, on that day; or in any other case, on the next business day after the day on which it was transmitted
Other electronic method	If the email or other electronic transmission is sent on a business day before 4.30pm, on that day; or in any other case, on the next business day after the day on which it was sent
Personal service	If the document is served personally before 4.30pm on a business day, it is served on that day; or in any other case, on the next business day after that day

In this context 'business day' means any day except Saturday, Sunday or a bank holiday; and 'bank holiday' includes Christmas Day and Good Friday.

Service of documents on children and protected parties - The rules relating to service on children and protected parties are contained in rule 6.13.

Claim Forms - The general rules about service are subject to the special rules about service of claim forms contained in rules 6.3 to 6.19.

Application to enter a restriction

Land Registry

RX1

If you need more room than is provided for in a panel, use continuation sheet CS and attach to this form.

1. **Administrative area and postcode** if known

2. **Title number(s)** CM987654

3. If you have already made this application by **outline application**, insert reference number:

4. **Property** *Insert address or other description.*

The restriction applied for is to affect *Place "X" in the appropriate box and complete as necessary.*

[x] the whole of each registered estate

[ ] the part(s) of the registered estate(s) shown on the attached plan by *State reference e.g. "edged red".*

[ ] the registered charge(s) dated in favour of referred to in the Charges Register

5. **Application and fee** *A fee calculator for all types of applications can be found on Land Registry's website at www.landregistry.gov.uk/fees*

Restriction Fee paid £ 40.00

Fee payment method: *Place "X" in the appropriate box.*

I wish to pay the appropriate fee payable under the current Land Registration Fee Order:

[x] by cheque or postal order, amount £ 40.00 made payable to "Land Registry".

[ ] by Direct Debit under an authorised agreement with Land Registry.

FOR OFFICIAL USE ONLY
Record of fee paid

Particulars of under/over payment

Fees debited £

Reference number

6. **Documents lodged with this application** *If this application is accompanied by either Form AP1 or FR1 please only complete the corresponding panel on Form AP1 or DL. Number the documents in sequence; copies should also be numbered and listed as separate documents, alternatively you may prefer to use Form DL. If you supply the original document and a certified copy, we shall assume that you request the return of the original; if a certified copy is not supplied, we may retain the original document and it may be destroyed.*

COPY INTERIM CHARGING ORDER

7. **The applicant is:** *Please provide the full name of the person applying for the restriction.*

The application has been lodged by:
Land Registry Key No. (if appropriate)
Name (if different from the applicant)
Address/DX No.

Reference JB/GOOD
E-mail

Telephone No. 01357 556442 | Fax No. 01357 84621

FOR OFFICIAL USE ONLY
Codes
Dealing

Status

8. Where you would like us to deal with someone else *We shall deal only with the applicant, or the person lodging the application if different, unless you place "X" against one or more of the statements below and give the necessary details.*

☐ Send title information document to the person shown below

☐ Raise any requisitions or queries with the person shown below

☐ Return original documents lodged with this form (see note in panel 6) to the person shown below
If this applies only to certain documents, please specify.

Name
Address/DX No.

Reference
E-mail

Telephone No.	Fax No.

9. Entitlement to apply for a restriction *Place "X" in the appropriate box.*

☐ The applicant is the registered proprietor of the registered estate/charge referred to in panel 4.

☐ The applicant is the person **entitled** to be registered as proprietor of the registered estate/charge referred to in panel 4. **Complete panel 12.**

☐ The consent of the registered proprietor of the registered estate/charge referred to in panel 4 accompanies this application or the applicant's conveyancer certifies that he holds this consent. **Complete panel 11.**

☐ The consent of the person **entitled** to be registered as proprietor of the registered estate/charge referred to in panel 4 accompanies this application or the applicant's conveyancer certifies that he holds this consent. **Complete panels 11 and 12.**

☒ Evidence that the applicant has sufficient interest in the making of the entry of the restriction applied for in panel 10 accompanies this application. **Complete panel 13.**

10. The applicant applies to enter the following restriction against the registered estate/charge referred to in panel 4: *Please set out the form of restriction required. Schedule 4 to the Land Registration Rules 2003 contains standard forms of restrictions. Use this form to apply for a standard form of restriction (as set out in Schedule 4 to the Land Registration Rules 2003) or, where appropriate, a restriction in another form. If the restriction is not a standard form of restriction, the registrar must be satisfied that the terms of the proposed restriction are reasonable and that applying the proposed restriction would be straightforward and not place an unreasonable burden on him. If the restriction requires notice to be given to a person, requires a person's consent or certificate or is a standard form restriction that refers to a named person,* ***include that person's address for service.***

11. Evidence of consent *Please complete this panel if instructed to do so in panel 9. Place "X" in the appropriate box.*

☐ The [registered proprietor of][person entitled to be registered as the proprietor of] the registered estate/charge referred to in panel 4 consents to the entry of the restriction and that person or their conveyancer has completed panel 15.

☐ I am the applicant's conveyancer and certify that I hold the consent referred to in panel 9.

☐ The consent referred to in panel 9 is contained on page ___ of the document numbered ___ referred to in [panel 6][Form AP1][Form DL].

12. Evidence of entitlement to be registered as proprietor *Please complete this panel if instructed to do so in panel 9. Place "X" in the appropriate box.*

☐ I am the applicant's conveyancer and certify that I am satisfied that the applicant/person consenting to this application is entitled to be registered as proprietor and that I hold the originals of the documents that contain evidence of that person's entitlement, or an application for registration of that person as proprietor is pending at Land Registry.

☐ Evidence that the applicant/person consenting to this application is entitled to be registered as proprietor is contained in the document(s) numbered ___ referred to in [panel 6][Form AP1][Form DL].

13. Evidence that the applicant has sufficient interest *Please complete this panel if instructed to do so in panel 9.*

State brief details of the applicant's interest in the making of the entry of the restriction applied for in panel 10.

Evidence of this interest is contained in the document(s) numbered referred to in [panel 6] [Form AP1][Form DL].

14. Signature of applicant or their conveyancer ______________________ **Date** ____________

15. Consent

Consent to the entry of the restriction specified in panel 10 is given by:

Names *BLOCK LETTERS*	**Signatures**
1.	1.
2.	2.
3.	3.

Claim Form (CPR Part 8)

In the NORTHAMPTON COUNTY COURT	
Claim No.	

Click here to clear your data after printing

SEAL

Claimant

TOM GOOD T/A GOOD FOOD & MANURE
1 CUCKOO LANE
BRAINTREE
ESSEX
CM6 3RT

Defendant(s)

MARGOT LEDBETTER
3 CUCKOO LANE
BRAINTREE
ESSEX
CM6 3RT

Does your claim include any issues under the Human Rights Act 1998? ☐ Yes ☑ No

Details of claim *(see also overleaf)*

APPLICATION FOR AN ORDER FOR SALE IN RESPECT OF THE FREEHOLD PROPERTY SITUATED AT 3 CUCKOO LANE, BRAINTREE, ESSEX, CM6 3RT PURSUANT TO SECTION 14 TRUSTS OF LAND AND APPOINTMENT OF TRUSTEES ACT 1996.

Defendant's name and address

MARGOT LEDBETTER
3 CUCKOO LANE
BRAINTREE
ESSEX
CM6 3RT

	£
Court fee	150.00
Solicitor's costs	69.50
Issue date	

The court office at

is open between 10 am and 4 pm Monday to Friday. When corresponding with the court, please address forms or letters to the Court Manager and quote the case number.

N208 Claim form (CPR Part 8) (10.00)

Printed on behalf of The Court Service

Claim No.	

Details of claim *(continued)*

1. The claimant obtained a final charging order in Northampton County Court under claim number 8NN123456 against the defendant, dated April 6, 2008.

2. The defendant has failed to pay the sum due under the Final Charging Order and the claimant therefore wishes to pursue further enforcement of the Final Charging Order by way of obtaining an Order For Sale.

3. The evidence in support of this claim is contained within the written statement of JOE BLOGGS annexed hereto.

4. Part 8 of the Civil Procedure Rules applies to this claim.

Statement of Truth

*(I believe)(The Claimant believes) that the facts stated in these particulars of claim are true.

* I am duly authorised by the claimant to sign this statement

Full name JOE BLOGGS

Name of claimant's solicitor's firm LA LAW SOLICITORS

signed________________ position or office held SOLICITOR

*(Claimant)(Litigation friend)(Claimant's solicitor) (if signing on behalf of firm or company)

**delete as appropriate*

LA LAW SOLICITORS
BOSTON HOUSE
NEW STREET
NOTTINGHAM
NN4 8SD

Claimant's or claimant's solicitor's address to which documents should be sent if different from overleaf. If you are prepared to accept service by DX, fax or e-mail, please add details.

IN THE NORTHAMPTON COUNTY COURT **CLAIM NO. 8NN123456**

B E T W E E N:

TOM GOOD
T/A GOOD FOOD & MANURE

Claimant

and

MARGOT LEDBETTER

Defendant

WITNESS STATEMENT IN SUPPORT OF CLAIM FOR ORDER FOR SALE

I, Joe Bloggs, Solicitor of LA Law Solicitors, Boston House, New Street, Nottingham, NN4 8SD on behalf of the above named claimant wish to rely on the following evidence in support of this claim:

1. Unless otherwise stated the contents of this statement are stated from my own knowledge, information or belief.

2. The claimant obtained a Final Charging Order in Northampton County Court, Case Number 8NN123456 dated 16th May 2008 against the above named defendant's interest in the freehold property known as 3 Cuckoo Lane, Braintree, Essex, CM6 3RT.

3. The Final Charging Order was in the sum of £1003.67, the full amount of which remains outstanding and due to the claimant.

4. From Office Copy Entries obtained from the Land Registry the claimant has been able to verify that the defendant is the joint proprietor of the aforementioned property, together with her husband, Jerry Ledbetter. The property is registered under Title No. CM987654 at the Peterborough Land Registry.

5. The defendant resides at the property with her spouse and joint proprietor, Jerry Ledbetter. There are not other occupiers of the property or dependents in occupation.

6. The claimant has been able to identify that one charge exists over the property held by Money Bank of 1 The High Street, Stirling Town. Unfortunately, despite repeated requests made to the bank they have declined to provide details of the amount required to redeem their charge at the present time.

7. The claimant has obtained a valuation of the property from Sell It & Rent Estate Agents, on the basis of an external valuation of the property as it has not been possible to gain access to the property for a full inspection and valuation. It is advised that the property is currently valued at £267,000.

8. There is no land charge of Class F or notice under section 31(10) of the Family Law Act 1996 registered against the property.

9. The claimant therefore seeks and order for sale and possession against the defendant in respect of the aforementioned property.

STATEMENT OF TRUTH

The Claimant believes the facts stated in this witness statement to be true.

Signed: ....

Full Name: ....

Date: ....

L A Law Solicitors
Boston House
New Street
Nottingham
NN4 8SD

Form 6.1

Rule 6.1

Statutory Demand under section 268(1)(a) of the Insolvency Act 1986. Debt for Liquidated Sum Payable Immediately

Notes for Creditor

- If the creditor is entitled to the debt by way of assignment, details of the original creditor and any intermediary assignees should be given in part C on page 3.
- If the amount of debt includes interest not previously notified to the debtor as included in the debtor's liability, details should be given, including the grounds upon which interest is charged. The amount of interest must be shown separately.
- Any other charge accruing due from time to time may be claimed. The amount or rate of the charge must be identified and the grounds on which it is claimed must be stated.
- In either case the amount claimed must be limited to that which has accrued due at the date of the demand.
- If the creditor holds any security the amount of the debt should be the sum the creditor is prepared to regard as unsecured for the purposes of this demand. Brief details of the total debt should be included and the nature of the security and the value put upon it by the creditor, as at the

Warning

- This is an **important** document. You should refer to the notes entitled "How to comply with a statutory demand or have it set aside".
- If you wish to have this demand set aside you must make application to do so **within 18 days** from its service on you.
- If you do not apply to set aside **within 18 days** or otherwise deal with this demand as set out in the notes **within 21 days** after its service on you, you could be made bankrupt and your property and goods taken away from you.
- Please read the demand and notes carefully. If you are in any doubt about your position you should seek advice **immediately** from a solicitor, a Citizen Advice Bureau, or a licensed insolvency practitioner.

Demand

To **MARGOT LEDBETTER**

Address **3 CUCKOO LANE, BRAINTREE, ESSEX, CM6 3R**

This demand is served on you by the creditor:

Name **TOM GOOD T/A GOOD FOOD & MANURE**

Address **1 CUCKOO LANE, BRAINTREE, ESSEX, CM6 3RT**

The creditor claims that you owe the sum of **£789.00**, full particulars of which are set out on page 2, and that it is payable immediately and, to the extent of the sum demanded, is unsecured.

The creditor demands that you pay the above debt or secure or compound for it to the creditor's satisfaction.

~~[The creditor making this demand is a Minister of the Crown or a Government Department, and it is intended to present a bankruptcy petition in the High Court.]~~

Signature of individual ______________________________

Name **JOE BLOGGS**
(BLOCK LETTERS)

Date ____

*Position with or relationship to creditor **SOLICITOR**

*I am authorised to make this demand on the creditor's behalf.

Address **LA LAW SOLICITORS, BOSTON HOUSE, NEW STREET, NOTTINGHAM, NN4 8 SD**

Tel. No. **01357 556442** Ref. **JB/GOOD**

*Delete if signed by the creditor himself

N.B. The person making this demand must complete the whole of pages 1, 2 and parts A, B and C (as applicable) on page 3.

Form 6.1 contd.

Particulars of Debt
(These particulars must include (a) when the debt was incurred, (b) the consideration for the debt (or if there is no consideration the way in which it arose) and (c) the amount due as at the date of this demand.)

1. The debtor contracted with the creditor in respect of the supply of goods, including vegetables and manure.

2. The creditor provided the debtor with an invoice in respect of the supply of these goods in the sum of £789.00.

3. Despite repeated requests for payment of the invoice the debtor has failed to pay the sum due. The creditor therefore believes that the debtor is unable to pay this debt.

Notes for Creditor
Please make sure that you have read the notes on page 1 before completing this page.

Note:
If space is insufficient continue on page 4 and clearly indicate on this page that you are doing so.

Form 6.1 contd.

Part A

Appropriate Court for Setting Aside Demand

Rule 6.4(2) of the Insolvency Rules 1986 states that the appropriate court is the court to which you would have to present your own bankruptcy petition in accordance with Rule 6.40(1) and 6.40(2). In accordance with those rules on present information the appropriate court is [the High Court of Justice] **[Chelmsford County Court]**
(address) **Priory Place, New London Road, Chelmsford, Essex, CM2 0PP**

Any application by you to set aside this demand should be made to that court.

Part B

The individual or individuals to whom any communication regarding this demand may be addressed is / are:

Name **JOE BLOGGS**
(BLOCK LETTERS)

Address **LA LAW SOLICITORS, BOSTON HOUSE, NEW STREET, NOTTINGHAM, NN4 8SD**

Telephone Number **01357 556442**

Reference **JB/GOOD**

Part C

For completion if the creditor is entitled to the debt by way of assignment

	Name	Date(s) of Assignment
Original creditor		
Assignees		

How to comply with a statutory demand or have it set aside (ACT WITHIN 18 DAYS)

If you wish to avoid a bankruptcy petition being presented against you, you must pay the debt shown on page 1, particulars of which are set out on page 2 of this notice, within the period of **21 days** after its service upon you. Alternatively, you can attempt to come to a settlement with the creditor. To do this you should:

- inform the individual (or one of the individuals) named in part B above immediately that you are willing and able to offer security for the debt to the creditor's satisfaction; or
- inform the individual (or one of the individuals) named in part B immediately that you are willing and able to compound for the debt to the creditor's satisfaction.

If you dispute the demand in whole or in part you should:

- contact the individual (or one of the individuals) named in part B immediately.

THERE ARE MORE IMPORTANT NOTES ON THE NEXT PAGE

Form 6.1 contd.

If you consider that you have grounds to have this demand set aside or if you do not quickly receive a satisfactory written reply from the individual named in part B whom you have contacted you should **apply within 18 days** from the date of service of this demand on you to the appropriate court shown in part A above to have the demand set aside.

Any application to set aside the demand (Form 6.4 in Schedule 4 to the Insolvency Rules 1986) should be made within 18 days from the date of service upon you and be supported by an affidavit (Form 6.5 in Schedule 4 to those Rules) stating the grounds on which the demand should be set aside. The forms may be obtained from the appropriate court when you attend to make the application.

Remember! – From the date of service on you of this document

(a) you have only 18 days to apply to the court to have the demand set aside, and

(b) you have only 21 days before the creditor may present a bankruptcy petition

Rule 6.1

Form 6.2

Statutory Demand under section 268(1)(a) of the Insolvency Act 1986. Debt for Liquidated Sum Payable Immediately Following a Judgment or Order of the Court

Notes for Creditor

- If the creditor is entitled to the debt by way of assignment, details of the original creditor and any intermediary assignees should be given in part C on page 3.
- If the amount of debt includes interest not previously notified to the debtor as included in the debtor's liability, details should be given, including the grounds upon which interest is charged. The amount of interest must be shown separately.
- Any other charge accruing due from time to time may be claimed. The amount or rate of the charge must be identified and the grounds on which it is claimed must be stated.
- In either case the amount claimed must be limited to that which has accrued due at the date of the demand.
- If the creditor holds any security the amount of the debt should be the sum the creditor is prepared to regard as unsecured for the purposes of the demand. Brief details of the total debt should be included and the nature of the security and the value put upon it by the creditor, as at the date of the demand, must be specified.
- Details of the judgment or order should be inserted, including details of the Division of the Court or District Registry and court reference, where judgment is obtained in the High Court.

Warning

- This is an **important** document. You should refer to the notes entitled "How to comply with a statutory demand or have it set aside".
- If you wish to have this demand set aside you must make application to do so **within 18 days** from its service on you.
- If you do not apply to set aside **within 18 days** or otherwise deal with this demand as set out in the notes **within 21 days** after its service on you, you could be made bankrupt and your property and goods taken away from you.
- Please read the demand and notes carefully. If you are in any doubt about your position you should seek advice **immediately** from a solicitor, a Citizens Advice Bureau, or a licensed insolvency practitioner.

Demand

To **MARGOT LEDBETTER**

Address **3 CUCKOO LANE, BRAINTREE, ESSEX, CM6 3RT**

This demand is served on you by the creditor:

Name **TOM GOOD T/A GOOD FOOD & MANURE**

Address **1 CUCKOO LANE, BRAINTREE, ESSEX, CM6 3RT**

The creditor claims that you owe the sum of **£805.88**, full particulars of which are set out on page 2, and that it is payable immediately and, to the extent of the sum demanded, is unsecured.

By a Judgment/Order of the **NORTHAMPTON COUNTY COURT** in proceedings entitled (Case) Number **8nn123456** between **TOM GOOD T/A GOOD FOOD & MANURE** Claimant and **MARGOT LEDBETTER** Defendant it was adjudged/ordered that you pay to the creditor the sum of **£648.88** and **£157.00** for costs.

The creditor demands that you pay the above debt or secure or compound for it to the creditor's satisfaction.

~~[The creditor making this demand is a Minister of the Crown or a Government Department, and it is intended to present a bankruptcy petition in the High Court in London.]~~

[Delete if inappropriate]

Signature of individual ____________________________

Name **JOE BLOGGS**

(BLOCK LETTERS)

Date ____

*Position with or relationship to creditor **SOLICITOR**

*I am authorised to make this demand on the creditor's behalf.

*Delete if signed by the creditor himself

Address **L A LAW SOLICITORS, BOSTON HOUSE, NEW STREET, NOTTINGHAM, NN4 8SD**

Tel. No. **01357 556442** Ref. **JB/GOOD**

N.B. The person making this demand must complete the whole of pages 1, 2 and parts A, B and C (as applicable) on page 3.

Form 6.2 contd.

Particulars of Debt
(These particulars must include (a) when the debt was incurred, (b) the consideration for the debt (or if there is no consideration the way in which it arose) and (c) the amount due as at the date of this demand.

1. The creditor issued a claim against the debtor in Northampton County Court under Claim No. 8NN123456 in respect of an unpaid invoice.

2. The creditor obtained judgment against the debtor on January 28, 2008 in the sum of £805.88.

3. The debtor has failed to pay the judgment debt and the creditor believes that the debtor is unable to pay the debt.

Notes for Creditor
Please make sure that you have read the notes on page 1 before completing this page.

Note:
If space is insufficient continue on page 4 and clearly indicate on this page that you are doing so.

Form 6.2 contd.

Part A

Appropriate Court for Setting Aside Demand

Rule 6.4(2) of the Insolvency Rules 1986 states that the appropriate court is the court to which you would have to present your own bankruptcy petition in accordance with Rule 6.40(1) and (2).

Any application by you to set aside this demand should be made to that court, or, if this demand is issued by a Minister of the Crown or a Government Department, you must apply to the High Court to set aside if it is intended to present a bankruptcy petition against you in the High Court (see page 1).

In accordance with those rules on present information the appropriate court is ~~[the High Court of Justice]~~

Chelmsford County Court]

(Address) **Priory Place, New London Road, Chelmsford, Essex, CM2 0PP**

Part B

The individual or individuals to whom any communication regarding this demand may be addressed is/are:

Name **JOE BLOGGS**
(BLOCK LETTERS)

Address **LA LAW SOLICITORS, BOSTON HOUSE, NEW STREET, NOTTINGHAM, NN4 8SD**

Telephone number **01357 556442**

Reference **JB/GOOD**

Part C

For completion if the creditor is entitled to the debt by way of assignment

	Name	Date(s) of Assignment
Original creditor		
Assignees		

THERE ARE IMPORTANT NOTES IN THE NEXT PAGE

Form 6.2 contd.

How to comply with a statutory demand or have it set aside (ACT WITHIN 18 DAYS)

If you wish to avoid a bankruptcy petition being presented against you, you must pay the debt shown on page 1, particulars of which are set out on page 2 of this notice, within the period of **21 days** after its service upon you. However if the demand follows (includes) a judgment or order of a County Court, any payment must be made to that County Court (quoting the Case No.). Alternatively, you can attempt to come to a settlement with the creditor. To do this you should:

- inform the individual (or one of the individuals) named in part B above immediately that you are willing and able to offer security for the debt to the creditor's satisfaction; or
- inform the individual (or one of the individuals) named in part B immediately that you are willing and able to compound for the debt to the creditor's satisfaction.

If you dispute the demand in whole or in part you should:

- contact the individual (or one of the individuals) named in part B immediately.

If you consider that you have grounds to have this demand set aside or if you do not quickly receive a satisfactory written reply from the individual named in part B whom you have contacted you should **apply within 18 days** from the date of service of this demand on you to the appropriate court shown in part A above to have the demand set aside.

Any application to set aside the demand (Form 6.4 in Schedule 4 to the Insolvency Rules 1986) should be made within 18 days from the date of service upon you and be supported by an affidavit (Form 6.5 in Schedule 4 to those Rules) stating the grounds on which the demand should be set aside. The forms may be obtained from the appropriate court when you attend to make the application.

Remember! –From the date of service on you of this document
(a) you have only 18 days to apply to the court to have the demand set aside, and
(b) you have only 21 days before the creditor may present a bankruptcy petition.

Form 6.7

Rule 6.6

Creditor's Bankruptcy Petition on Failure to Comply with a Statutory Demand for a Liquidated Sum Payable Immediately

(a) Insert full name(s) and address(es) of petitioner(s)

I/ (a) TOM GOOD T/A GOOD FOOD & MANURE, 1 CUCKOO LANE, BRAINTREE, ESSEX, CM6 3RT

(b) Insert full name, place of residence and occupation (if any) of debtor

petition the court that a bankruptcy order may be made against (b) MARGOT LEDBETTER, 3 CUCKOO LANE, BRAINTREE, ESSEX, CM6 3RT

(c) Insert in full any other name(s) by which the debtor is or has been known

[also known as (c)]

[and carrying on business as (d)]

(d) Insert trading name (adding "with another or others", if this is so), business address and nature of business

(e) Insert any other address or addresses at which the debtor has resided at or after the time the petitiion debt was incurred

[and lately residing at (e)]

[and lately carrying on business as (f)

(f) Give the same details as specified in note (d) above for any other businesses which have been carried on at or after the time the petition debt was incurred

and say as follows:—

1. (g) The debtor's centre of main interests has been at 3 CUCKOO LANE, BRAINTREE, ESSEX, CM6 3RT

(g) Delete as applicable

OR

The debtor carries on business as an insurance undertaking; a credit institution; an investment undertaking providing services involving the holding of funds or securities for third parties; or a collective investment undertaking as referred to in Article 1.2 of the EC Regulation

OR

The debtor's centre of main interests is not within a member State

(h) Or as the case may be following the terms of Rule 6.9

2. The debtor has for the greater part of six months immediately preceding the presentation of this petition (g) resided at 3 CUCKOO LANE, BRAINTREE, ESSEX, CM6 3RT

within the district of this court (h)

Under the EC Regulation:

(i) The centre of main interests should correspond to the place where the debtor conducts the administration of his interests on a regular basis.

(ii) Establishment is defined as "any place of operations where the debtor carries out a non-transitory economic activity with human means and goods".

(j) Please give the amount of debt(s), what they relate to and when they were incurred. Please show separately the amount or rate of any interest or other charge not previously notified to the debtor and the reasons why you are claiming it

3. The debtor is justly and truly indebted to us in the aggregate sum of £(j) 789.00

4. The above-mentioned debt is for a liquidated sum payable immediately and the debtor appears to be unable to pay it.

(k) Insert date of service of a statutory demand

(l) State manner of service of demand

5. On (k) 1 February 2008
a statutory demand was served upon the debtor by (l) FRED BROWN, PROCESS SERVER OF SHERLOCK & POIROT PLC
in respect of the above-mentioned debt. To the best of my knowledge and belief the demand has neither been complied with nor set aside in accordance with the Rules and no application to set it aside is outstanding

(m) If 3 weeks have not elapsed since service of statutory demand give reasons for earlier presentation of petition

(m)

6. I/ do not, nor does any person on our behalf, hold any security on the debtor's estate, or any part thereof, for the payment of the above-mentioned sum

OR

I/ hold security for the payment of (g) [part of] the above-mentioned sum.
I/ will give up such security for the benefit of all the creditors in the event of a bankruptcy order being made.

OR

I/ hold security for the payment of part of the above-mentioned sum and we estimate the value of such security to be £ . This petition is not made in respect of the secured part of our debt.

Endorsement

This petition having been presented to the court on ________________________
it is ordered that the petition shall be heard as follows:—

Date ____

Time ____________________________________ hours

Place ____

(n) Insert name of debtor

and you, the above-named (n) MARGOT LEDBETTER, 3 CUCKOO LANE, BRAINTREE, ESSEX, CM6 3RT, are to take notice that if you intend to oppose the petition you must not later than 7 days before the day fixed for the next hearing

(i) file in court a notice [in Form 6.19] specifying the grounds on which you object to the making of a bankruptcy order; and

(ii) send a copy of the notice to the petitioner or his solicitor.

(o) Only to be completed where the petitioning creditor is represented by a solicitor

The solicitor to the petitioning creditor is:—(o)

Name	JOE BLOGGS
Address	LA LAW SOLICITORS, BOSTON HOUSE, NEW STREET, NOTTINGHAM, NN4 8SD
Telephone Number	01357 556442
Reference	JB/GOOD

[illegible]

Appendix C

Tables of Information

Matrix for Information Sources In A Debt Recovery Team

Provider	Nature of Service	Website Address
EQUIFAX/EXPERIAN/ CALL-CREDIT	for business information—limited and non limited businesses—checks solvency/credit history/phone numbers/addresses	www.myequifax.co.uk/ www.experian.co.uk/ www.callcredit.co.uk
192.com	Checks addresses/phone numbers/ price of house	www.192.com
TRACING AGENCY # 1	Sub-contracted tracing service	
ADMAR	Subscription service to trace phone numbers—will show ex-directory address as well	www.admar.co.uk
ROYAL MAIL	Checks addresses/postcodes	www.royalmail.com
HM LAND REGISTRY	Checks Land Registry records—for charges/proprietor—cost £3.00 per search	www.landreaistry.qov.uk
GOOGLE	Put name of individual/business into Google and as a wild card see what comes out—surprising what can be found!!!!	www.google.co.uk
COMPANIES HOUSE	The official UK government register of UK companies	www.companieshouse.qov.uk
ASSOCIATION OF BRITISH INVESTIGATORS	Searchable database of private investigators	www.theabi.org.uk
LAW SOCIETY	Representative body for solicitors in England and Wales	www.lawsociety.org.uk
CITIZENS ADVICE BUREAU	The Citizens Advice service helps people resolve their legal, money and other problems by providing free, independent and confidential advice, and by influencing policy-makers.	www.citizensadvice.org.uk
DIRECTGOV	Public services information all in one place	www.directgov.qov.uk
YELL.COM	Allows you to search companies by name or area.	www.yell.com

Provider	Nature of Service	Website Address
RISK DISC	Search for all UK registered companies	www.riskdisk.com
ASKALIX	UK business directory and finder services from Askali × Company details finder, UK business guide and online directory enquiries.	www.askalix.com
STREETMAP	Online maps with detailed streetmaps of Great Britain. Includes search by postcode, place name, London streetname or OS grid reference.	www.streetmap.co.uk
THE INSOLVENCY SERVICE WEBSITE	Deals with insolvency matters in England and Wales and some limited insolvency matters in Scotland, administer and investigate the affairs of bankrupts, of companies and partnerships wound up by the court, and establish why they became insolvent—check individual bankruptcy and Individual Voluntary Arrangements	www.insolvency.gov.uk
LATE PAYMENT LEGISLATION AND ONLINE CALCULATOR	This web site provides a simple guide to using the Late Payment Legislation in the UK. If you run a business in the UK this legislation allows you to charge interest where a customer is late in paying their invoices. This site also provides a calculator that you can use to work out how much interest you can claim on an outstanding debt.	www.late-payment-law.co.uk
HER MAJESTY'S COURT SERVICE	They are responsible for managing the magistrates' courts, the Crown Court, county courts, the High Court and Court of Appeal in England and Wales. This site contains a wide range of information including: small claims, divorce proceedings, civil partnership dissolution, adoption, wills and probate	www.hmcourts-service.qov.uk
HOUSE PRICES	Searches the UK Land Registry database by postcode or address for recent house prices in England and Wales.	www.houseprices.co.uk

Provider	Nature of Service	Website Address
POSTCODE ANYWHERE	Postcode Anywhere offers web services to lookup UK and international addresses, provide a store locator function, validate bank details, plan routes etc.	www.postcodeanywhere.co.uk
REGISTRY TRUST	Operates the Registry of Judgments, Orders and Fines for England and Wales on behalf of the Department for Constitutional Affairs	www.registry-trust.org.uk
THOMSONS DIRECTORY	Similar to Yell.co.uk. Allows you to search of a business by name, type and area	www.thomsonlocal.com
BRITISH TELECOM	A free directory service to be able to locate addresses and telephone numbers for individuals and businesses.	www.bt.com
UPMYSTREET	A free property service allowing users to make enquiries regarding the price of property in a particular area, local authority information. As well as information regarding recent activity concerning sales of property.	www.upmystreet.com
aRMadillo	An online service allowing users to access a variety of company information for companies in the UK and worldwide	www.rmonline.com
MULTIMAP	Can assist in locating an address, where you have a postcode and need clarification as to the exact location of the property	www.multimap.co.uk
INFORMATION COMMISSIONER'S OFFICE	Can be used as a source of information almost in reverse to check if a debtor has notified his or her business under the Data Protection Act which will in turn confirm the current address of the debtor	www.ico.gov.uk

Useful Organisations

Type Of Organisation	Organisation title	Contact Details
Trade Bodies	Association of Civil Enforcement Agencies	ACEA 513 Bradford Road BATLEY West Yorkshire WF17 8LL Tel: 01924 350090 www.acea.org.uk
	British Bankers' Association	Pinners Hall 105-108 Old Broad Street London EC2N 1EX Tel: 020 72168 800 www.bba.org.uk
	Consumer Credit Association	Queens House Queens Road Chester CH1 3BQ Tel: 01244 312044 www.ccauk.org
	Consumer Credit Trade Association	Suite 4 The Wave 1 View Croft Road Shipley BD17 7DU Tel: 01274 714959 www.ccta.co.uk
	Credit Services Association	Wingrove House 2nd Floor East Ponteland Rd Newcastle Upon Tyne NE5 3AJ Tel: (UK) 0191 286 5656 www.csa-uk.com
	Enforcement Services Association (formally Certified Bailiffs Association)	Park House 10 Park Street Bristol BS1 5HX Tel: 0117 907 4771 www.ensas.org.uk
	Finance & Leasing	Imperial House 2nd Floor 15-19 Kingsway London

Type Of Organisation	Organisation title	Contact Details
		WC2B 6UN Tel: 020 7836 6511 www.fla.org.uk
	Insolvency Practitioners' Association	Valiant House 4-10 Heneage Lane London EC3A 5DQ Tel: 02076235108 www.insolvency-practitioners.org.uk
Ombudsmen and Regulatory Bodies	Information Commissioner's Office (formally Office of the Data Protection Registrar)	Wycliffe House Water Lane Wilmslow SK9 5AF Tel: 01625 545 745 www.ico.gov.uk
	The Law Society (England and Wales)	113 Chancery Lane London WC2A 1PL Tel: 020 7242 1222 www.lawsociety.org.uk
	Office of Fair Trading (OFT)	Fleetbank House 2-6 Salisbury Square London EC4Y 8JX Tel: 020 7211 8000 www.oft.gov.uk
	Office of Gas and Electricity Markets (Ofgem)	9 Millbank London SW1P 3GE Tel: 020 7901 7295 www.ofgem.gov.uk
	Office of Communications (Ofcom)	Ofcom Riverside House 2a Southwark Bridge Road London SE1 9HA Tel: 020 7981 3000 www.ofcom.org.uk
	Office of Water Services (Ofwat)	Ofwat Centre City Tower 7 Hill Street Birmingham B5 4UA United Kingdom

Type Of Organisation	Organisation title	Contact Details
		Tel: 01216 251 300 www.ofwat.gov.uk
Organisations Giving Advice Or Representing Advice Networks:	Association of British Credit Unions Ltd.	ABCUL Holyoake House Hanover Street Manchester M60 0AS Tel: 01618 323 694 www.abcul.org
	Business Debtline	Tel: 0800 1976 026 www.bdl.org.uk
	adviceUK (formally Federation of Information and Advice Centres	12th Floor New London Bridge House 25 London Bridge Street London SE1 9SG Tel: 020 7407 4070 www.adviceuk.org.uk
	Money Advice Trust	The Money Advice Trust 21 Garlick Hill London EC4V 2AU Tel: 020 7489 7796 www.moneyadvicetrust.org
	Citizens Advice	Myddelton House 115-123 Pentonville Road London N1 9LZ Tel: 020 7833 2181 www.citizensadvice.org.uk
	National Consumer Council	20 Grosvenor Gargens London SW1W 0DH Tel: 020 7730 3469 www.ncc.org.uk
	National Debtline	Tel: 0808 808 4000 www.nationaldebtline.co.uk

Look-Up Table For Foreign Judgment Enforcement – As At August 2008

Country	Reciprocal Treaty	Statutory Instrument	Form of Certificate For Outgoing Judgment	Explanatory Notes
Anguilla	The Administration of Justice Act 1920	S.I. 1984 No. 129 and Pt II of AJA 1920 extends to the countries specified in Sched.I to that Order which has been amended by the Judgments (Administration of Justice Act 1920, Pt II) (Amendment) Order 1985 (S.I. 1985 No. 1994)	Form 110	
Antigua and Barbuda	The Administration of Justice Act 1920	S.I. 1984 No. 129 and Pt II of AJA 1920 extends to the countries specified in Sched.I to that Order which has been amended by the Judgments (Administration of Justice Act 1920, Pt II) (Amendment) Order 1985 (S.I. 1985 No. 1994)	Form 110	
Australia	The Foreign Judgments (Reciprocal Enforcement) Act 1933	S.I. 1994 No. 1901	Form 110	
Austria	Council Regulation (EU) 44/2001 and now Council Regulation 805/2004	S.I. 1962 No. 1339	Form N219/219A	
Bahamas	The Administration of Justice Act 1920	S.I. 1984 No. 129 and Pt II of AJA 1920 extends to the countries specified in Sched.I to that Order which has been amended by the Judgments (Administration of Justice Act 1920, Pt II) (Amendment) Order 1985 (S.I. 1985 No. 1994)	Form 110	
Barbados	The Administration of Justice Act 1920	S.I. 1984 No. 129 and Pt II of AJA 1920 extends to the countries specified in Sched.I to that Order which has been amended by the Judgments (Administration of Justice Act 1920, Pt II) (Amendment) Order 1985 (S.I. 1985 No. 1994)	Form 110	

Country	Reciprocal Treaty	Statutory Instrument	Form of Certificate For Outgoing Judgment	Explanatory Notes
Belgium	Council Regulation (EU) 44/2001 and now Council Regulation 805/2004	S.R. & O. 1936 No. 1169.	Form N219/219A	
Belize	The Administration of Justice Act 1920	S.I. 1984 No. 129 and Pt II of AJA 1920 extends to the countries specified in Sched.I to that Order which has been amended by the Judgments (Administration of Justice Act 1920, Pt II) (Amendment) Order 1985 (S.I. 1985 No. 1994)	Form 110	
Bermuda	The Administration of Justice Act 1920	S.I. 1984 No. 129 and Pt II of AJA 1920 extends to the countries specified in Sched.I to that Order which has been amended by the Judgments (Administration of Justice Act 1920, Pt II) (Amendment) Order 1985 (S.I. 1985 No. 1994)	Form 110	
Botswana	The Administration of Justice Act 1920	S.I. 1984 No. 129 and Pt II of AJA 1920 extends to the countries specified in Sched.I to that Order which has been amended by the Judgments (Administration of Justice Act 1920, Pt II) (Amendment) Order 1985 (S.I. 1985 No. 1994)	Form 110	
British Indian Ocean Territory	The Administration of Justice Act 1920	S.I. 1984 No. 129 and Pt II of AJA 1920 extends to the countries specified in Sched.I to that Order which has been amended by the Judgments (Administration of Justice Act 1920, Pt II) (Amendment) Order 1985 (S.I. 1985 No. 1994)	Form 110	
British Virgin Islands	The Administration of Justice Act 1920	S.I. 1984 No. 129 and Pt II of AJA 1920 extends to the countries specified in Sched.I to that Order which has been amended by the Judgments (Administration of Justice Act 1920, Pt II) (Amendment) Order 1985 (S.I. 1985 No. 1994)	Form 110	

Country	Reciprocal Treaty	Statutory Instrument	Form of Certificate For Outgoing Judgment	Explanatory Notes
Canada	The Foreign Judgments (Reciprocal Enforcement) Act 1933	S.I. 1987 No. 468 as amended by S.I. 1987 No. 2211, S.'I. 1988 No. 1304 and SI. 1988, No. 1853 S.I. 1989 No. 987 S.I. 1991 No. 1724 S.I. 1992 No. 1731	Form 110	The Federal Court of Canada and any court to the province of British Columbia, Manitoba, New Brunswick, Nova Scotia, Ontario, Prince Edward Island, Saskatchewan, or the Yukon Territory Northwest Territories, Newfoundland, Alberta
Cayman Islands	The Administration of Justice Act 1920	S.I. 1984 No. 129 and Pt II of AJA 1920 extends to the countries specified in Sched.I to that Order which has been amended by the Judgments (Administration of Justice Act 1920, Pt II) (Amendment) Order 1985 (S.I. 1985 No. 1994)	Form 110	
Christmas Island	The Administration of Justice Act 1920	S.I. 1984 No. 129 and Pt II of AJA 1920 extends to the countries specified in Sched.I to that Order which has been amended by the Judgments (Administration of Justice Act 1920, Pt II) (Amendment) Order 1985 (S.I. 1985 No. 1994)	Form 110	
Cocos (Keeling) Islands	The Administration of Justice Act 1920	S.I. 1984 No. 129 and Pt II of AJA 1920 extends to the countries specified in Sched.I to that Order which has been amended by the Judgments (Administration of Justice Act 1920, Pt II) (Amendment) Order 1985 (S.I. 1985 No. 1994)	Form 110	

Country	Reciprocal Treaty	Statutory Instrument	Form of Certificate For Outgoing Judgment	Explanatory Notes
Czech Republic	Council Regulation (EU) 44/2001 and now Council Regulation 805/2004		Form N219/219A	
Denmark	The Civil Jurisdiction & Judgment Act 1982		Form 110	
Dominica	The Administration of Justice Act 1920	S.I. 1984 No. 129 and Pt II of AJA 1920 extends to the countries specified in Sched.I to that Order which has been amended by the Judgments (Administration of Justice Act 1920, Pt II) (Amendment) Order 1985 (S.I. 1985 No. 1994)	Form 110	
Estonia	Council Regulation (EU) 44/2001 and now Council Regulation 805/2004		Form N219/219A	
Falkland Islands	The Administration of Justice Act 1920	S.I. 1984 No. 129 and Pt II of AJA 1920 extends to the countries specified in Sched.I to that Order which has been amended by the Judgments (Administration of Justice Act 1920, Pt II) (Amendment) Order 1985 (S.I. 1985 No. 1994)	Form 110	
Fiji	The Administration of Justice Act 1920	S.I. 1984 No. 129 and Pt II of AJA 1920 extends to the countries specified in Sched.I to that Order which has been amended by the Judgments (Administration of Justice Act 1920, Pt II) (Amendment) Order 1985 (S.I. 1985 No. 1994)	Form 110	
Finland	Council Regulation (EU) 44/2001 and now Council Regulation 805/2004		Form N219/219A	•

Country	Reciprocal Treaty	Statutory Instrument	Form of Certificate For Outgoing Judgment	Explanatory Notes
France	Council Regulation (EU) 44/2001 and now Council Regulation 805/2004	S. R. & O. 1936 No. 609.	Form N219/219A	
Germany	Council Regulation (EU) 44/2001 and now Council Regulation 805/2004	S.I. 1961 No. 1199	Form N219/219A	
Ghana	The Administration of Justice Act 1920	S.I. 1984 No. 129 and Pt II of AJA 1920 extends to the countries specified in Sched.I to that Order which has been amended by the Judgments (Administration of Justice Act 1920, Pt II) (Amendment) Order 1985 (S.I. 1985 No. 1994)	Form 110	
Gibraltar	The Civil Jurisdiction & Judgment Act 1982		Form 110	
Greece/ Cyprus	Council Regulation (EU) 44/2001 and now Council Regulation 805/2004	S.I. 1984 No. 129 and Pt II of AJA 1920 extends to the countries specified in Sched.I to that Order which has been amended by the Judgments (Administration of Justice Act 1920, Pt II) (Amendment) Order 1985 (S.I. 1985 No. 1994)	Form N219/219A	
Grenada	The Administration of Justice Act 1920	S.I. 1984 No. 129 and Pt II of AJA 1920 extends to the countries specified in Sched.I to that Order which has been amended by the Judgments (Administration of Justice Act 1920, Pt II) (Amendment) Order 1985 (S.I. 1985 No. 1994)	Form 110	
Guyana	The Administration of Justice Act 1920	S.I. 1984 No. 129 and Pt II of AJA 1920 extends to the countries specified in Sched.I to that Order which has been amended by the Judgments (Administration of Justice Act 1920, Pt II)	Form 110	

Country	Reciprocal Treaty	Statutory Instrument	Form of Certificate For Outgoing Judgment	Explanatory Notes
		(Amendment) Order 1985 (S.I. 1985 No. 1994)		
Hungary	Council Regulation (EU) 44/2001 and now Council Regulation 805/2004		Form N219/219A	
Iceland	The Civil Jurisdiction & Judgment Act 1982		Form 110	
Island of Guernsey	The Foreign Judgments (Reciprocal Enforcement) Act 1933	S.I. 1973 No. 610.	Form 110	
Isle of Man	The Foreign Judgments (Reciprocal Enforcement) Act 1933	S.I. 1973 No. 611.	Form 110	The courts in this jurisdiction will only recognise a High Court judgment which includes a County Court judgment transferred to the High Court for enforcement
Israel	The Foreign Judgments (Reciprocal Enforcement) Act 1933	S.I. 1971 No. 1039	Form 110	
Italy	Council Regulation (EU) 44/2001 and now Council Regulation 805/2004	S.I. 1973 No. 1894.	Form N219/219A	
Jamaica	The Administration of Justice Act 1920	S.I. 1984 No. 129 and Pt II of AJA 1920 extends to the countries specified in Sched.I to that Order which has been amended	Form 110	

Country	Reciprocal Treaty	Statutory Instrument	Form of Certificate For Outgoing Judgment	Explanatory Notes
		by the Judgments (Administration of Justice Act 1920, Pt II) (Amendment) Order 1985 (S.I. 1985 No. 1994)		
Jersey (Bailiwick of)	The Foreign Judgments (Reciprocal Enforcement) Act 1933	S.I. 1973 No. 612.	Form 110	
Kenya	The Administration of Justice Act 1920	S.I. 1984 No. 129 and Pt II of AJA 1920 extends to the countries specified in Sched.I to that Order which has been amended by the Judgments (Administration of Justice Act 1920, Pt II) (Amendment) Order 1985 (S.I. 1985 No. 1994)	Form 110	
Kiribati	The Administration of Justice Act 1920	S.I. 1984 No. 129 and Pt II of AJA 1920 extends to the countries specified in Sched.I to that Order which has been amended by the Judgments (Administration of Justice Act 1920, Pt II) (Amendment) Order 1985 (S.I. 1985 No. 1994)	Form 110	
Latvia	Council Regulation (EU) 44/2001 and now Council Regulation 805/2004		Form N219/219A	
Lesotho	The Administration of Justice Act 1920	S.I. 1984 No. 129 and Pt II of AJA 1920 extends to the countries specified in Sched.I to that Order which has been amended by the Judgments (Administration of Justice Act 1920, Pt II) (Amendment) Order 1985 (S.I. 1985 No. 1994)	Form 110	
Lithuania	Council Regulation (EU) 44/2001 and now Council Regulation 805/2004		Form N219/219A	
Luxembourg	Council Regulation (EU)		Form N219/219A	

Country	Reciprocal Treaty	Statutory Instrument	Form of Certificate For Outgoing Judgment	Explanatory Notes
	44/2001 and now Council Regulation 805/2016			
Malawi	The Administration of Justice Act 1920	S.I. 1984 No. 129 and Pt II of AJA 1920 extends to the countries specified in Sched.I to that Order which has been amended by the Judgments (Administration of Justice Act 1920, Pt II) (Amendment) Order 1985 (S.I. 1985 No. 1994)	Form 110	
Malaysia	The Administration of Justice Act 1920	S.I. 1984 No. 129 and Pt II of AJA 1920 extends to the countries specified in Sched.I to that Order which has been amended by the Judgments (Administration of Justice Act 1920, Pt II) (Amendment) Order 1985 (S.I. 1985 No. 1994)	Form 110	
Malta	Council Regulation (EU) 44/2001 and now Council Regulation 805/2004	S.I. 1984 No. 129 and Pt II of AJA 1920 extends to the countries specified in Sched.I to that Order which has been amended by the Judgments (Administration of Justice Act 1920, Pt II) (Amendment) Order 1985 (S.I. 1985 No. 1994)	Form N219/219A	
Mauritius	The Administration of Justice Act 1920	S.I. 1984 No. 129 and Pt II of AJA 1920 extends to the countries specified in Sched.I to that Order which has been amended by the Judgments (Administration of Justice Act 1920, Pt II) (Amendment) Order 1985 (S.I. 1985 No. 1994)	Form 110	
Montserrat	The Administration of Justice Act 1920	S.I. 1984 No. 129 and Pt II of AJA 1920 extends to the countries specified in Sched.I to that Order which has been amended by the Judgments (Administration of Justice Act 1920, Pt II) (Amendment) Order 1985 (S.I. 1985 No. 1994)	Form 110	-
Netherlands	Council Regulation (EU) 44/2001 and	S.I. 1969 No. 1063	Form N219/219A	

Country	Reciprocal Treaty	Statutory Instrument	Form of Certificate For Outgoing Judgment	Explanatory Notes
	now Council Regulation 805/2018			
New Zealand	The Administration of Justice Act 1920	S.I. 1984 No. 129 and Pt II of AJA 1920 extends to the countries specified in Sched.I to that Order which has been amended by the Judgments (Administration of Justice Act 1920, Pt II) (Amendment) Order 1985 (S.I. 1985 No. 1994)	Form 110	
Nigeria	The Administration of Justice Act 1920	S.I. 1984 No. 129 and Pt II of AJA 1920 extends to the countries specified in Sched.I to that Order which has been amended by the Judgments (Administration of Justice Act 1920, Pt II) (Amendment) Order 1985 (S.I. 1985 No. 1994)	Form 110	
Northern Ireland (simplified procedure)	The Civil Jurisdiction & Judgment Act 1982		Form 111	
Norway	The Civil Jurisdiction & Judgment Act 1982	S.I. 1962 No. 636.	Form 110	
Pakistan	The Foreign Judgments (Reciprocal Enforcement) Act 1933	S.I. 1958 No. 141 and see Pakistan Act 1990.	Form 110	
Papua New Guinea	The Administration of Justice Act 1920	S.I. 1984 No. 129 and Pt II of AJA 1920 extends to the countries specified in Sched.I to that Order which has been amended by the Judgments (Administration of Justice Act 1920, Pt II) (Amendment) Order 1985 (S.I. 1985 No. 1994)	Form 110	
Poland	Council Regulation (EU) 44/2001 and now Council Regulation 805/2004		Form N219/219A	

Country	Reciprocal Treaty	Statutory Instrument	Form of Certificate For Outgoing Judgment	Explanatory Notes
Portugal	Council Regulation (EU) 44/2001 and now Council Regulation 805/2004		Form N219/219A	
Republic of Cyprus	The Administration of Justice Act 1920		Form 110	
Republic of India	The Foreign Judgments (Reciprocal Enforcement) Act 1933	S.I. 1958 No. 425.	Form 110	Territories named in schedule to Order in Council—SI 1958 No 425
Republic of Ireland	Council Regulation (EU) 44/2001 and now Council Regulation 805/2004		Form N219/219A	
Scotland (simplified Procedure)	The Civil Jurisdiction & Judgment Act 1982		Form 111	
Seychelles	The Administration of Justice Act 1920	S.I. 1984 No. 129 and Pt II of AJA 1920 extends to the countries specified in Sched.I to that Order which has been amended by the Judgments (Administration of Justice Act 1920, Pt II) (Amendment) Order 1985 (S.I. 1985 No. 1994)	Form 110	
Sierra Leone	The Administration of Justice Act 1920	S.I. 1984 No. 129 and Pt II of AJA 1920 extends to the countries specified in Sched.I to that Order which has been amended by the Judgments (Administration of Justice Act 1920, Pt II) (Amendment) Order 1985 (S.I. 1985 No. 1994)	Form 110	
Singapore	The Administration of Justice Act 1920	S.I. 1984 No. 129 and Pt II of AJA 1920 extends to the countries specified in Sched.I to that Order which has been amended	Form 110	

Country	Reciprocal Treaty	Statutory Instrument	Form of Certificate For Outgoing Judgment	Explanatory Notes
		by the Judgments (Administration of Justice Act 1920, Pt II) (Amendment) Order 1985 (S.I. 1985 No. 1994)		
Slovakia	Council Regulation (EU) 44/2001 and now Council Regulation 805/2004		Form N219/219A	
Slovenia	Council Regulation (EU) 44/2001 and now Council Regulation 805/2004		Form N219/219A	
Solomon Islands	The Administration of Justice Act 1920	S.I. 1984 No. 129 and Pt II of AJA 1920 extends to the countries specified in Sched.I to that Order which has been amended by the Judgments (Administration of Justice Act 1920, Pt II) (Amendment) Order 1985 (S.I. 1985 No. 1994)	Form 110	
Sovereign Base Area of Akrotiri and Dhekelia in Cyprus	The Administration of Justice Act 1920	S.I. 1984 No. 129 and Pt II of AJA 1920 extends to the countries specified in Sched.I to that Order which has been amended by the Judgments (Administration of Justice Act 1920, Pt II) (Amendment) Order 1985 (S.I. 1985 No. 1994)	Form 110	
Spain	Council Regulation (EU) 44/2001 and now Council Regulation 805/2004		Form N219/219A	
Sri Lanka	The Administration of Justice Act 1920	S.I. 1984 No. 129 and Pt II of AJA 1920 extends to the countries specified in Sched.I to that Order which has been amended by the Judgments (Administration of Justice Act 1920, Pt II) (Amendment) Order 1985 (S.I. 1985 No. 1994)	Form 110	

Country	Reciprocal Treaty	Statutory Instrument	Form of Certificate For Outgoing Judgment	Explanatory Notes
St Christopher and Nevis	The Administration of Justice Act 1920	S.I. 1984 No. 129 and Pt II of AJA 1920 extends to the countries specified in Sched.I to that Order which has been amended by the Judgments (Administration of Justice Act 1920, Pt II) (Amendment) Order 1985 (S.I. 1985 No. 1994)	Form 110	
St Helena	The Administration of Justice Act 1920	S.I. 1984 No. 129 and Pt II of AJA 1920 extends to the countries specified in Sched.I to that Order which has been amended by the Judgments (Administration of Justice Act 1920, Pt II) (Amendment) Order 1985 (S.I. 1985 No. 1994)	Form 110	
St Lucia	The Administration of Justice Act 1920	S.I. 1984 No. 129 and Pt II of AJA 1920 extends to the countries specified in Sched.I to that Order which has been amended by the Judgments (Administration of Justice Act 1920, Pt II) (Amendment) Order 1985 (S.I. 1985 No. 1994)	Form 110	
St Vincent and the Grenadines	The Administration of Justice Act 1920	S.I. 1984 No. 129 and Pt II of AJA 1920 extends to the countries specified in Sched.I to that Order which has been amended by the Judgments (Administration of Justice Act 1920, Pt II) (Amendment) Order 1985 (S.I. 1985 No. 1994)	Form 110	
Suriname	The Foreign Judgments (Reciprocal Enforcement) Act 1933	S.I. 1981 No. 735.	Form 110	
Swaziland	The Administration of Justice Act 1920	S.I. 1984 No. 129 and Pt II of AJA 1920 extends to the countries specified in Sched.I to that Order which has been amended by the Judgments (Administration of Justice Act 1920, Pt II) (Amendment) Order 1985 (S.I. 1985 No. 1994)	Form 110	
Sweden	Council Regulation (EU)		Form N219/219A	

Country	Reciprocal Treaty	Statutory Instrument	Form of Certificate For Outgoing Judgment	Explanatory Notes
	44/2001 and now Council Regulation 805/2004			
Switzer-land	The Civil Jurisdiction & Judgment Act 1982		Form 110	
Tanzania	The Admin-istration of Justice Act 1920	S.I. 1984 No. 129 and Pt II of AJA 1920 extends to the coun-tries specified in Sched.I to that Order which has been amended by the Judgments (Administra-tion of Justice Act 1920, Pt II) (Amendment) Order 1985 (S.I. 1985 No. 1994)	Form 110	
Tasmania	The Admin-istration of Justice Act 1920	S.I. 1984 No. 129 and Pt II of AJA 1920 extends to the coun-tries specified in Sched.I to that Order which has been amended by the Judgments (Administra-tion of Justice Act 1920, Pt II) (Amendment) Order 1985 (S.I. 1985 No. 1994)	Form 110	
Terri-tory of Norfolk Island	The Admin-istration of Justice Act 1920	S.I. 1984 No. 129 and Pt II of AJA 1920 extends to the coun-tries specified in Sched.I to that Order which has been amended by the Judgments (Administra-tion of Justice Act 1920, Pt II) (Amendment) Order 1985 (S.I. 1985 No. 1994)	Form 110	
The Gambia	The Admin-istration of Justice Act 1920		Form 110	
Tonga	The Foreign Judgments (Reciprocal Enforcement) Act 1933	S.I. 1980 No. 1523.	Form 110	
Trinidad and Tobago	The Admin-istration of Justice Act 1920	S.I. 1984 No. 129 and Pt II of AJA 1920 extends to the coun-tries specified in Sched.I to that Order which has been amended by the Judgments (Administra-tion of Justice Act 1920, Pt II)	Form 110	

Country	Reciprocal Treaty	Statutory Instrument	Form of Certificate For Outgoing Judgment	Explanatory Notes
		(Amendment) Order 1985 (S.I. 1985 No. 1994)		
Turks and Caicos Islands	The Administration of Justice Act 1920	S.I. 1984 No. 129 and Pt II of AJA 1920 extends to the countries specified in Sched.I to that Order which has been amended by the Judgments (Administration of Justice Act 1920, Pt II) (Amendment) Order 1985 (S.I. 1985 No. 1994)	Form 110	
Tuvalu	The Administration of Justice Act 1920	S.I. 1984 No. 129 and Pt II of AJA 1920 extends to the countries specified in Sched.I to that Order which has been amended by the Judgments (Administration of Justice Act 1920, Pt II) (Amendment) Order 1985 (S.I. 1985 No. 1994)	Form 110	
Uganda	The Administration of Justice Act 1920	S.I. 1984 No. 129 and Pt II of AJA., 1920 extends to the countries specified in Sched.I to that Order which has been amended by the Judgments (Administration of Justice Act 1920, Pt II) (Amendment) Order 1985 (S.I. 1985 No. 1994)	Form 110	
Zambia	The Administration of Justice Act 1920	S.I. 1984 No. 129 and Pt II of AJA 1920 extends to the countries specified in Sched.I to that Order which has been amended by the Judgments (Administration of Justice Act 1920, Pt II) (Amendment) Order 1985 (S.I. 1985 No. 1994)	Form 110	
Zimbabwe	The Administration of Justice Act 1920	S.I. 1984 No. 129 and Pt II of AJA 1920 extends to the countries specified in Sched.I to that Order which has been amended by the Judgments (Administration of Justice Act 1920, Pt II) (Amendment) Order 1985 (S.I. 1985 No. 1994)	Form 110	

Determining Jurisdiction where the Defendant is Domiciled in an EU State

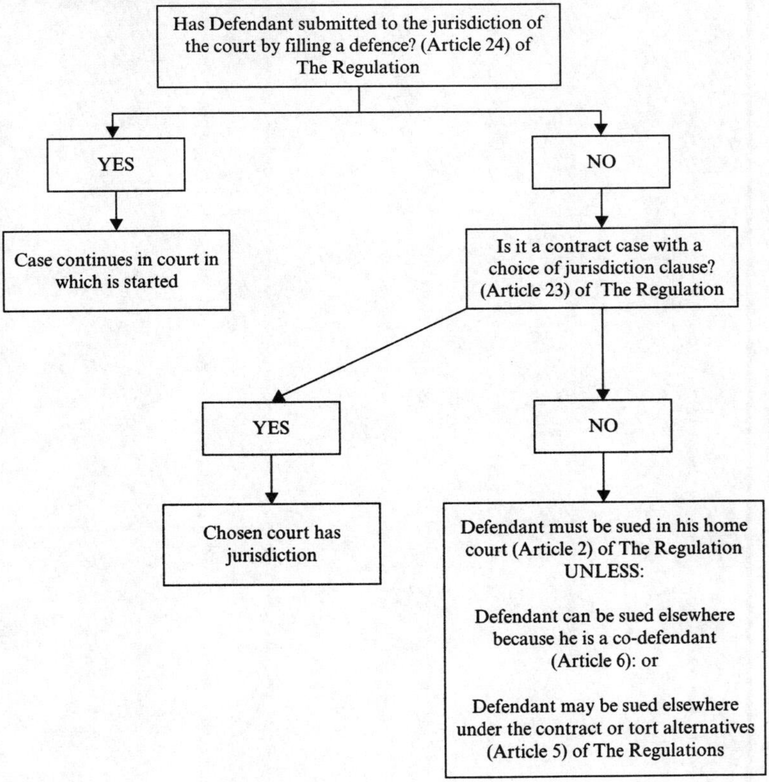

Index